The Essential SAMPLER QUILT Book

LYNNE EDWARDS

The Essential SAMPLER QUILT Book

40 Techniques for Machine and Hand Patchwork

LYNNE EDWARDS

D&C
David and Charles
www.rucraft.co.uk

To all those quilters world-wide who have kindly bought, borrowed or shared both the original Sampler Quilt Book *and* The New Sampler Quilt Book *over the last fourteen years. I am constantly amazed by the wonderful quilts that have been produced using them, and as always am determined to take the entire credit for everything...*

A DAVID & CHARLES BOOK

David & Charles is an F+W Media Inc. company
4700 East Galbraith Road, Cincinnati, OH 45236

First published in the UK and US in 2010

Some of the text and images contained in this edition were first published as *The Sampler Quilt Book* and *The New Sampler Quilt Book*.

A catalogue record for this book is available from the British Library.

ISBN-13: 978-0-7153-3613-7 paperback
ISBN-10: 0-7153-3613-4 paperback

Printed in China by RR Donnelley
for David & Charles
Brunel House Newton Abbot Devon

Publisher Ali Myer
Commissioning Editors Jane Trollope and Cheryl Brown
Assistant Editor Juliet Lines
Project Editor Lin Clements
Art Editor Martin Smith
Designer Victoria Marks
Photographers Karl Adamson and Kim Sayer
Production Controller Bev Richardson
Pre Press Natasha Jorden

Photograph on page 2: *Lynne Edwards began her sampler quilt as the teaching sample for her second sampler quilt course. For more details about the border design, see page 246.*

Contents

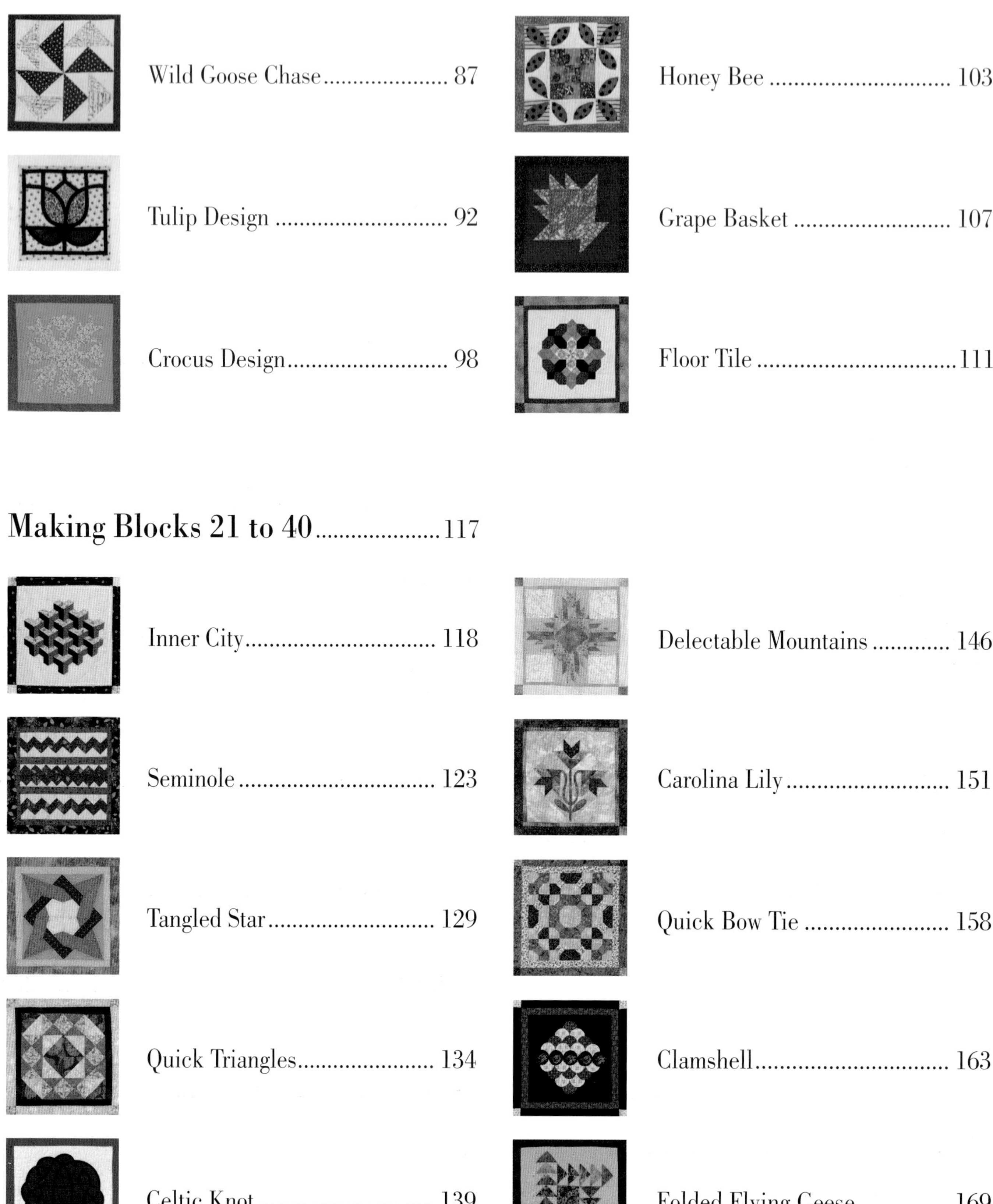

Making Blocks 21 to 40 117

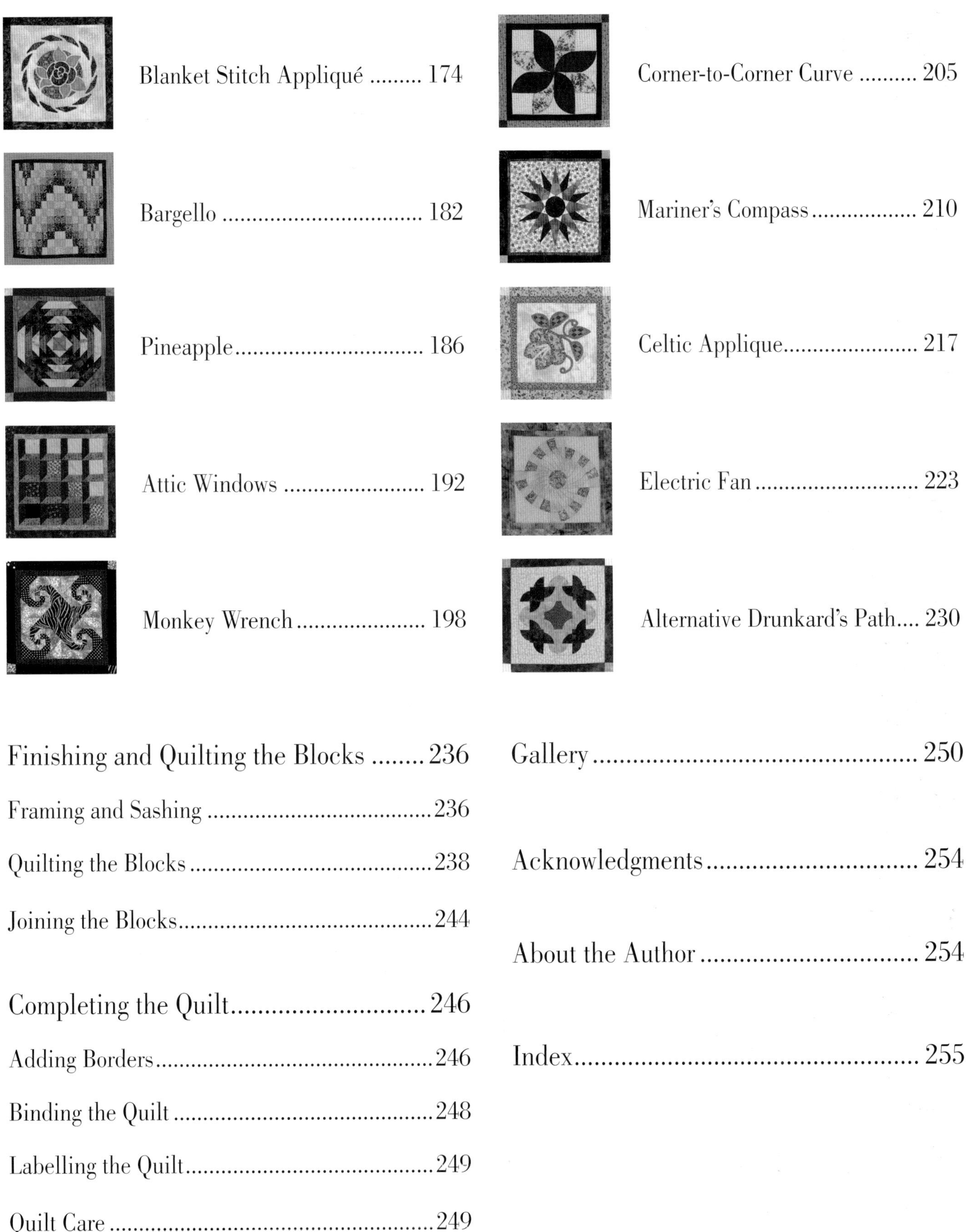

Introduction

I am such a fortunate quilter: I have around 120 students who come to me regularly for a whole day's quilt-making in a local village hall. There are eight groups and they each come twelve times a year, tackling designs and techniques that I offer them or pursuing their own projects with my help. I try not to let them know just how proficient they are in case they all stop coming, but I must admit that the quality of their work both technically and aesthetically is quite amazing. And they all started by making a sampler quilt.

The first group of total beginners, all those years ago in 1991, followed the course for a year, with five full-day sessions over each of three terms. They finished the course, completed the quilts and we had a modest quilt show to show them off, where I recruited two more groups who wanted to do the course over the next year. What I hadn't expected was that the first group would not leave. They wanted to continue with the delights of making quilts, still in the company of their fellow students, now good friends of course. After three years I had four groups ongoing, all of whom had learned the basic skills by making the first beginner's sampler quilt. It was then that I was asked by publishers David & Charles to convert the course into a book so that a wider audience could be reached. All the quilts used in the book were the quilts of these students, so not made by experts, and were their own choice of colours and fabrics – a comfort and inspiration to the prospective reader picking up the book and hoping to make a start.

When the first *Sampler Quilt Book* was published my students became very nostalgic about the course they had toiled through in past years. Misty-eyed they declared that they had never learned so much nor achieved as much as then. (They had, of course, forgotten how hard they had worked…) Couldn't they do another structured course, they asked, a more advanced one with all the blocks and techniques that had not been covered in the first sampler quilt? So that was the start of the second volume, *The New Sampler Quilt Book*, based on the course that more than a hundred willing victims undertook. Like the first book, there were twenty techniques, which were more complex (although not necessarily more difficult), and the resulting quilts were richer and even more impressive – real heirlooms to be treasured.

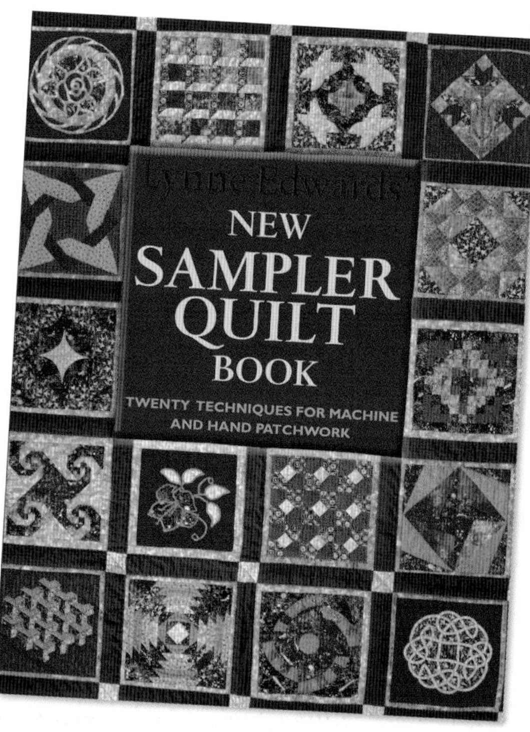

The original Sampler Quilt Book *is shown here with its most recent cover, featuring Pam Croger's quilt. Three different quilts were used as the cover during the book's lifetime – Hazel Hurst's rich green quilt, Collie Parker's red, white and blue quilt for the US edition and finally Pam's for the paperback version.* The New Sampler Quilt Book *stayed with Pat Mitchells' heraldic red and gold quilt on its cover throughout.*

Pauline Bugg's magnificent sampler quilt is based on the blocks from The New Sampler Quilt Book. *It is beautifully crafted and heavily hand-quilted – a true heirloom quilt.*

"When I first joined my quilting group, The Shotesham Quilters in Norfolk, I knew I had a lot to learn. Most of the members had just finished making their own sampler quilts and they looked wonderful but technically difficult. However, I was persuaded that I could make one too and was introduced to Lynne's sampler books and assured that I would find them easy to follow – they were! My quilt took about six months to piece and, with my new-found love of hand-quilting, was completed over a period of two years. It gave me the confidence to go on and develop my quilting skills." **Pauline Bugg**

Over the years I have seen many quilts made from each book, as teachers throughout the world have been kind enough to use them as a basis for their beginners' classes. Photos turn up regularly from the proud owners, who cannot know the huge pleasure they have given me by sending them. More and more of the quilts have used blocks from both books and it is obvious that many quilters have started by dutifully working their way through the first volume and then just couldn't resist poaching a few from the second. That is why it seemed such a good idea to combine the two books as one in this volume – *The Essential Sampler Quilt Book*.

This is a new edition to mark David & Charles' fifty years in publishing, and we felt that a new edition deserved colour throughout all the instructions, plus forty new quilts! Time moves on and there is as much a fashion in the world of fabric as there is in the clothes of each era. All the quilts chosen for this book have been made in recent years, which gives a new look to what is essentially a timeless craft.

Making a sampler quilt is an ideal way to try a variety of different techniques without ending up with a pile of unfinished samples. Skills are acquired for future projects and new techniques become unexpected favourites. Others may fall into the 'never again' category, but at least you have found out that it's not for you. One technique in *The New Sampler Quilt Book* that many found tricky was reverse appliqué, so I have taken the opportunity with this edition of keeping the lovely retro rose design but replacing the technique with blanket-stitch appliqué, which is a favourite of mine and is one that most quilters really enjoy. We are, after all, doing this for pleasure.

Left *Collie Parker's quilt was chosen to be used on the cover of the US edition of the original* Sampler Quilt Book. *A fitting choice, as when making it she was inspired by the American tradition, especially those quilts that display bold colour contrasts and clear designs.*

Right *Jean Hatherley's quilt shown in* The New Sampler Quilt Book *was inspirational for its calm balance of colours and the stunning use of the Delectable Mountains design for the final border around the quilt.*

The blocks are a mixture of hand and machine work and are sequenced in order so that the skills learned from one block may be used in other later block designs. In this edition of course there are far too many blocks to be used in just one quilt, so there are more choices. You may decide to start by using just the first part of the book and working through what was the original Sampler Quilt Course from beginning to end, but it is more likely that you will use some of the more basic blocks from the earlier pages and also some from the more complex designs that appear further on in the book, dipping into it to choose designs or techniques that appeal to you. These can be combined with others to make a large quilt or used on their own in your personal projects.

Once the blocks are made they are framed and then quilted individually before being joined together in the 'quilt-as-you-go' technique. I used this method in both of the original books and although the final joining together can be a bit tedious, it does mean that the quilting is easier and more portable and the quilts do get finished.

Many of the quilts shown are a mixture of blocks from the first and the second Sampler Quilt books. Some quilts also include extra blocks chosen and constructed by the maker that do not appear anywhere else in these pages, either because they omitted some of mine or because they needed more blocks for their king-sized quilts. If these are the very blocks that you really want to make, then I apologise. The trouble with giving quilters more skills and the confidence to pursue their own ideas is that they do just that, whether it suits me or not...

Left *My original sampler quilt started in the way all my quilts begin – a pile of fabrics that I kept patting and stroking and rearranging. I had collected four different Indian Madras cotton fabrics, which were in plain colours but woven in two tones to give a subtle, shot effect. These were combined with many different Liberty Lawn prints to make the quilt which is still used in our house today.*

Right *My second sampler quilt used a wide variety of fabrics, some of them from a range designed by American quilt artist Nancy Crow, plus many others. By the time I made this quilt the choice of fabrics was so much more than when I first started making quilts.*

Getting Started

This section gives you all the information you need to start your sampler quilt and will be very useful to beginners. Basic equipment is described opposite and the Basic Techniques you will need are on page 15.

Fabrics and Wadding

Before we get to the equipment and techniques you will need there are some questions about fabric and wadding (batting) that need to be discussed first.

How Much Fabric do I Need?

For a single bed quilt you will need a total of about 6yd (5.5m) of 45in (115cm) wide fabric for the front of the quilt. For a double bed quilt about 9yd (8.25m) is needed. To begin with it is better to buy small amounts, ½yd (45.7cm) or so, of six to eight fabrics and then see how the quilt develops. This is risky I know, but if you have bought three yards of one fabric you will feel obliged to use it, even if the quilt is moving in another direction where that particular fabric does not belong. Once a few blocks have been made you will be able to add fabrics more easily, as you will see which fabrics and colours are working well together. If one of your favourites is no longer available, find another fabric similar in colour, which will add to the richness of the quilt. You will be surprised how far ½yd (45.7cm) will go.

With the 'quilt-as-you-go' technique, a whole piece of fabric for the backing is not required as each block is backed individually. For this sampler quilt, each of the blocks is backed with a square of fabric 17½ x 17½in (44.5 x 44.5cm), so you can cut these as you go along. As a guide you need 6yd (5.5m) of 45in (115cm) wide backing fabric for a single bed quilt and about 8yd (7.4m) for all twenty blocks plus borders. This is a lot of fabric, so shop around for something you like that is not too expensive. I used one backing fabric for the blocks and another to back the borders which means I get patchwork on both sides of the quilt.

How do I Choose Colours?

Colour is very personal and is strongly influenced by fashion but it is probably best to start with a fabric you really like. If you want your quilt to be essentially one colour then make sure there is plenty of variation in the shades you use, both light and dark. If you want a real contrast of colours, like a red and white quilt, add textures, spots, checks and small and large prints to the basic red and white scheme.

The sampler quilt is quite complex in design and probably looks best with a limited number of colours. Begin by choosing one fabric in a colour you really want to use and then find two or three more that are similar. Try to stick to medium-weight cotton fabrics for the quilt as these are easier to handle and to use together. A mix of patterned and plain or slightly textured fabrics will give balance to the quilt.

Many of the blocks have a background area that supports the main design. Find a fabric that will look good in a supporting role with your first collection. I used two similar creamy-beige fabrics for my background areas (see picture on page 2), but one would do to begin with and you may decide in time to keep to that one fabric throughout. Finally, take all your chosen pieces and pick a third colour and even a fourth if you wish, which will add some interest to the quilt. Small amounts of several fabrics will allow you to build up a palette of shades to dip into as you choose for each block. Bear in mind that the main area of regret with students is that they did not restrict their palette of colours enough but added more and more as they went along.

What About the Wadding?

The amount of wadding (batting) needed – the layer of padding between the front and back of the quilt – will be similar to the fabric backing. There are now more options for wadding available. I used an heirloom wadding 80% cotton 20% polyester, which was a joy to quilt. It is much thinner than the usual two ounce polyester but made a much heavier quilt. Take the advice of other quilters when choosing wadding. A factor to be considered is how much you intend to quilt your blocks – some waddings specify quite close areas of quilting while others allow large spaces between quilting lines.

How do I Prepare the Fabrics?

It is safest to wash all fabrics before use. However, if, like me, you enjoy working with fresh, crisp unwashed fabrics, you must at least test any strong or dark fabrics for colourfastness before you begin. Wash these separately with a gentle non-biological liquid soap or detergent and check that the colour does not leach out into the water. Reds, indigo and dark browns are all colours to be tested as they can be the ruin of your quilt. Specialist quilt fabrics are not likely to shrink but I am not so sure about furnishing cottons or fashion fabrics, so always wash them before use. Try to iron the fabrics while they are still slightly damp to ensure a smooth finish.

Basic Equipment

There is an increasingly wide range of tools and gadgets available from specialist shops and quilt shows. If you are a beginner it is probably best to stick to the basic equipment listed here.

Equipment for Hand Sewing

Needles: Try to buy packets of one size only – it's more economical. Sharps size 9 or 10 are best for piecing and appliqué. Betweens size 9 or 10 are best for quilting.

Pins: My current favourite are silk pins, which are very fine but strong. Otherwise I use long, fine dressmaker's pins (extra-fine, extra-long), although other people favour the coloured, glass-headed type as they are easier to hold and find. Buy the smaller, fine variety rather than huge quilt pins.

Thimble: The use of a thimble is your choice but I feel that one is needed for quilting, to protect the middle finger of your dominant hand. A flat-topped one is the best shape.

Thread: For sewing cotton fabrics I like to use a good quality, pure cotton thread, although cotton-coated polyester is a good alternative. Try to match the colour of the thread to the fabrics. If using a mixture of colours, it is best to go for a darker rather than a lighter shade. For quilting, pure cotton quilting thread is ideal. It is stronger, thicker and waxed to give a smooth thread that tangles less than ordinary sewing thread.

Scissors: You will need a sharp, medium-sized pair of scissors for cutting fabric, plus a larger pair for paper cutting. A pair of small, sharp scissors with good points will be useful for clipping seams and trimming threads.

Fabric Markers: You will need a fabric marker to mark template shapes on to fabric and indicate quilting lines. Beware of spirit pens though, even if water erasable. They make a harsh line and it is not known yet whether their chemicals will eventually rot fabric. Specialist quilt shops sell silver, white and yellow marking pencils that can be sharpened to a fine point. Read the packaging carefully before you use them; if it says 'will not fade' it's fine for marking around templates but is not suitable for quilting. Always test the marker on a spare piece of fabric before you start work and check it can be erased. You can buy a fabric eraser for use with these markers. For quilting I use Aquarelle coloured pencils in the softest quality, bought from art shops. Choose a shade similar to the fabric but dark enough to be seen clearly. The line wears off the fabric as it is worked and can be sponged if necessary to remove final traces.

Tape Measure: Use an extra long tape measure l00in (2.5m) or longer with metric markings on the reverse.

Bias Bars: These are produced specifically for Celtic patchwork, where narrow strips of fabric are appliquéd on a background in interlaced patterns. There are several widths of bar, from ⅛in (3mm) to ½in (1.3cm). A ¼in (6mm) bar is used for the Celtic Knot block, and a narrower ⅛in (3mm) bar for the Celtic Appliqué block.

Masking Tape: Special ¼in (6mm) masking tape is sold in quilt shops which is really useful for marking straight lines for quilting. Avoid the wider varieties sold in stationers and do-it-yourself shops as they are not low-tack. Do not leave any tape on the fabric any longer than necessary just in case it leaves a mark.

Equipment for Making Templates

Many of the block designs use templates transferred on to card or template plastic. Accuracy is critical so you will need very sharp pencils, pencil sharpener, eraser, ruler, tracing paper and card or template plastic.

Template plastic: This is widely available from specialist quilt shops and other sewing equipment outlets. It can be used over and over again. The plastic is clear and firm, yet pliable and easy to cut with scissors. It is available in two types: a plain, clear one, and one marked with a measured grid.

Graph paper: This is very useful for drafting your own patterns and borders. Quilt shops often have A4 pads marked in ¼in (6mm) squares. Art shops sometimes stock large sheets of graph paper marked in inches, but beware of buying any with 1/10in (2.5mm) markings, as they don't show ¼in (6mm) divisions.

Freezer Paper: This is becoming very popular for appliqué work. It looks like greaseproof paper but is slightly thicker and has a shiny side which sticks to the fabric when it is ironed. Thus it keeps small appliqué shapes firm as they are stitched in place. After use the paper can be peeled off without leaving any marks and be reused. Currently freezer paper is available from specialist quilt shops. A good substitute is the thick paper used to wrap packs of photocopying paper.

Equipment for Machine Work

Sewing Machine: This does not have to be a state of the art model, just a reliable one you enjoy using. Use a size 11/80 machine needle for medium-weight cotton fabrics and change after at least every eight sewing hours. A straight-stitch foot is ideal for machine patchwork. You need to stitch straight seams that are exactly ¼in (6mm) from the needle, so a narrow straight-stitch foot is very helpful. So too is the ¼in (6mm) foot that some manufacturers have produced especially for quilters. A walking foot is useful for stitching through layers of fabric and wadding, as it prevents the top fabric from creeping ahead of the other layers and producing a twisted effect. It also makes sewing on the final binding to the quilt much easier and is essential for machine quilting.

Thread: Use the same cotton or cotton-coated polyester thread as for hand sewing. Choose one manufacturer and thread type and stick to this for both top and bobbin thread.

Stitch Ripper: I use this as an extra finger to hold fabric in place while feeding it under the machine foot. It can also prevent the seam allowances from being pushed in the wrong direction by the machine foot as you sew.

Pins: For any machine work I prefer silk pins or extra-fine, extra-long pins as they slip out of the fabric so easily.

Equipment for Rotary Cutting

Rotary Cutter, Ruler and Mat: Once you start using these you will wonder how you ever managed without them. There are several different mats on the market, but do get one with an inch grid marked on. The most useful size for patchwork is the larger one, 23 x 17in. Always follow the instructions printed on the mat and store flat out of direct sunlight. The mat is self-healing when a rotary cutter is used on it. Do use the appropriate cutter as craft knives and other blades will do real damage to the mat.

Cutters come in several sizes, all of which I use for different tasks. The small one (28mm diameter) easily cuts two layers of fabric and is ideal for cutting curves. The larger version (45mm) is the most useful for all cutting tasks. There is also a really large cutter (60mm) that I use for all my serious cutting of up to eight layers of fabric, but it is not needed for the projects in this book. The blades on rotary cutters do become blunt with use and must be replaced at intervals.

Special rulers must be used with the mat and cutter because the rotary cutter will shave off the edges of wooden, plastic and even metal rulers. Rotary rulers are about ⅛in (3mm) thick and are made of tough acrylic. Choose one with markings that you feel comfortable reading and which measures up to 24in. This size will work well on folded fabric and on a medium-sized cutting mat. A 12½in square Perspex ruler is also useful.

Other Useful Items

Display Board: A piece of white felt or flannelette stretched over a board is good for planning your designs, as the cut pieces will 'stick' to the fabric without pins. A large cork or polystyrene tile also works well, but with these you will need pins to keep the pieces in position.

Light Box: A light box for tracing designs on to fabric can be bought from business supply shops, but is expensive. All you really need is a flat, clear surface lit from below so that lines to be traced are highlighted through the fabric. A glass-topped table with a light beneath will give the same effect. If all else fails, tape the design to a window, tape the fabric over the top and trace the outline.

Basic Techniques

This section looks at some of the basic techniques you need to master to make the sampler quilt.

Making Templates

The blocks in this sampler quilt use specific shapes joined together to create the design. These shapes are provided with the individual block instructions and should be made into templates to be used as required. Templates are made by tracing a shape and transferring it on to card or special template plastic. If using card, first trace the shape on to tracing paper. When tracing a straight-lined shape, such as a diamond, mark the corners with a dot and carefully join the dots with a ruler and a sharp pencil. Mark the arrow to show the direction of the grain of the fabric. Cut out the traced shape roughly, keeping about ¼in (6mm) outside the drawn outline. Stick this on to card and then cut out the exact outline through both tracing paper and card. Cut just inside the drawn lines as this keeps the measurements accurate as you draw round the template on the fabric.

If using template plastic, trace over the outline and grain arrow in the way described above. Cut out the template carefully with scissors, again cutting just inside the lines to keep the measurements accurate. Label each template clearly and put them all in an envelope or transparent wallet so that you can use them again.

Pressing

A good iron and ironing board are essential for all sewing work. Press all your fabric before use, as creased fabric leads to inaccuracy. When pressing seams in patchwork, press from the front and use a dry iron as steam can distort the fabric, especially on bias seams. Resist the temptation to press seams in patchwork from the back – you could press little pleats in the fabric over the seams which you only discover when you turn the piece over to the front. These tiny, roll-over creases are hard to press out and can lead to inaccuracy.

Setting Up the Machine

It is important to have your sewing machine and chair at the right height and an adjustable office chair might be a good investment. If you cannot leave your sewing machine permanently in position, do all the preliminary cutting work first and then clear a space for the machine.

Thread the machine ready for use. If it has an extension plate that fits on to create a larger surface, do use it as it supports the patchwork and stops it from pulling away from the needle as you stitch. Set the stitch length to a shorter stitch than required for dressmaking – about two-thirds the usual size or about fifteen stitches to the inch. This will be small enough to prevent the seams from coming undone when they are cut, but not so small that you can't unpick them.

Many people find stitching a straight line very difficult. If you fit a ¼in (6mm) foot on your machine, it really will help.

One trick is to stick a strip of masking tape on to the machine exactly ¼in (6mm) away from the needle. This makes a good edge to line your fabric against as you sew. Use the point of a stitch ripper to help guide the fabric accurately while stitching.

There is a useful test to find out whether your ¼in (6mm) seam is accurate. The seam may be just right mathematically but because the seams are pressed to one side rather than pressed open, it makes the seams a tiny bit wider, so you need to stitch a slightly 'skinny' or 'scant' ¼in (6mm) to finish up with the correct sizing.

Take a strip of one of your fabrics 2in (5cm) wide and about 18in (45.7cm) long and cut it into three lengths (Fig 1a). Stitch these three lengths together with a ¼in (6mm) seam. Press the seams to one side, from the front of the work so that the seams are really flat (Fig 1b). Now measure the work from side to side – it should be *exactly* 5in (12.7cm). If it is smaller than this your seams are too wide; if it is more than 5in (12.7cm) your seams are too narrow. Try the test again, adjusting the position of your masking tape until you get exactly the right seam allowance. Once this has been done you are set up for all your future patchwork. Press in this direction from the front of the work.

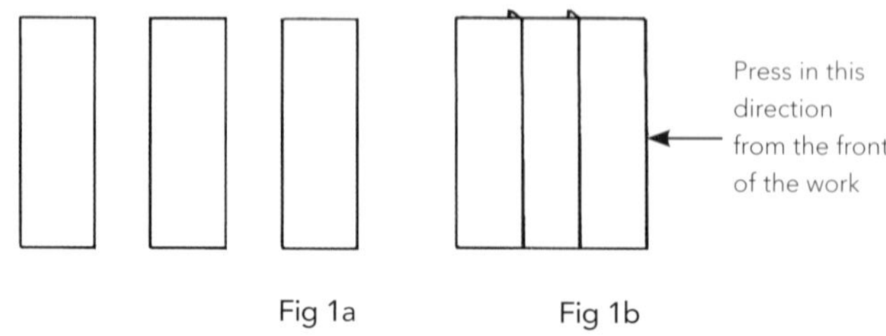

Fig 1a

Fig 1b

Rotary Cutting

To cut fabric, place it on the cutting mat and align the woven threads of the fabric (called the grain) with the gridlines on the mat. Position the ruler on the fabric and hold it firmly so your hand forms an arch and is not lying flat, as there is more strength in your fingers than in the flat of your hand. Hold the handle at an angle of 45° to the mat, not leaning to one side or the other. The flatter side of the cutter should be against the side of the ruler, not the side with the assembly nut (see photograph below). Only snap down the safety guard when you are ready to cut. Left-handed users should cut from the left side rather than from the right. Get into the habit of always cutting *away* from you, so start at the near side of the mat and begin cutting before the blade reaches the fabric, pressing down firmly and evenly in one continuous movement. If the ruler has a tendency to slip to one side as you cut, stop cutting and move your hand crab-like up the ruler before starting to cut again.

Cutting Strips

Remember that strips cut from the width of the fabric will be stretchy, so whenever possible cut strips down the side parallel to the selvedge. If you are working with more than a couple of yards or metres of fabric, cutting from the long side of the fabric will also keep the length intact for use in borders later.

1 Turn the cutting mat so that the longer side runs from top to bottom to give a longer cutting distance. If the piece of fabric is too long for the mat, fold it carefully as many times as needed to make it fit on to the cutting mat with the selvedge edges exactly on top of each other. Place the fabric on the mat with the folded edge along a *horizontal* gridline. This is very important to avoid getting V-shapes in the final long strip (see picture 1 below).

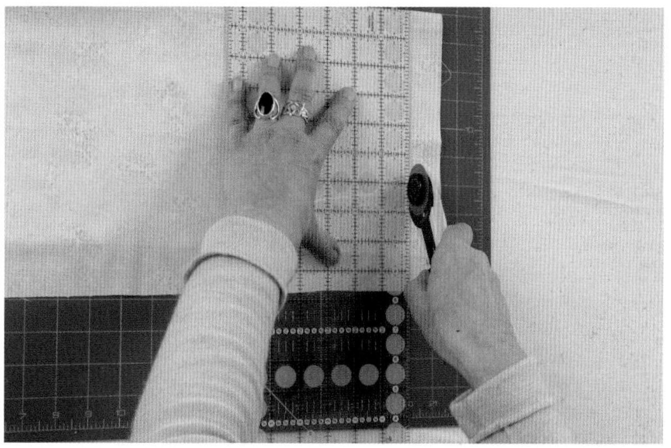

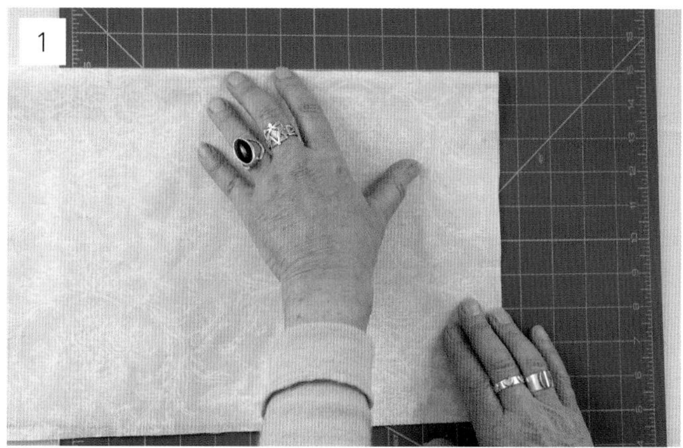

2 Place the ruler on one of the *vertical* gridlines on the mat and trim off the selvedges (picture 2a). To cut a strip of a measured width, use the marked measurements at the top and bottom of the mat. I actually count the number of inches along the top markings on the mat. Move the ruler to this position, hold it firmly and cut along its edge (2b). Before moving the ruler, check that all the layers have been completely cut through. If not, re-cut the whole strip rather than saw at the offending section (2c).

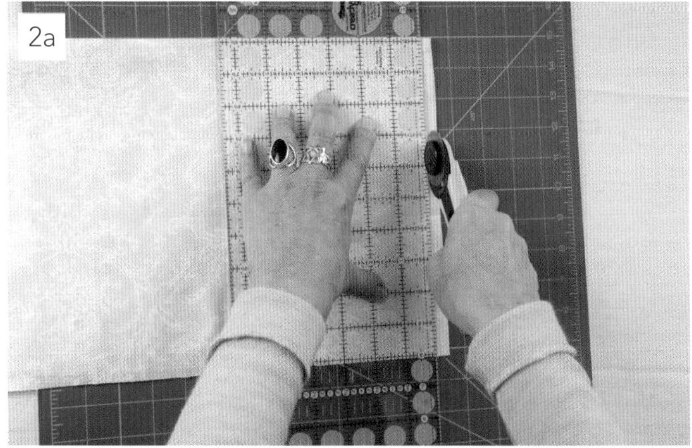
2a

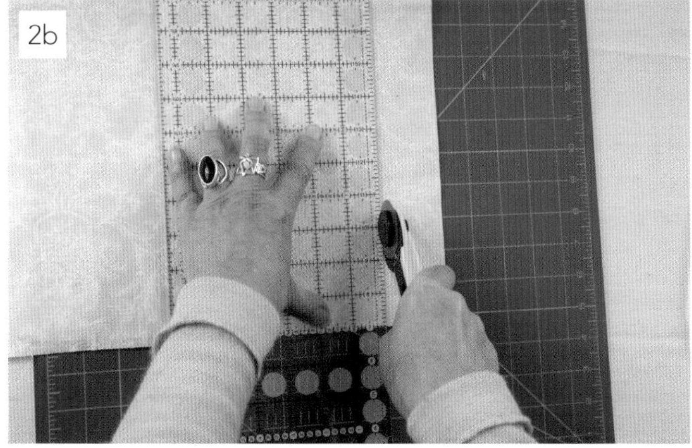
2b

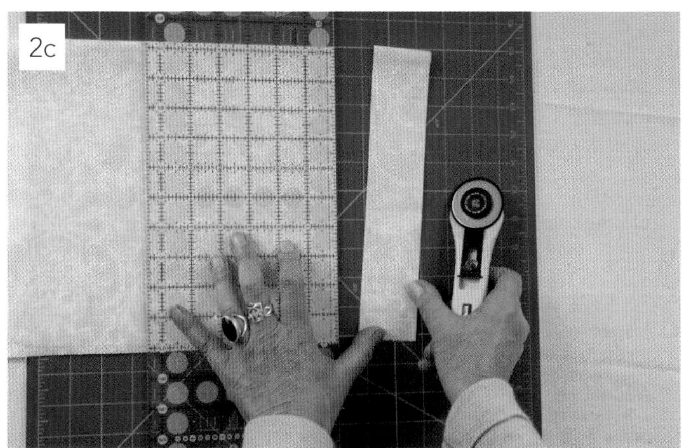
2c

3 Lift the ruler and reposition it for cutting the next strip. Continue to cut until the required number of strips have been cut (3).

3

Alternative Method for Cutting Strips

For years I cut all my strips in the way just described, using the measurements on the cutting mat as my guide. I still always straighten the folded edges as written above, as I find it avoids getting that horrid kink in the centre. Having done this, I tend to cut the strips themselves using the measurements on the ruler as my guide rather than the markings on the mat. This has extra value in that the cutting mat no longer gets worn out on certain marked lines with the constant use. It also makes cutting complicated measurements far easier to manage.

When cutting strips or drawing a grid for quick pieced triangles, measurements like 3⅞in (9.8cm) are quite common. It is all too easy to mis-measure when using the mat markings as a guide. Instead, after trimming the selvedges, turn the mat through 180° without disturbing the fabric, or walk around the mat to the other side – see photo 1 below. Start cutting from the left-hand side, instead of from the right. If you are left-handed reverse these directions. See overleaf for sequence.

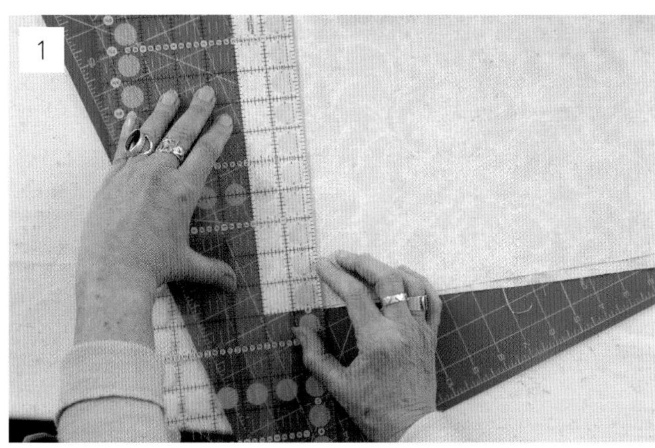
1

Look at the markings on your ruler: many have an extra half inch added to one long side. If yours is like this, turn the ruler so the marked half inch line is on the left-hand side and the whole inches are nearest the edge of the fabric (picture 2a).

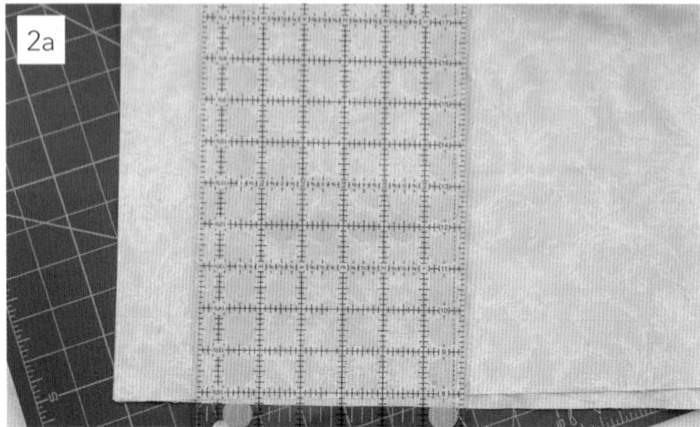

To cut a strip of 3in, move the ruler over the fabric until the cut edge lines up with the 3in line on the ruler. The fabric you see trapped under the ruler is the strip that you want (2b).

Cut along the right side of the ruler and remove the cut strip. Left-handers will work from left to right, cutting along the left side of the ruler each time. Continue to do this across the fabric as many times as required (2c).

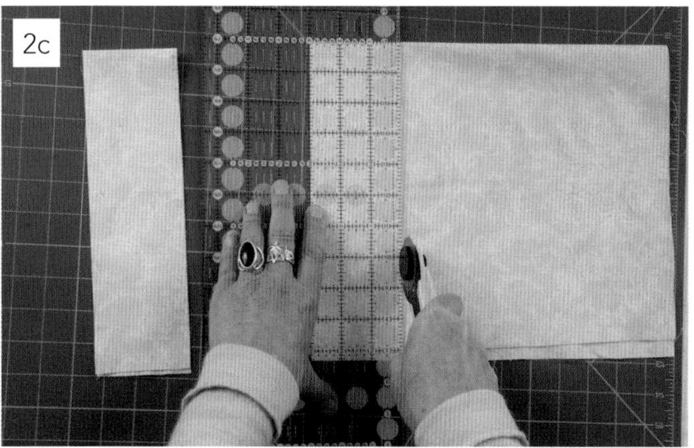

Cutting Half Inch Measurements

Many patchwork designs use strips and squares of whole inch measurements like 3in or 4in in the finished design. These need to be cut with an extra half inch added for the seam allowances, so quilters find themselves having to cut more of these awkward measurements, like 3½in or 4½in, than they do of whole inches. Rulers that have an extra half inch added on one side make this easier to do. When you need to cut a measurement that includes a half inch, just turn the ruler round through 180°. The extra half inch strip on the ruler will be on the right-hand edge. Left-handers should work from the right, with the extra half inch strip on the ruler on the left-hand edge.

Make a cut along the right side of the ruler and then remove the cut strip (see picture 1 below).

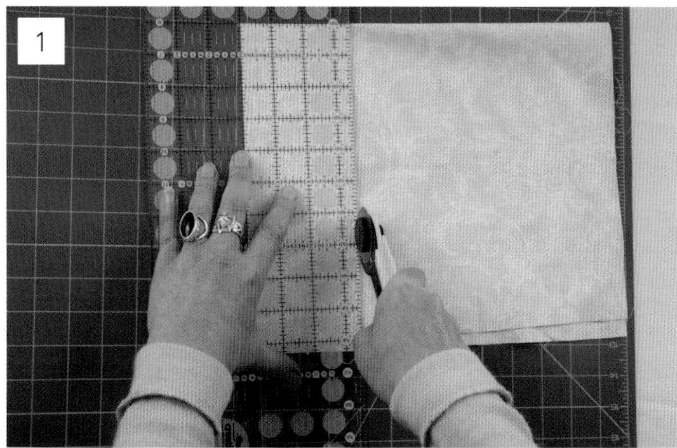

To cut a 3½in strip, move the ruler across the fabric as usual until the line marked 3½in matches the cut edge of the fabric. Cut along the edge of the ruler to make the strip (2).

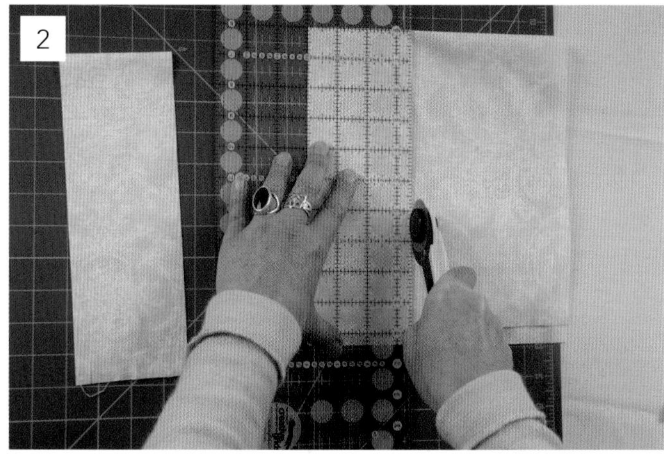

Cutting a Square

If the fabric will fit on to the mat without hanging over the edge, place it down with the grain parallel to the mat's gridlines. Straighten one edge of the fabric by lining the ruler up with a vertical gridline and cutting against it. Without moving the fabric, cut a second vertical line at the desired distance from the first one (count the squares to check). Turn the mat through 90° and trim the other two sides of the square the same way. If the piece of fabric is too big for the mat, you could cut out the square roughly first and then trim it on the mat as described above or alternatively use one of the large square rulers.

1 Use a square ruler larger than the square of fabric that you want to cut. It doesn't have to be the same size – larger is fine. Place a corner of the fabric on the cutting mat and position the square ruler on it so that about ½in of fabric extends beyond it on two sides (see picture 1 below). Position the ruler with the diagonal marking running from top right to bottom left and the marked numbers increasing towards bottom left, with the extra half inch strip to the left and bottom of the ruler. Left-handers should position the ruler with the diagonal line running from top left to bottom right and the extra half inch strip to the right and along the bottom of the ruler. Match the grain of the fabric (the direction of the woven threads) with the top and side of the ruler.

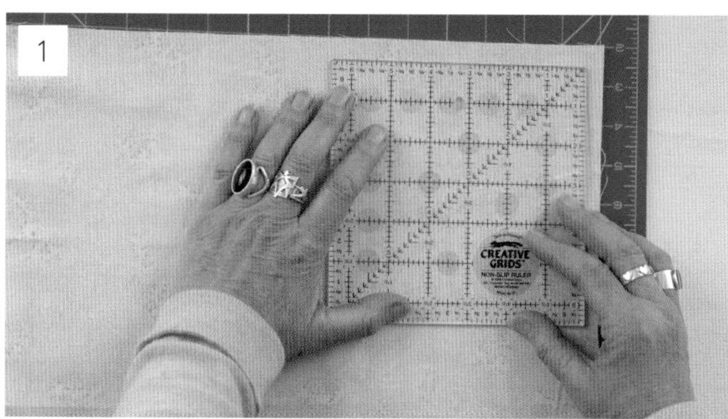
1

2 Trim along these two sides with a rotary cutter (as shown in picture 2 below). Left-handers should cut along the left side and across the top.

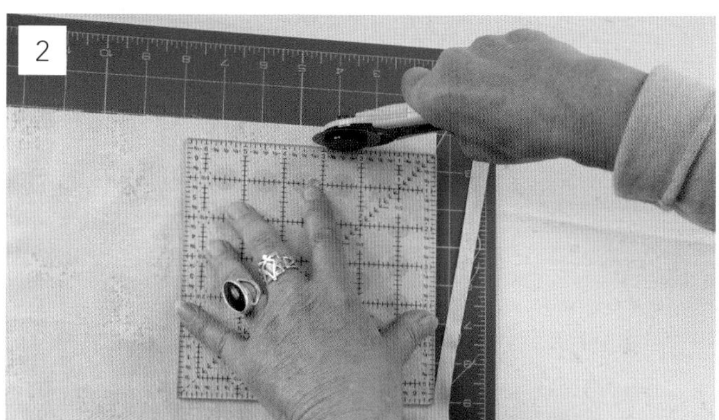
2

3 Turn the fabric round through 180° so that the two cut edges are at the bottom left of the mat. Place the square ruler on the fabric with the ruler markings in the same position as before. Move the ruler over the two cut edges of the fabric until the chosen measurement on the two sides of the ruler lines up with the cut edges (picture 3a). Trim the remaining two sides to complete the square (3b).

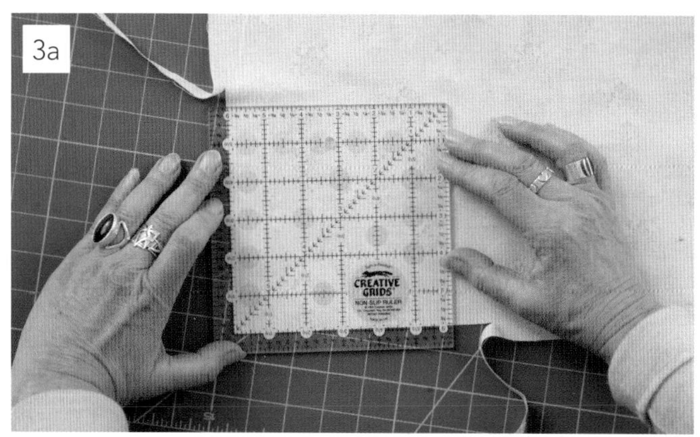
3a

3b

4 To cut a square that has a half inch in its measurement, such as 12½in just turn the ruler around so that the diagonal marking is still in the same position, but the extra half inch strips are along the top edge and the right side of the ruler (picture 4). For left-handers, the extra half inch strips should be along the top and on the left side of the square ruler. Trim along the top and side edge as usual to cut the required square.

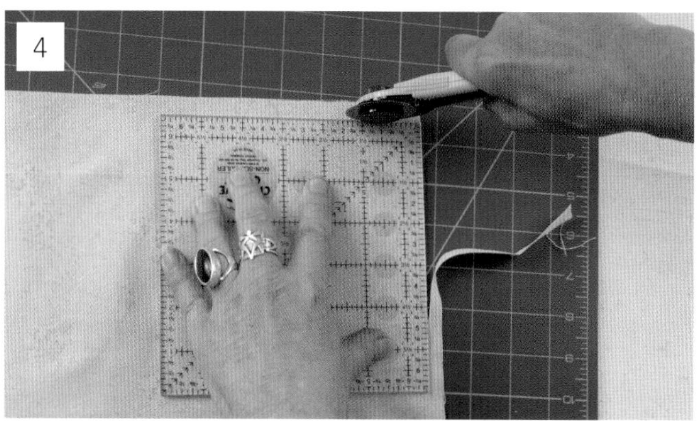
4

Making Blocks 1 to 20

Each block for this essential sampler quilt is fully described, with guidance in selecting colours and fabrics, step-by-step instructions and clear diagrams throughout. Look at the photographs of the different quilts throughout the book to get some ideas for your own colour schemes. The following section describes blocks 1 to 20, with blocks 21 to 40 beginning on page 116.

The blocks are presented in sequence, so the skills learned in one design are built upon in the following techniques, and probably the best way to use the book is to work through the designs one by one. However, feel free to leave out blocks that do not appeal to you, or make more of the ones you really love. It is, after all, your quilt and you are allowed to pick and choose. The advantage of making and quilting the blocks individually and then assembling them at the end is that you can decide how many to make. Whether they finish up as a huge king-size quilt, a cot quilt or just a series of cushions is up to you.

English Patchwork

Tumbling Blocks

Patchwork over papers is a traditional English method of patchwork. Many people believe – incorrectly – that hand stitching hexagons is the only form of patchwork there is, whilst those more experienced in quilt-making often see the hexagon as a design cliché lacking in imagination and creativity. Although this can be true, I have seen some really beautiful hexagon quilts made in recent years where scraps of many fabrics have been blended and balanced for colour and design. These quilts are destined to become heirlooms, to be passed on and treasured for their looks as well as for their nostalgic content. The almost mindless repetition involved in this method of sewing is wonderfully

soothing and therapeutic to do, and I have seen many a quilter abandon a challenging project in times of stress, unhappiness or sheer fatigue to take up a piece of English patchwork over papers.

It is not just hexagons that are stitched in this way but any geometric shape that does not fit neatly into squares and rows, such as diamonds, octagons and equilateral triangles. The papers give a rigid outline to the shapes that makes it easy to join them together with great accuracy. Once completed, the papers are all removed and can be re-used on another project.

For the sampler quilt I have chosen a design called Tumbling Blocks, an arrangement of diamonds that gives the illusion of a three-dimensional tower of blocks. It is also known as Baby's Blocks.

Colour Choices

The design is made up of groups of three diamonds arranged to form a hexagon. To obtain the three-dimensional effect use three different fabrics: one dark, one light and one medium. Place the three fabrics alongside each other to check that one stands out as being lighter and another is definitely darker. The third fabric will lie between these two extremes as a medium tone. The contrasts do not have to be great but should be enough to register on the eye, or the illusion of a tower of bricks will be lost. Half-closing your eyes when looking at the fabrics will help you see the difference in tone.

A fourth fabric is required for the background on which the Tumbling Blocks tower sits. You may like to use the same background fabric for all of your blocks to give continuity to the quilt, or you may decide to vary the background from block to block. A plain fabric is the obvious choice but you could also consider a small print or textured design, even a small check or spot will read from a distance as plain but could add interest.

The possibilities are there for you to make your own personal choice. Do not rush it: place the three fabrics for the Tumbling Blocks in the middle of your background choice and consider the effect. If you're not sure, try another background and then go back to the first. If you're still unsure, make the Tumbling Blocks first, then arrange them on various fabrics to see what looks best. All the time you are sewing the diamonds you can be quietly thinking about the options for the background and could well come to a decision before you get anywhere near the final stage.

Construction

1 Make a template by tracing the diamond shape from Fig 1, cutting it out and sticking it on to card, or use template plastic, see page 15 for instructions on making templates.

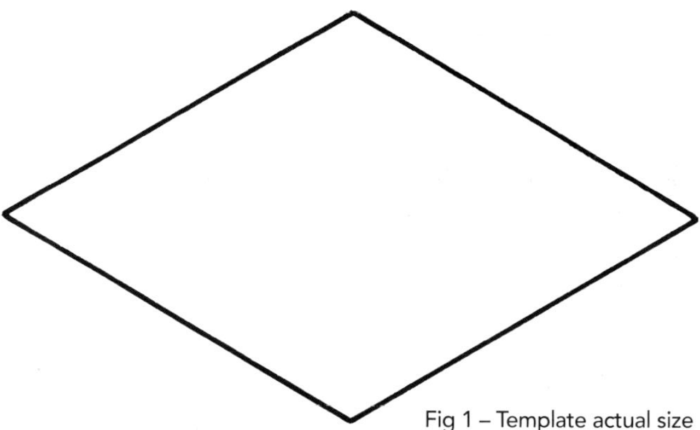

Fig 1 – Template actual size

2 Using a really sharp pencil to keep the shape accurate, draw round the template on to thick paper – the cartridge paper in children's drawing books is ideal. Do not use card as it is too thick. Mark the corners of the diamonds by continuing the drawn lines to just beyond the template corners so that they cross. This cross marks the exact corner and will make cutting out more accurate (Fig 2).

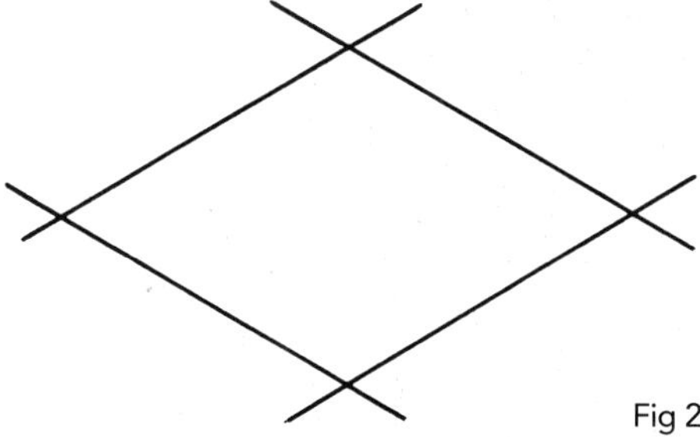

Fig 2

3 Cut out eighteen paper diamonds, cutting just inside the drawn lines to prevent the shape becoming larger than the original diamond.

4 On the wrong side of each fabric, pin six paper shapes, following the straight grain of the fabric and leaving a ¼in (6mm) gap around each paper as shown in Fig 3.

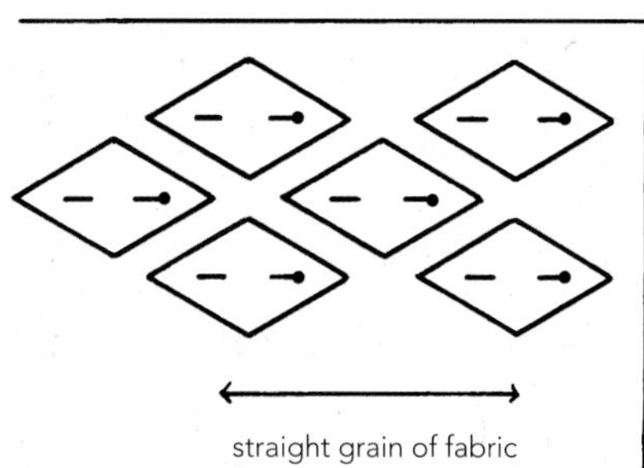

Fig 3

5 Cut around each paper adding a ¼in (6mm) seam allowance on all sides. This does not have to be carefully measured and marked as it is not critical if you are a little generous. However, try to avoid cutting a seam allowance less than ¼in (6mm) as this makes tacking (basting) difficult. The points at the long corners can be shortened to leave a ¼in (6mm) margin of fabric beyond the paper (Fig 4).

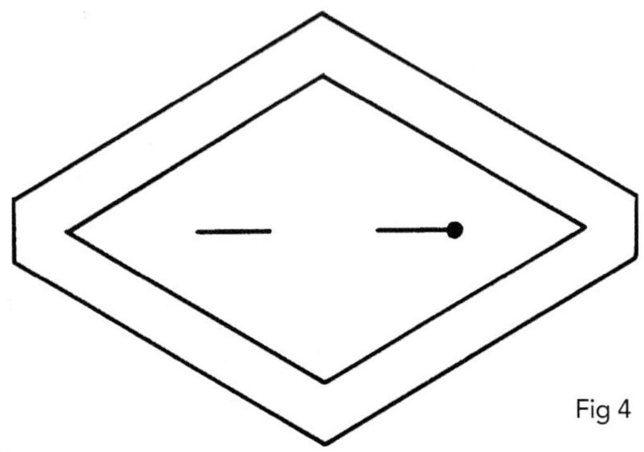

Fig 4

6 Thread a needle with tacking (basting) thread – I use either crewel needles or sharps size 8 or 9. Begin with a knot and tack fabric to paper by folding the seam allowance tightly over the paper and stitching it down. The corner of folded fabric extending beyond the diamond can be ignored at this stage (Fig 5). Turn the tacked shape over and check that the corners exactly outline the shape of the paper beneath it (Fig 6). Remove the pins.

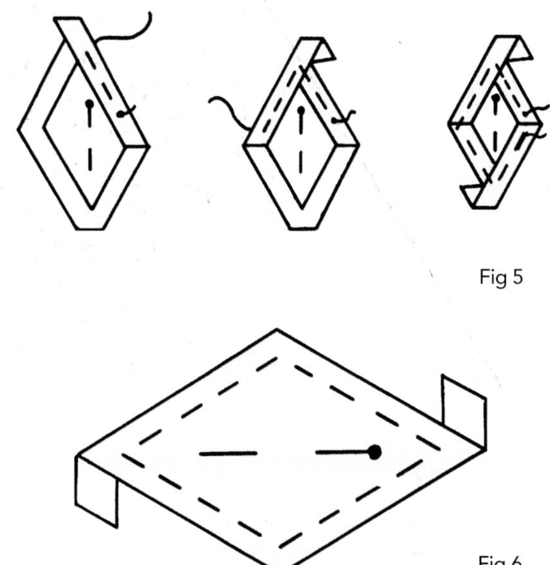

Fig 5

Fig 6

7 Arrange one light, one medium and one dark diamond in the desired design (Fig 7). I have put the lightest fabric horizontally across the top of each block, but you may like to arrange them differently. As long as all six blocks are identical you can place the diamonds however you like. Thread a needle with no more than 18in (46.7cm) of toning thread. If stitching two different coloured fabrics together, match the thread to the darker fabric as it is always less obvious than the lighter.

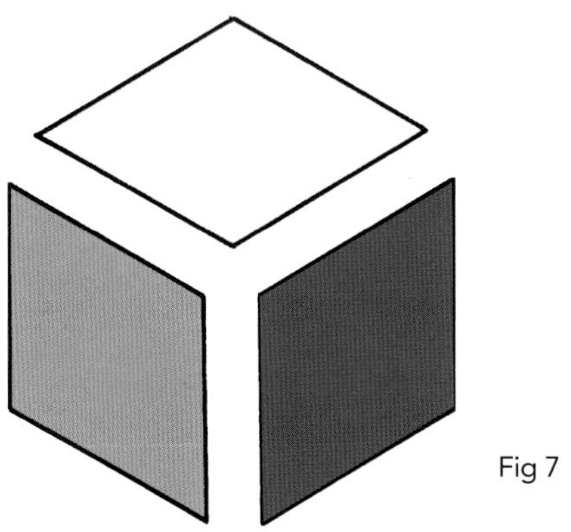

Fig 7

Take two diamond shapes and place them right sides together ready to sew. If one edge seems longer than the other, (this happens more often than you would think, so do not blame yourself) place them so that the shorter edge is lying on top as you work. As you sew the top layer stretches, just as it does on a sewing machine, so you can ease the shorter edge to fit the longer. Fix the corner you are working towards with a pin (Fig 8) so that as you sew the two corners will match exactly.

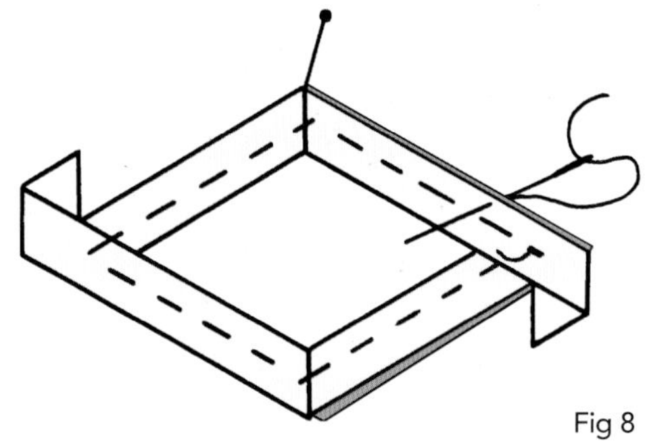

Fig 8

8 Starting with a double stitch to secure the thread, oversew with small even stitches, making sure that the two sets of corners match exactly. The stitches

"I've enjoyed sewing all my life but this was my very first attempt at quilting. The sampler quilt took me nearly two years to make but I felt a great sense of achievement when it was completed." **June Turner**

should be about the same distance apart as small machine stitches (Fig 9). If you stitch too closely you can weaken the fabric and make almost a satin stitch effect which will prevent the finished seam from lying flat.

As you sew the corners, push the seam allowances to one side so that they stick out beyond the edges (Fig 10). Once the papers are removed these extra flaps dovetail in with each other without adding extra bulk. Do not be tempted to trim down these flaps as this can weaken the seams. Finish sewing with a double stitch and cut the thread, leaving about ¼in (6mm) for safety.

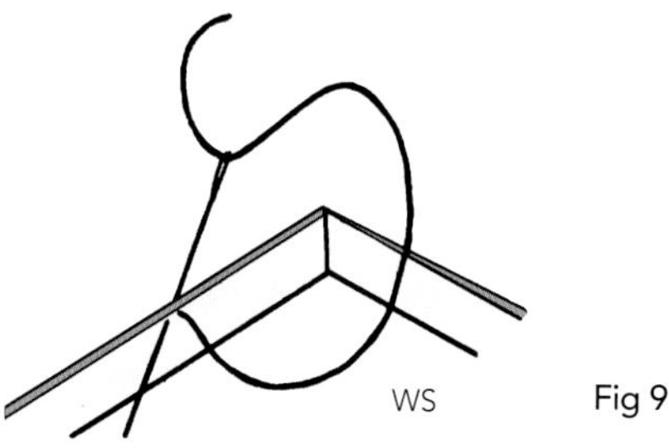

Fig 9

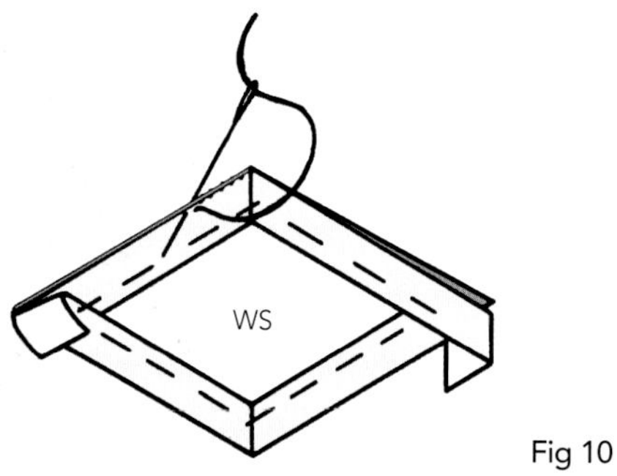

Fig 10

9 Open out the two diamonds and attach diamond three in the same way, sewing another double stitch at the centre of all three diamonds to strengthen it.

10 Assemble all six hexagons in this way and join them together to make the tower shape (Fig 11). Press before removing the papers so that the outer seam allowances remain turned under. Remove tacking by undoing the final stitch and pulling firmly on the knot to pull the tacking thread out in one length. The papers can then be lifted out and stored. Tack around the edges of the tower shape to keep the seam allowances in place, folding back any flaps that are sticking out under the main shape and including these in the tacking.

Fig 11

11 Cut a 13in (33cm) square of fabric for the background. Although the finished size will be 12½in (31.7cm) square, when one fabric is stitched on to another (known as appliqué), the bottom fabric often draws up slightly to finish up smaller than when you started. By using a 13in (33cm) square it can be accurately trimmed to 12½in (31.7cm) once the tower has been stitched in place.

12 Place the tower centrally on the background fabric. It helps if you fold the square in four and crease lightly with your fingers – the creases then make guidelines for positioning the tower. Pin or tack the tower on to the background square.

13 Using a shade of thread to match the tower and not the background, sew the tower on to the background, keeping stitches small and even. Sew a double stitch at each corner to secure it (Fig 12).

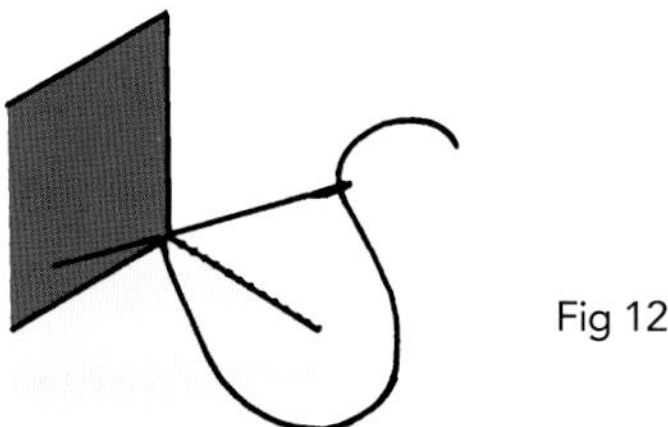

Fig 12

14 Before an appliquéd shape is quilted its thickness can be reduced by cutting the background fabric away from behind the appliqué. This is not compulsory and if you are nervous about doing this, leave it. However, it does make the whole piece easier to quilt and allows it to lie flatter.

Turn the block to the back and, with your fingers, just pull away the backing from the appliqué at the centre. Make a small cut in the backing fabric. Once you have done this, carefully cut away the backing up to ¼in (6mm) from the stitching line of the appliqué, leaving the appliqué itself intact (Fig 13).

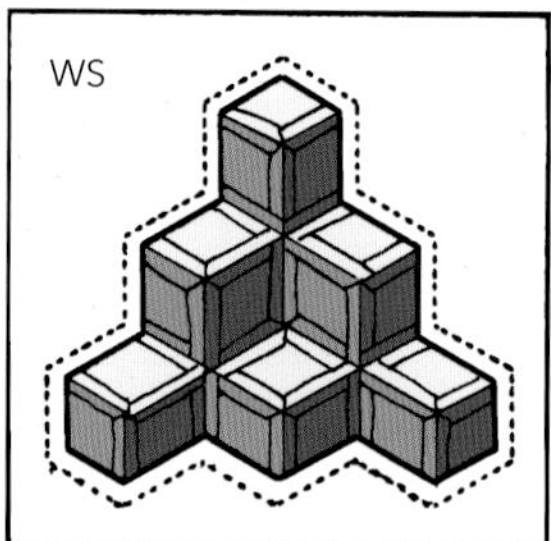

Fig 13

15 Trim the finished block to an exact 12½in (31.7cm) square and add the framing and sashing strips – see page 236. If you have not yet chosen the sashing fabric, leave the block until you have completed enough other blocks to help you decide.

Machined Strip Patchwork

Rail Fence

This block is a traditional strip design which, in the past, has been made by hand using a template for each strip. We can now use a rotary cutter and ruler to cut the strips and a sewing machine to stitch the block quickly and accurately. The Rail Fence design is made by sewing together three long strips of different fabrics and then re-cutting this band into squares. The squares are then arranged and joined together to make the block. This quickly made design can be used very effectively to make a larger quilt, turning the blocks through 90° each time so that the strips make a pattern of steps running diagonally across the quilt.

Colour Choices

For this block you need three fabrics. The same combination of fabrics used in Tumbling Blocks (page 22) could be used again or a new selection made. Fold the fabrics into narrow strips and place them next to each other on a flat surface so that you can see how effective they look together. If you are unsure about the effect, cut four strips of each fabric measuring ½ x 1½in (1.3 x 3.8cm) and play around with them, arranging them in various combinations until you get the best effect. Stick the chosen arrangement on to card or paper.

Construction

1 From each fabric cut one strip measuring 2½in (6.3cm) wide and 28in (71.1cm) long (Fig 1). If you are trying to cut your strips parallel to the selvedge and cannot cut a strip 28in (71.1cm) long, cut two 14in (35.5cm) long strips of each fabric instead. See page 16 for instructions on cutting strips.

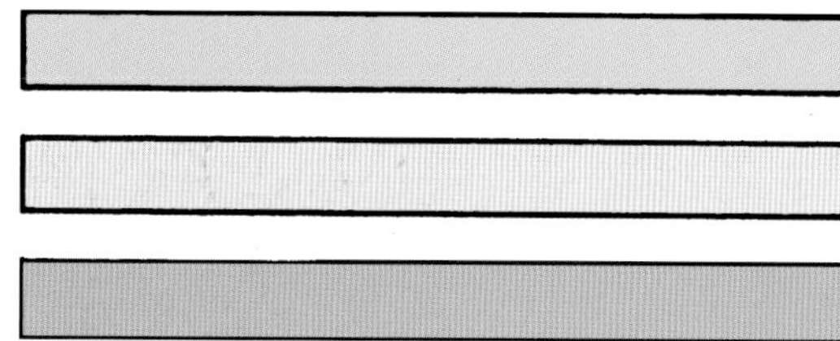

Fig 1

2 Set the stitch length on your sewing machine to about two-thirds the size of the usual dressmaking stitch, small enough to prevent the seams from coming undone when the strips are cut across, but not so small that you could never unpick the stitches if you had to. See page 15 for setting up the machine. Be careful to ensure that the sewn seams are a scant ¼in (6mm). A strip of masking tape stuck on to the machine plate at the correct distance from the needle can provide a useful guide.

Stitch the three strips together: I do not use pins but stop every 3–4in (7.6–10.2cm) and line up the next section of fabric edges as I go. Try not to stretch the strips but guide them gently, using small scissors or the point of a seam ripper to keep the edges in position. Alternate the direction you sew the strips to keep the band straight not slightly rippled (Fig 2).

Fig 2

3 Press the band from the front with the seams all in one direction (Fig 3). See page 15 for general advice on pressing work.

Fig 3

4 Place the fabric band horizontally on the cutting board, lining up the top edge with one of the horizontal markings on the board. If you are lucky the band will be perfect and lie flat, although it is more likely to have a slightly wavy or rippled effect, the result of joining together three different fabrics. You cannot help this so just place the band as flat as possible and continue.

Measure the width of the band. If you have stitched an accurate scant ¼in (6mm) the band should be 6½in (16.5cm). Using the rotary ruler and cutter, trim one end of the band to straighten it and cut four sections each 6½in (16.5cm) long, to make four squares (Fig 4).

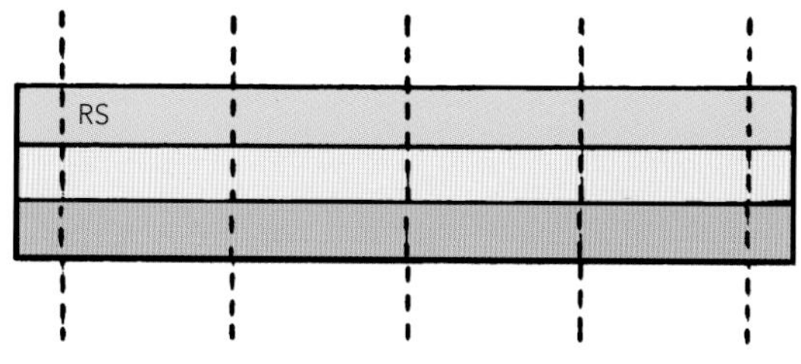

Fig 4

Note: If your band does not measure 6½in (16.5cm), even if it is only ⅛in (3mm) out, take the measurement you have and cut the four squares to match it. This way you will have true squares, even if they are slightly more or less than intended. You can make adjustments later on if necessary.

5 Arrange the four squares to make the block design (Fig 5). Pin and machine stitch the top two squares together with a ¼in (6mm) seam. If you place the pins at right angles to the seams you will be able to stitch right up to each pin before removing it (Fig 6 overleaf).

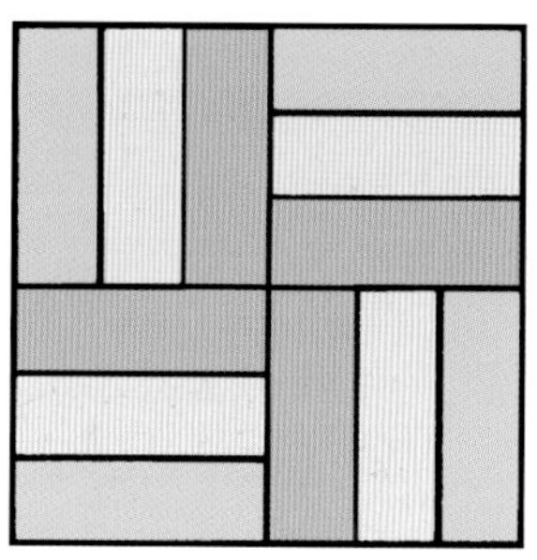

Fig 5

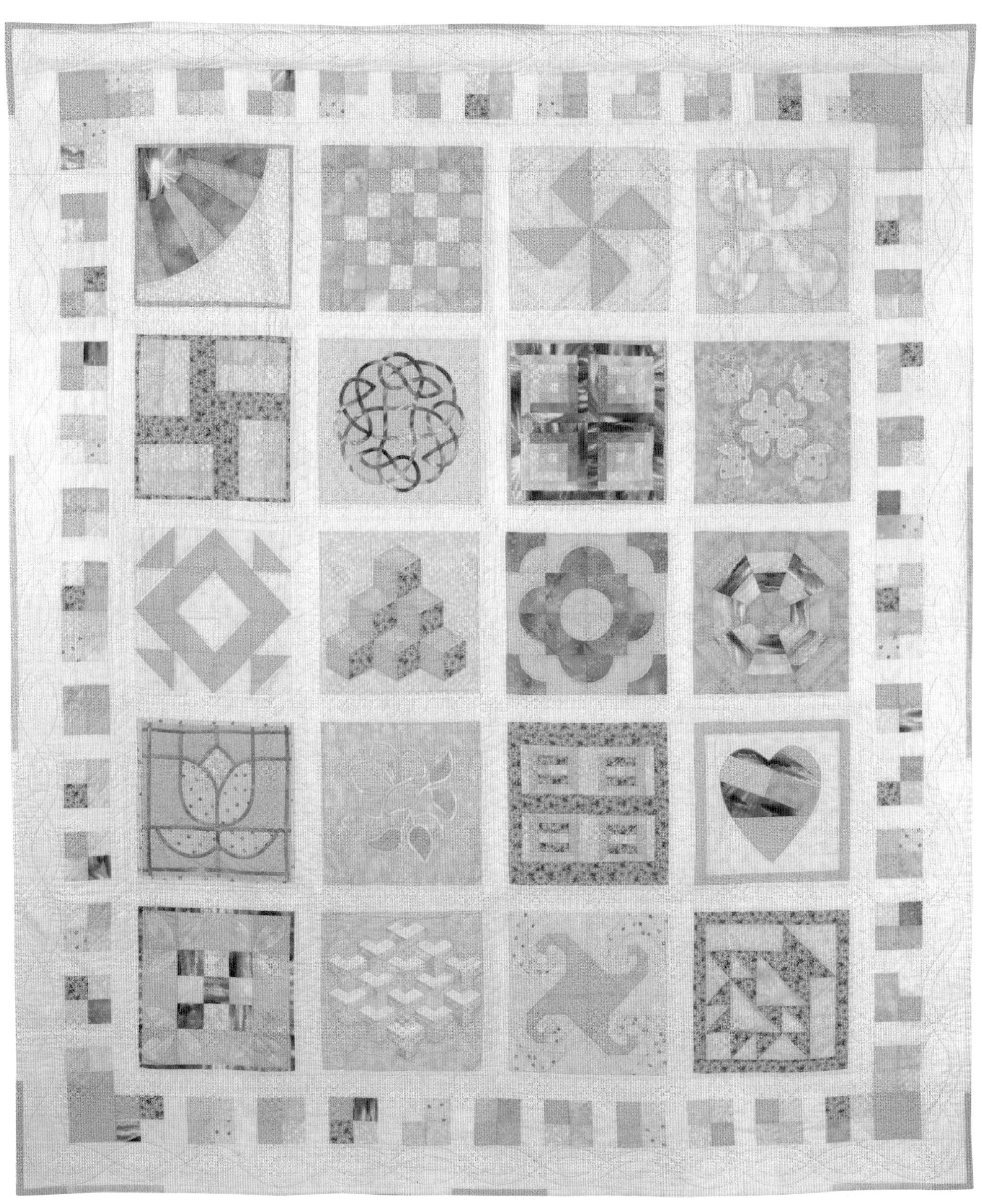

"This is the first sampler quilt that I made and I was so pleased when it won the Visitor's Choice prize at our local show. It remains my most enjoyable quilting experience." **Carol Wood**

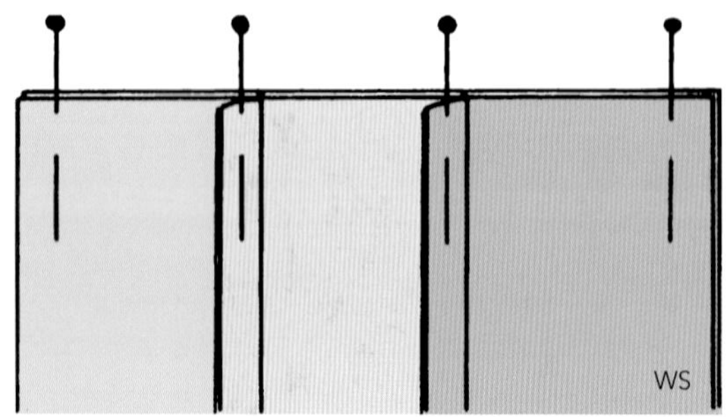

Fig 6

If the two edges do not match exactly and one is shorter than the other, pin and stitch with the shorter edge on top, as this will stretch slightly as you stitch and should ease the problem. Press the seams to one side from the front of the joined squares.

6 Pin and machine stitch the second pair of squares. Press the seams in the opposite direction to the first half (Fig 7).

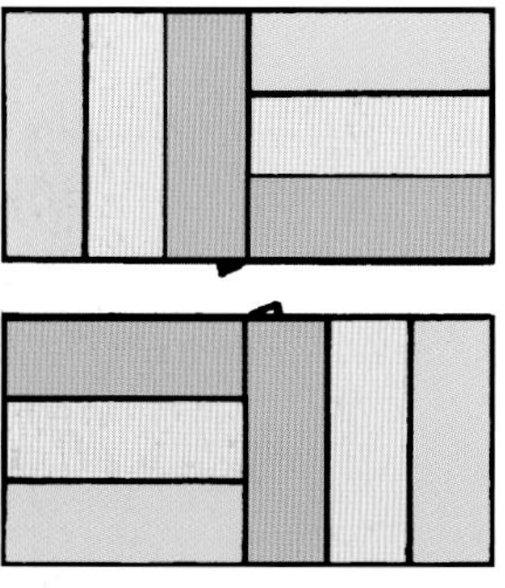

Fig 7

7 Join the two halves by stitching across with a ¼in (6mm) seam, taking care to match the centre seams. Pressing the centre seams of each half in opposite directions will help you to match them accurately, as they lock into each other as you sew. Pin diagonally as this helps to keep both sets of seam allowances flat while stitching (Fig 8). The final long seam can be pressed to one side or, if this makes it too bulky, press the seam open (Fig 9).

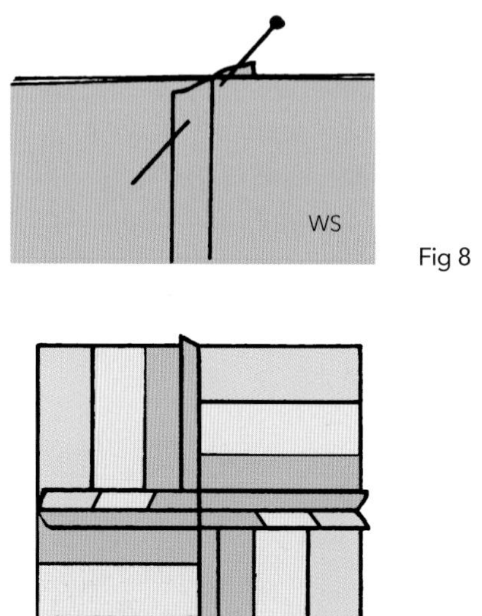

Fig 8

Fig 9

8 Trim the block to an exact 12½in (31.7cm) square. If it is too small, cut it down a little more and add an extra border with a fabric that frames the block well. See page 236 for instructions on trimming and bordering blocks. This border can then be trimmed down to make the completed block exactly 12½in (31.7cm) square. If you have chosen the fabric for the framing sashing strips, add them following the instructions on page 236. If not, just leave your decision until you have made a few more blocks.

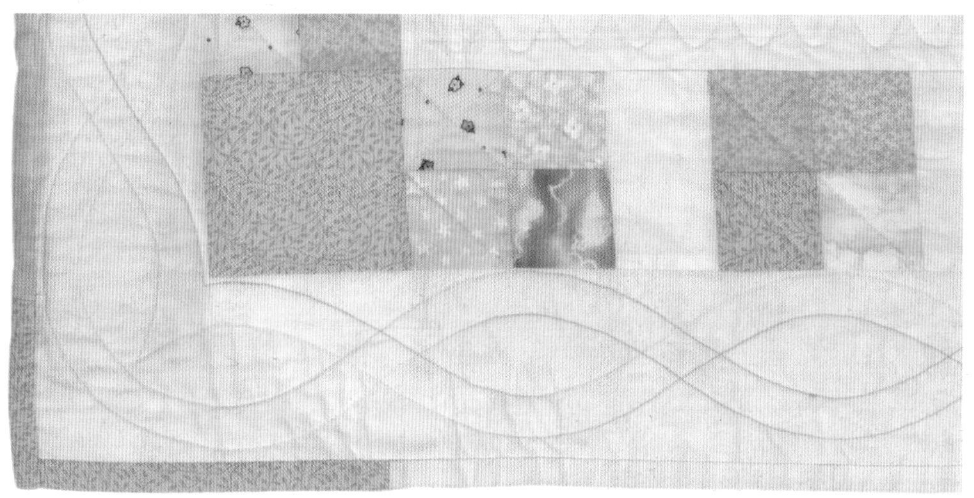

Carol Wood used a simple border of four-patch blocks around her quilt, with machine quilting beyond it on the final frame of background fabric. The quilting design on the outer border is enhanced by the use of a variegated thread for the machine stitching.

American Pieced Patchwork

Maple Leaf

It was seeing the quilt collection in the American Museum at Claverton Manor near Bath in the UK that started my life-long love affair with quilts and quilt-making. I had only ever seen museum exhibits of Victorian hexagon or octagon quilts – often unfinished – and until then had no idea what a wonderfully rich mix of shape and colour had been established in traditional American quilts.

The Americans view the idea of piecing patchwork using papers as near madness. They have their own technique of hand-piecing that evolved when the early settlers from Europe found themselves facing cruel winters without sufficient warm covers. They needed to make thick blankets as quickly as

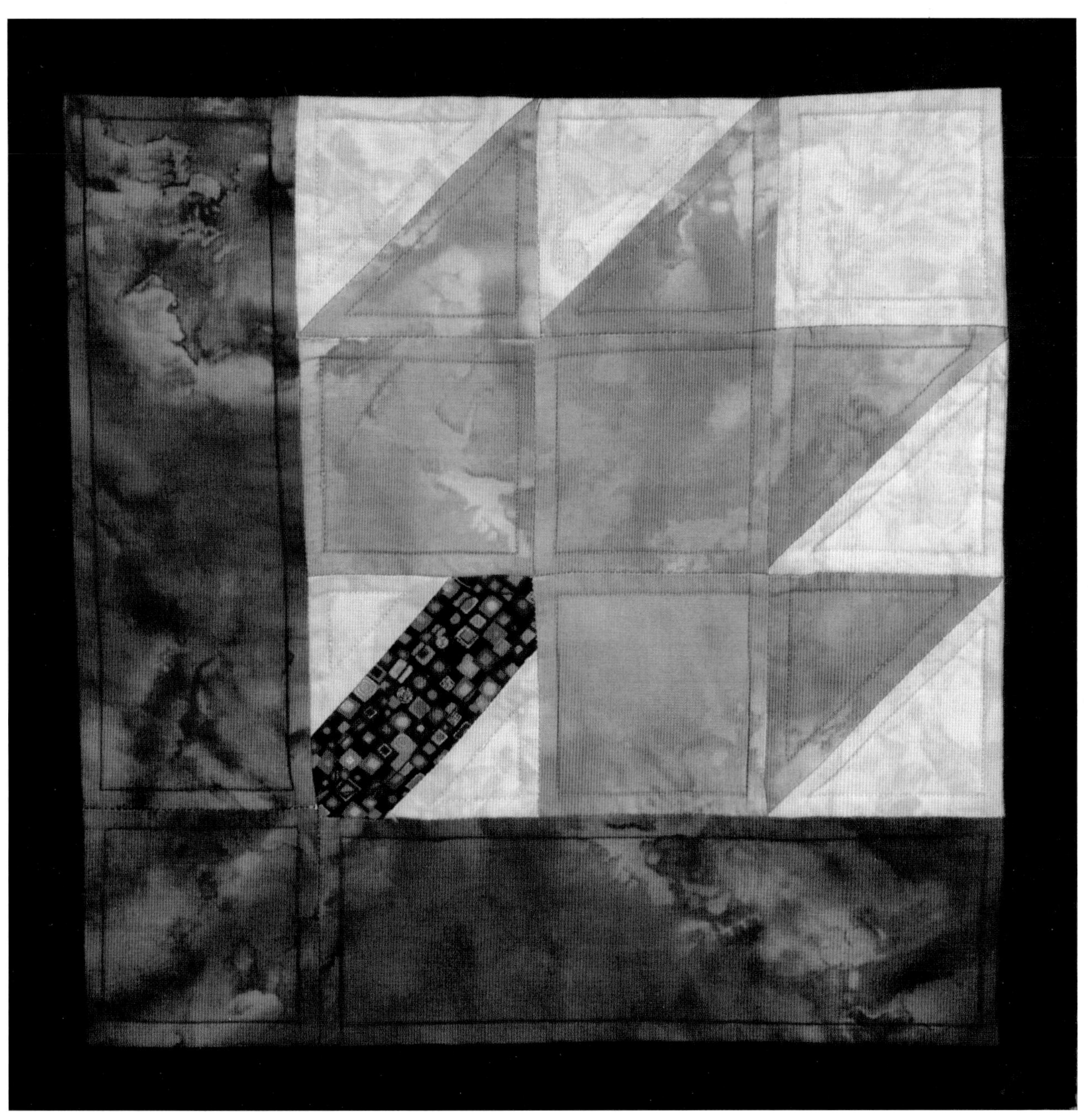

possible from the few scraps and rags available, so they joined squares, rectangles and strips into a blanket-shaped piece. Another similar shape was made and a filling of shredded rags, wool and scraps was placed between the two to give some warmth. To keep the filling in place an even running stitch was made through all the layers.

In time the makers of these quilts used the traditions of quilt-making that had been brought with them from Europe to turn the random piecing of patches into regular designs. The designs took the form of squares, called blocks, of sizes varying from 10in (25.4cm) to 16in (40.7cm) or 18in (45.7cm), which were repeated and joined to make quilts. There are now hundreds of traditional block designs, many appearing in different areas of the United States under a variety of names. Their names reflect the life and times of those early settlers: Bear's Paws, Goose Tracks, Hovering Hawks. Others show a religious influence: Jacob's Ladder, Hosannah, Steps to the Altar. Some blocks have been named after a person, which makes you wonder who they were.

The stitching in these blocks did not need to be as strong as that in English patchwork because the quilting stitches, which crossed and re-crossed the quilt through all the layers, reinforced the fabrics and took the strain off the linking stitches. The traditional American method of patchwork uses templates to mark the fabrics and the pieces are then joined by matching up and stitching along the drawn lines.

The block I have chosen to introduce this most commonly used hand technique is the Maple Leaf. It is a design based on nine squares, some of which are divided into smaller shapes. Any pattern which has these nine basic squares is called a Nine-Patch and many Nine-Patch designs can be found amongst the traditional patchwork blocks. A border strip has been added to the left side and along the bottom of the block. I especially like the diagonal slant to this block as it gives a lovely feeling of movement when repeated on a large quilt. It is ideal for a corner block in a sampler quilt where it draws the eye from the corner into the main quilt (Fig 1).

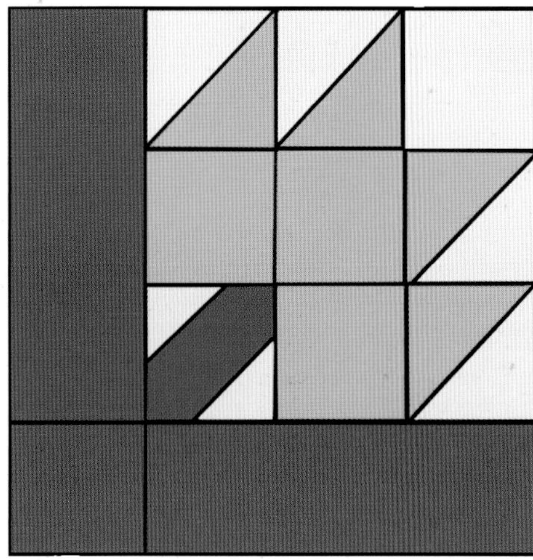

Fig 1

Colour Choices

This simple block needs two fabrics, one for the leaf itself and one for the background, plus a third fabric for the border strips. The corner square at the bottom left corner of the design could be made from the leaf fabric, the background fabric or another fabric altogether. Do not think that because you are piecing a leaf, it has to be a correct leaf colour; the shape is a maple leaf and the colours can be whatever suits your own quilt. You do not need a large square of background fabric as you did for the Tumbling Blocks. Here every piece is cut to shape and joined with its neighbour to form the complete block.

Construction

1 Make templates by tracing the five shapes from Fig 2 on page 35, cutting them out and sticking them on to card, or use template plastic. See page 15 for instructions on making templates.

2 On the wrong side of each fabric, draw accurately around the templates using a sharp marking pencil. This marks the sewing line. Allow at least ½in (1.3cm) between each drawn outline so that a seam allowance of ¼in (6mm) can be added to each shape when cutting out (see Fig 3). For the leaf you will need three of square A, four of triangle B and one of stem C. Save space by arranging the shapes on the fabric as shown in Fig 4. For the background you need one of square A, four of triangle B and two of triangle D. For the border you need two of rectangle E and one of square A.

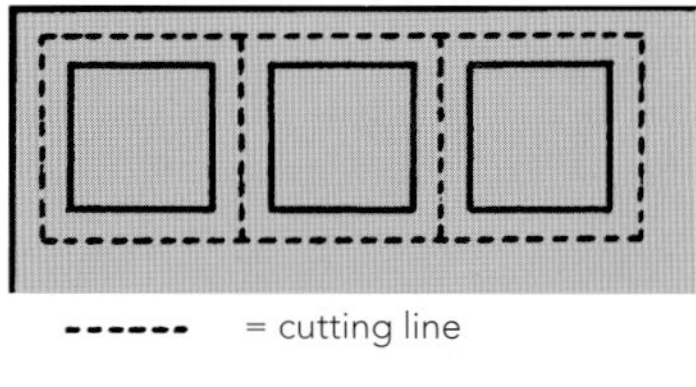

Fig 3

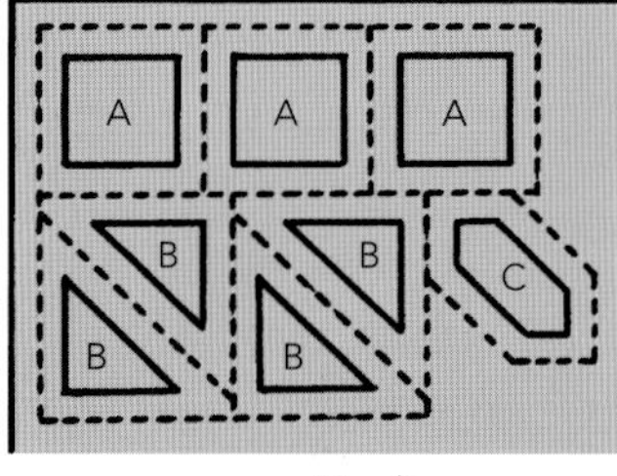

Fig 4

3 Cut out each shape to include the ¼in (6mm) seam allowance, either by eye or more accurately by measuring. In time you get used to judging this distance and you may find it quicker to cut without extra markings. As with English patchwork, the exact width of the seam allowance is not critical, so judging by eye is perfectly acceptable if you feel comfortable doing it this way.

"I made this quilt at a beginners' course organized by Crystal Quilters in Stourbridge, hence the quilted crystals in each corner. My start point was the multicoloured small print fabric which I loved and incorporated into every block. Making the quilt taught me so much. It won the Visitor's Choice prize at my first group show in 2007 and is still one of my favourite pieces of work." **Angela Lloyd**

4 Arrange the cut pieces on a flat surface or pin them in position on a polystyrene tile or display board. Final adjustments to the design can then be made at this stage.

5 Do not try to assemble the leaf and then join on the background pieces. Instead, assemble each of the nine squares in the following way (Fig 5).

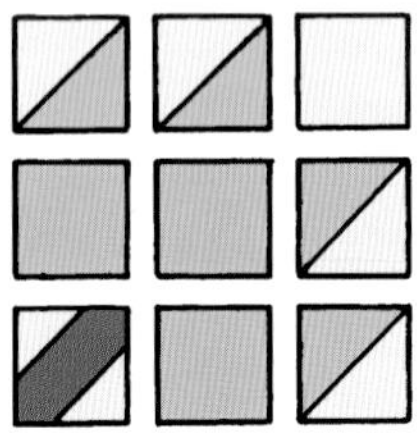

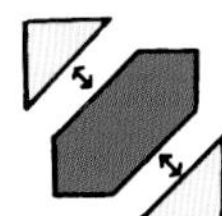

Fig 5

Place the first two triangles together, right sides facing. The pencil markings will be on the outside and must be positioned *exactly* on top of each other as they indicate the sewing lines. Align the starting points of the sewing lines by pushing a pin through both layers of fabric until the head is on the surface of the top fabric. Repeat this to mark the finishing point (Fig 6). Reposition the pins at right angles to the seam. Add more pins along the seamline, matching the marked lines (Fig 7).

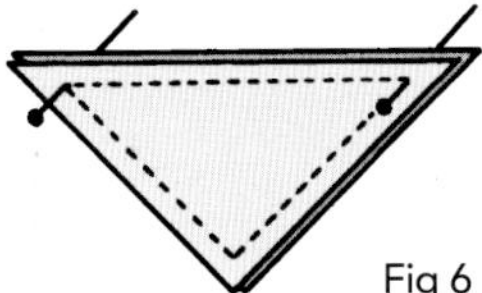

Fig 6

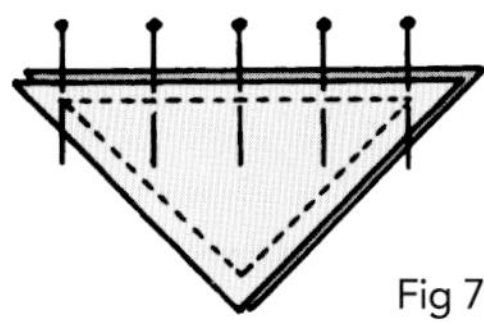

Fig 7

6 Starting with a double stitch, sew along the pencilled line with small running stitches about the same length as machine stitches, loading several stitches on to the needle at a time. Begin each run of stitches with a backstitch to secure the work firmly. Finish the seam exactly at the end of the marked line with several backstitches (Fig 8). Do not sew into the seam allowances – these are left free so that once the block is complete the seams may be pressed to one side. They are never pressed open, as the hand-sewn stitches are not strong enough.

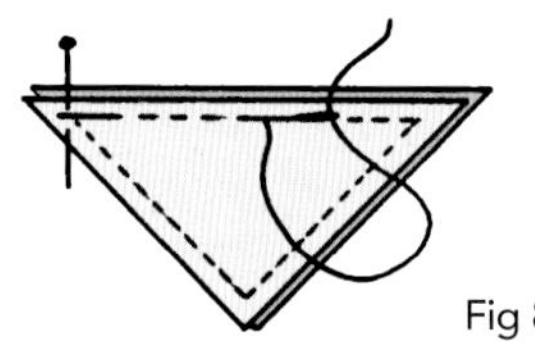

Fig 8

7 Once all nine squares are assembled, sew together the horizontal rows of three squares, pinning and matching the seams as before (Fig 9). Join the top two rows by placing them right sides together, matching seams. Push a pin exactly through the seams and corners on each piece. Reposition the pins at right angles to the seams and add more along the seamlines, matching the marked lines (Fig 10). As before, sew together without sewing into the seam allowances, instead, sew up to each seam and make a backstitch. Pass the needle through the seam allowances to the other side. Backstitch again and continue sewing (Fig 11). Join on the third row in the same way.

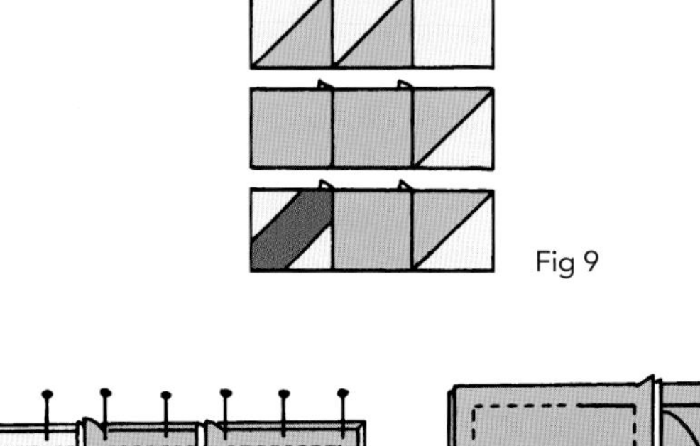

Fig 9

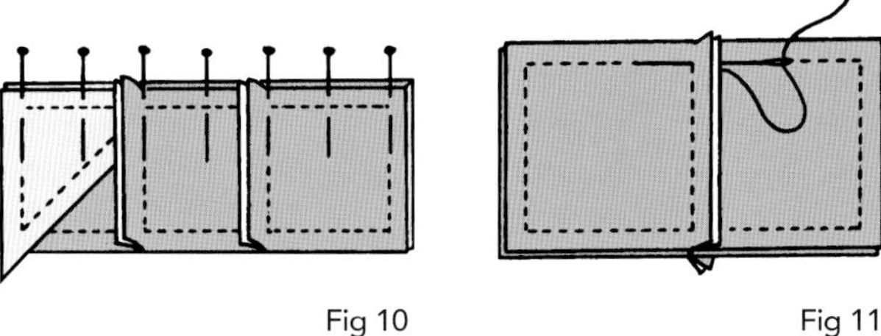

Fig 10

Fig 11

8 Attach a border strip to the side of the block using the same method. Join the remaining square and border strip together. Finally, sew these along the bottom edge to complete the block.

9 Measure the block, it should be 12½in (31.7cm) square. If it needs trimming, trim away on the two border sides only so that you do not trim off the corners of the maple leaf (Fig 12).

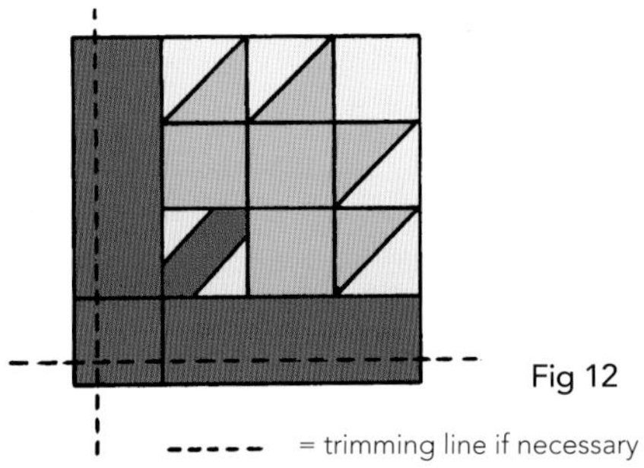

Fig 12

10 Add the framing sashing strips if you are ready to, see page 236 for instructions.

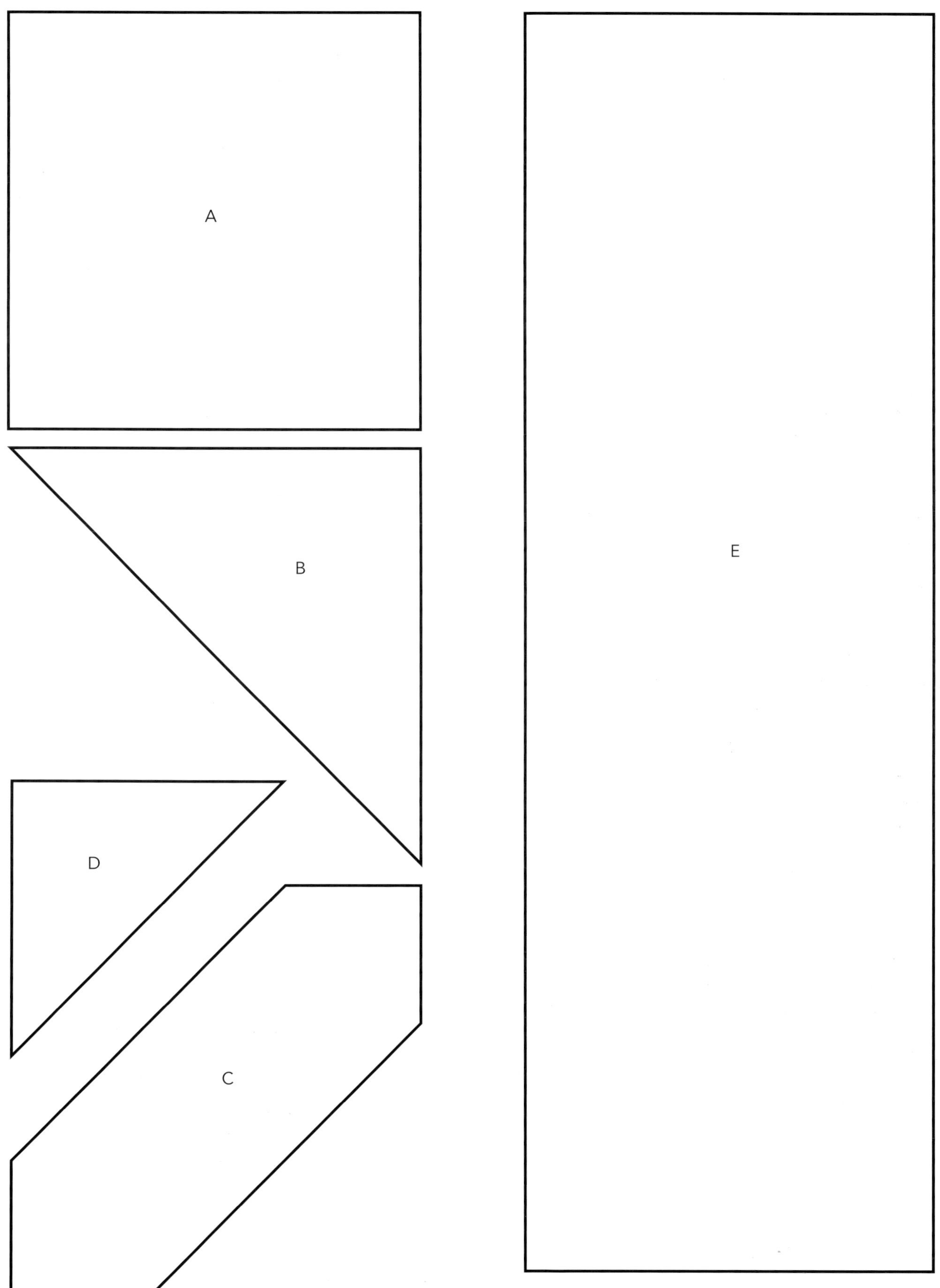

Fig 2 – Templates actual size

Quick Machined Squares

Trip Around the World

This simple design of squares is a traditional pattern frequently found in Amish quilts. The Amish are a religious sect now found mainly in Pennsylvania, Ohio and Indiana in the United States. They left Alsace, on the borders of France and Germany, to avoid persecution in the eighteenth century, and founded their own farming communities in the New World based on their beliefs. They live a simple life set apart as much as possible from the surrounding world. They have no connection by telephone or electricity lines or water or gas pipes. They are excellent farmers, sharing basic equipment that is pulled by horses or man-powered. The communities follow a strict code in

the way they decorate their houses and in their clothing. Everything is simple and plain, using Nature's colours only. They make all their family clothes, using black, white, greys, browns, greens, blues and mauves. The dresses are very simple and are worn with a white bonnet and a black or white cape and apron. No fancy frills or even patterned fabrics are used in their clothing, or in the quilts for which they are famous. The simple designs use a mixture of clear, plain colours and have a strength and elegance that is enhanced by wonderful hand-quilting. Amish quilts, especially antique ones, have been likened to modern abstract art and are now collectors' items, commanding very high prices.

The Trip Around the World design is based on simple squares using several colours. The central square represents the world and each surrounding row is a new colour, making a diamond design around the single central square (Fig 1).There must be an odd number of squares in each row, such as nine, eleven or fifteen, so that there is one square in the centre of the block for the focus (the world). For the 12in (30.5cm) block in the sampler quilt I have used seven squares in each row so that the piecing is not too fiddly, making a total of forty-nine squares.

Fig 1

Colour Choices

If you wish you can use seven colours, changing them for each circuit of squares. This can look very busy so you may wish to limit the fabrics to four or five; Fig 2 shows three different arrangements of squares to give you some ideas. Most books suggest that when planning the colours for a design like this you should draw out the block on squared paper and colour it in to see the different effects. This is fine, but I find it very difficult to relate the shaded pencil colours to actual fabric. Ideally you should just cut lots of fabric squares and play with them, but this inevitably leads to waste; also it takes a strong person to discard twenty cut squares of one fabric in favour of another because the original idea did not work as well as you had hoped. I favour a compromise: from each fabric cut a strip ½in (1.3cm) wide and 10–12in (25.4–30.5cm) long. From these cut off ½in (1.3cm) squares. Now play with these small pieces until you find the design you like best. There is little wastage using these narrow strips and you will get a good idea of what the completed block will look like. Either stick the chosen arrangement on to card or paper or draw a plan of it on squared paper to keep as a reference. Using a felt board is ideal as the fabric squares can be placed on it and they will stay in position without pinning, see Basic Equipment page 15.

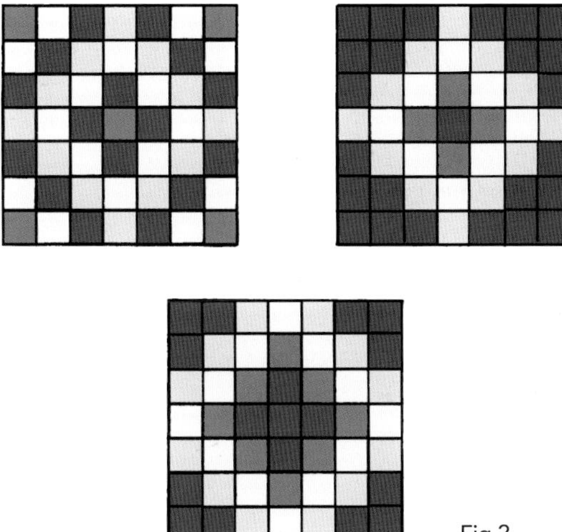

Fig 2

Construction

1 From your chosen fabrics cut strips 2¼in (5.7cm) wide. The length of each strip will vary according to how many 2¼in (5.7cm) squares are needed for your design. Place each strip horizontally on the cutting board, lining the top long edge with a horizontal marking line on the board. Cut pieces from each strip to make squares 2¼in (5.7cm) in size (Fig 3).

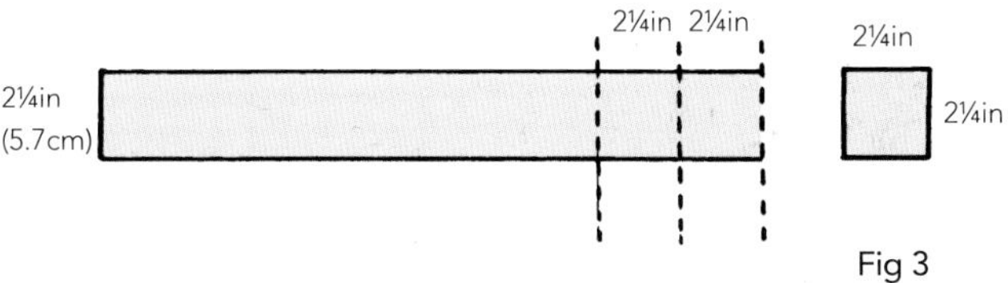

Fig 3

2 Arrange the squares in your chosen design and check that it looks as good as it seemed when you made it with the tiny squares.

3 Stitching an exact ¼in (6mm) seam at all times, machine together the squares from the top row of the design. Position the squares by matching them edge to edge so that there is no need to pin them together. If you use a smaller stitch (about two-thirds normal size) there is no need to secure the ends by reversing the stitching. If the design is symmetrical (and it should be!), row one should be the same as row seven, row two the same as row six and row three the same as row five. Row four is the centre row and is unique (Fig 4 overleaf).

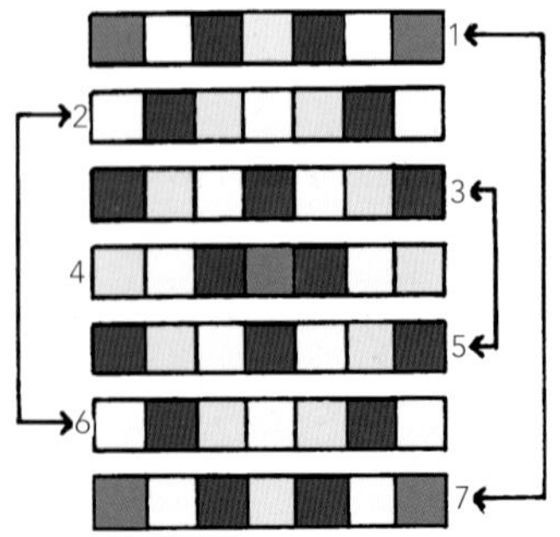

Fig 4

Consider streamlining your stitching and saving time and thread by sewing each pair of identical rows at the same time. Stitch together the first pair of squares in row one, stopping at the last stitch on the fabric. Take the identical pair of squares from row seven and place them right sides together matching the edges. Without lifting the pressure foot, slip this pair under the front of the foot and continue sewing (Fig 5).

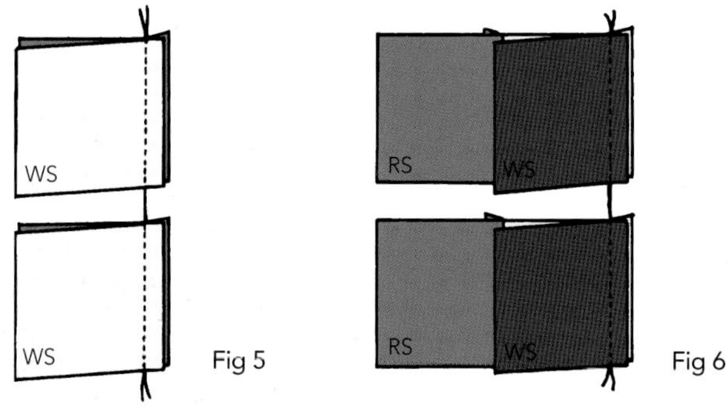

Fig 5

Fig 6

A short length of machined stitches will separate each pair of squares. Remove the squares from the machine and cut the threads to separate them. Open out the joined squares from row one and place the third square in position. Stitch down this seam and continue stitching the identical seam for row seven (Fig 6).

Remove the pieces from the machine and cut the threads to separate them. Continue to do this for each square that you add, stitching row one first and then row seven.

Do the same for rows two and six and for rows three and five. This technique is called stringing or chaining. If you find it simpler to join each row individually, do so – use the method you are comfortable with.

4 Press from the front, ironing the seams of row one in one direction and those in row two the opposite way. Continue to press each row with seams alternately pressed to the right and left.

5 Pin together rows one and two, matching the seams carefully. This is made easier by the pressed seams which lock into each other (Fig 7). Pin diagonally across the seam allowances to keep them flat while stitching (Fig 8).

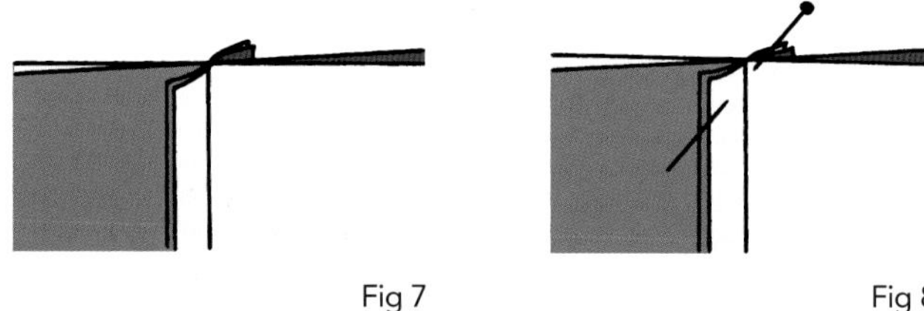

Fig 7

Fig 8

6 If the squares do not all match each other and a little 'easing' has to be done, stitch with the shorter edge on top, as this will stretch as you sew. Stitch row one and row two together. Continue to pin and stitch each row until the block is completed.

7 Press from the front with the seams to one side as before. If the seams are too bulky, press these final long seams open from the back of the work.

8 Measure the completed block, it should be slightly more than 12½in (31.7cm) square and will need to be centred and trimmed down on all four sides to an exact 12½in (31.7cm) square. See page 236 for instructions on trimming the blocks.

9 Add the final sashing strips if you are ready to – see page 236 for instructions.

Pauline Wilson added several borders to frame her quilt, including a simple row of squares and a wider border with this lovely hand-quilted design of hearts running along it.

"This is my first quilt, and it began with a gorgeous pack of fat quarters. I did not have a clue about what I was doing but with the help and support of my teacher, our quilting group and Lynne's sampler book I have found a wonderful pastime and most rewarding hobby – there is no stopping me now!" **Pauline Wilson**

American Pieced Patchwork

Card Trick

This block uses only two templates, fewer than the Maple Leaf, but the pieces are smaller so there is more work involved. When I made my own sampler quilt I made the finished size of the Card Trick block exactly 12in (30.5cm), but I altered the size to a 9in (22.8cm) block with an added surrounding border for the students in case the completed blocks finished up a little bigger than planned, trimming the block down to size would have cut off all those lovely points around the outside edges and spoiled the effect. Please don't misunderstand me – I did not assume that everyone's block would be inaccurate. This was just a contingency plan so that *if* any block was too big, it would

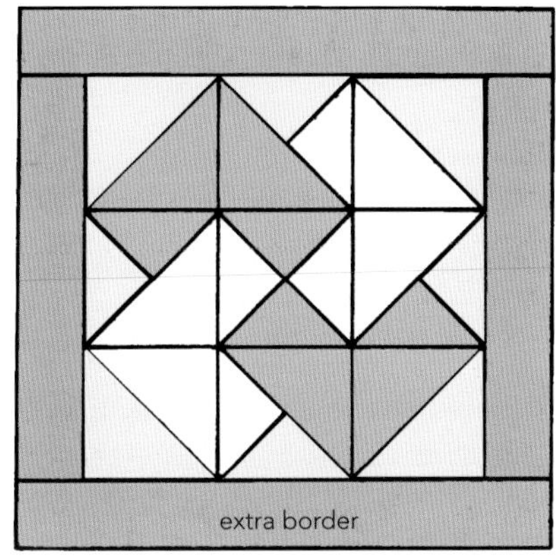

Fig 1

not matter. When you are a beginner I feel you need every bit of help available. Also I liked the smaller scale of the 9in (22.8cm) block, and wished I had made mine that size (Fig 1).

The templates here are for a 12in (30.5cm) block, but if you prefer the smaller version it is very easy to draft your own templates. The block is based on nine squares, three rows of three squares, which is known as a Nine-Patch. To make a 9in (22.8cm) block, each square needs to measure 3 x 3in (7.6 x 7.6cm). Draw a 3in (7.6cm) square on graph paper or template plastic, keeping the lines as accurate as possible. Divide the square with a diagonal line (Fig 2). One of the resulting triangles is used as the larger template, A. Draw another diagonal line from one comer, stopping at the centre point so that the second large triangle is now divided into two. Either of these two smaller triangles is template B. If working on graph paper, cut roughly around the square, stick it on to card and then cut the two triangular templates A and B from it. See page 15 for making templates.

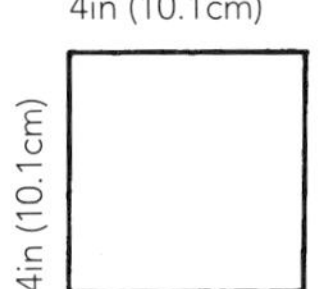

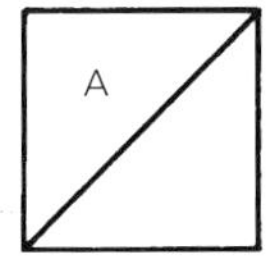

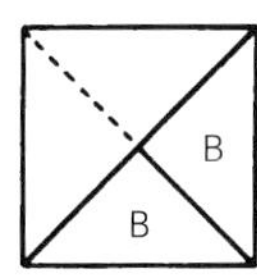

Fig 2

Colour Choices

The Card Trick block is given its name because it looks like a handful of playing cards spread out in a fan shape. There are four 'cards' made from two fabrics placed alternately, although four different fabrics can be used. Another fabric is needed for the background. As with the Maple Leaf, this background is not just a large square on to which the cards are stitched. Instead, every piece is cut to shape and joined with its neighbour to make the block. The 'card' fabrics need to balance each other in their density of colour. In other words, you do not want one colour that is much stronger than the others. Arrange the 'card' fabrics in a cross shape on a piece of the background fabric. Stand back and half close your eyes. If one fabric seems to dominate, change it. It is easier to achieve a balance if you just use two fabrics for the cards, as in Fig 1. The background can be dark, as in Fig 1, or much lighter. You may, of course, use one fabric throughout the sampler quilt for all the backgrounds of the blocks. Remember that with the 9in (22.8cm) block an edging border of at least 1½in (3.8cm) finished width has to be added to increase it to the required 12in (30.5cm) block, so the fabric for this also has to be considered. Any extra borders around blocks like this should not be of the same fabric as the sashing strips, so if you have not made a decision on the sashing fabric, you may need to before you can go much further.

Construction

1 Make card templates by tracing triangles A and B from Fig 3 on page 44, cutting them out and sticking them on to card, or use template plastic. If you want to make the smaller block draft your own templates as explained earlier, see page 15 for instructions on making templates.

2 On the wrong side of each fabric draw accurately around the templates using a sharp marking pencil. This marks the sewing line. Allow at least ½in (1.3cm) between each drawn outline so that the seam allowance of ¼in (6mm) can be added to each shape when cutting out.

If you are using two fabrics for the 'cards' you will need four of triangle A and four of triangle B from each fabric. (If using four fabrics you need two of each triangle from each fabric.) You also need four of each triangle from the background fabric. Save space by arranging the shapes on the fabric as shown in Fig 4.

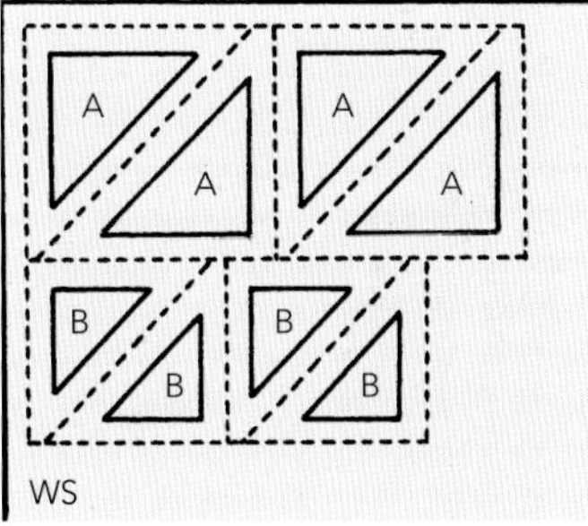

Fig 4

3 Cut out each shape to include the ¼in (6mm) seam allowance, either by eye or more accurately by measuring. In time you get used to judging this distance, and as the exact width of the seam allowance is not critical in American piecing judging by eye is perfectly acceptable if you feel comfortable doing it this way.

4 Arrange the cut pieces on a flat surface or pin them in position on a polystyrene tile or board. Final adjustments to the design can be made at this stage.

5 Do not try to assemble the 'cards' and then join on the background pieces. Instead, assemble each of the nine squares in the following way (Fig 5). Place the first two triangles together with right sides facing. The pencil markings will be on the outside and must be positioned *exactly* on top of each other as they indicate the sewing lines. Align the starting points of the sewing lines by pushing a pin through both layers of fabric until the head is on the surface of the top fabric. Repeat this to mark the finishing point (Fig 6). Reposition the pins at right angles to the seam. Add more pins along the seamline, matching the marked lines (Fig 7).

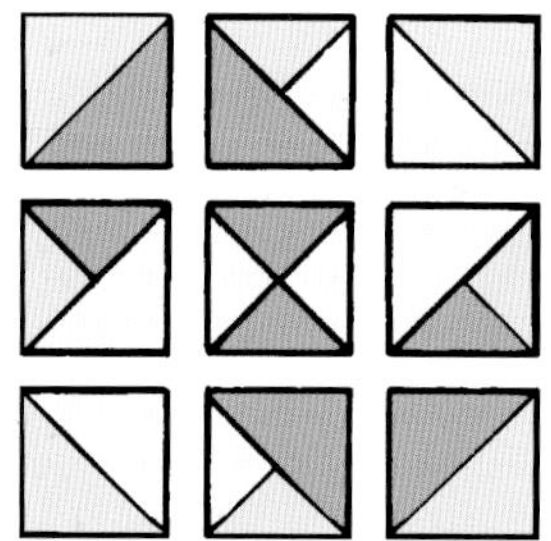
Fig 5

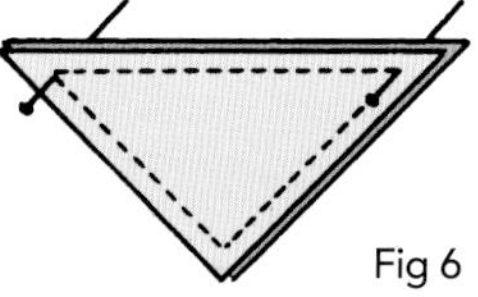
Fig 6

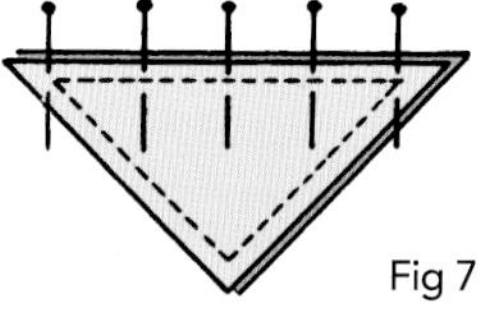
Fig 7

6 Starting with a double stitch, sew along the pencilled line with small running stitches about the same length as machine stitches, loading several stitches on to the needle at a time. Begin each run of stitches with a backstitch to secure the work firmly. Finish the seam exactly at the end of the marked line with several backstitches (Fig 8). Do not sew into the seam allowances – these are left free so that once the block is complete the seams may be pressed to one side. They are never pressed open, as the hand-sewn stitches are not strong enough. There is no set rule for which way each seam is finally pressed – just press them to avoid too much bulk building up on the back.

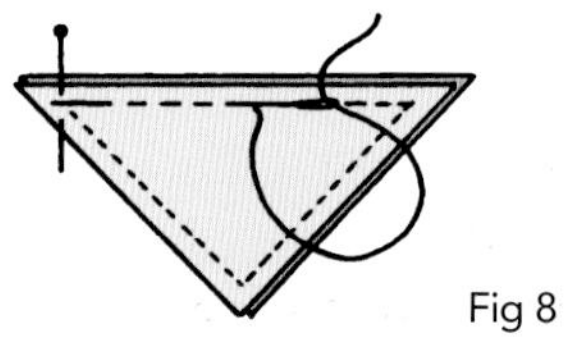
Fig 8

7 The squares made from three pieces need to be sewn in two stages. First join together the two smaller triangles and then sew the halves together to make the square, pinning and matching the seams as before (Fig 9). When sewing this second seam, do not sew over the seam allowances in the middle. Instead, sew up to the seam and make a backstitch. Pass the needle through the seam allowances to the other side. Backstitch again and continue sewing (Fig 10). For the central square sew the triangles into pairs and then join the two halves together (Fig 11).

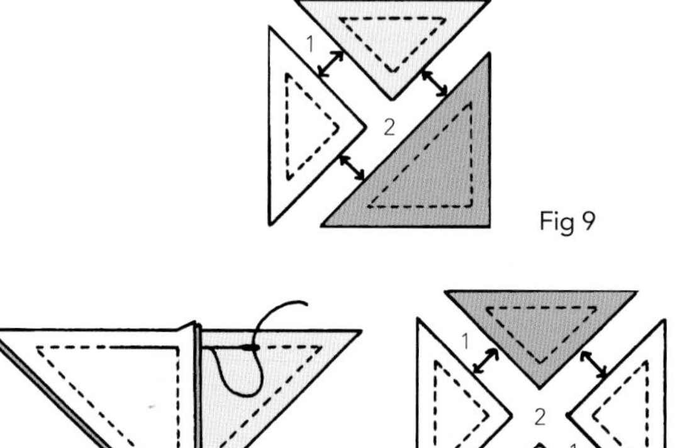

Fig 9

Fig 10

Fig 11

Once the nine squares are assembled, sew together the horizontal rows of three squares, pinning and matching the seams as before (Fig 12).

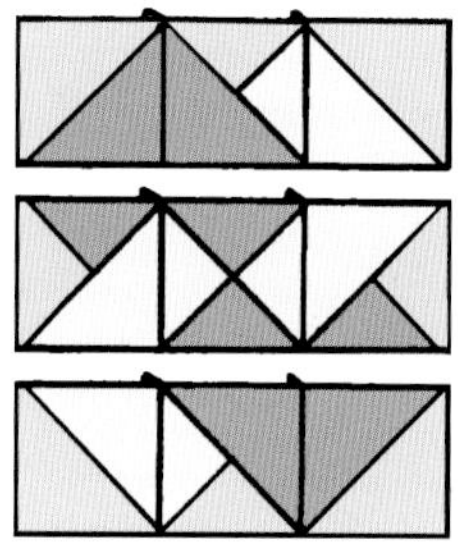
Fig 12

8 Join the top two rows by placing them right sides together, matching seams. Push a pin exactly through the seams and corners on each piece. Reposition these pins at right angles to the seams and add more along the seamline, matching the marked lines (Fig 13). Stitch together without sewing over the seam allowances as before. Join on the third row in the same way.

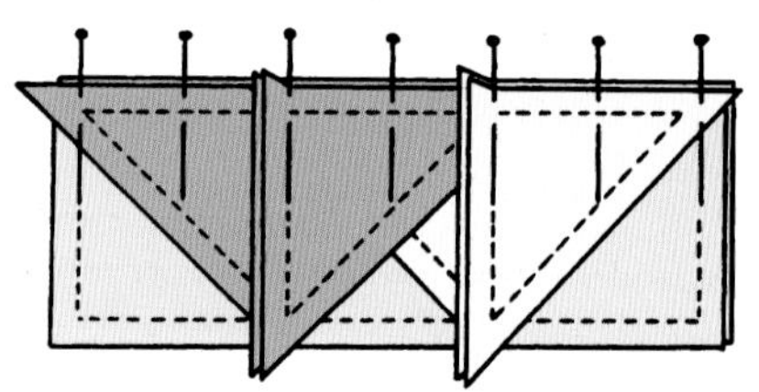
Fig 13

"Since acquiring Lynne's first book I couldn't wait to start my first sampler quilt using the bright colours I love. With help and encouragement from Kate Badrick I became addicted. Both my daughters are quilters. I now have to teach my four granddaughters! Thanks Lynne." **Linda Riceman**

9 If you have chosen to make a larger block, it is now complete, ready for the final sashing strips to be added. If you are making the smaller block it will now need a border. Cut four strips from your chosen fabric, two measuring 2¼ x 9½in (5.7 x 24.2cm) and two measuring 2¼ x 13in (5.7 x 33cm). Using a sharp marking pencil draw a line on the wrong side of each fabric strip ¼in (6mm) away from one long edge. Mark the line as shown in Fig 14.

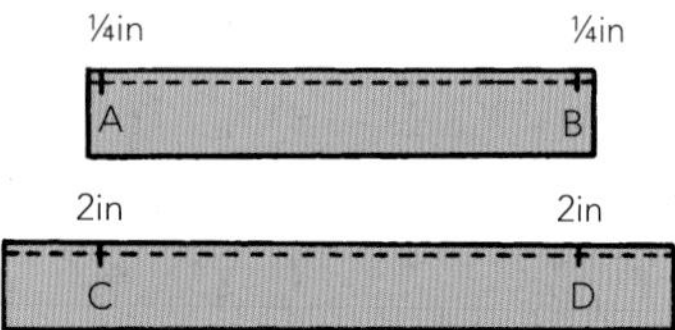

Fig 14

10 With right sides together, pin each shorter strip to opposite sides of the block, matching the marked lines. Marks A and B should match the drawn corners of the block. Use pins as before (Fig 15).

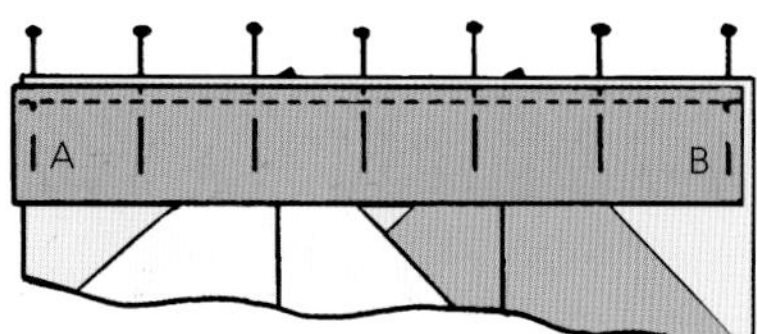

Fig 15

As the block will have been pressed on completion, all the seam allowances will be pressed in the chosen directions. Because of this, these border strips can be stitched on through all the seam allowances if you prefer. Stitch from one end of the strip to the other, not just from A to B. You can stitch these strips on to the block by hand or by machine. Use a machine foot that lets you see the pencilled line as you stitch – a straight stitch foot is ideal – as you need to sew *exactly* along the drawn line.

Press the two strips outwards. With right sides together, pin the longer strips to the other two sides of the block, matching the marking lines. Marks C and D should be matched with the corners of the block (Fig 16). Stitch along the drawn lines from one end of the strip to the other, not just from C to D. Press the strips outwards.

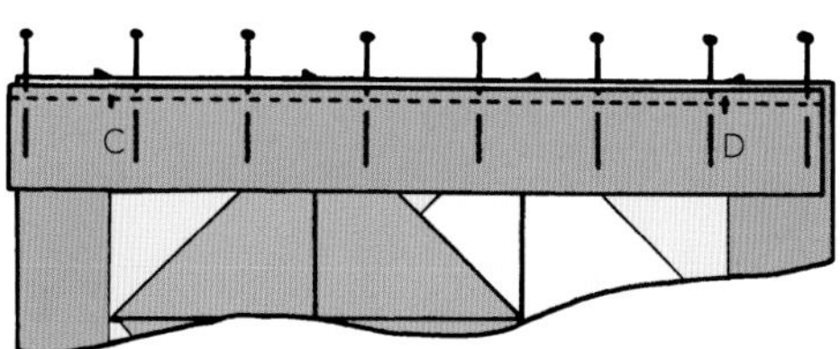

Fig 16

11 Measure the block, it should be a little more than 12½in (31.7cm) square. Trim it to an exact 12½in (31.7cm) square. See page 236 for instructions on trimming blocks. Add the framing sashing strips if you are ready to, see page 236 for instructions.

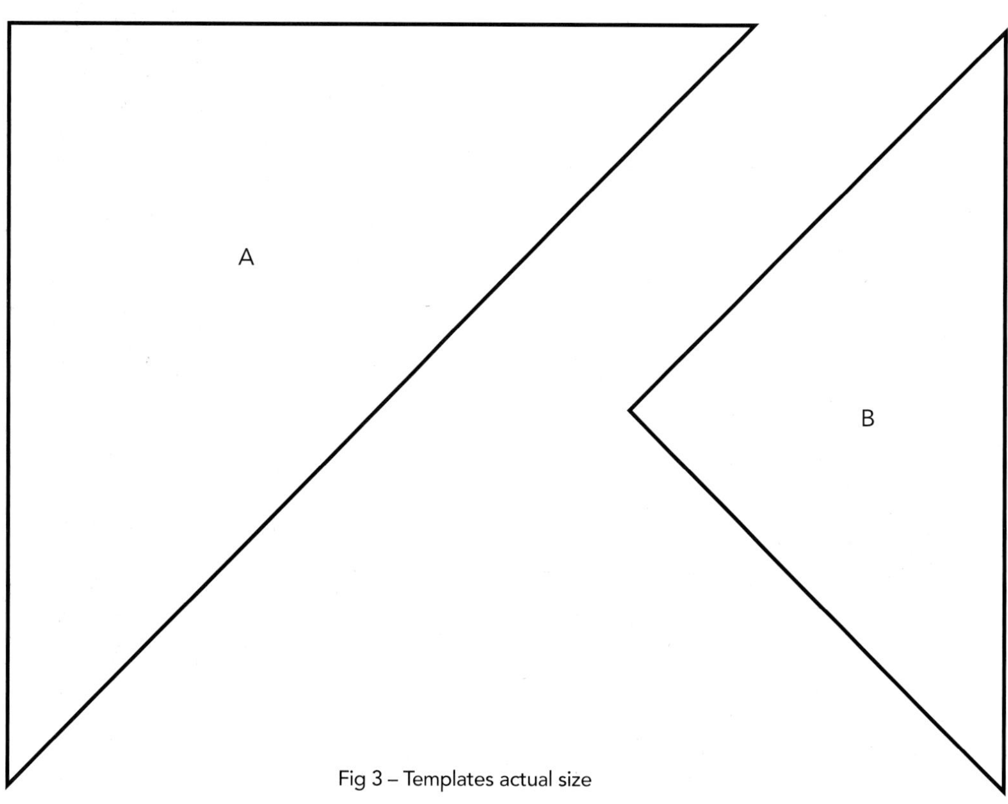

Fig 3 – Templates actual size

Machined Strip Patchwork

Strip Rail

I first saw this pattern in an American book about quick machined patchwork without templates written by Trudie Hughes, a very clever quilter whose books are always an inspiration and whose techniques are speedy and exciting.

Like Rail Fence, this design uses long strips of fabric which are stitched into a band and then cut. Diagonal cutting and stitching creates a strongly diagonal feeling to the block, so it makes a good choice for a corner of your sampler quilt. Very exciting quilt designs can be made from the repeated block, especially if it is placed 'on point', with the corners of the block at the top, bottom and sides and extra fabric added to make a square (Fig 1). Several lovely quilt-sized patterns

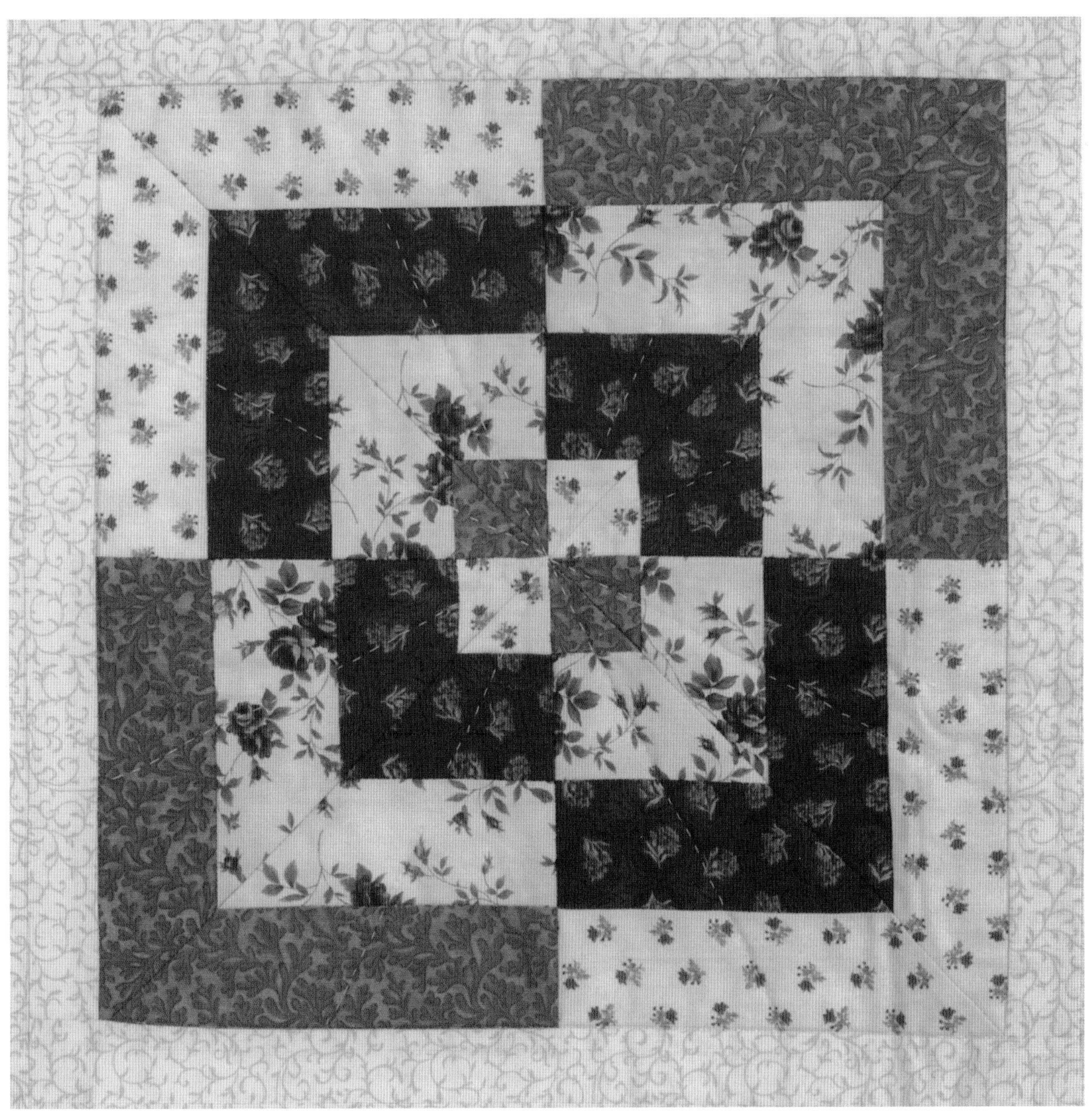

based on Strip Bow (the arrangement shown in Fig 1) can be found in Trudie Hughes' book *Template-Free Quiltmaking* published by the American publisher That Patchwork Place.

Fig 1

Colour Choices

Four fabrics are used in this block and they could be full of contrasts or could graduate in colour from light to dark across the strips. The strongest fabrics are most effective when used on the outside rather than on the inside of the band of four. Take your chosen fabrics and fold them into narrow strips. Place them in order on a flat surface so that you can judge the effect. Rearrange them if necessary until you are happy with the sequence.

Construction

1 From each fabric cut two sets of strips each measuring 2⅛in (5.3cm) wide and 15in (38cm) long (Fig 2), see page 16 for instructions on cutting strips.

Fig 2

2 Set the stitch length on your sewing machine to about two-thirds the size of the usual dressmaking stitch, to prevent the seams from coming undone when the strips are cut across. As usual, the seams need to be a scant ¼in (6mm). Use a strip of masking tape to help you accurately stitch the seams (see page 15 for setting up the machine). Stitch the four strips together, alternating the direction you sew the strips to keep the band straight and not slightly rippled (Fig 3).

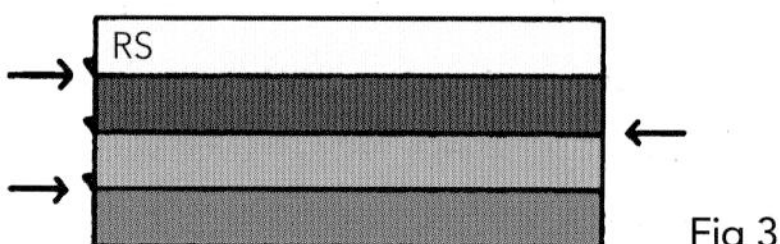

Fig 3

3 Press one band of strips from the *front* with the seams pressed towards the top of the band. Press the second band from the *front* with the seams pressed down towards the bottom of the band (Fig 4). See page 15 for general advice on pressing.

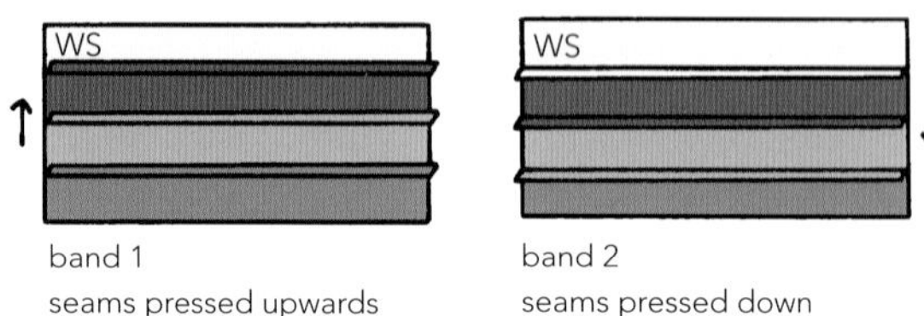

Fig 4

4 Take band one and place it horizontally on the cutting board right side up, lining up the top edge with one of the horizontal markings on the board. If the band is slightly rippled, do not worry, just pat it as flat as you can and carry on. Four different fabrics cannot be expected to lay completely flat when joined. If they do, take all the credit; if they do not, blame the fabric!

Take band two and place it right side down on top of band one, matching colours and seams carefully. The seam allowances go in opposite directions, which helps to line up the seams of the two bands (Fig 5).

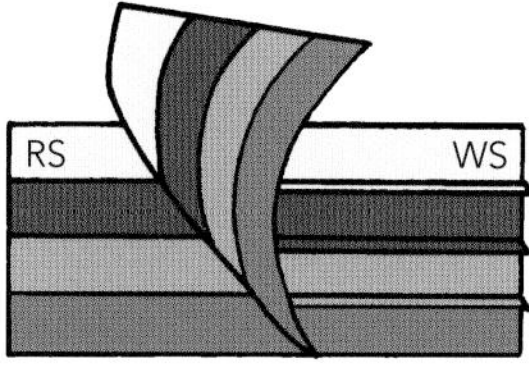

Fig 5

5 Measure the width of the bands. If you have stitched an accurate scant ¼in (6mm) seam the bands should measure 7in (17.8cm). Using the rotary ruler and cutter, trim one end of the layered bands to straighten them and cut off two sections each 7in (17.8cm) long, to make two layered squares (Fig 6).

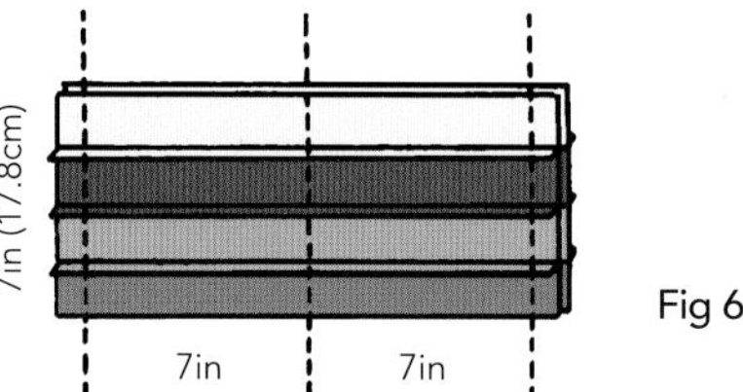

Fig 6

Note*:* If your bands do not measure 7in (17.8cm), even if they are only ⅛in (3mm) out, take the measurement you have and cut the squares to match it. If the two bands are not identical in width it is worth re-stitching one of them so that they match each other. Always work from the final width measurement of both bands to cut your squares; this way you will finish up with true squares, even if they are slightly more or slightly less than they are supposed to be. You can adjust that later if necessary.

"I knew the finished look I wanted for this quilt – rich, warm colours with a cream sashing and border, found at Birmingham NEC in August 2008 where Lynne was promoting her latest book Cathedral Windows Quilts. *Not in my wildest dreams could I imagine my quilt would feature in her third sampler book!"* **Liz Parsons**

6 Keeping the two layers matching exactly, cut each square diagonally in one direction (Fig 7). Each double layer of triangles is now ready to sew.

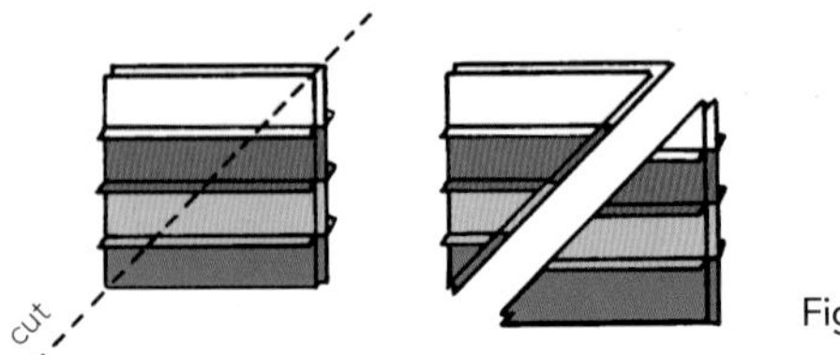

Fig 7

7 Pin the diagonal edges together on all four pairs of triangles, matching the seams. Handle the pieces carefully as the cut edges are on the bias (the diagonal grain of the fabric) and will be very stretchy. This stretchiness can be a help, though, if you have to do a bit of easing to make the seams match. Machine stitch along each diagonal seam. Press from the front of the work, pressing the seam allowances to one side. The resulting four squares show two different colour arrangements (Fig 8).

8 Arrange the four squares until you find a design you like, two alternatives are shown in Fig 9, although more are possible, so keep moving the squares around until you find your favourite.

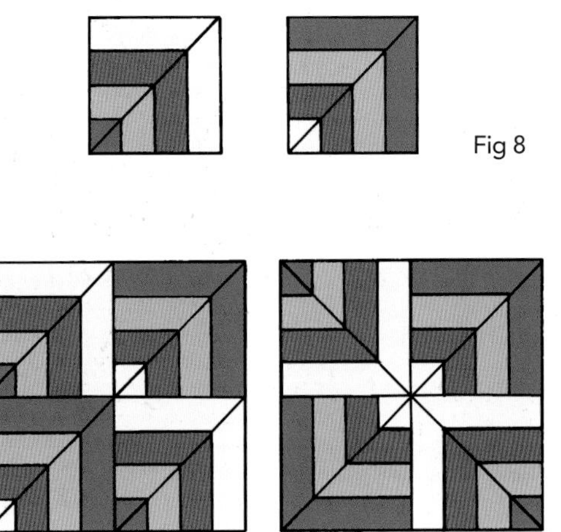
Fig 8

Fig 9

9 Pin and machine stitch the top two squares together with a ¼in (6mm) seam. If you place the pins at right angles to the seams you will be able to stitch right up to each pin before you need to remove it (Fig 10).

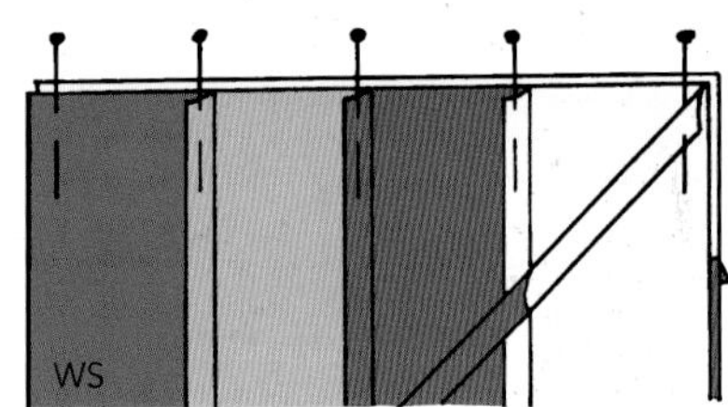

Fig 10

If the two edges do not match exactly and one is shorter than the other, pin and stitch with the shorter edge on top, as this will stretch slightly as you stitch and should ease the problem. Press the seams to one side from the front of the joined squares.

10 Pin and machine stitch the second pair of squares. Press the seams in the opposite direction to the first half (Fig 11).

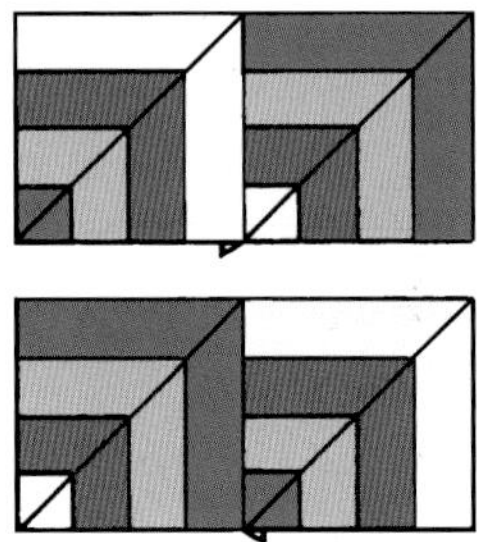
Fig 11

11 Join the two halves by stitching across with a ¼in (6mm) seam, taking care to match the centre seams. Pressing the centre seams of each half in opposite directions will help you to match them accurately, as they lock into each other as you sew. Pin diagonally as this helps to keep both sets of seam allowances flat while stitching (Fig 12). The final long seam can be pressed to one side or, if this makes it too bulky, press the seam open.

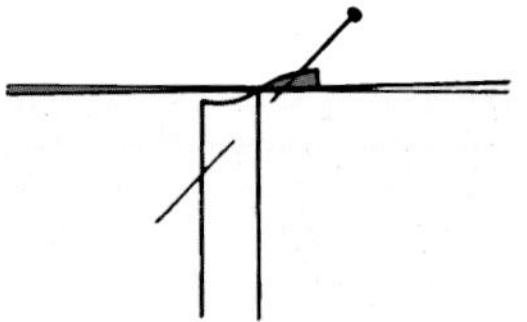
Fig 12

12 The finished block should measure slightly more than 12½in (31.7cm) square. If this is the case, centre it on a cutting board and trim it down to an exact 12½in (31.7cm) square. See page 236 for instructions on trimming the blocks. Add the framing sashing strips, following the instructions on page 236.

Drunkard's Path

This interesting design originated in England where it was known as Robbing Peter to Pay Paul. It then travelled to America with the early settlers who gradually developed a whole series of designs based on sixteen squares, each of which is divided into two parts, a quadrant (quarter circle) and the remainder of the square (see Fig 1 overleaf). As the block patterns evolved they were given a variety of fascinating names including Wanderer in the Wilderness, Solomon's Puzzle, Old Maid's Puzzle and the most well known, Drunkard's Path. You might like to consider the alternative method of creating a Drunkard's Path block, which is described on page 230.

Drunkard's Path

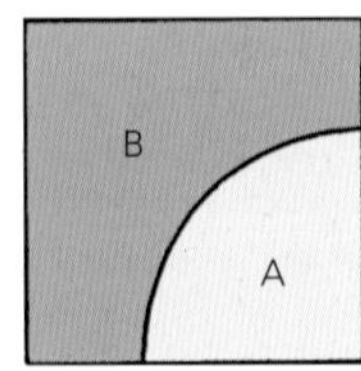

Fig 1

The arrangement of the sixteen squares, four in each of four rows, changes the block design so much that it is quite possible to include several Drunkard's Path blocks in a sampler quilt without anyone realizing that they are the same basic design; Fig 2 below shows six different arrangements, each using just two fabrics. This block is another that is constructed by American piecing, with the new problem of sewing the curved seam that joins shapes A and B to make a square. There are sixteen of these seams in the block, so by the time you have finished you should have become quite used to it! This traditional curved seam block, and its many variations, is a great favourite of mine.

Colour Choices

The designs in Fig 2 use two fabrics only, although you might like to use more, as shown in Fig 3. As you have now made quite a number of blocks, it is always a good idea to lay them all out while you choose the fabric for this design. If there is one fabric that seems to jar you must decide whether it was a mistake or whether you just need to use more of it in future blocks. Assemble your fabrics according to which arrangement of Drunkard's Path you have chosen and decide which fabric is to go where in the design. You may find it easier to make a rough sketch or tracing of the block and colour it in so that you know how many of each shape you need to cut out from each fabric.

Fig 2

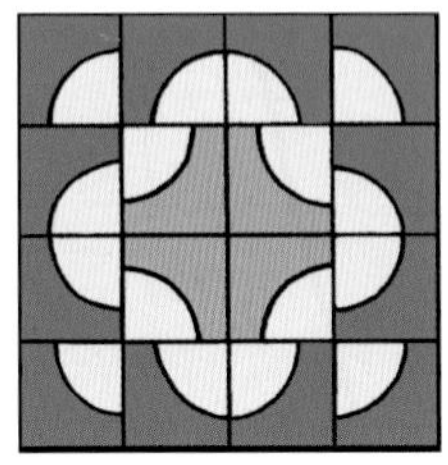

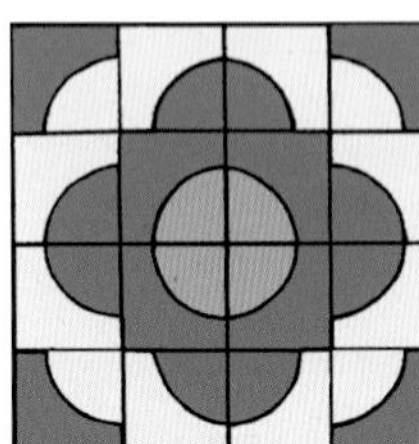

Fig 3

Construction

1 Make card templates by tracing templates A and B from Fig 4 below and cutting them out. These are combined to make a 3in (7.6cm) square, and sixteen squares will make the block. Stick the traced shapes on to card, or use template plastic, see page 15 for instructions on making templates.

2 Use your coloured drawing of the block to check how many of each template shape you need in each fabric. For instance, for the Drunkard's Path block shown first in Fig 2 you need eight of template A and eight of template B from each of the two fabrics.

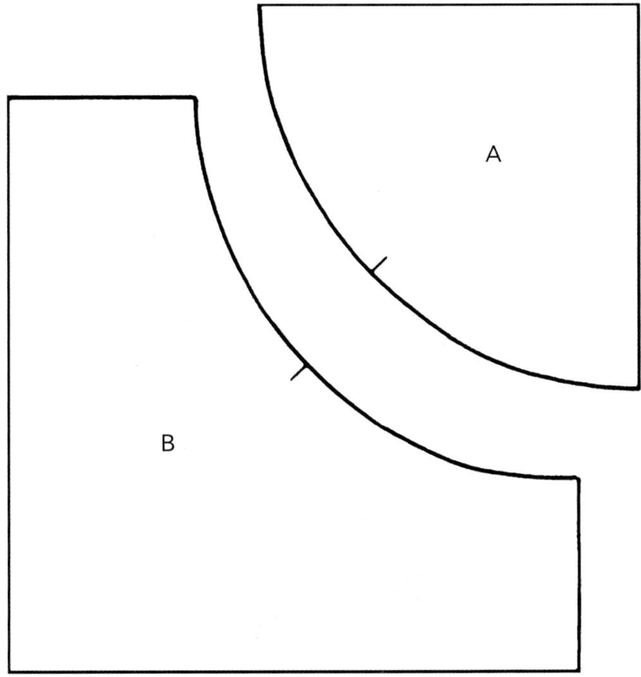

Fig 4 – Templates actual size

3 On the wrong side of each fabric draw accurately around the templates using a sharp marking pencil. This marks the sewing line. Mark the centre point on each curve in the seam allowance (Fig 5). Allow at least ½in (1.3cm) between each drawn outline so that a seam allowance of ¼in (6mm) can be added to each shape when cutting out. Save space by arranging the shapes on the fabric as shown in Fig 6.

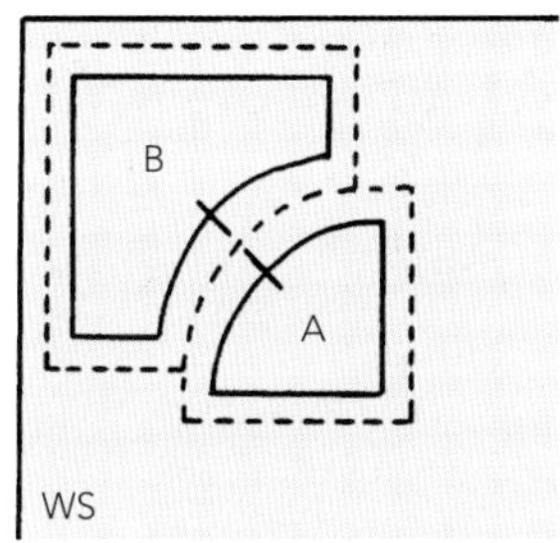

Fig 5

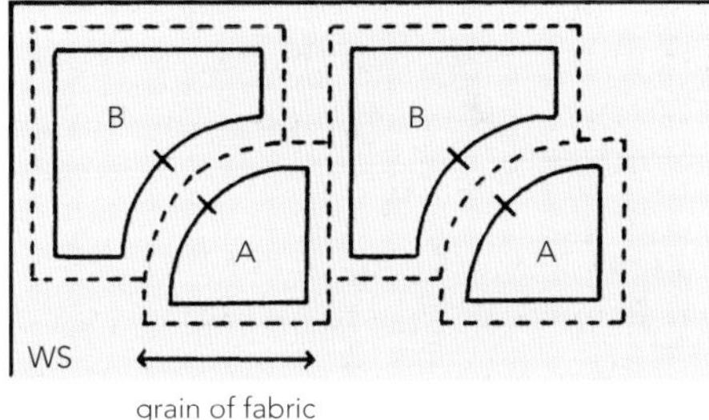

Fig 6

4 Cut out each shape to include the ¼in (6mm) seam allowance, do this either by eye or more accurately by measuring.

5 Arrange the cut pieces on a flat surface or pin them in position on a polystyrene tile or board. You may find that you rearrange the pieces to make a completely new design. Always keep an open and flexible attitude as you work and be prepared to change your mind if you come up with a better alternative.

6 Take the two shapes A and B which make up one of the sixteen squares in the design. Using a small pair of scissors with sharp points, clip the curved seam alllowance on shape B, snipping at roughly ¼in (6mm) intervals, going nearly but not quite to the drawn line (Fig 7).

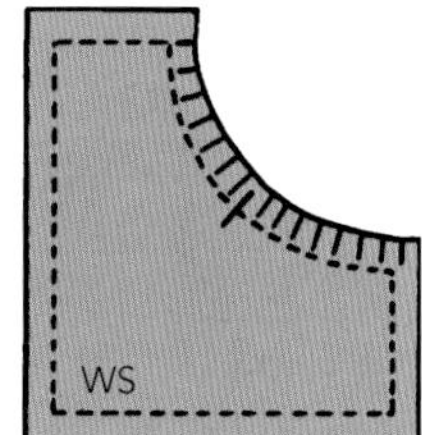

Fig 7

7 Joining shape A to shape B seems straightforward when the pieces are arranged in the block, but they do not seem to match at all when you place them right sides together ready for pinning. The only way you can make them fit each other is by curving the pieces in your hand as you pin, like setting in a sleeve in dressmaking. Match the centre marks on each piece by pushing a pin through both layers of fabric until the head is on the surface of the top fabric. Reposition the pin at right angles to the seam. I find it easier to sew if I arrange the pins with the points outwards (see Fig 8), that way I don't bleed all over the fabric! Swing one corner of shape A round to match the corner of shape B, lining up the straight outer edges of both pieces. Align the corners of the sewing lines by pushing through a pin (Fig 9). Swing the other corner of shape A round and match and pin the drawn corners, aligning the two straight edges. The resultant shape cannot be held flat – it takes on a deep curve as in Fig 10. More pins are needed to fix one drawn line exactly on top of the other, so match and pin the two pieces at intervals no greater than ½in (1.3cm), closer if you need to. This makes a real hedgehog of a seam, bristling with pins, but it is the only way to keep the lines matching exactly (Fig 11).

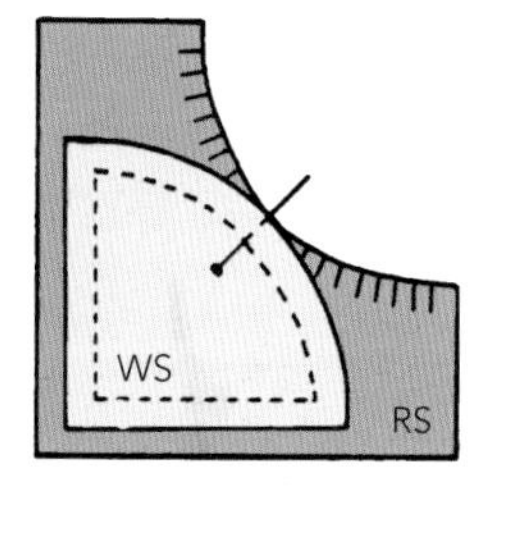

Fig 8

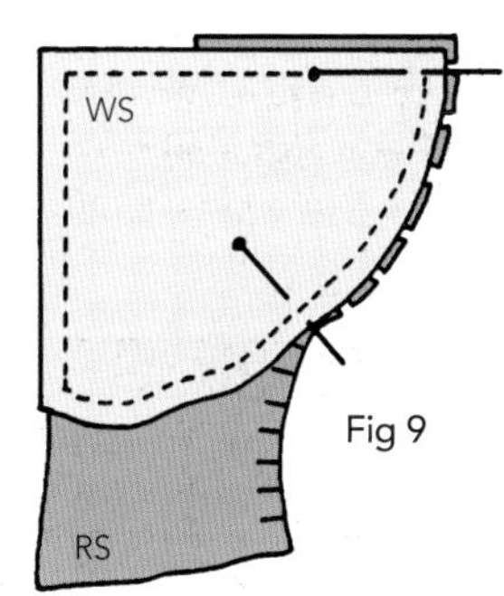

Fig 9

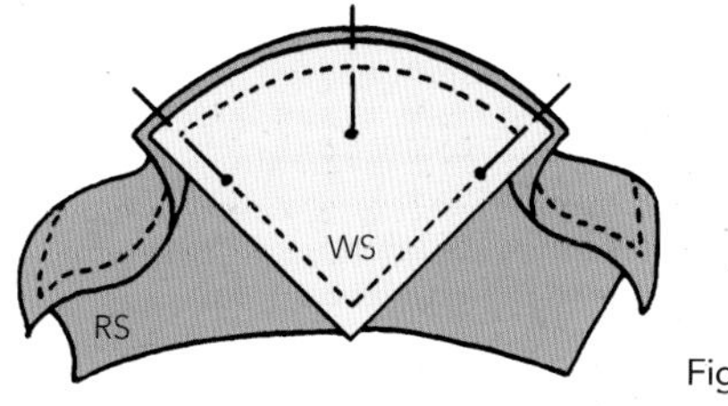

Fig 10

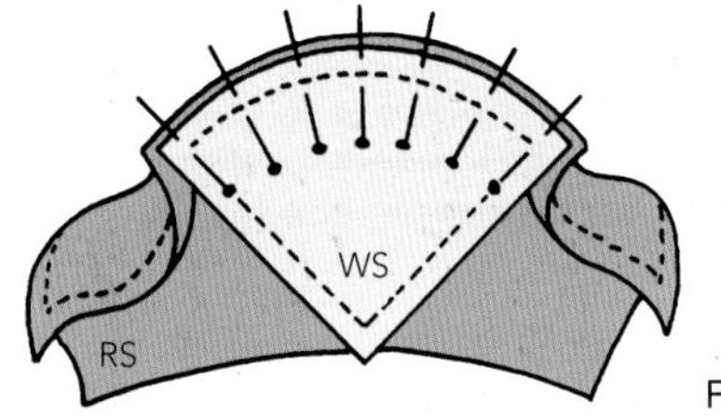

Fig 11

8 Sew along the pencilled line with small running stitches removing the pins as you go, see Maple Leaf step 6 on page 34 for more detailed instructions. Do not sew into the seam allowances at either end of the curve (Fig 12). You may find it easier to pin the curve with shape B on the top so that the seam curves away from you. Alternatively you may find it easier to ease in the fullness by curving it over your hand while you pin and sew (Fig 13). Try both ways and see which you prefer.

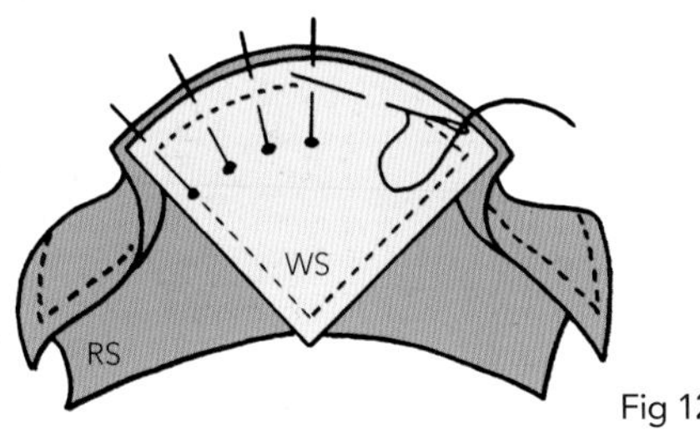

Fig 12

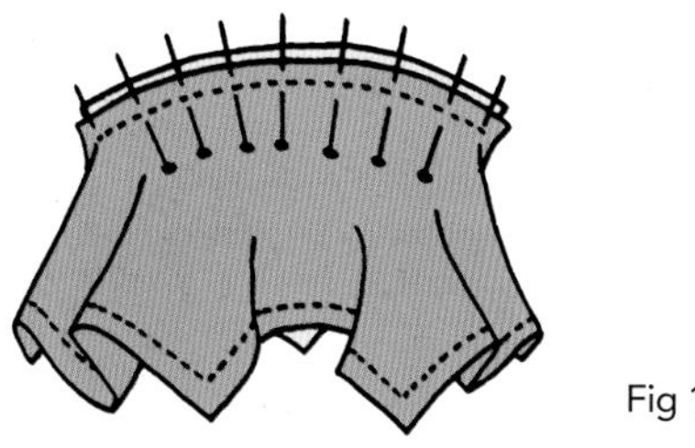
Fig 13

9 Press the completed square from the front with the curved seam towards the larger shape B. This way the clipped edges spread and help reduce the bulk of the seam so that it lies flat (Fig 14).

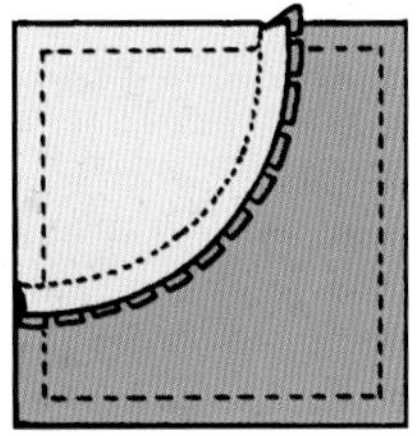
Fig 14

10 Assemble each of the sixteen squares in this way, then arrange them into your chosen design. Join the squares into horizontal rows, pinning and matching the seams in the usual way. Join the rows together to complete the block. Just this once I break the rule of not sewing across the seam allowances when stitching across the curved seam as it has already been pressed to one side (shown in Fig 14). I sew from one marked corner of the square to the other, sewing right across the pressed curved seam allowances (Fig 15).

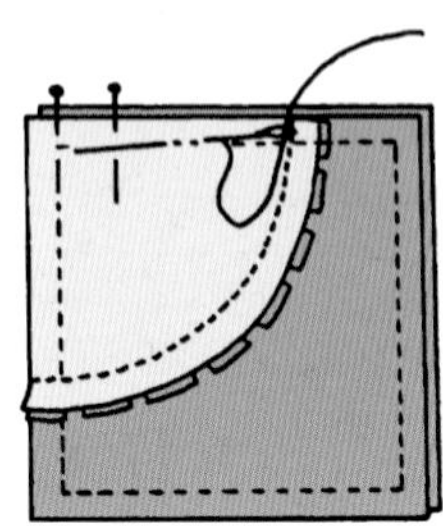
Fig 15

It is quite possible to assemble the squares of this block by machine if you prefer. Pin the two squares together, matching the drawn lines in the same way as for hand piecing. Machine stitch carefully along the drawn line using a straight stitch foot so that you can see exactly where you are stitching. It is usual when machine stitching the marked lines to sew beyond the drawn lines into the seam allowances, right across the fabric from edge to edge.

Join each row of four squares. Press from the front, ironing the seams of row one in one direction, those in row two the opposite way and so on, as in the Trip Around the World block. When you join the rows together, match and pin the drawn lines carefully and machine stitch along the drawn line right across the fabric, stitching through all the seam allowances.

Note: Do not attempt to machine the curved seam itself on this 3in (7.6cm) square, you are likely to trap tiny pleats in the seam as you sew.

11 Press the completed block from the front and measure it, it should be 12½in (31.7cm) square. If it is not, make adjustments to bring it to the exact size by trimming or adding a narrow border. See page 236 for instructions on trimming and bordering blocks.

12 Add the framing sashing strips, following the instructions on page 236.

"This quilt is special to me as it was on my mother's bed during the last few weeks of her life. I was inspired to make it by some beautiful winter fabrics I found at a quilt show, and enjoyed choosing blocks from Lynne's books that would best show them off." **Theresa Stredder**

Machined Strip Patchwork

Spider's Web

This kaleidoscopic design used to be painstakingly hand-pieced, using templates to get all the little strips. With rotary cutters and quick piecing techniques it has become another one of those clever join-the-strips-cut-it-up-again processes. It looks wonderful when all eight segments have been joined to form the final design, so that the eight points all meet in the centre. Many patchwork designs have six or eight corners meeting and they do not always work out as well as the maker hopes. The trick is to get it right at each stage of construction so that mistakes are corrected as you go along rather than finishing up with a jumble of points and angles at the end and with no idea how to correct them.

Colour Choices

For this block four fabrics are used in a sequence of strips, so look at the blocks you have already completed to see which fabrics could be re-introduced. You may already have a block that uses four fabrics that you could use again. The fabrics are joined to form a long band, which is then cut and turned in alternate directions, so that the top and bottom colours come together to form the centre and the two middle colours alternate with each other in the design (Fig 1). Cut out the corner triangles when the web has been made as it will be much easier to choose the fabric which looks best then.

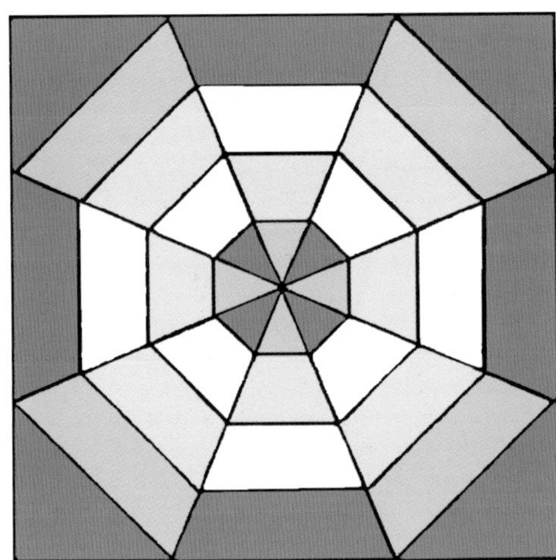

Fig 1

Construction

1 Make templates A and B from Fig 2 overleaf in the usual way, see page 15 for instructions on making templates. Mark the three dotted lines and the three dots on template A. Push a large pin through each dot on template A to make a hole – it needs to be big enough to take the point of a pencil so you can mark fabric through it.

2 Cut a strip 2 x 30in (5 x 76cm) from each of your four chosen fabrics.

3 Machine stitch the strips together with the usual small stitch and a ¼in (6mm) seam allowance. Remember to alternate the direction you sew the strips as explained in Rail Fence page 28. Press the band from the front with the seams all in one direction (Fig 3).

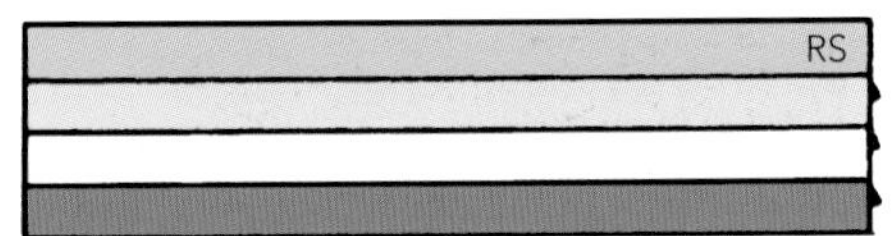

Fig 3

4 Place the fabric band on a cutting board wrong side up. Place template A on the band – it should fit exactly from top to bottom with the stitched seams matching the dotted lines on the template (Fig 4). If it does not, it is worth re-stitching the seams to get a good fit. It is important that the template fits properly top to bottom; if the seamlines do not match the dotted lines on the template, do not worry too much.

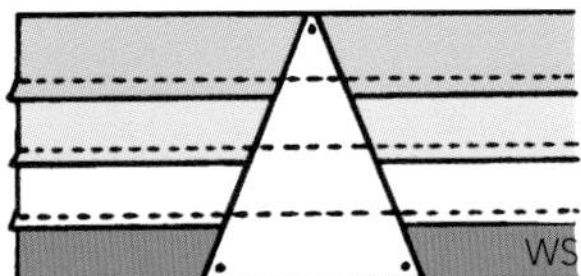

Fig 4

Using a sharp pencil, draw down both sides of the template and mark the dots. Move the template along the band, turning it through 180° to fit against the first drawn shape, now draw round the template again. Continue this way until eight shapes have been marked on the band (Fig 5). If two shapes do not fit against each other accurately, leave a small gap between them if necessary – the band is long enough to allow you to do this (Fig 6). Mark the dots on each shape.

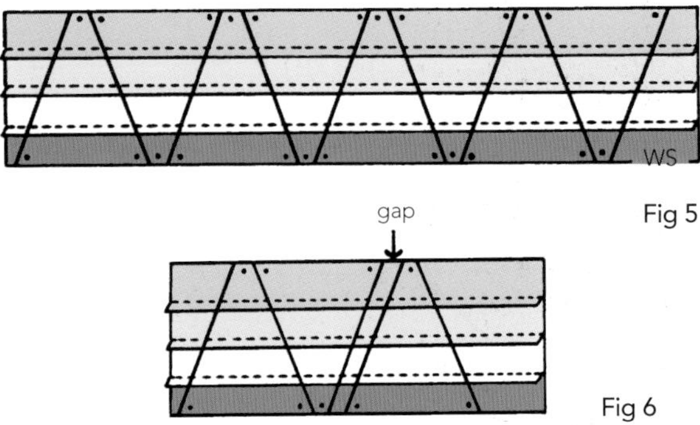

Fig 5

Fig 6

5 Use a rotary cutter and ruler to cut the drawn lines. Now arrange the eight triangular shapes to make a spider's web.

6 First join the triangles in pairs, matching the seams carefully and stitching right through the marked dots on both pieces (Fig 7). Take care that each pair is exactly the same as the others (Fig 8) and not

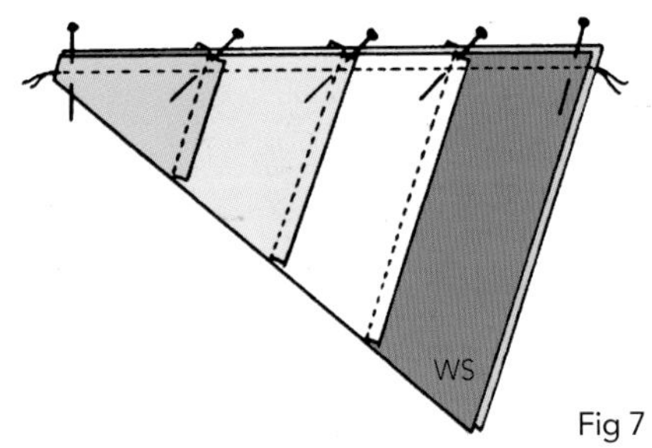

Fig 7

stitched together in the reverse order (Fig 9), otherwise they will not fit together to make the design. Press the seams from the front to one side.

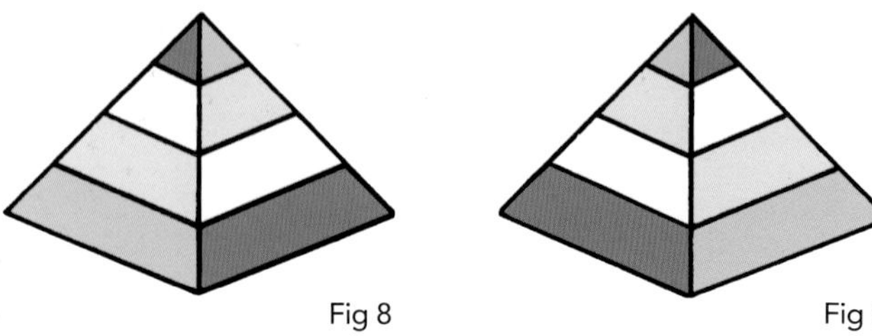

Fig 8 Fig 9

"This sampler quilt was my first attempt at a large project. It proved a challenge in more ways than one and took almost a year to complete, although I learnt new techniques with each block. My choice of colours was uncharacteristic for me, as I usually opt for subtle shades. I was very pleased with the result and am now much more adventurous with my colour choices."

Jan Evers

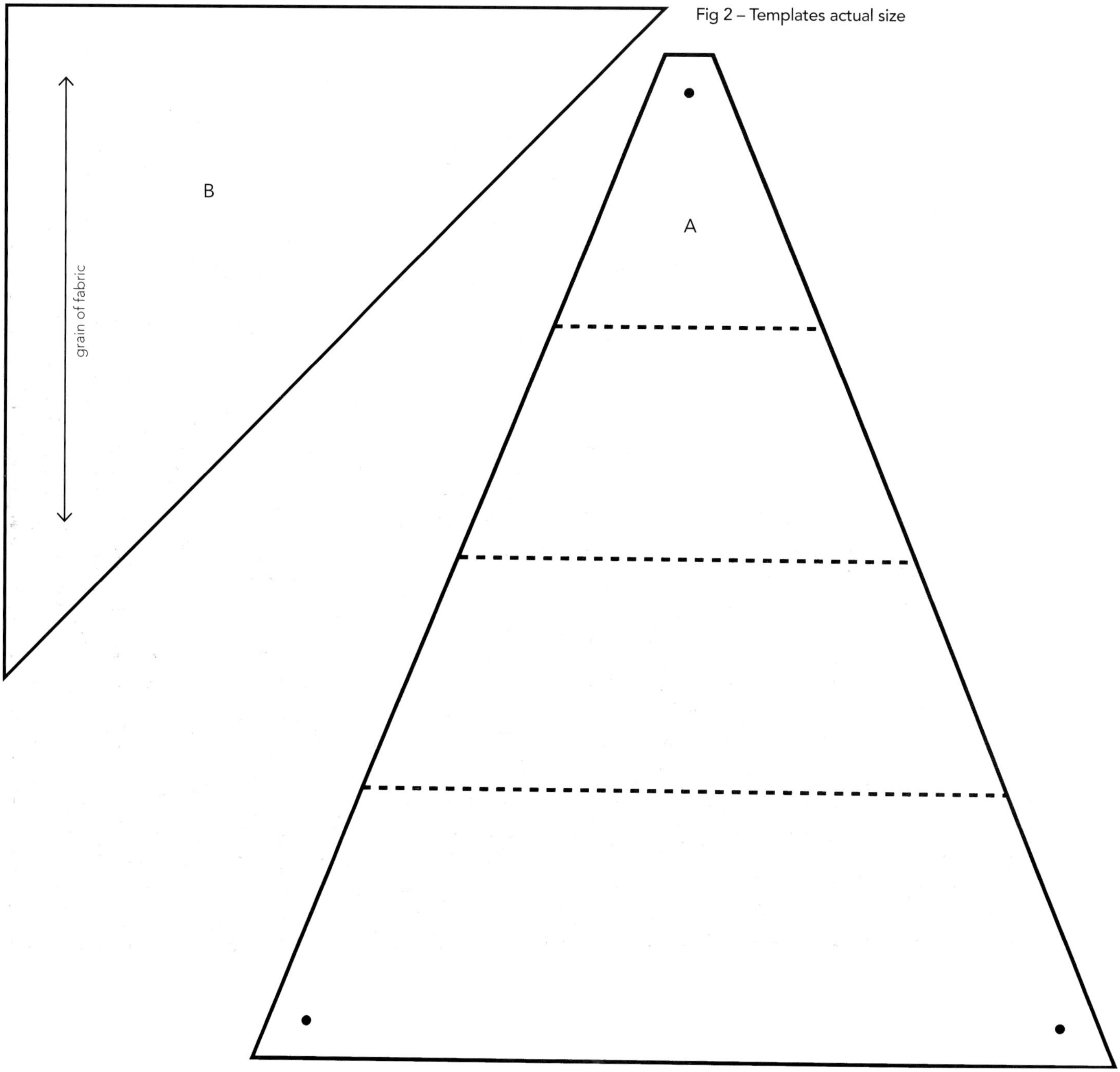

Fig 2 – Templates actual size

B

grain of fabric

A

7 Now pin two pieces together matching dots carefully and stitch through them as accurately as possible. Do not have your machine stitch length set too small in case you need to unpick the stitches at some stage. Repeat this process with the other two pieces. Now comes quality control time. Open out each half and inspect them from the front. You are aiming to have the two inner fabrics meeting in an arrowhead exactly ¼in (6mm) away from the top edges of the fabrics (Fig 10).

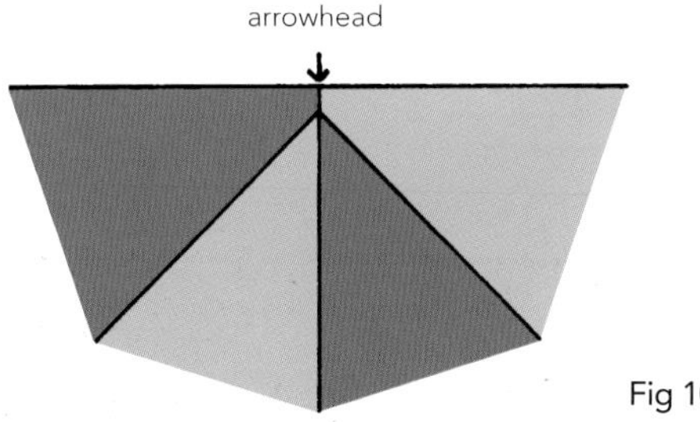

Fig 10

If you have successfully matched the arrowheads but it is less than ¼in (6mm) from the top edges, re-sew the centre seam (the last one to have been sewn), stitching just inside the original stitches – there is no need to unpick these stitches as they are now in the seam allowance. However, if the arrowheads are *not* matching but look like Fig 11, unpick the centre seam, match the dots more carefully and stitch again. If you take time to get the two halves of the web right at this stage they will match more accurately in the final long seam. When you are happy with the arrowheads, press from the front, pressing the seams to one side.

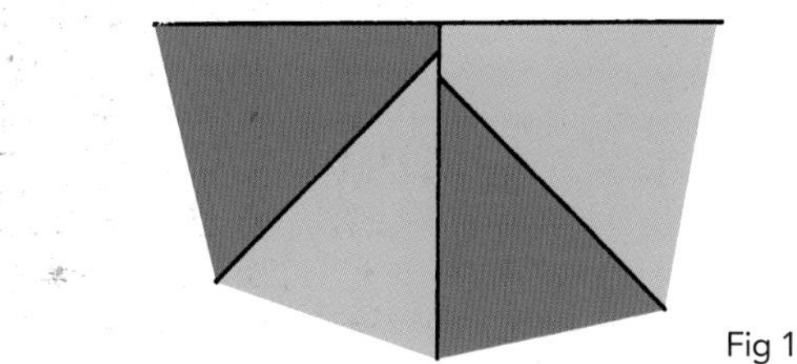

Fig 11

8 Pin the two halves together, matching the seams along the edges and taking care to position the tips of the two arrowheads in the centre exactly on top of each other. Check by peeling the top half back with the pin. When the arrowheads match, hold them in position firmly and pin on both sides of the centre seam. I use extra-long, extra-fine pins so that I can machine stitch over them if necessary (Fig 12). Stitch the seam.

Now check from the front. If you have lost the tips of the arrowheads your seam allowance was too wide. Finger press the seam open and check how the centre looks – this can make quite a difference to the balance of the central eight points. If you are unhappy with the result, unpick 2in (5cm) or so either side of the centre and try again. Do the best you can and remember that only you will notice if it is not perfect. Finally, press the long seam open from the back of the work.

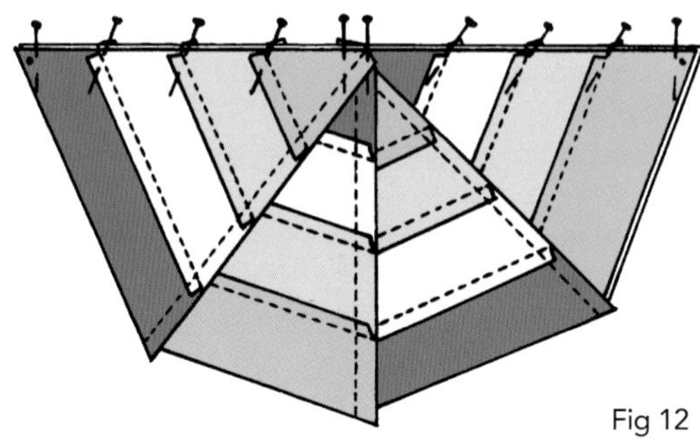

Fig 12

9 The large triangles from template B form the four corners of the block. They can be placed adjacent to the sides or edges that use fabric one or adjacent to the sides using fabric four (Fig 13), so choose the fabric that works best for these corners. Draw round the template on the wrong side of the chosen fabric four times and cut out exactly on the line as no extra seam allowance is needed.

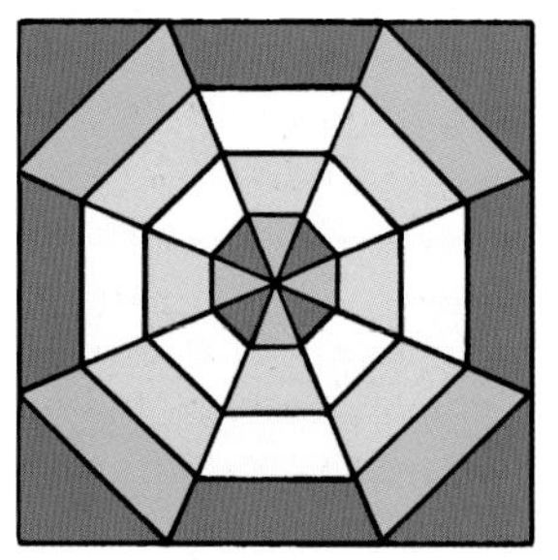

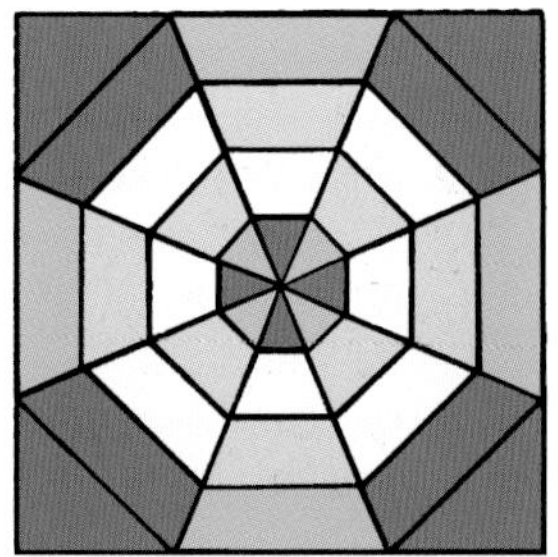

Fig 13

10 With right sides together, pin and stitch each corner to the block, matching the long edge of shape B with the outer edge of the block as shown in Fig 14 below.

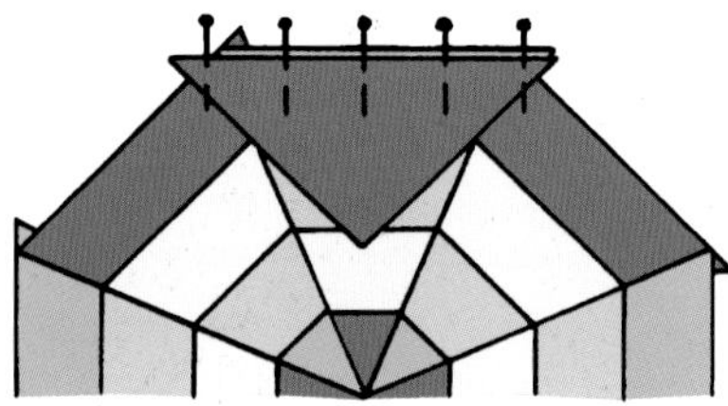

Fig 14

11 Press the corners with the seams outwards. Trim the block to an exact 12½in (31.7cm) square. See page 236 for instructions on trimming blocks. Add the framing sashing strips, see page 236 for instructions.

Pieced Patchwork

Grandmother's Fan

This traditional block has always been pieced by hand, but nearly all of it can be machine-pieced if you prefer. It features the curving lines used in Drunkard's Path, but on a larger scale to give a fan shape. The fan is divided into six sections, although in old quilts it can often be seen with up to ten divisions. Compared with piecing the Drunkard's Path curves this one is really quick and easy. There are only two curves to be pieced and one of them is so large it hardly seems like a curve at all. The centre of Grandmother's Fan is not in the middle of the block but in the corner, which makes it an ideal design to use in a corner of the sampler quilt where it gives weight and encourages the eye to move inwards.

Colour Choices

The fan has six segments that can be made from six different fabrics or, as shown in Fig 1, from three fabrics repeated in sequence. A striking design can also be made with just two contrasting fabrics used alternately in the segments. The background is quite a large, empty area of fabric, so if you choose a plain fabric you may need to break it up visually with quilting. The central quadrant is like the eye of a flower and should be strong enough to give the fan a focus without dominating everything else. If you are not sure which centre or background fabrics will look best, cut and piece together the fan before making a decision.

Fig 1

Construction

1 Make templates A and B from Fig 2 below – see page 15 for instructions on making templates. The background shape is too large for a template to be given here, so make it in the following way.

On a large piece of graph paper draw a 12in (30.5cm) square. Set a pair of compasses at a distance of 10in (25.4cm). I use an extra long pencil in the compasses. Fix the point of the compasses in a corner of the drawn square and draw a quadrant as in Fig 3. The shaded section of the square will be your template. If you cannot make your compasses reach to 10in (25.4cm) use a ruler and mark 10in (25.4cm) at roughly ½in (1.3cm) intervals. Join these marks by eye to make the curve (Fig 4). Mark the centre of the curve by placing a ruler diagonally across two corners of the square and marking the point where the ruler crosses the curve. Stick the template on to card.

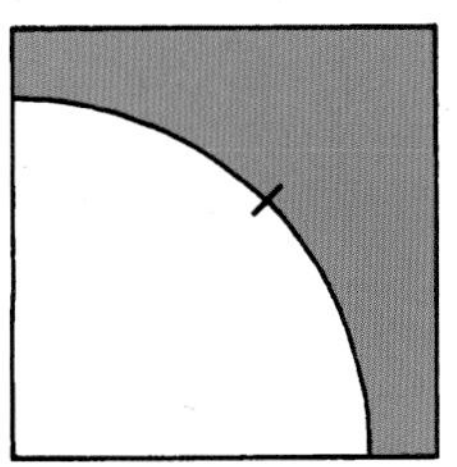

Fig 3

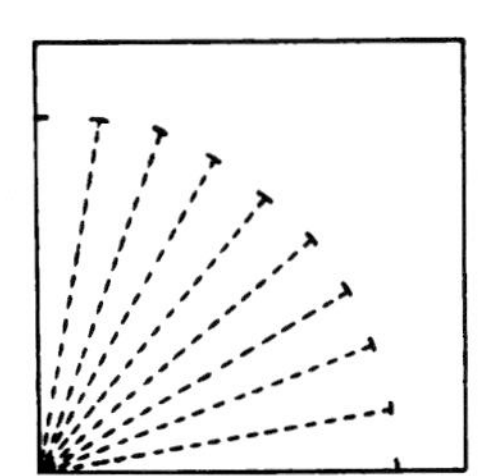

Fig 4

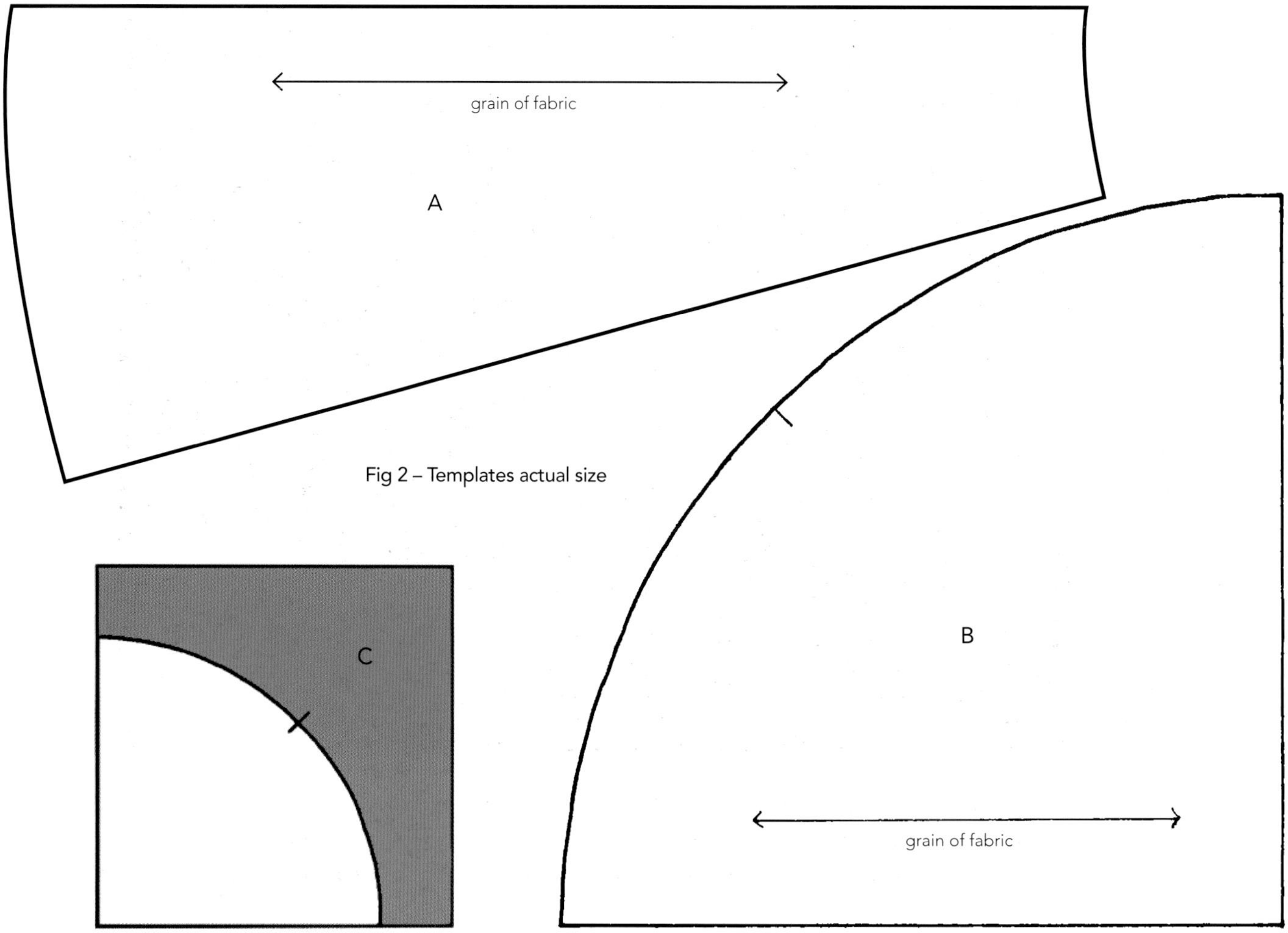

grain of fabric

A

Fig 2 – Templates actual size

B

grain of fabric

C

"This was my first quilt and, as a complete novice, all the different techniques were a revelation. I didn't have a 'stash' and kept running out of fabric. Needless to say I now have enough fabric to keep me quilt-making for years." **Kath Cadman**

2 On the wrong side of your chosen fabrics draw accurately around fan template A using a sharp marking pencil. This marks the sewing line. Allow at least ½in (1.3cm) between each drawn outline so that a seam allowance of ¼in (6mm) can be added to each shape when cutting out (Fig 5). You need six shape A pieces. You also need one shape B and one shape C.

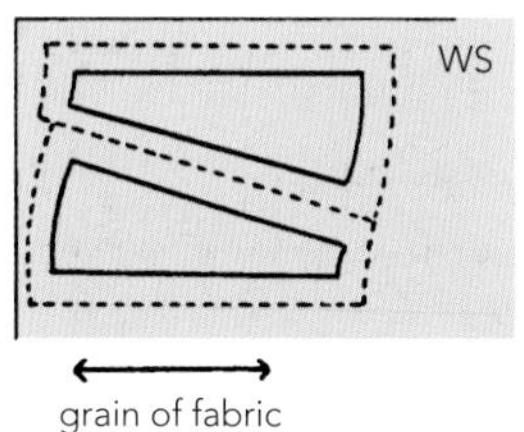

Fig 5

3 Cut out each shape to include the ¼in (6mm) seam allowance, judging this by eye.

4 Arrange the segments of the fan on a flat surface or pin them in position on a polystyrene tile or board. Move them around to check that you like the sequence of fabrics. At the same time see how effective your chosen centre and background fabrics are. There is still time to make changes before joining everything together.

5 Take the first two segments of shape A and place them right sides together, matching the drawn lines with pins (Fig 6) as in the Maple Leaf block page 34. Stitch along the drawn lines either by hand or machine. If by hand, sew along the lines but not into the seam allowances at either end. If by machine, stitch along the lines from one end of the fabric to the other including the seam allowances (Fig 7). Join all six pieces of the fan together in this way. Press the seams from the front of the work to one side.

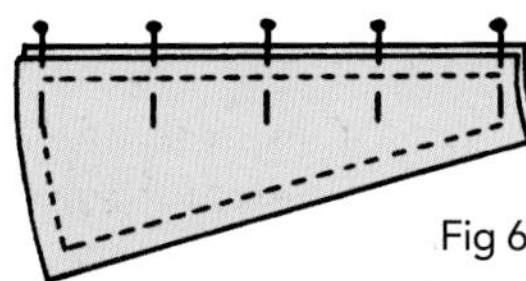

Fig 6

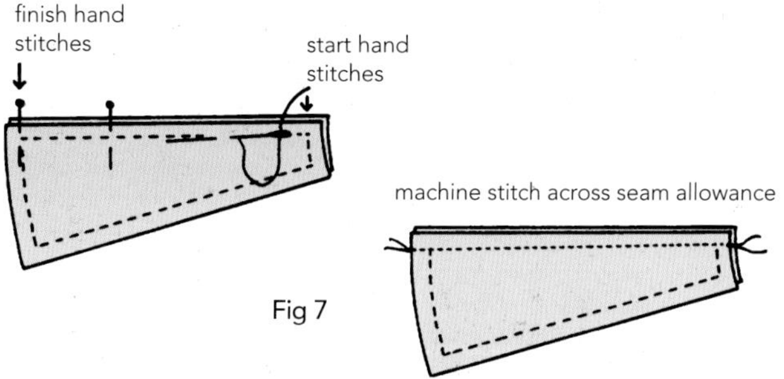

Fig 7

6 Clip the seam allowance of the fan along the smaller curved edge (Fig 8). Pin and sew the fan to the centre piece B in the same way as described for Drunkard's Path on page 52. I like sewing this by hand, but do try it by machine if you want to. Press the seam towards the fan, pressing from the front.

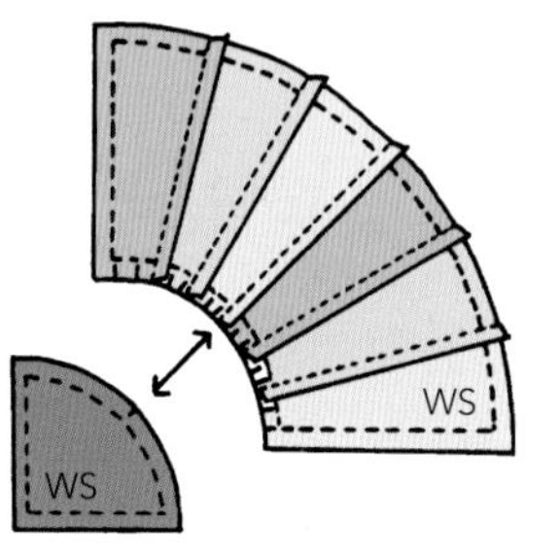

Fig 8

7 Clip the seam allowance of the curved edge of the large background piece. Pin the longer curve of the fan to the clipped edge of the background, matching corners and centres carefully (Fig 9), as described in Drunkard's Path page 52. Press the seam towards the background fabric.

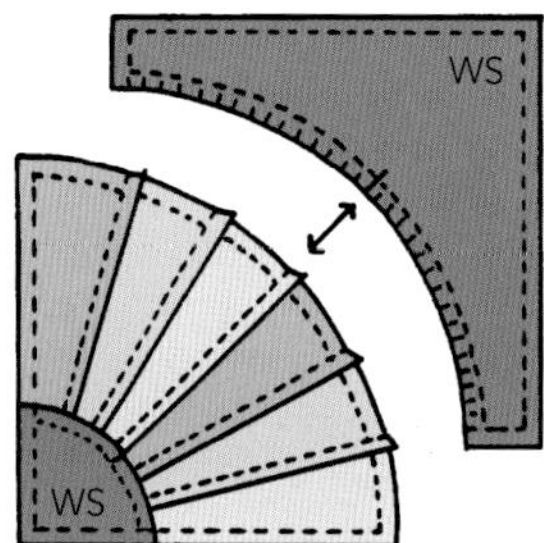

Fig 9

8 Measure the completed block, it should be 12½in (31.7cm) square. If it needs trimming, trim away from the two sides of the background fabric *only*, leaving the fan its full size. See page 236 for instructions on trimming the blocks.

9 Add the framing sashing strips, following the instructions given on page 236.

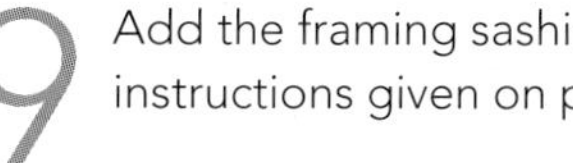

Quick Machined Strip Patchwork

Log Cabin

Log Cabin quilts have been part of the European quilt heritage for several hundred years. The design appears in Dutch, Swedish and British quilts of the 19th century and earlier and it is likely that settlers took it to America where it has become one of the most popular of the traditional quilt patterns.

The design is made of rectangular strips of light and dark fabrics arranged around a central square. Traditionally the strips represented the wooden logs that made up the pioneer's log cabin. The central square was either red to represent the fire in the hearth or yellow for the welcoming light in the window. Light and dark scraps of fabric were cut

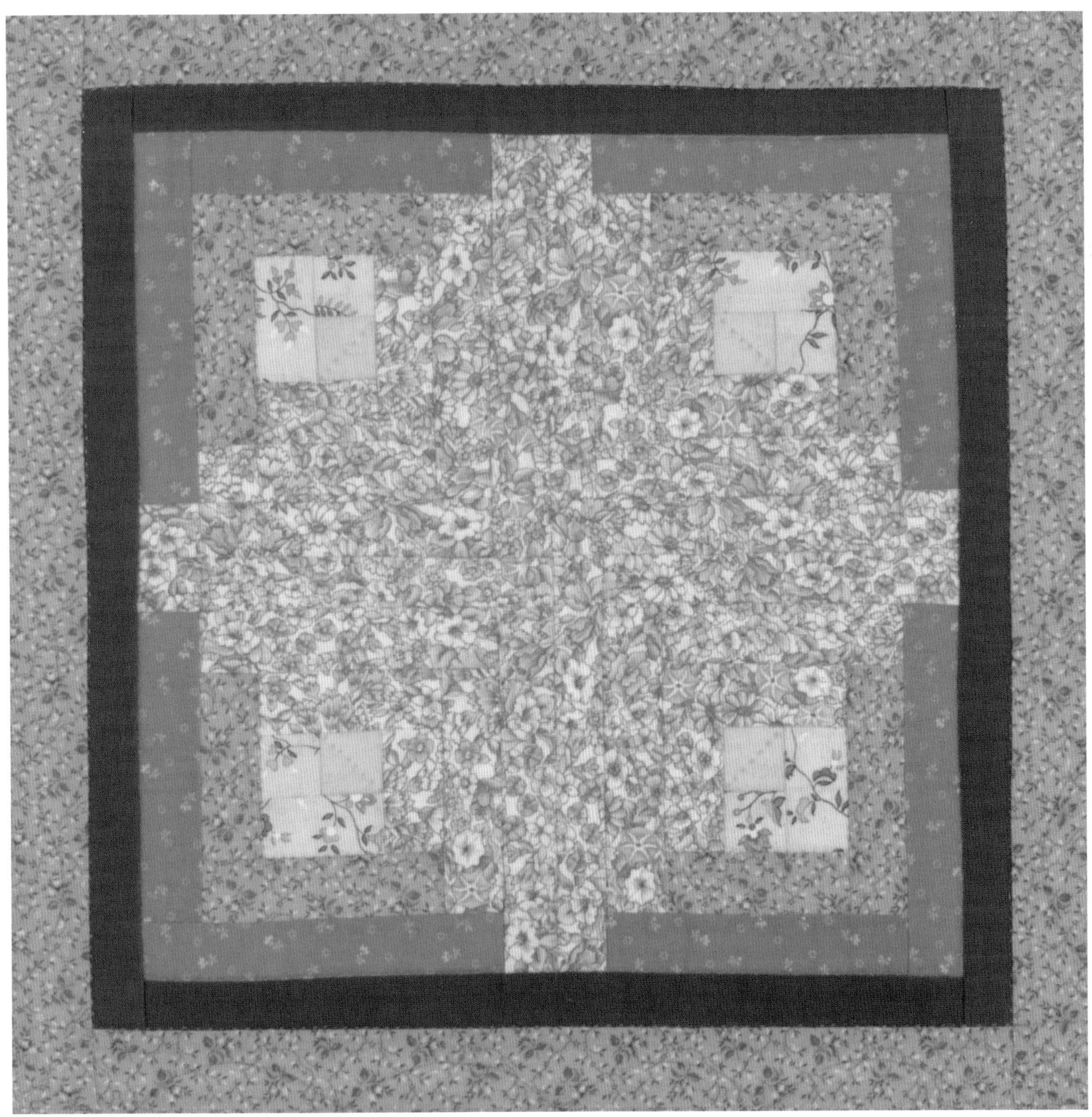

into strips of the correct length using templates, and then pieced together around the centres to make squares which showed strongly contrasting areas of light and dark (Fig 1).

Fig 1

This is still the way the design is worked today, but modern cutting and stitching techniques have revolutionized the speed and accuracy with which a quilt can be assembled. In the sampler quilt four identical squares of Log Cabin are made at the same time in a mass production method. These are then joined together to make the final block.

Colour Choices

Choosing fabric for Log Cabin is always tortuous. You need two sets of fabric showing a distinct difference from each other – a dark set contrasting with a light set, or a set of plain shades against patterned, or even a complete change of colour like red fabrics against black. Within these sets the fabrics should be similar so that they blend together without one standing out against the others too much.

Lay your fabrics out on a flat surface, overlapping so that you get an idea what ¾in (1.9cm) strips will look like when stitched together. Arrange them in the two sets and avoid using a fabric that does not obviously belong in either set. For instance if you are using dark green fabrics with light cream fabrics do not include a medium green and cream print which could be part of either set. You will lose the element of contrast that gives the block its distinctive appearance. If you have a limited number of fabrics to choose from you could restrict them to two fabrics in each set and use them alternately as in Fig 2. The central square does not have to be the traditional red or yellow, it can be anything you like. You may prefer a strong spot of colour for each centre or a colour that does not match either set of strips but gently complements them. Study some of the Log Cabin blocks in the sampler quilts shown in this book and choose whichever effect you like best.

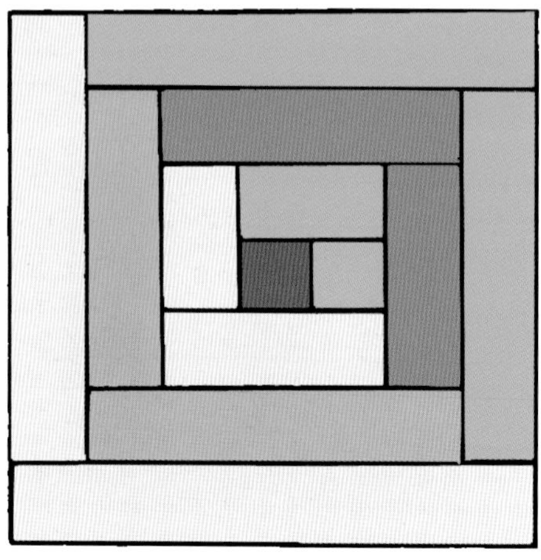
Fig 2

Construction

1 Cut strips 1¼in (3.2cm) wide from each fabric and arrange them at the side of the sewing machine in the order they will be used. A total length of approximately 3¼yd (3m) of strips for each set is needed.

2 Cut a short strip about 7in (17.8cm) long and 1¼in (3.2cm) wide from the centre fabric. Cut pieces from this strip to give four 1¼in (3.2cm) squares (Fig 3).

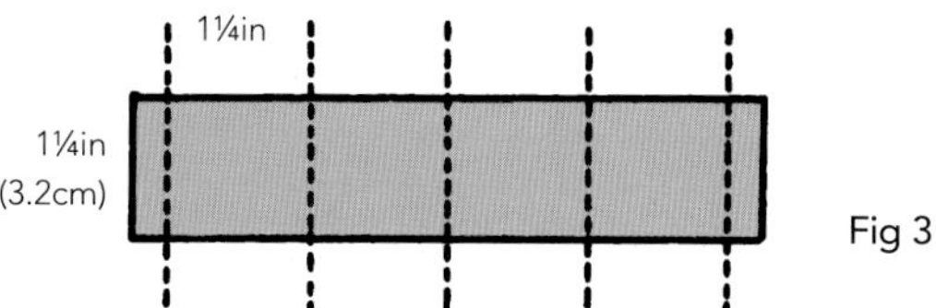

Fig 3

3 Stick a small square of masking tape on to the back of one of these central squares, avoiding the ¼in (6mm) seam allowance. Label the tape with numbers 1, 2, 3 and 4, as shown in Fig 4. The numbers give a guide to where each strip will be stitched.

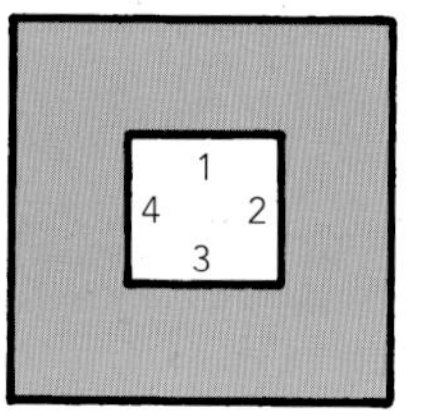

Fig 4

4 Choose the fabric you wish to use first and place it right side *up* on the machine in the correct position for a ¼in (6mm) seam to be sewn. Lower the pressure foot and wind the needle down into the fabric. Now the pressure foot can be lifted and the central squares added without the first strip slipping out of position.

5 Place the first square right side *down* on the strip with side 1 on the masking tape as the edge to be stitched. Using a short stitch and a ¼in (6mm) seam, sew the central square on to the strip. Sew onwards a few stitches and place a second square right side *down* on the strip. Sew this square in position then add the third and fourth squares in the same way (Fig 5).

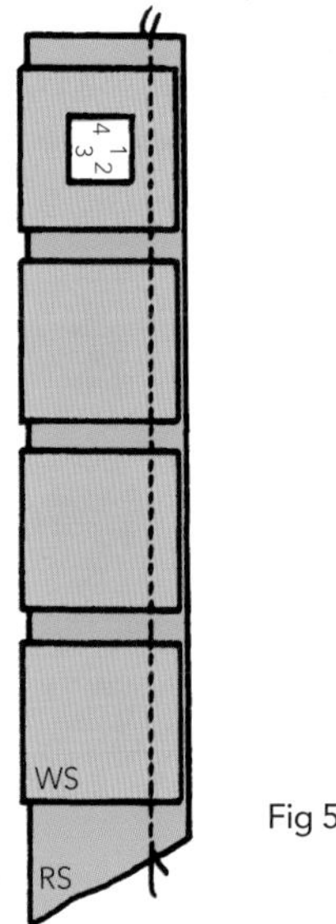

Fig 5

6 Remove the strip from the machine and carefully trim it to match the central squares exactly, using either sharp scissors or a rotary cutter (Fig 6). Finger press the seams away from the squares by holding the central square between your finger and thumb and pushing the strip away from the centre with your thumbs, pressing the seam firmly (Fig 7).

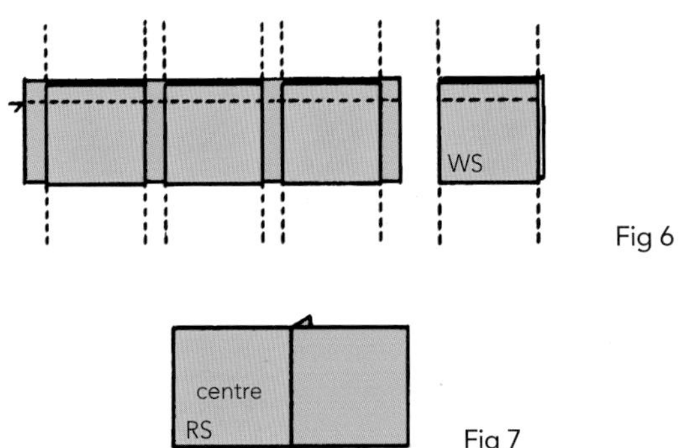

Fig 6

Fig 7

7 In building up the Log Cabin rounds of strips surrounding the centre, each fabric is always used twice, making an L-shape. So put the same fabric strip on the sewing machine again, right side *up* and wind the needle down into the fabric. Take the original block with its piece of masking tape and place it right side *down* on the strip with side two at the edge to be sewn (Fig 8). Sew down this edge and place the second block on the strip in the same way.

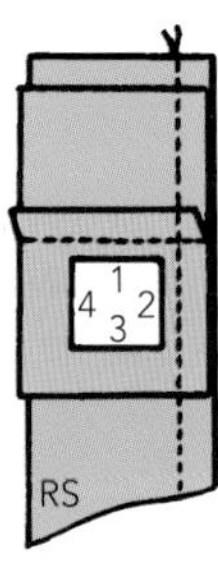

Fig 8

8 The first block is your model and the next three blocks must follow the same arrangement as they are positioned on the strip. Sew down and add the third and fourth blocks to match (Fig 9).

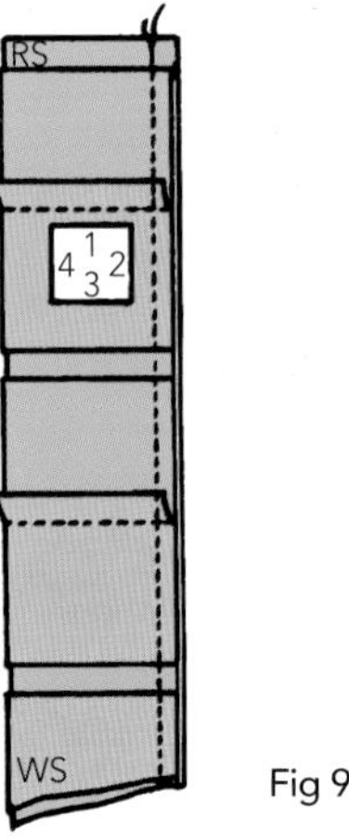

Fig 9

9 Trim the strip to match exactly the edges of the four blocks (Fig 10). Finger press the seams away from the centre square (Fig 11).

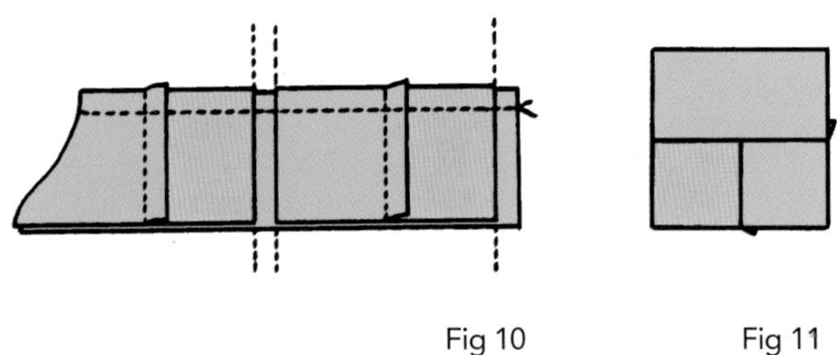
Fig 10

Fig 11

10 Having sewn on two strips from the first fabric, take a strip of fabric from the contrasting set and fix it under the machine, right side *up* with the needle wound down into it. If you were using dark fabrics, now change to light, or go from plain to patterned. Position the original block with side 3 on the masking tape at the sewing edge (Fig 12). Sew down this edge and add the remaining three blocks to match the first (Fig 13). Trim the strips to match each block and finger press the seams away from the centre (Fig 14).

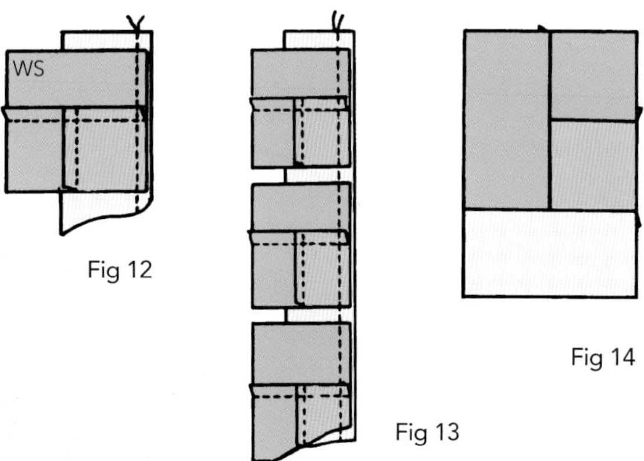

Fig 12

Fig 13

Fig 14

11 Using a strip of the same fabric (remember, always use each fabric *twice* to make an L-shape), follow the same procedure, sewing the strip on to side 4. You now have a complete round of strips surrounding the central square (Fig 15).

Now you have completed this much there is a quick way to see at a glance which side is the next to be stitched. Look at the block and find the edge which has two seams along it – this is the side which is to be stitched next (Fig 16).

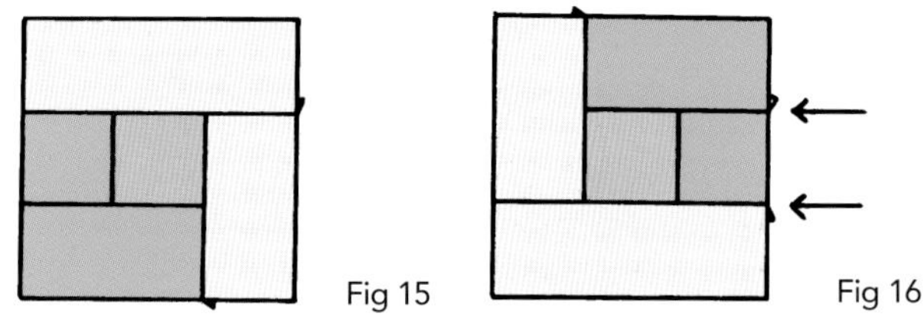

Fig 15

Fig 16

12 Continue building up the design, referring to the numbers on the masking tape square. Sides 1 and 2 always have the same set of fabrics against them and sides 3 and 4 always have the contrasting set of fabrics. Remember to use each fabric *twice* to make the L-shape. The sequence of fabrics is: two sides from first fabric from set one, two sides from first fabric from set two, two sides from second fabric from set one, two sides from second fabric from set two and so on.

13 When three rounds of strips have been sewn, check against Fig 1 that you have attached the correct number of strips and then press each square from the front.

14 Arrange the four squares in the design you like best. Pin and machine stitch the top two squares together with a ¼in (6mm) seam as usual. If the two edges do not match exactly and one is shorter than the other, pin and stitch with the shorter edge on top as this will stretch slightly as you work and should ease the problem. Press the seam from the front to one side.

15 Pin and stitch the second pair of squares, pressing the centre seams in the opposite direction to the first half (Fig 17).

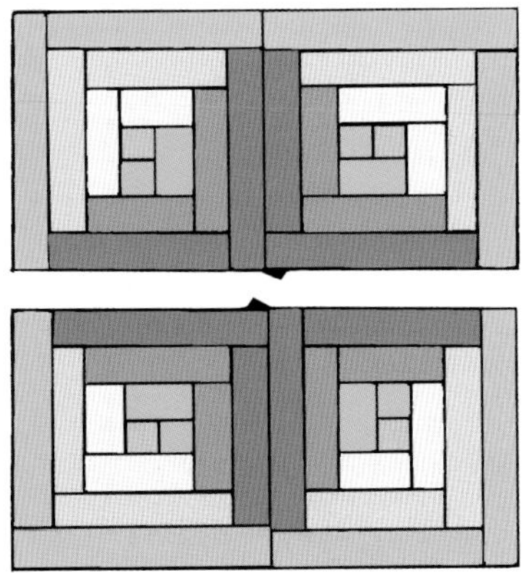

Fig 17

16 Join the two halves, matching the centre seams carefully. The final long seam can be pressed to one side, or if this makes it too bulky, press the seam allowances open.

17 Measure the completed block, it should be about 11in (28cm) square. Choose a fabric to use as an extra frame around the block before the sashing. Cut strips 1½in (3.8cm) wide for this frame and then attach them. See page 236 for instructions on trimming and adding frames. Trim the block to an exact 12½in (31.7cm) square. Add the framing sashing strips – see page 236 for instructions.

*"*Lynne's Sampler Quilt Book *came out just as I was starting quilting and it was very inspiring. I liked the 'quilt-as-you-go' method that allowed me to take small pieces of work away on holiday, which I did over several years between other projects. This quilt now has pride of place in my guest room."* **Jan Farris**

Quick Machined Strip Patchwork

Courthouse Steps

The Log Cabin design is so versatile and there are so many different variations of it that we could fill the book with just this one classic block and all the quilts that can be made with it. It is particularly stunning used throughout a large quilt, so this is one technique I would recommend for future projects. This is where the sampler quilt scores: try one block and if you like it, you know you will be happy embarking on a larger design sometime.

The variation shown here is the Courthouse Steps, which is made using the same quick machined method as the classic Log Cabin, but looks very different as the strips are joined on opposite sides of the block each time, which makes a more

symmetrical design (see Fig 1). As with Log Cabin, four Courthouse Steps units are made at the same time and then joined together to make the block for the sampler quilt.

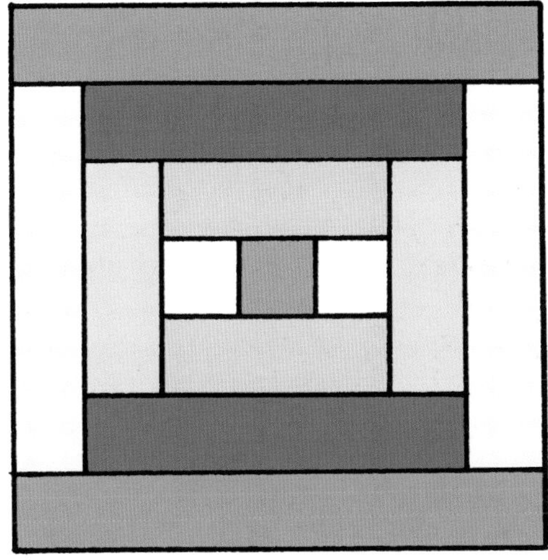

Fig 1

Colour Choices

Courthouse Steps is a variation of Log Cabin and the colour choices present exactly the same dilemmas (see Log Cabin Colour Choices page 64). There are still two sets of colours to be selected and arranged in an order that pleases the eye and where it is easy to see which fabric belongs to which team of fabrics. The only difference in this block is the way that the chosen sets of fabrics are stitched around the centre square, so all the advice for fabric selection given for the original Log Cabin block applies here.

Construction

1 Proceed exactly as for Log Cabin (see pages 64–66), cutting similar strips and centres. Mark the centres with the masking tape as before if you feel you need that extra guidance to positioning the strips as you make the blocks.

2 Add the first fabric two times, but at *opposite* sides of the centre square (sides 1 and 3 marked on the masking tape) as shown in Fig 2 below. Once sewn, finger press the seams away from the centre square.

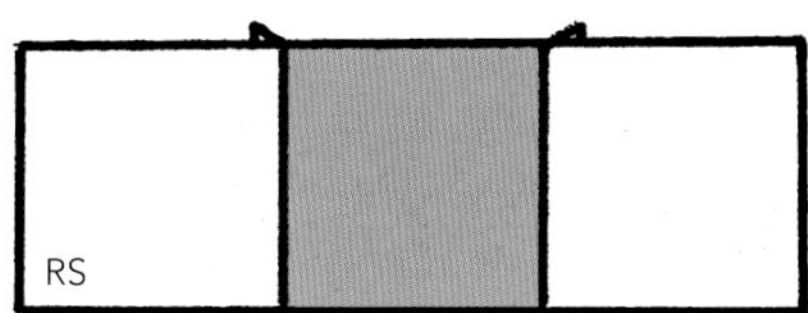

Fig 2

3 The first contrasting fabric is used next. It is also used twice – stitching it on to sides 2 and 4 (Fig 3), making the first complete round of strips surrounding the centre square. Finger press the seam away from the centre square as before.

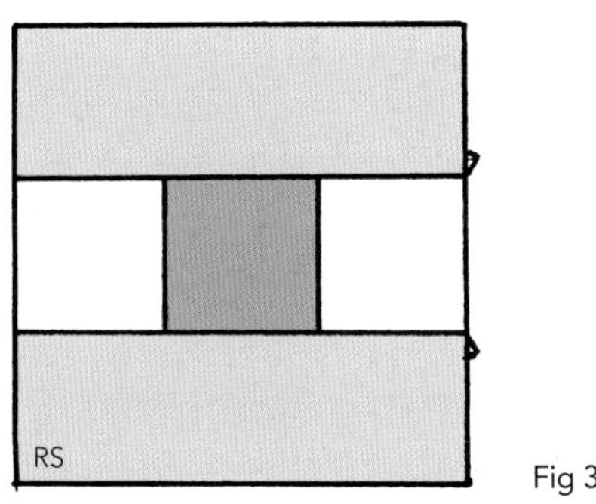

Fig 3

4 Look at the block and you will see that there are *two* sides that have two seams along their edges (Fig 4). These are the sides that will be stitched next.

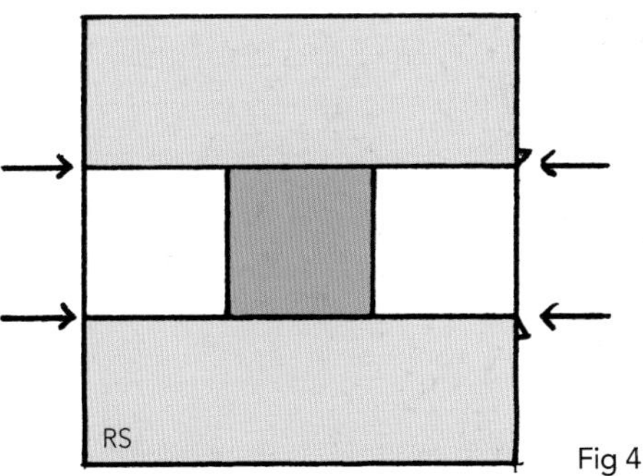

Fig 4

5 Take the second fabric from the first set and stitch it to each of the sides with the two seams along them (sides 1 and 3 on the masking tape) as in Fig 5. Finger press seams away from the centre.

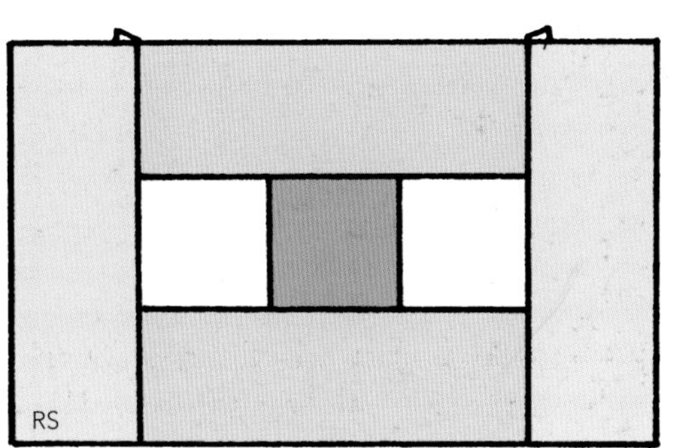

Fig 5

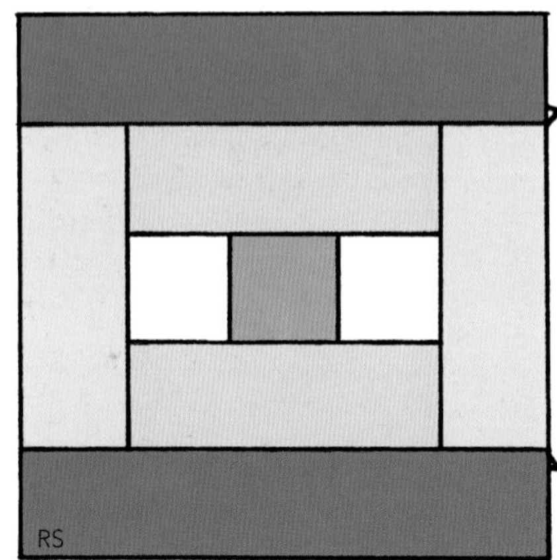

Fig 6

6 Look again for the two seams along the edges of the blocks. Take the second contrasting fabric and stitch it to each of the sides with the two seams along them (sides 2 and 4 on the masking tape), as in Fig 6. Finger press the seams away from the centre as usual.

7 Continue building up the design, referring to the masking tape square if necessary. Sides 1 and 3 should always have the first set of fabrics against them and sides 2 and 4 always have the contrasting set of fabrics. When three rounds of strips have been stitched, check against Fig 1 that you have attached the correct number of strips in the correct position and press each square from the front.

8 Arrange the four squares in the design you like best. They could be in vertical columns of colour as in Fig 7a or the spinning arrangement shown in Fig 7b.

9 Follow the instructions in the Log Cabin block on page 66 steps 14–17 to trim each square and stitch them together to make the Courthouse Steps block.

Fig 7a

Fig 7b

Gill Peskett needed to make her quilt larger and so added five more blocks, using these calming 'Boxed Square' blocks to create quiet spaces amongst the complex Sampler Quilt designs.

"This was my first quilt, which was started with Kate Badrick and finished with Lynne Edwards. On pinning up the twenty finished blocks it looked too busy, so Lynne suggested the boxed square spacer blocks to calm it down, which I think works really well." **Gill Peskett**

Dresden Plate

There are many patchwork blocks based on the circular plate design and Dresden Plate is the most popular and well known of these. The number of segments in the plate varies from eight to twenty, while the outer edges may be all curved, all pointed or a mixture of the two. No particular number or layout is obligatory, so it can be varied at the whim of the maker. This simple block is often used for a large quilt, with the fans repeated and combined to make stunning designs. Here the Dresden Plate has twelve sections, four with pointed edges to give a stronger accent at the top, bottom and two sides (Fig 1). The segments are joined together to make the plate, which is then appliquéd on to a

background. The outer edges have to be turned over and tacked (basted) before being stitched to the background. Finally, the central circle is appliquéd in position. So this block is as much about appliqué as it is about piecing.

Fig 1

Colour Choices

This is another block, like Grandmother's Fan and Tumbling Blocks, that has a design set on a background, so when choosing the fabrics arrange them on the background fabric to get an idea of how they look. You may be varying your backgrounds or keeping them all one colour, but you need to pin up or lay out all the completed blocks to check how the selection and balance of colours is looking. If it is not possible to pin them on to a vertical surface, lay them on the floor and view them from as great a distance as possible – stand on a chair or even a step-ladder. Note the fabrics you need to use more of and what is needed to keep a good balance. You will be surprised at how much easier this gets as you complete more blocks.

For the segments choose a selection of three fabrics that are equal in tone. Try to avoid one that is much stronger than the others or use it for the pointed-edged segments to make a cross. You can leave the decision about the central circle until later if you are not sure what to use at this stage.

Construction

1 Make templates A, B and C from Fig 2 below in the usual way – see page 15 for instructions on making templates.

2 On the wrong side of your chosen fabrics draw accurately around template A and template B using a sharp marking pencil. You need eight A shapes and four B shapes. Mark the lines X in the seam allowances on each piece (Fig 3). Allow at least ½in (1.3cm) between each drawn outline so that a seam allowance of ¼in (6mm) can be added to each shape when cutting out. Save space by arranging the shapes as in Fig 4.

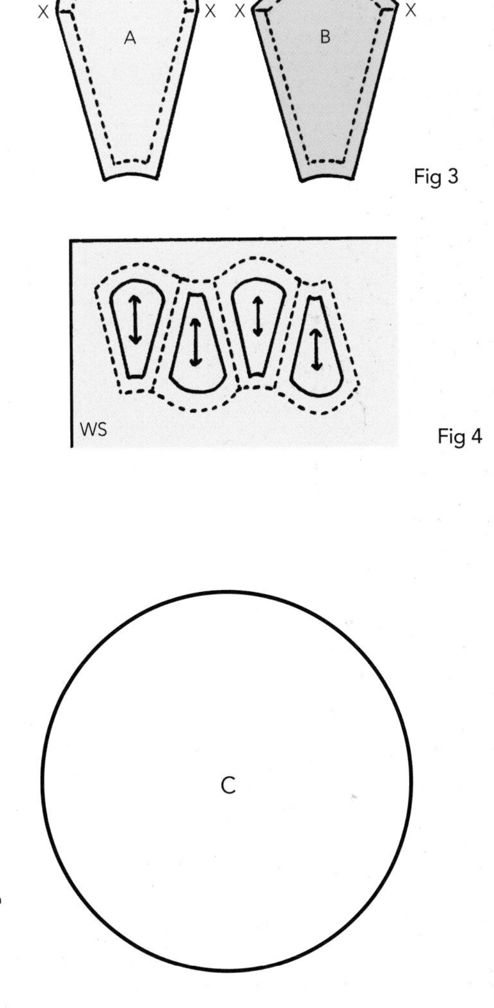

Fig 3

Fig 4

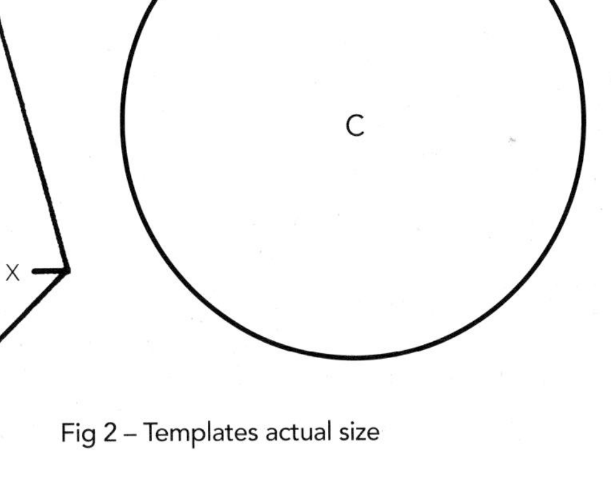

Fig 2 – Templates actual size

3 Cut out each shape to include the ¼in (6mm) seam allowance, judging this by eye or by measuring.

4 Arrange the segments on the background fabric to check that you are happy with the sequence of fabrics before stitching them together.

5 Take two adjacent segments and place them right sides together, matching the drawn lines with pins from the corner to the lines marked X (Fig 5), as in Maple Leaf page 34. Stitch along the drawn lines either by hand or machine, beginning and finishing at the comer of the design and at X (Fig 6).

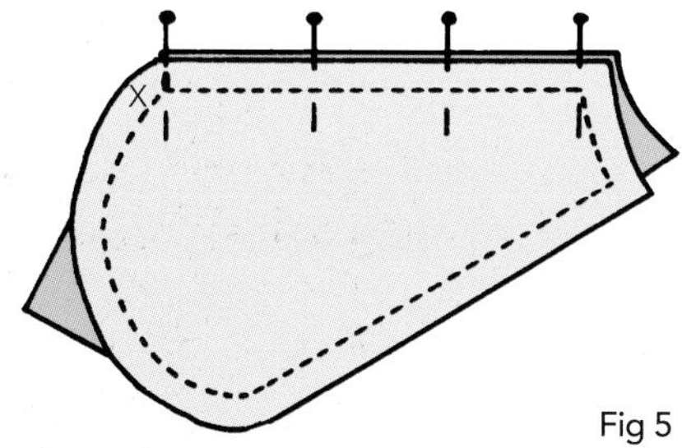

Fig 5

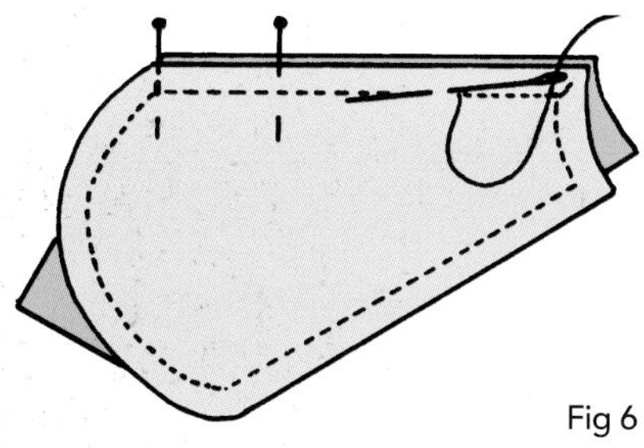
Fig 6

Join all twelve segments together in this way to make a complete circle (Fig 7). Press the seams from the front of the work to one side.

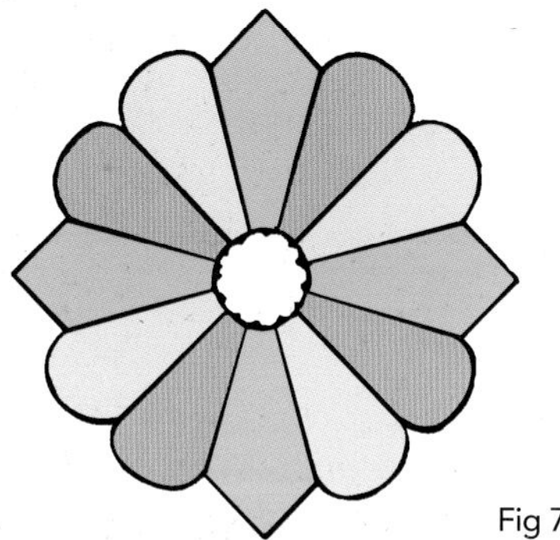
Fig 7

6 Turn the 'plate' to the wrong side and carefully clip the seam allowance of the curved outer edge, snipping at roughly ¼in (6mm) intervals, going nearly but not quite to the drawn line. The seam allowances along the outer edge of the 'plate' need to be turned to the back of the work and tacked (basted). The turning lines are most easily marked by the traditional technique called needle-marking, as follows.

Lay the 'plate' right side down on a pad of folded fabric (a folded flannelette sheet is ideal). Position template A on one of the curved segments, exactly on the drawn outline. Using a large blunt tapestry needle, trace around the curved edge of the template, holding the needle at an angle and pressing firmly. You should find that the needle has pressed a crease along the drawn curved line (Fig 8). Repeat this on all eight curved edges, then use template B to needle-mark the pointed edges of the remaining four segments.

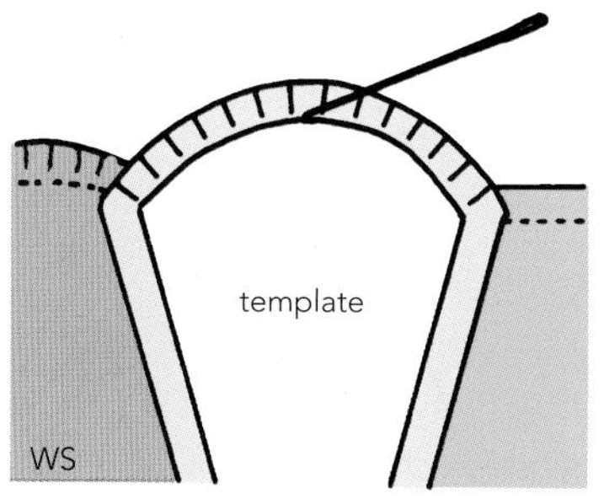

Fig 8

7 Turn over the 'plate' to its front and, following the creased lines, turn under the outer edges to the back of the work, tacking them down with small running stitches as you go (Fig 9). Do not press this tacked edge. It will be easier to appliqué the 'plate' on to the background in a really smooth curve if the edge is unpressed so that any little irregularities along it can be adjusted as it is stitched.

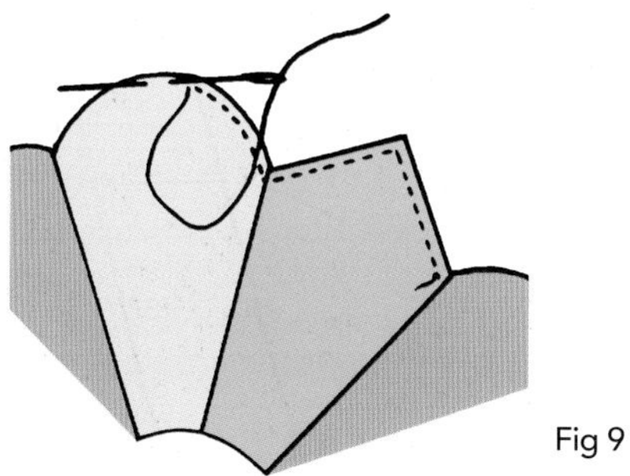
Fig 9

8 Cut a 13in (33cm) square of fabric for the background. This allows for any pulling in of the background when the 'plate' is appliqué on to it and can be trimmed to the exact size later on.

"This was the first quilt I made. I used Lynne's book and had one of Lynne's friends, Kate Badrick, teaching me, which made the whole thing fun and enjoyable. I even had my children and husband helping me choose materials and selecting patterns, so it was a real family effort!" **Kirsty Gowler**

Fold the background square of fabric into quarters and press lightly to mark the centre. Unfold it and position on the 'plate', centring the creased lines within the hole in the plate (Fig 10).

Pin or tack the 'plate' on to the background and using thread to match the fabrics of it and not the background, sew the 'plate' in position using small, even slip stitches (Fig 11). Sew a double stitch at each inner comer to secure it. Press from the front.

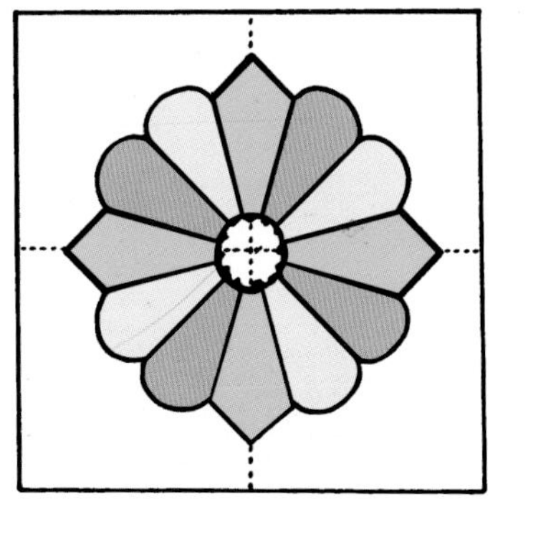

Fig 10

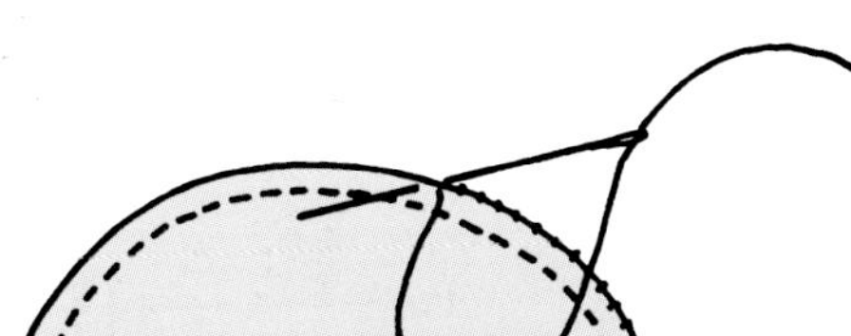

Fig 11

9 On the wrong side of your chosen fabric draw around circle template C from page 73 and cut it out with a ¼in (6mm) seam allowance added. Make a line of small tacking stitches close to the outer edge of the fabric circle (Fig 12a). Place the card template on the wrong side of the fabric and pull the tacking stitches so that the edges of the fabric are gathered tightly over the card (Fig 12b). Secure with a double stitch and press lightly from the front. Remove the card circle by bending it slightly. Pin the fabric on to the centre of the 'plate' and stitch in place.

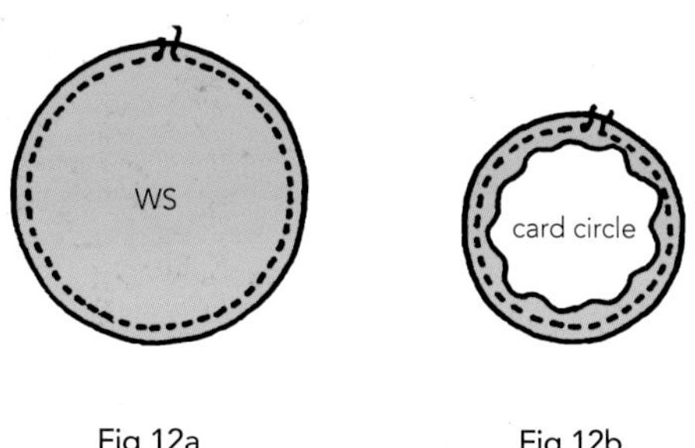

Fig 12a Fig 12b

Alternatively, you might like to try freezer paper to make the circle in this design, see Basic Equipment page 14. On the freezer paper draw round template C and cut it out exactly. Iron the circle, shiny side *down*, on to the wrong side of the fabric. Cut around it with a ¼in (6mm) seam allowance. Clip the curve nearly but not quite to the freezer paper (Fig 13a). Carefully peel off the circle, replacing it in exactly the same position but with the shiny side facing *upwards* (Fig 13b). Using the tip of an iron, push the seam allowance over the freezer paper, sticking it down as you go (Fig 13c). Take care not to press in any tiny pleats on the outer edge but keep the curve smooth. If there are areas you are not happy with, just peel the fabric back and re-press in the correct position. Place the circle of fabric in the centre of the 'plate' and press. This will fix it on to the background while you stitch it in place.

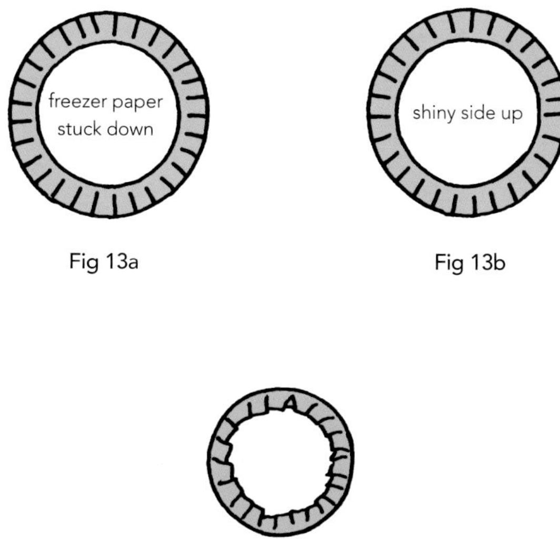

Fig 13a Fig 13b

Fig 13c

10 If you use freezer paper, cut away the background fabric after the block has been completed to remove the paper and reduce the layers for quilting. If the centre has been appliquéd in the normal way it is up to you whether you cut the background away, although it does allow the block to lie flatter and will be easier to quilt. See Tumbling Blocks page 26 for instructions on cutting away the background.

11 Trim the block to an exact 12½in (31.7cm) square. See page 236 for instructions on trimming blocks.

12 Add the framing sashing strips, see page 236 for instructions.

Quick Machined Patchwork

Triangles

Patchwork designs worked by the early American pioneers depended greatly on the simple square, as it provided a way of making a quilt from scraps quickly and with little wastage. Large squares were often combined with groups of four smaller squares in a checker-board arrangement to create more elaborate designs and as a way of using up scraps. An exciting progression from these squares was to divide the square diagonally into two right-angled triangles (see Fig 1 overleaf). These triangles were combined with squares and other triangles to create a huge number of block patterns, as well as decorative borders and edgings (Fig 2). The usual method of making these designs was to

make a template, cut out the shapes, then piece them together by hand or machine, following the drawn sewing lines in the American piecing technique. However, there is a quicker and easier way of turning the triangles into squares by using rotary equipment and a sewing machine. You still have the tiresome task of joining the squares and matching the corners (remember the centre of Spider's Web?), but the preliminary cutting and stitching is simplified.

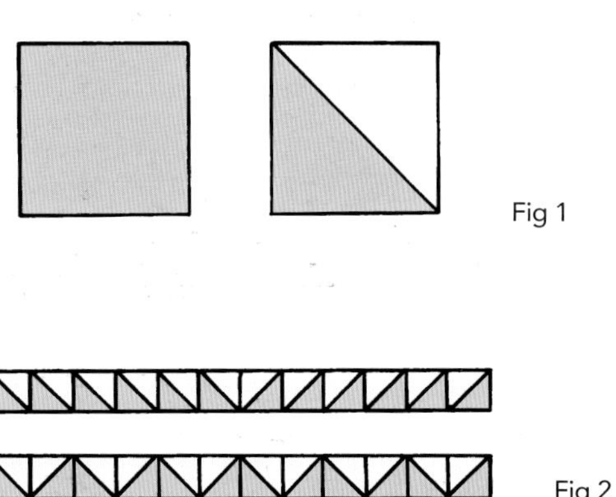

Fig 1

Fig 2

This amazing piece of lateral thinking was first devised by American quilter Barbara Johannah and is based on a drawn grid of squares, the size of which depends on the final size required. When planning a machined design that uses 3in (7.6cm) squares finished size, you must cut 3½in (8.9cm) squares to allow for the ¼in (6mm) seam allowance on all sides (Fig 3a). In other words, you always begin with a cut square that measures the finished size *plus* ½in (1.3cm). For a finished square measuring 3in (7.6cm) made up of two triangles, the starting measurement has to allow for the diagonal seam across the square and must be 3⅞in (9.8cm) square (Fig 3b). In other words, for your drawn grid you always add ⅞in (2.2cm) to the final measurement. A tiresome business, but one not to be avoided if the work is going to finish up exactly the size you want.

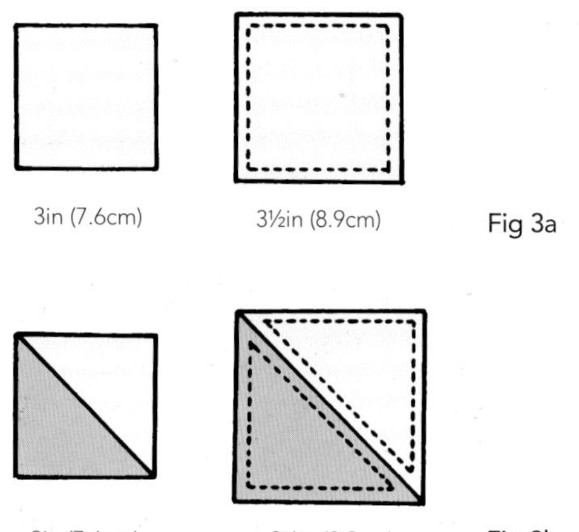

Fig 3a

Fig 3b

Colour Choices

Six block designs are shown in Figs 4a to 4f. Each one uses just two fabrics and because the designs are so varied it is quite possible to make more than one block for the sampler quilt without any similarity between them.

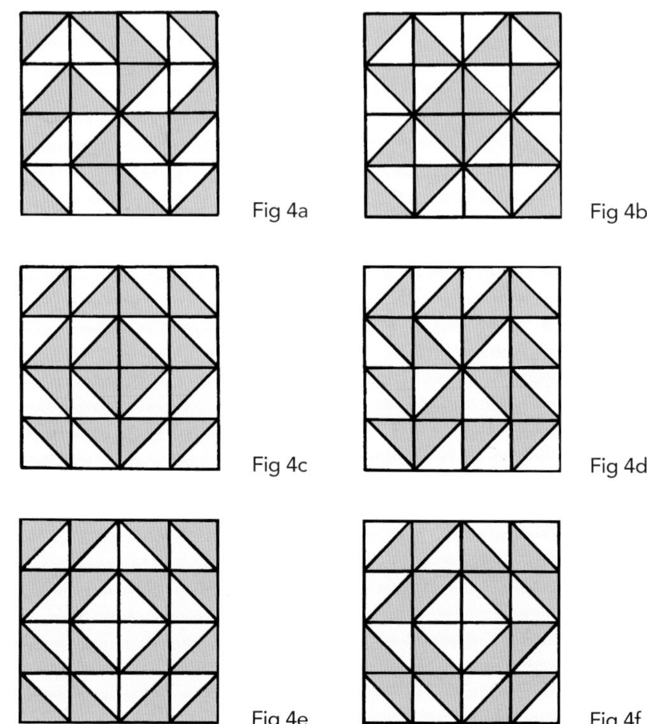

Fig 4a

Fig 4b

Fig 4c

Fig 4d

Fig 4e

Fig 4f

Construction

1 From each of the two chosen fabrics cut a piece measuring about 16½ x 9in (42 x 22.8cm). Place them right sides together and press. This will help keep the two layers in place.

2 Place the two layers of fabric on a cutting board. On the top fabric you are going to draw a grid of eight squares – two rows of four – each square measuring 3⅞in (9.8cm) square (Fig 5). To do this accurately it is better to use the measurements on the ruler rather than those on the cutting board.

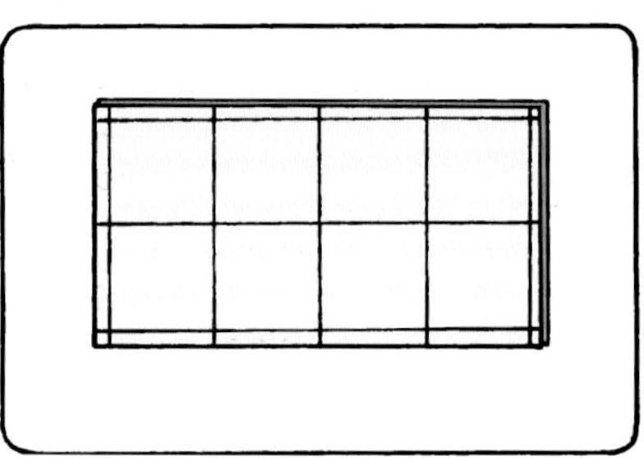

Fig 5

Find the line or marks on the ruler that are 3⅞in (9.8cm) from one edge. Mark this distance by sticking a small piece of tape at each end of the ruler on the 3⅞in (9.8cm) line (Fig 6).

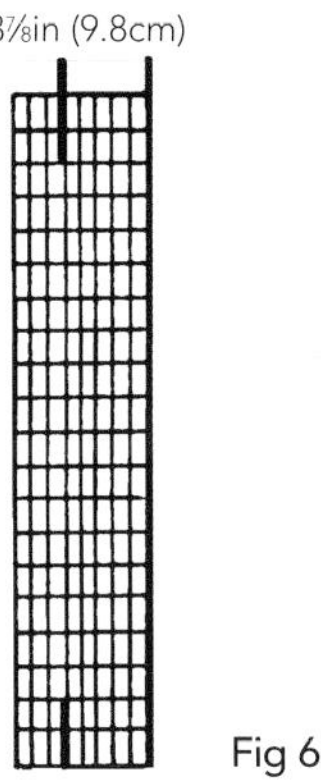

Fig 6

Place the ruler vertically about ¼in (6mm) from the left-hand edge of the fabrics (Fig 7a). Using a marking pencil, draw a line from top to bottom of the fabric along the ruler's edge. Move the ruler across the fabric to the right until the marked 3⅞in (9.8cm) line is exactly on top of the drawn line (Fig 7b). Draw a line along the ruler's edge.

Once again move the ruler across the fabric to the right until the new drawn line lies exactly under the 3⅞in (9.8cm) line on the ruler. Draw a line along the ruler's edge. Repeat this twice until five vertical lines have been drawn on to the fabric at 3⅞in (9.8cm) intervals. Left-handed quilters should begin marking from the right-hand side and move the ruler across the fabric to the left.

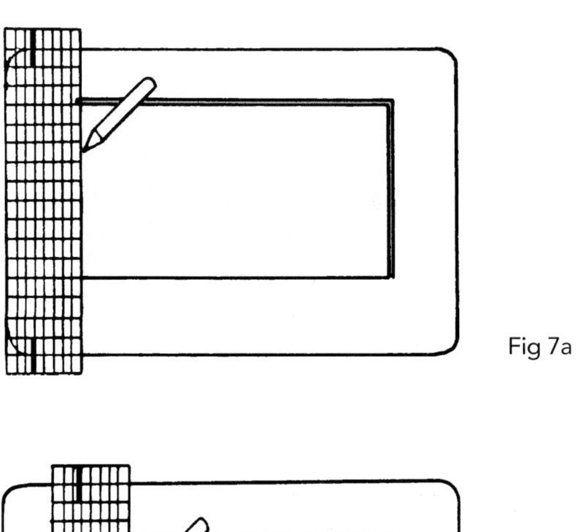
Fig 7a

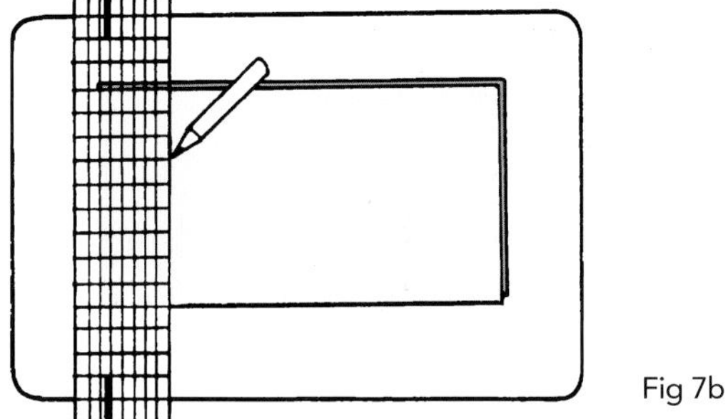
Fig 7b

3 Turn the ruler horizontally and draw a line on the fabric about ¼in (6mm) from the bottom edges (Fig 7c). In the same way as before, move the ruler upwards over the fabric until the 3⅞in (9.8cm) line is exactly on top of the drawn line (Fig 7d). Draw a line along the ruler's edge. Repeat this once more to complete the grid of two rows of four squares.

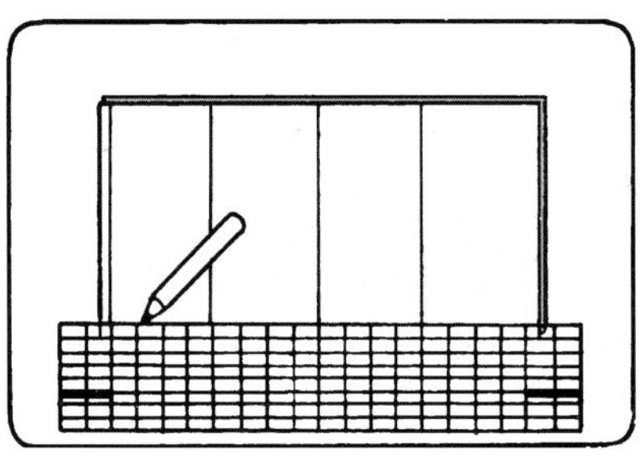
Fig 7c

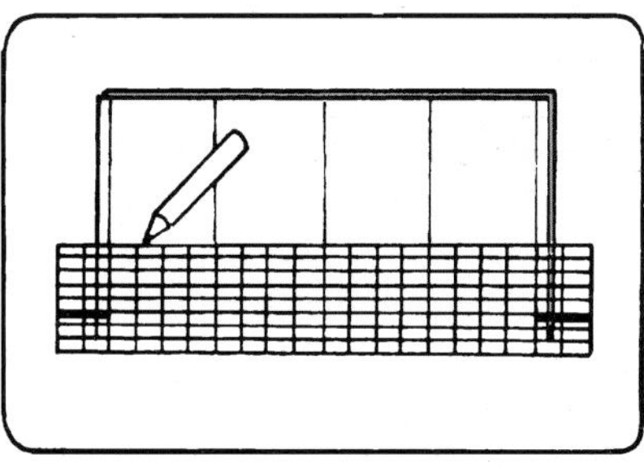
Fig 7d

4 Draw diagonal lines across each square in one direction only (Fig 8).

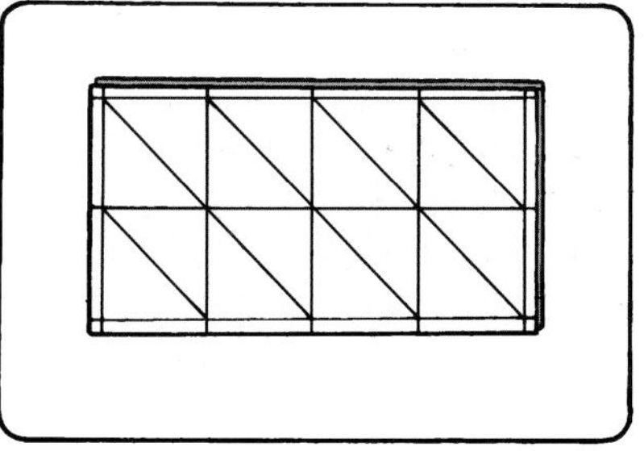
Fig 8

5 Pin the two fabrics together with eight to ten pins to hold the layers while stitching. Machine a line of stitching on either side of the drawn diagonal lines at a distance of exactly ¼in (6mm) using a slightly smaller stitch as usual (Fig 9)

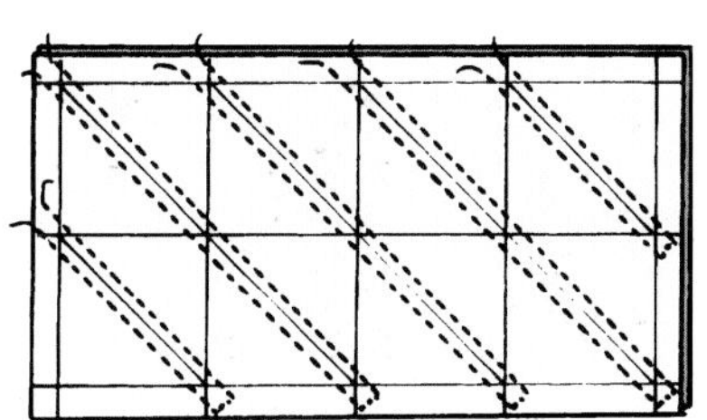
Fig 9

If you have a strip of masking tape stuck on to your machine plate as a stitching guide you will not be able to see it through the layers of fabric, so another way of stitching accurately must be found – try the following.

a Use a special ¼in (6mm) foot on the machine.

b If your machine has the facility, move the machine needle until the distance between it and the side of your usual machine foot is exactly ¼in (6mm).

c Using a different colour marking pencil to prevent confusion, draw in a line ¼in (6mm) away from the diagonal line on both sides.

6 Once the pairs of lines have been stitched, remove the fabrics from the machine and place them on the cutting board. Using a ruler and cutter, cut along all the drawn vertical lines. Without moving the fabric, cut along the drawn horizontal lines. Finally, cut along the drawn diagonal lines (Fig 10). You will find that a miracle has happened and that when you pick up each triangle of fabric, it has been stitched to another and you have a pieced square made of two triangles of two different fabrics. Some of the triangles will have a line of stitches across one corner (Fig 11). Loosen these gently by pulling the fabrics apart – they will easily come undone and the threads can be removed. Press each square from the front with the seams towards the darker fabric.

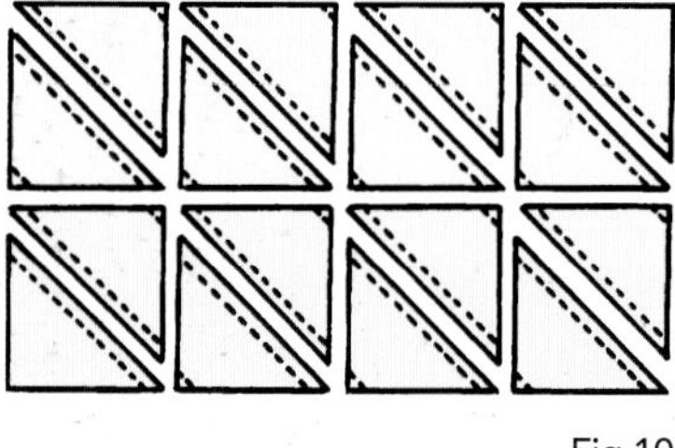

Fig 10

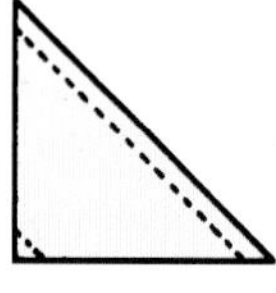

Fig 11

7 Arrange the sixteen squares in your chosen design. If they do not all fit together perfectly, remember that you can swap the squares around because they are all identical.

8 Sew together the top four squares to make a row. If you have a design where two triangles meet in a point, check that once they are joined the two triangles meet in an arrowhead ¼in (6mm) from the top edges of the fabric (Fig 12), see Spider's Web page 58. From the front press all seams on row one in one direction.

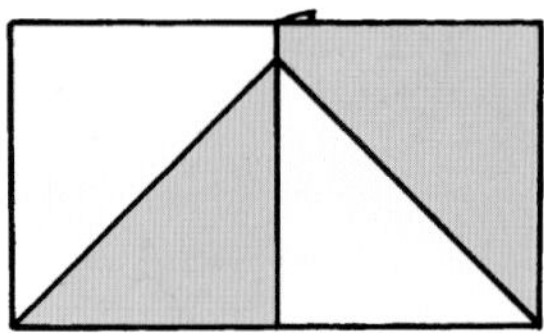

Fig 12

9 Join together the four squares in row two. From the front press the seams in the opposite direction to row one. Join rows one and two, matching seams carefully. Repeat with rows three and four until the block is completed.

10 Press the completed block from the front and measure, it should be exactly 12½in (31.7cm) square. If it is not, trim or add a small border. See page 236 for instructions on trimming the blocks and adding borders.

11 Add the framing sashing strips, following the instructions on page 236.

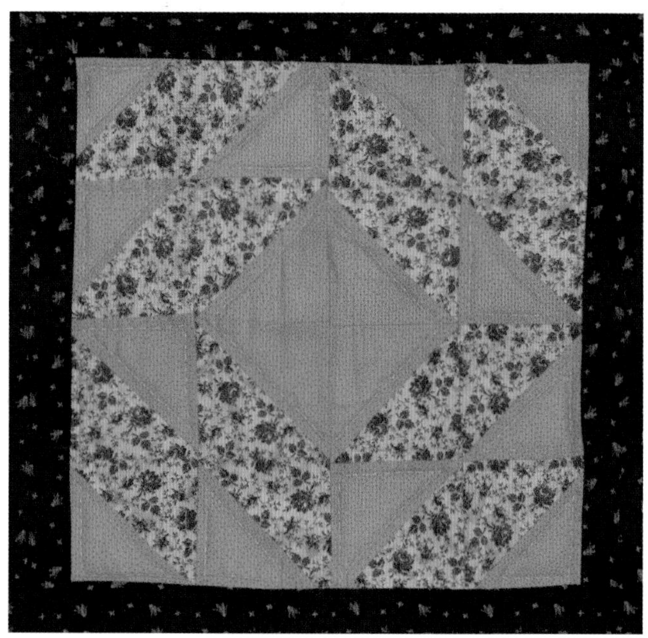

Christine Askew added a second version of the Triangles block to her quilt, using a different pair of fabrics and arranging the pieces in an alternative design as shown here.

"On holiday in Norfolk in July 2004 I saw a beautiful patchwork quilt and declared, 'I'm going to make one of those when I get home'. Having no idea how to get started, my husband bought me Lynne Edwards' **Sampler Quilt Book** *for my birthday. Fabrics were chosen in a palette of colours I liked and work began. The quilt was completed in April 2005, the bedroom decorated and a new bed chosen to match the quilt."* **Christine Askew**

Hand Appliqué

Rose of Sharon

Appliqué is a technique often used in quilt-making and many of the traditional appliqué designs, which include simplified flowers, leaves and wreaths, are used together with piecing and quilting to create beautiful quilts. The appliqué block for the sampler quilt is the Rose of Sharon design, which I chose partly for its good looks and partly because the design combines all the possibly tricky elements of appliqué – sharp points, deep V-shapes, curves and overlapping pieces. By the time you have finished stitching it you should be ready for any appliqué design that takes your fancy in the future. It is always a much-admired block in everyone's sampler quilt.

Colour Choices

This design gives you a chance to use up all the small pieces of fabric you may have as none of the appliqué pieces are very big, although you will need a 13in (33cm) square of background fabric which will be trimmed down to a 12½in (31.7cm) square once the appliqué has been completed. Cut out and arrange one section of the design on the background square (Fig 2 page 86) before you begin sewing to check that you like the arrangement of fabrics.

Construction

Before beginning any appliqué design you must do some planning. Firstly, the appliqué shapes should always be cut so that when they are sewn in position the straight grain of all the fabrics matches the straight grain of the background fabric. The straight grain is marked on the templates here with a double-headed arrow. Secondly, the appliqué shapes must be attached in the right order so that the top shapes are added last. Where two shapes meet, the seam allowance of the bottom background piece is left unturned. The second piece is then placed overlapping this raw edge. In Fig 2 the dotted lines indicate where the seam allowances are left unturned and overlapped by another shape. Small arrowheads indicate edges where the seam allowances have been turned under and tacked (basted).

1 For the background cut a 13in (33cm) square of fabric. Fold it diagonally into four to find the centre point, then finger press. Trace the design layout in Fig 2 on to paper. Place the fabric square over the design layout, positioning the centre of the fabric over the central cross on circle E and a diagonal fold over the broken positioning line. Draw very lightly with a marking pencil about ⅛in (3mm) inside the lines of the design to give an indication where the appliqué pieces will be positioned. Do not draw exact outlines in case these show around the edges of the appliquéd shapes after stitching. If the fabric is not fine enough to trace through, use a light box, see Basic Equipment page 15. Turn the fabric and position another diagonal fold over the positioning line on the layout. Draw the guidelines for each shape as before. Repeat this with the other two diagonal fold lines until the complete appliqué design has been marked on the fabric.

2 Make templates A, B D and E from Fig 1 on page 86 in the usual way (see page 15 for instructions on making templates). Template C is for the inner flower and is optional. If the fabric for the outer flower D is very busy you may feel that you do not need the extra layer, in which case omit template C.

3 The outlines of the appliqué shapes can now be transferred to the fabrics in two ways – choose whichever way you prefer.

a Hold the card template in position on the front of the appliqué fabric and draw round it lightly with a sharp marking pencil.

b Draw round the template on the wrong side of the appliqué fabric. Place the fabric on a pad of folded fabric, wrong side up. Hold the card template in position on the drawn outline and, using a large blunt-ended needle, run the point very firmly around the edge of the template. This is the needle-marking technique used in the Dresden Plate block on page 74.

Both of these techniques work well. You may find that your fabric does not crease well enough for needle-marking, or that a marking pencil does not show clearly on the fabric. My advise is to try both methods and use whichever one is the more efficient.

For the design you will need four of shape A, eight of shape B, four of shape C, four of shape D and one of E.

4 Once the outlines have been transferred to the appliqué fabric, cut them out adding a ¼in (6mm) seam allowance. Using sharp scissors clip any curved edges at right angles to the pencil line, nearly but not quite to the line itself. Outer points should be left unclipped for ½in (1.3cm) either side of the point while V-shaped edges need to be clipped cleanly to the pencil line (Fig 3).

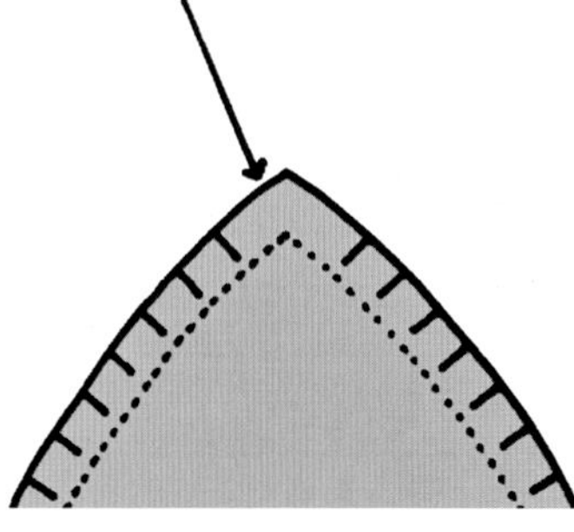

Fig 3

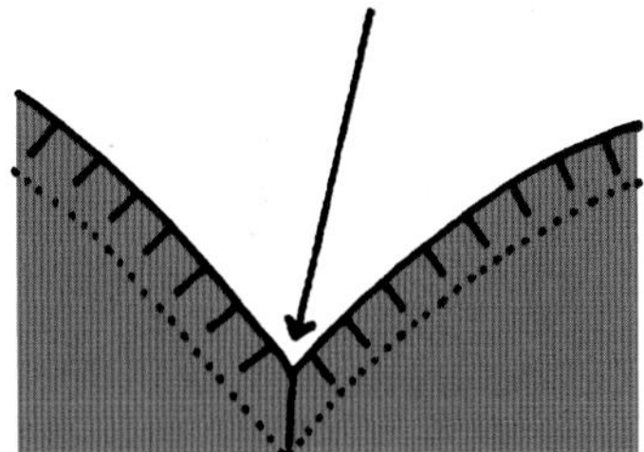

5 Begin with shape A – Fig 4a shows the edges that are to be clipped and turned under. Clip to the line at the points marked X so that the narrow stem shape can be turned under. The two unturned edges will be overlapped by shapes B. Turn the appropriate seam allowances to the back after clipping, following the pencil line or needle-marked fold exactly and tack (baste) with small running stitches, as in Dresden Plate. Do not press the tacked appliqué pieces as it will be easier to ease out any irregularities in the edges as you stitch if they are unpressed.

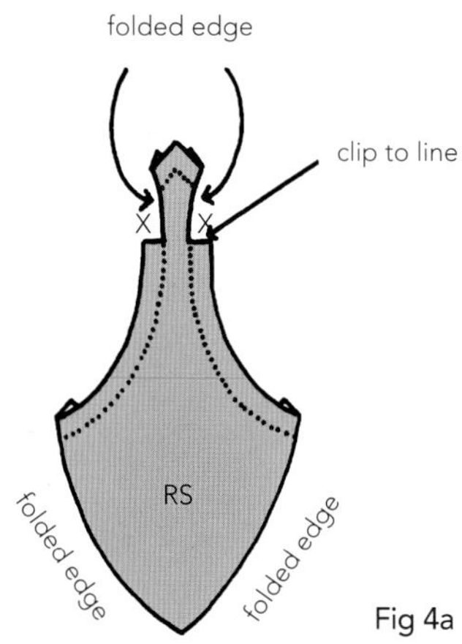

Fig 4a

6 Clip and tack under all edges of shape B. The sharp corners can be folded over neatly in three stages, as shown in Fig 4b.

7 Clip and tack under shapes C (if used) and D on the outer curves only (Fig 4c).

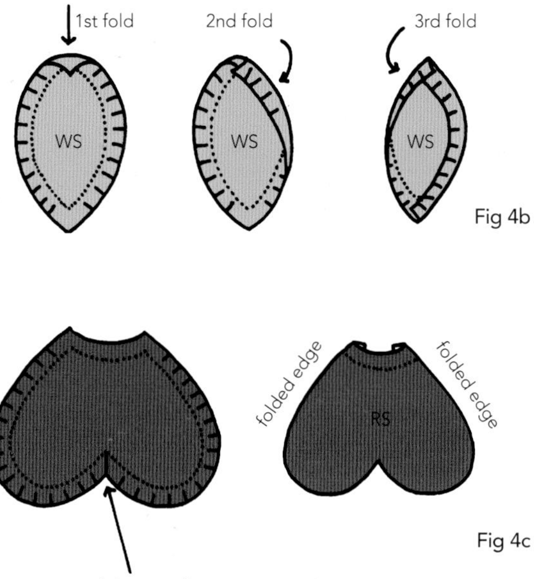

Fig 4b

Fig 4c

8 Shape E can be made either by gathering the fabric circle around a card template or by using freezer paper. Follow the instructions given in the Dresden Plate on page 76.

9 Arrange the tacked shapes in position on the background, beginning with A, then B, C, D and finally E. Make sure that each shape overlaps the previous one by ¼in (6mm). Pin or tack each piece in place (Fig 5).

Fig 5

10 Stitch each shape on to the background with small even slipstitches, beginning with shape A and working towards the centre (Fig 6). Match the sewing threads to the appliqué fabrics, not the background. In the V-shaped areas of any shape that have been clipped right up to the line, reinforce with two or three stitches in the inner corner (Fig 7).

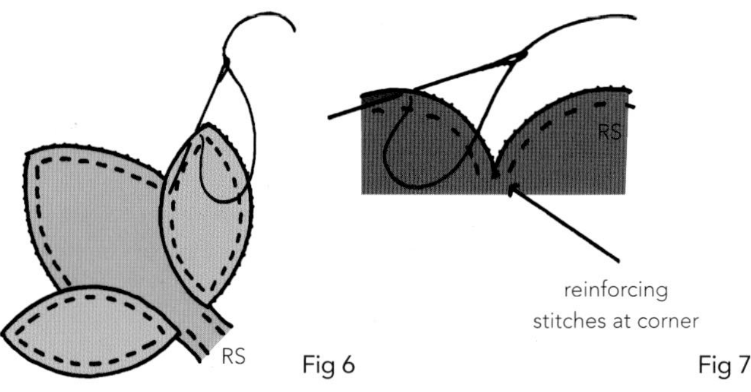

Fig 6

Fig 7

11 Once the appliqué has been completed, remove the tacking stitches. If you wish, the layers can be reduced by cutting away the background fabric behind the appliqué. This is your choice, although if freezer paper has been used for the central circle then the background fabric *has* to be cut away so that the paper can be removed.

12 Trim the background fabric to an exact 12½in (31.7cm) square.

13 Add the framing sashing strips as usual, following the instructions on page 236.

"This sampler quilt, my first, will always remind me of a wonderful year – not only the arrival of my son's first child Grace and my daughter's engagement but also the great pleasure derived from every stitch in the making of this quilt." **Julie Moreland**

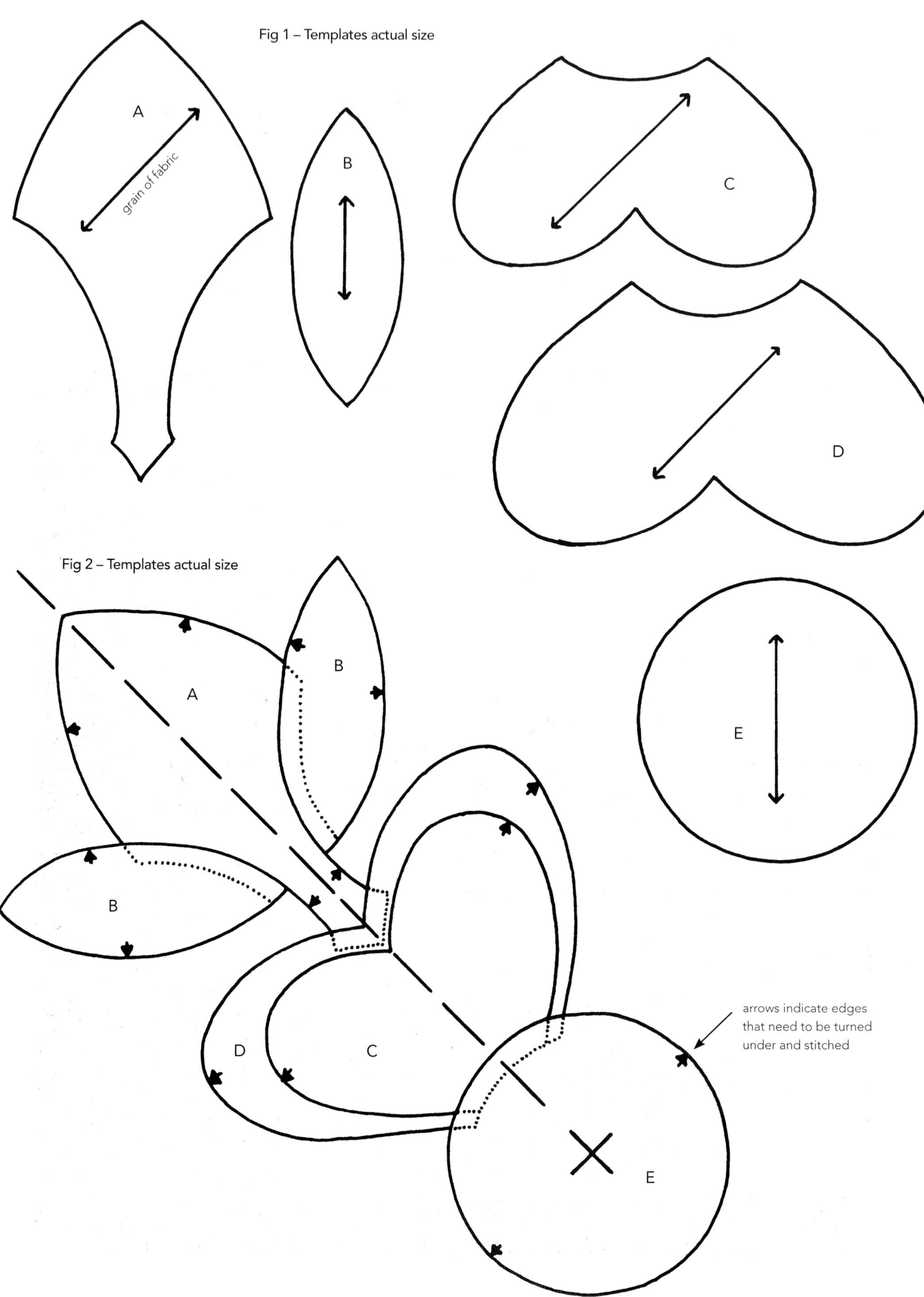
Fig 1 – Templates actual size
A
grain of fabric
B
C
D
Fig 2 – Templates actual size
A
B
B
D
C
E
E
arrows indicate edges that need to be turned under and stitched

Quick Machine Patchwork

Wild Goose Chase

This block is based on Flying Geese, which is a favourite pattern, appearing in many quilts both as blocks (see Figs 1a, lb, and 1c overleaf) and as borders (Fig 1d). The block for the sampler quilt is called Dutchman's Puzzle, but it is also known as Wild Goose Chase, which I prefer as it conjures up the desperate chase for the perfect fabric for the quilt! Traditionally this design was laboriously pieced using templates and American piecing. Pauline Adams, a very clever quilt-maker from Hertfordshire, has worked out this ingenious machined method. Flying Geese is often used as a border design, with the 'goose' triangles following each other around the quilt.

Fig 1a

Fig 1b

Fig 1c

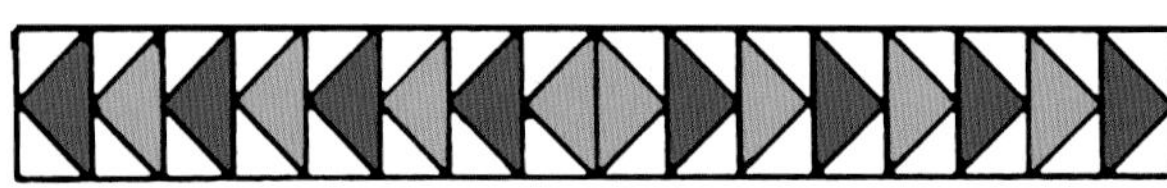
Fig 1d

The quick method of sewing half-square triangles (see page 78) was based on the principle that if you want to finish up with a square of a certain size, you must start with a square that is ⅞in (2.2cm) larger (Fig 2a). This includes the ¼in (6mm) seam allowance round the edges plus the diagonal seam that joins the two triangles.

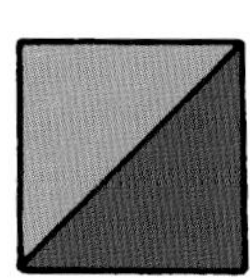
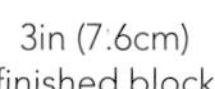
3in (7.6cm)
finished block

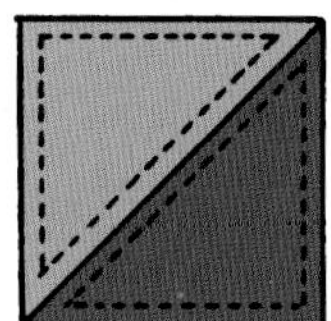
3⅞in (9.8cm)
start size

Fig 2a

There is a similar formula for cutting a square divided into four triangles. The final size required needs to have an extra 1¼in (3.2cm) added to it at the start. This extra includes the ¼in (6mm) seam allowance round the edges plus the two diagonal seams (Fig 2b). Do not ask me to explain this: someone has done lots of hard sums to give us this formula, just accept it gratefully. Pauline Adams' method uses both of these principles. If you are very mathematical, you may be able to fathom the logic behind it. If you are like me you will just follow the instructions and be amazed at the result.

3in (7.6cm)
finished block

4¼in (10.6cm)
start size

Fig 2b

Colour Choices

The block uses two main colours for large triangles, known in the pattern as 'geese', and one background shade for the smaller triangles, which represent the 'sky' (Fig 3). When you get to this block you may be running short of some fabrics, so it is best to check with the sizes given below to ensure you have enough for your chosen shades.

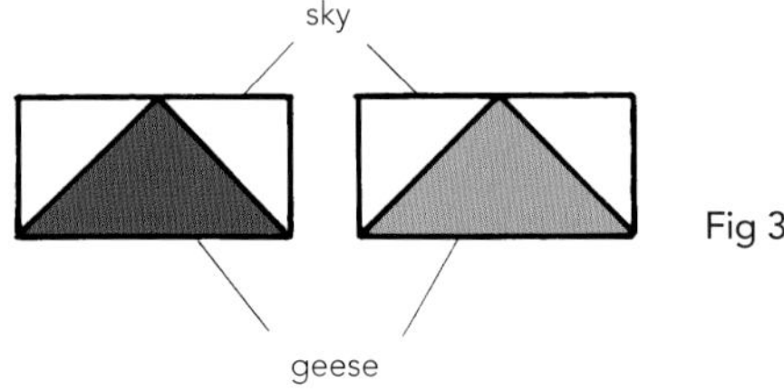

Fig 3

Construction

The design is made from eight Flying Geese, the final size of each unit being 6 x 3in (15.2 x 7.6cm).
The large squares are cut 1¼in (3.2cm) larger than the final size: 6in + 1¼in = 7¼in (15.2cm + 3.2cm = 18.4cm) square.
The small squares are cut ⅞in (2.2cm) larger than the final size: 3in + ⅞ in =3⅞in (7.6cm + 2.2cm = 9.8cm) square.

1 Cut a 7¼in (18.4cm) square from each of the two fabrics you are using for the geese. Draw the diagonals on the *right side* of each square with a sharp marking pencil (Fig 4).

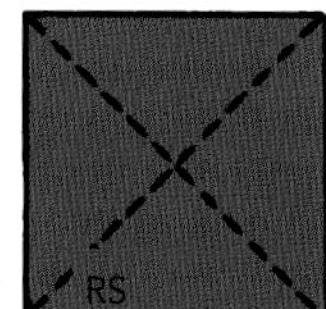

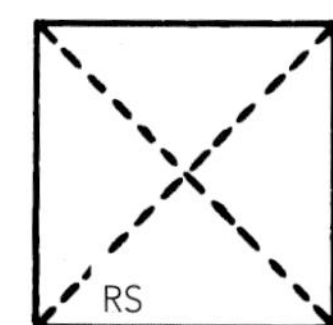

Fig 4

2 Cut eight 3⅞in (9.8cm) squares from the sky fabric by cutting a strip 3⅞in (9.8cm) wide and cutting off 3⅞in (9.8cm) lengths (Fig 5). Draw one diagonal on the *wrong side* of each of these (Fig 6).

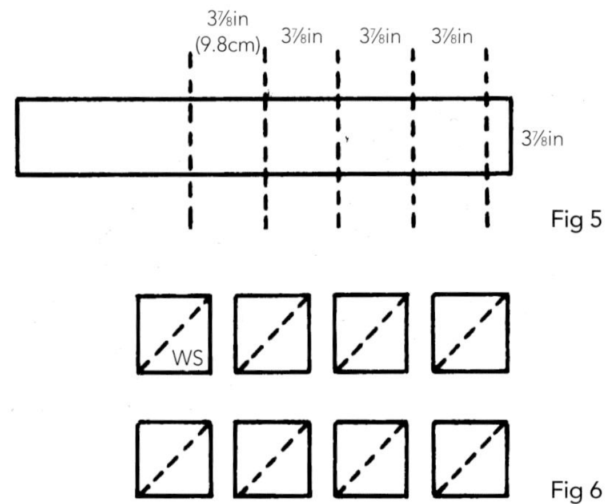

Fig 5

Fig 6

3 With right sides together, pin two of the smaller squares on to one of the larger squares, lining up the drawn diagonal lines. The two corners of the smaller squares will overlap in the centre (Fig 7a). Trim off these corners following the drawn line on the large square so that the two smaller squares meet but do not overlap (Fig 7b).

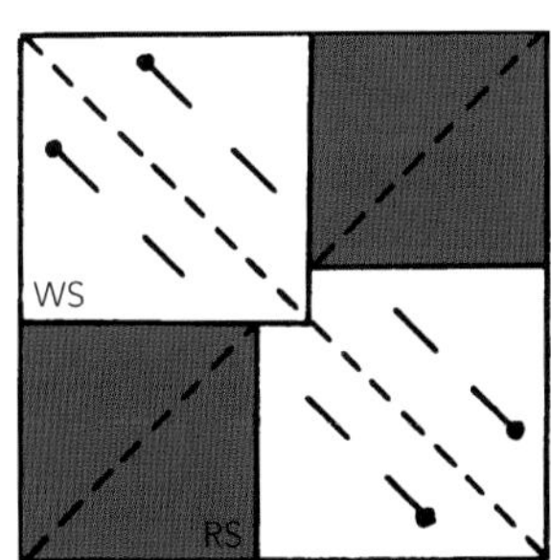

Fig 7a

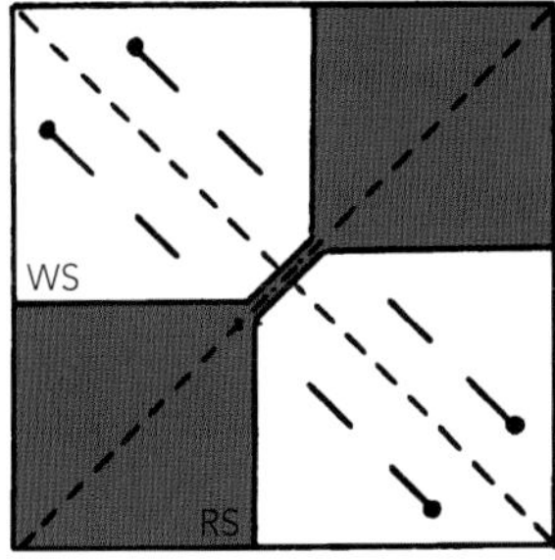

Fig 7b

4 On the smaller squares machine stitch a seam on either side of the drawn diagonal lines exactly ¼in (6mm) from the line (Fig 8). This is the same technique used in Triangles on page 78.

5 Cut along the drawn diagonal line between the two stitched lines (Fig 9).

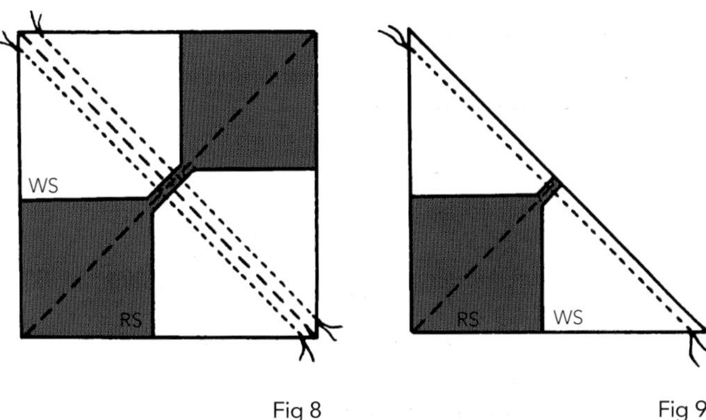

Fig 8 Fig 9

6 Take one section and finger press the small triangular pieces away from the main triangle (Fig 10).

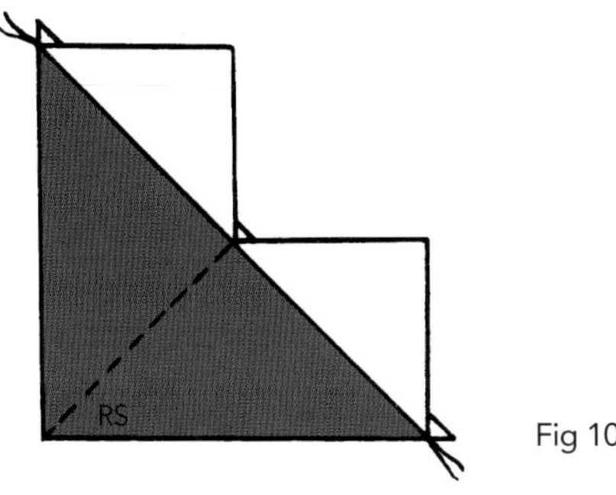

Fig 10

7 With right sides together, pin a small square on to the main triangle, matching the drawn diagonals as before (Fig 11a). Machine a seam on either side of the diagonal line on the small square, exactly ¼in (6mm) from the line (Fig 11b). Cut along the drawn line between the two stitched lines (Fig 11c).

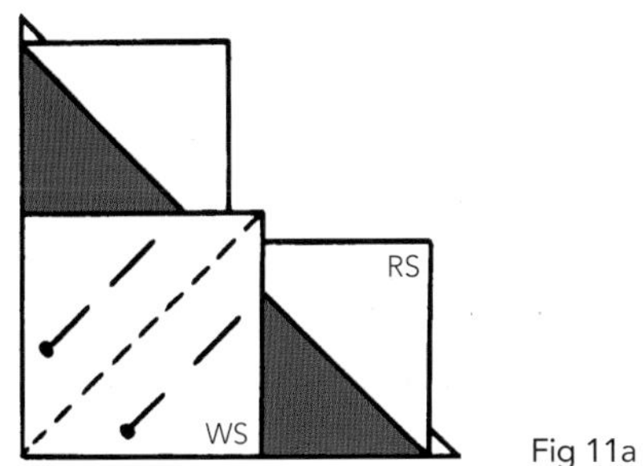

Fig 11a

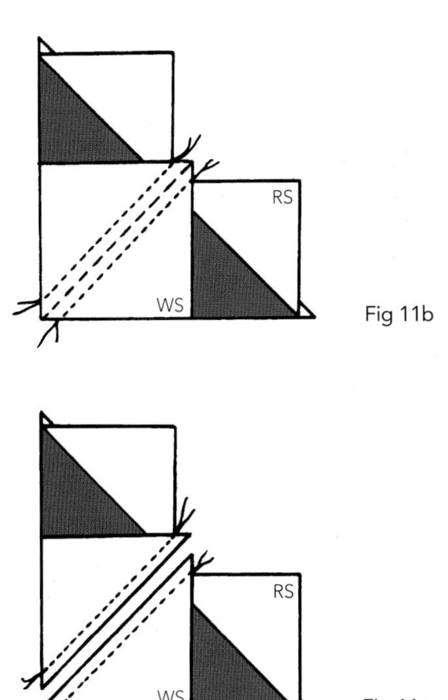

Fig 11b

Fig 11c

8 Repeat this with the other section and one small square. Press each piece from the front, with the seams lying towards the smaller triangles. You will now have four identical Flying Geese (Fig 12a)

9 Repeat the entire process, using the second large square of fabric and the remaining four smaller squares. This will give you four Flying Geese in the second colour combination (Fig 12b).

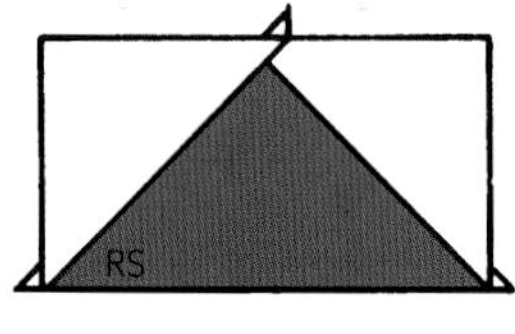

Fig 12a

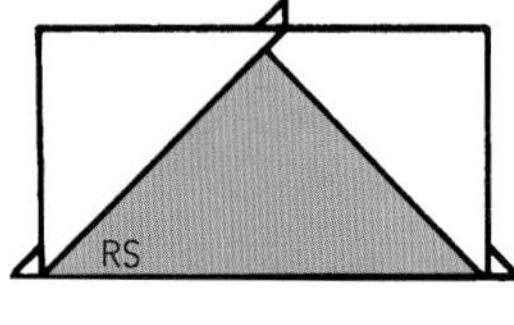

Fig 12b

10 Arrange the eight Flying Geese in the design shown in Fig 1a on page 88, or any other arrangement that looks good. Join the Flying Geese into pairs, pinning them as shown in Fig 13a, so that when you stitch you sew through the crossed seams in the centre (Fig 13b). If you stitch right through this cross of stitches you will not cut off the point of the large triangle. After all, who wants Flying Geese with bent beaks?

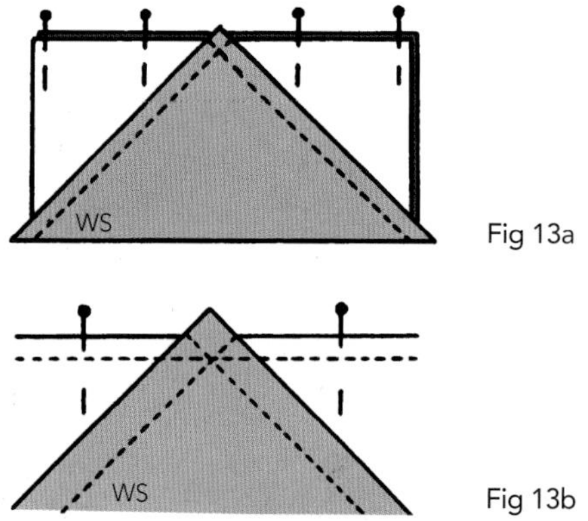

Fig 13a

Fig 13b

11 Press seams to one side from the front of the work (Fig 14). Now arrange the four sections in the design. Join the top two together so that the two seams meet in an arrowhead ¼in (6mm) from the edge (Fig 15). Press the seam to one side. Join the bottom pair, pressing the seam in the opposite direction. Sew the two halves together, matching the centre seams carefully. Either press this long seam to one side or press it open, whichever gives a flatter result.

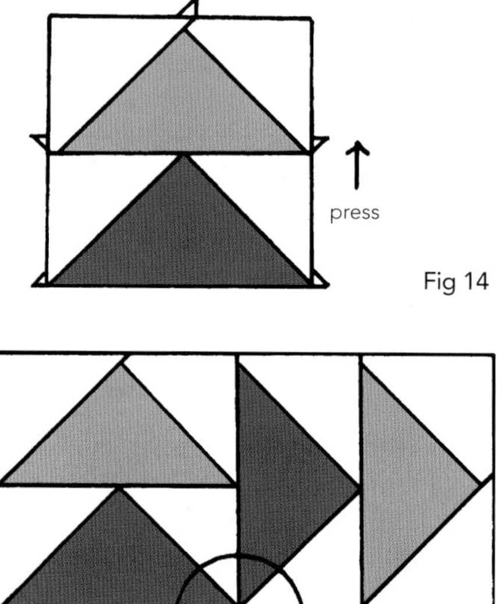

Fig 14

Fig 15

12 Measure the completed block – it should be 12½in (31.7cm) square. If the block is too big, try taking in the seams a little rather than trimming down the outside edges, as losing the sharp points can spoil the design. If the block is too small, add a narrow border to bring it up to size. See page 236 for instructions on trimming and adding borders. Add the framing sashing strips, see page 236 for instructions.

Jean Parson has used the same Flying Geese design as a border around her quilt. This is a very popular choice of border design, as the blocks are quickly made and very effective arranged around a quilt like this.

"This quilt, which I've called 'Novice Star', was my first experience of patchwork and quilting. I learnt a new skill with each block under the excellent guidance of Alison Maudlin." **Jean Parsons**

Stained Glass Patchwork

Tulip Design

Stained glass has been used to enhance the windows of churches and houses for hundreds of years. The depth of colour from light pouring through tinted glass outlined by black leading gives a stunning effect. Stained glass patchwork, which is a variation of hand appliqué, aims to create the same effect with fabric. The coloured sections are tacked (basted) into position on the background fabric and then the edges are covered by narrow strips of black fabric to give the impression of the lead strips in stained glass. There have been some wonderful large quilt designs made using this technique, some with a stained glass look to them, others re-interpreting Art Deco themes to great effect.

Colour Choices

If you were planning a wall hanging of a stained glass design your chosen fabrics would probably imitate the brilliance and jewel-like quality of true stained glass as closely as possible. However, these strong colours may not be appropriate for the sampler quilt, so just follow the technique using colours that complement the blocks you have already made. The edging round each area of colour can be of any fabric you wish. It does not even have to be a plain colour – striped or patterned fabrics can look wonderful. The background area needs to be a 13in (33cm) square, while the bias strips (strips cut diagonally across the fabric) for the 'leading' can be cut from a piece measuring 14in (35.5cm) square.

Construction

1 Draw a 13in (33cm) square on a large sheet of tracing paper. I do this by laying the paper on a cutting board, using the board markings to find the four corners of the square. I mark these with dots and then join up the dots with a long ruler to make the square. Mark the centre vertical line with a dotted line (Fig 1a) using the same technique. Mark the centre point O on this line.

2 Trace the design in Fig 2 page 97 on to one half of the tracing paper, matching the centre lines and point O. Continue drawing the lines of the design to meet the edges of the paper square (Fig 1b). From point O measure along the centre dotted line 5¼in (13.3cm) above and 5¼in (13.3cm) below. Mark both these points. From each point draw a horizontal line across the designs to the edge of the paper square. Turn the paper over and trace the other half of the design, matching the centre lines and both halves of the design exactly (Fig 1b). Include the arrows that show the direction of the straight grain of the fabric.

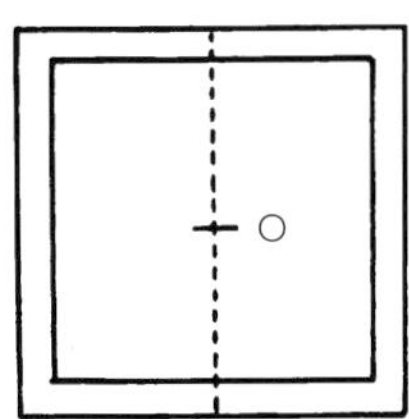

Fig 1a

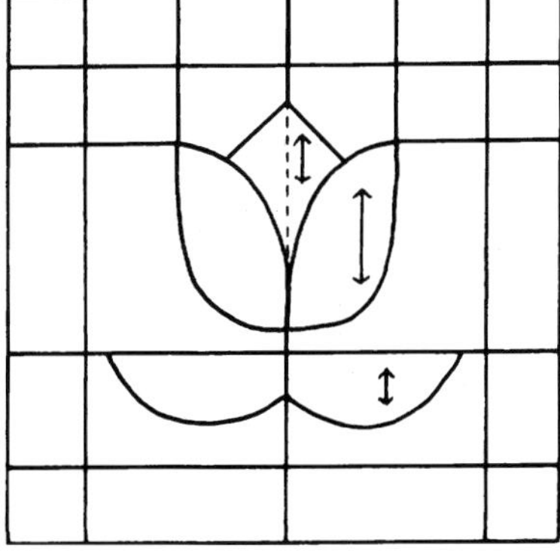

Fig 1b

3 Now cut a 13in (33cm) square of fabric for the background. Fold it in half vertically and crease it lightly to mark the centre line.

4 Place the fabric square over the design layout, matching the creased line with the central dotted line on the tracing. Trace the design on to the fabric with a sharp marking pencil. Use a light box if necessary, see Basic Equipment page 15.

5 Cut shapes A, B and C from the tracing paper (Fig 3). Use these as patterns by pinning them on to the right side of the chosen fabrics, matching the grain arrows on the tracings with the straight grain of the fabric (the direction of the woven threads). Cut around each shape exactly, no extra seam allowance is needed. Use a single layer of fabric for shape A and a double layer (right sides together) for shapes B and C to give one centre tulip petal, two side petals and two leaves.

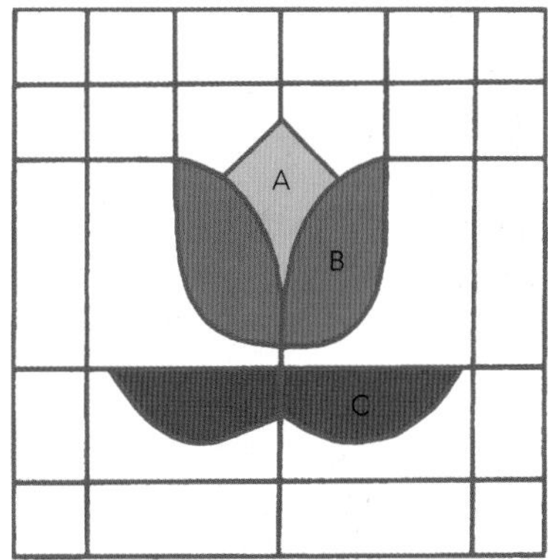

Fig 3

6 Pin each piece in position on the background square so that the raw edges of each shape butts against its neighbour. Tack (baste) in place (Fig 4).

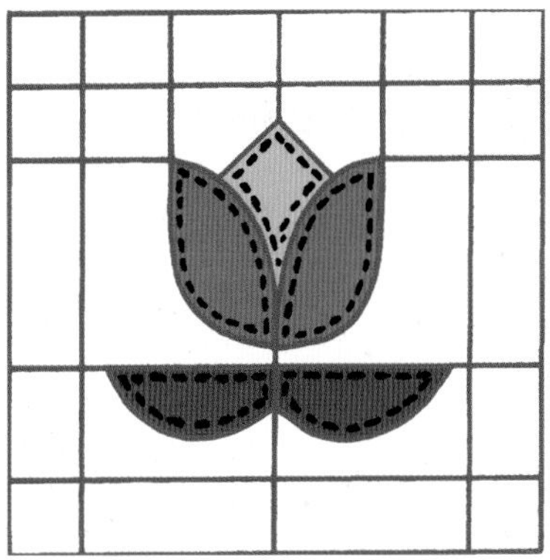

Fig 4

7 The 'leading' strips must be cut on the bias of the fabric because they need to stretch slightly to curve around the shapes without puckering – 1in (2.5cm) wide bias strips are needed for this design. To cut the strips place a single layer of fabric across one of the 45° lines on a cutting board. Cut along the line with a rotary ruler and cutter (Fig 5). Turn the fabric so that the cut edge is on the left and move the ruler over it until the cut edge lines up with the required width on the ruler. Cut along the right side of the ruler. Repeat this across the fabric (Fig 6). Left-handers should cut their strips from the right, not the left.

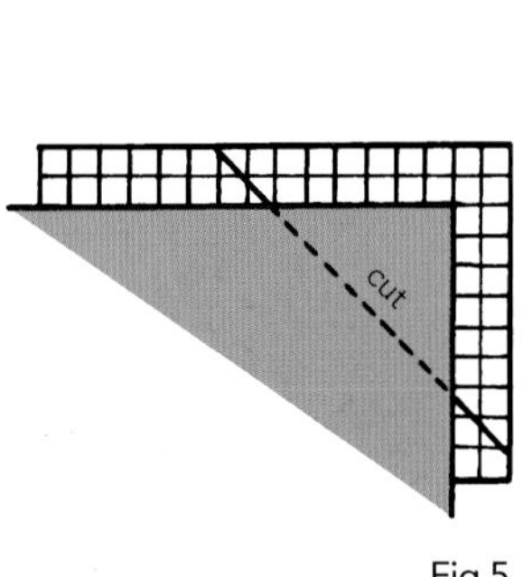

Fig 5

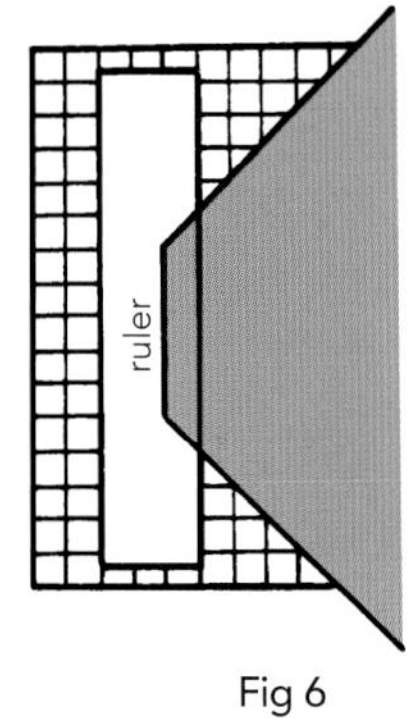

Fig 6

There are two gadgets available that will help quilters make folded bias strips: a Bias-Maker or Bias Bars, see Basic Equipment page 14. Each one uses a different procedure so try them both, if possible, and use whichever you prefer.

With a Bias-Maker, use the ½in (1.3cm) version and follow the manufacturer's instructions for pulling the strip of bias fabric through the gadget. Press the bias strip with a steam iron as it appears in its folded form from the narrower end of the Bias-Maker (Fig 7). This will make a length of bias that looks exactly like commercial bias binding and is about ½in (1.3cm) wide, which is a little too wide for this design. To narrow the folded strip, refold one side across the back and press with a steam iron (Fig 8).

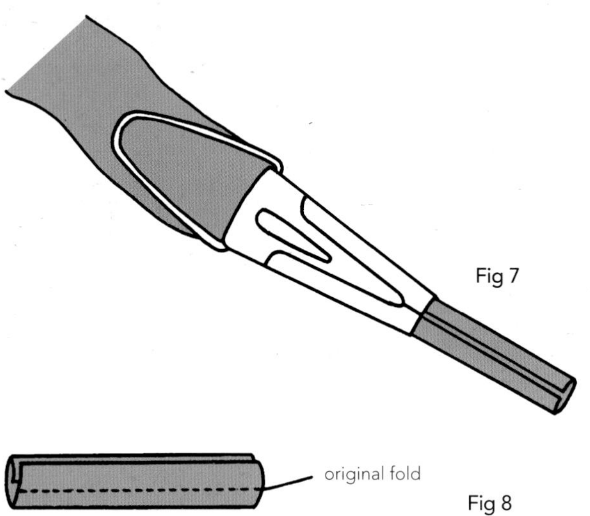

Fig 7

Fig 8

With Bias Bars, use a ¼in (6mm) width bar. With wrong sides facing, fold the 1in (2.5cm) wide bias strip of fabric in half. Using a slightly smaller stitch than normal, machine stitch a ¼in (6mm) seam down the length of the strip to make a tube. Always make a short sample length first to check that the Bias Bar will just slip into the tube – it needs to fit really snugly without any slack (Fig 9a). Trim the seams to a scant ⅛in (3mm) (Fig 9b). Slide the Bias Bar into the tube, twisting the fabric so that both seam and seam allowance lie across one flat side of the bar and cannot be seen from the other side (Fig 9c). With the bar in place, press the seam allowance to one side. Slide the tube gradually off the bar, pressing firmly as you go.

Fig 9a

Fig 9b

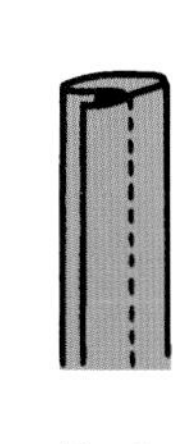
Fig 9c

You do not need a continuous length of bias for the design. The sequence for adding the strips has been planned so that as many bias ends as possible are concealed beneath other strips. The suggested order of stitching the Tulip Block is shown in Fig 10.

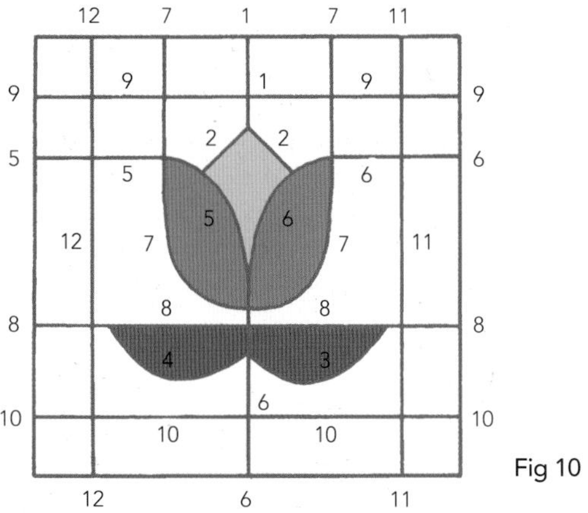

Fig 10

"This quilt was based around the small floral print, which I loved. It is my first sampler quilt and has increased my knowledge of colours and techniques. I especially enjoyed the appliquéd butterflies and the Flying Geese. It was made in the company of enthusiastic quilters with an encouraging tutor, Jan Jones." **Pippa Higgitt**

8 Take a length of pressed bias tubing slightly longer than line one in Fig 10, using the design (Fig 2 opposite) for measurement. Pin the strip so that the drawn line on the fabric lies midway underneath it. Trim the ends exactly to match the end of the drawn line (Fig 11).

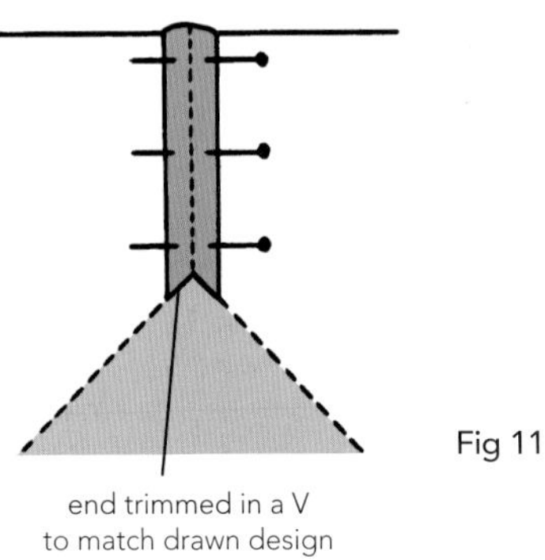

Fig 11

9 Matching the sewing thread to the strip, not the background, sew both sides of the strip in turn on to the background with small even slip stitches.

10 Cut a length of pressed bias tubing slightly longer than the V-shaped line two in Fig 10. Fold it into a mitred corner about halfway along and pin in position with the corner covering the end of strip one and the drawn guideline midway beneath it (Fig 12). Trim the ends of the strip to match the ends of the drawn lines. Sew the strip in place on the background.

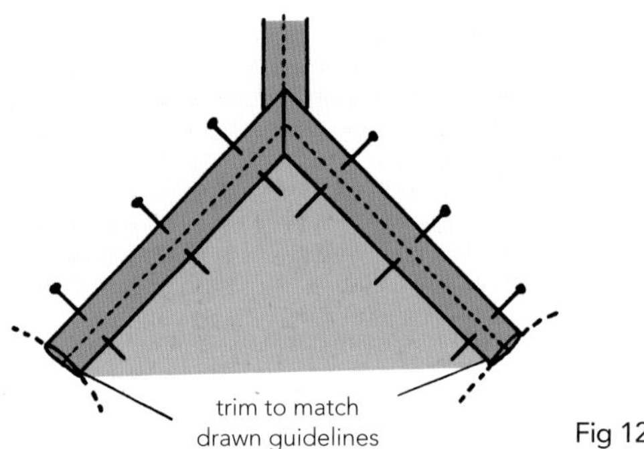

Fig 12

11 Cut a length of pressed bias tubing slightly longer than line 3 in Fig 10. This is a curved line, so must be treated slightly differently. The strip must be positioned half on the tacked leaf C and half on the background (Fig 13).

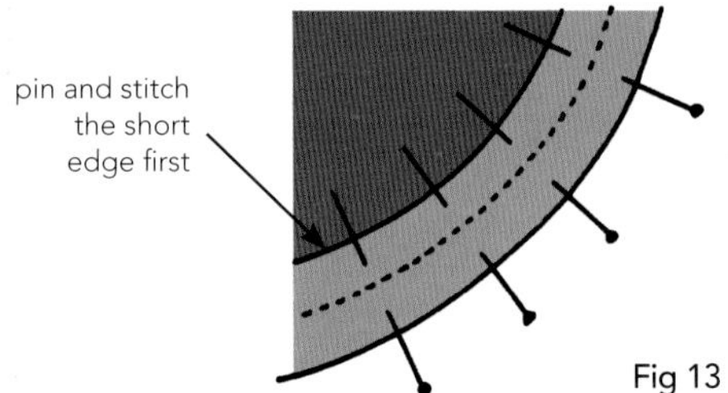

Fig 13

Pin and sew the shorter inside edge of the curve first. The longer outside edge can then be stretched slightly when sewing to fit the curve (Fig 14). If you fix the longer edge first the shorter edge will finish up with little pleats in it. Trim the ends of the strip to match the drawn guidelines.

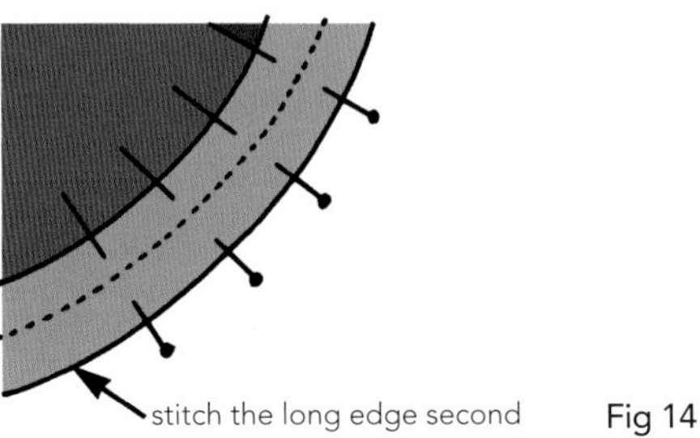

Fig 14

12 Continue to pin and stitch each length of pressed bias tubing in turn, following the sequence shown in Fig 10.

13 Remove tacking (basting) and press. Trim the background fabric to an exact 12½in (31.7cm) square. Add the framing sashing strips as usual, following the instructions on page 236.

This is a very different interpretation of the stained-glass effect Tulip block by Davina Wing – bright, unconventional and full of fun!

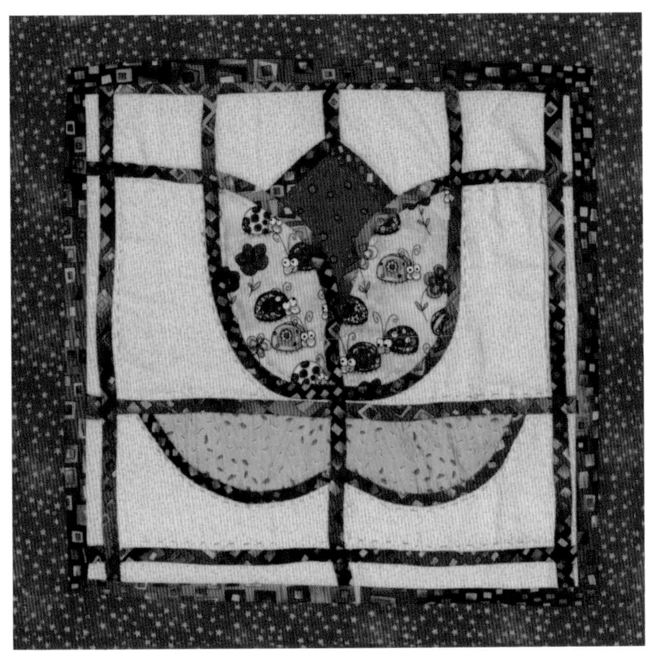

Fig 2 – Template actual size

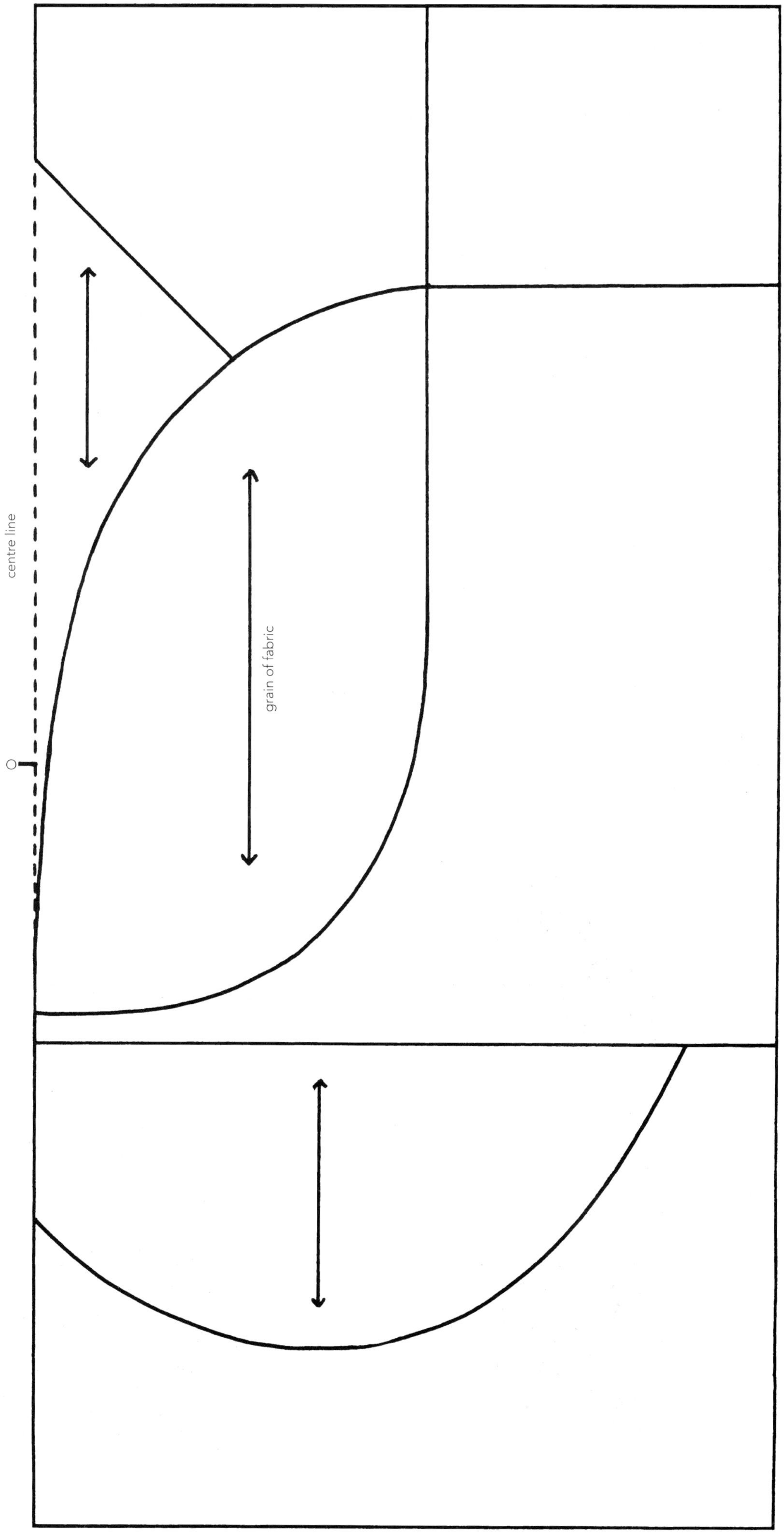

centre line

grain of fabric

Hawaiian Appliqué

Crocus Design

American missionaries introduced patchwork techniques to Hawaii in the 1820s and since then the native Hawaiian have developed their own colourful interpretation of hand appliqué quilts. Quilt-sized pieces of paper are folded into eighths and then cut to create patterns which represent the flowers, fruit and leaves of the Hawaiian islands. This paper is then unfolded and the pattern used to cut out the huge fabric appliqué motif which is tacked (basted) in place on the contrasting quilt background.

In traditional Hawaiian designs colours are clear and vibrant such as red, green or blue on white and only plain fabrics are used. The appliqué edges are stroked under with the point of

a needle and stitched on to the background in one process. Quilting lines follow the outline of the appliquéd design and are repeated to the edge of the quilt, just like contour lines on a map or waves lapping outwards (Fig 1).

This appliqué technique (known as needle-turning) using a design based on folded paper shapes, can be scaled down and adapted for a block in the sampler quilt. Rather than copy the exotic tropical plants of Hawaii, I felt it was more appropriate to use a design taken from the English garden, in this case a crocus with its characteristic long, pointed leaves. Many students have insisted that the flower looks more like a tulip than a crocus, but as there is already a tulip in the stained glass block I am sticking to the crocus label.

Fig 1

Colour Choices

A 13in (33cm) square piece of background fabric is needed for the background. The appliqué design is cut from a folded 11in (28cm) square of fabric. Just because traditional Hawaiian quilts use strong, plain colours do not feel that you must do the same. An American visiting one of my classes was horrified when she saw the soft colours and patterned fabrics being used with casual abandon as backgrounds or appliqué. As always, use the technique but choose fabrics that suit the balance of your collection of blocks.

Construction

1 With right sides together fold the smaller fabric square (the appliqué fabric) in half (Fig 2a). Fold it in half again (Fig 2b). Finally, fold it diagonally (Fig 2c). Follow Figs 2a, 2b and 2c carefully and check that the centre of the fabric square is positioned as shown. If it is not you may end up with several pieces of fabric instead of one whole one. Press the folded fabric firmly to give nice, sharp folds.

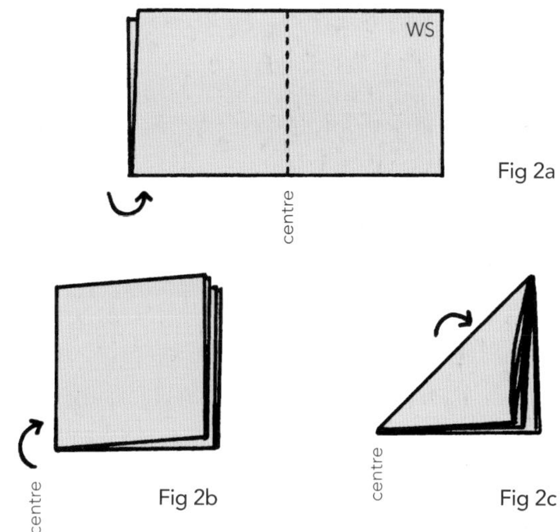

Fig 2a

Fig 2b

Fig 2c

2 Make a template of the appliqué design given in Fig 3 page 102 by tracing it on to card, or use template plastic – see page 15 for instructions on making templates.

3 Place the template on the folded triangle of fabric, matching the centres. Check that the bias and straight edges of the fabric match the bias and straight markings on the template (Fig 4). Draw round the template using a sharp marking pencil.

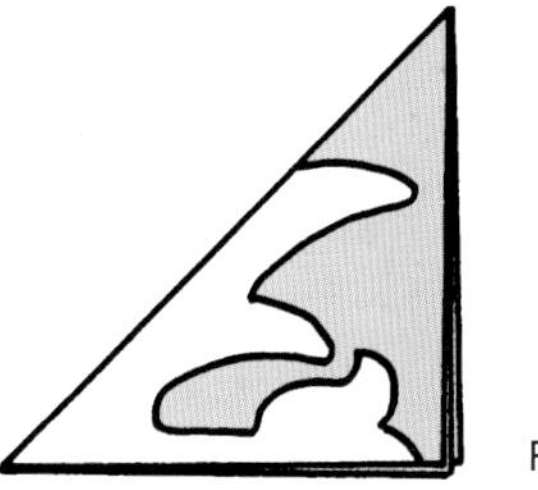

Fig 4

4 Secure the layers of folded fabric with two or three pins. Using very sharp scissors, cut out the drawn outline through all eight layers, holding the fabric firmly so that none of the layers can slip.

5 Fold the background square into eighths in the same way as before. Press lightly with an iron to make guidelines for positioning the appliqué.

6 Unfold the background fabric and lay it on a flat surface. Place the folded appliqué on to the background with the centres matching (Fig 5a). Unfold the appliqué design section by section (Figs 5b and 5c) until the whole design is revealed (Fig 5d). Check that the fold lines on the appliqué design are lying exactly on the guideline folds in the background fabric.

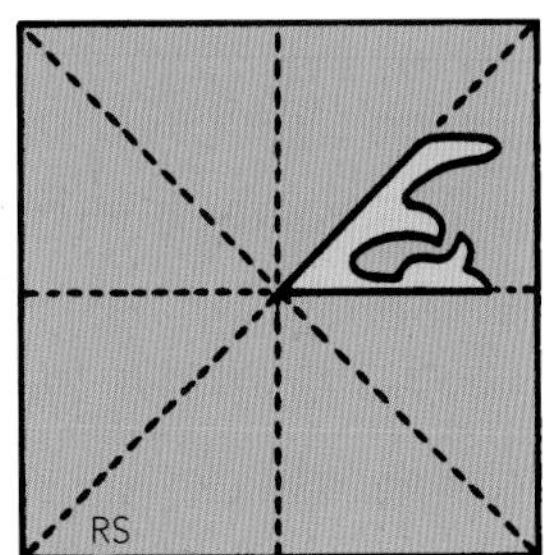

Fig 5a

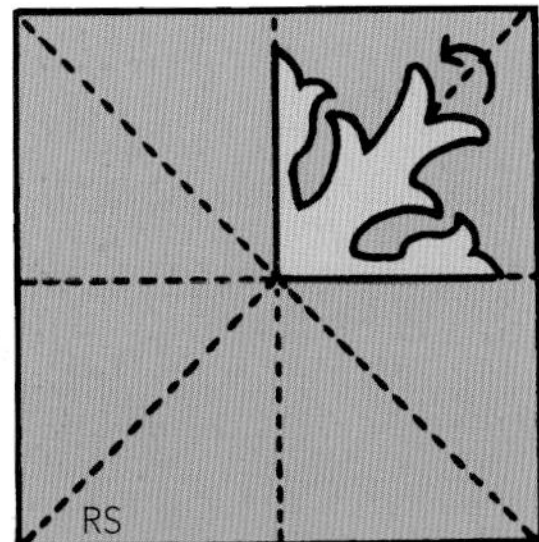

Fig 5b

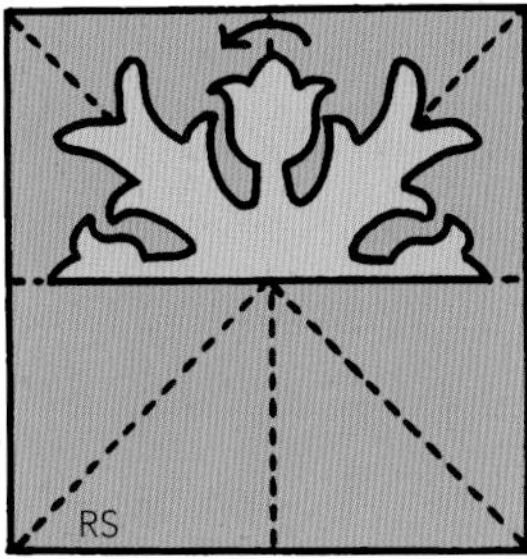

Fig 5c

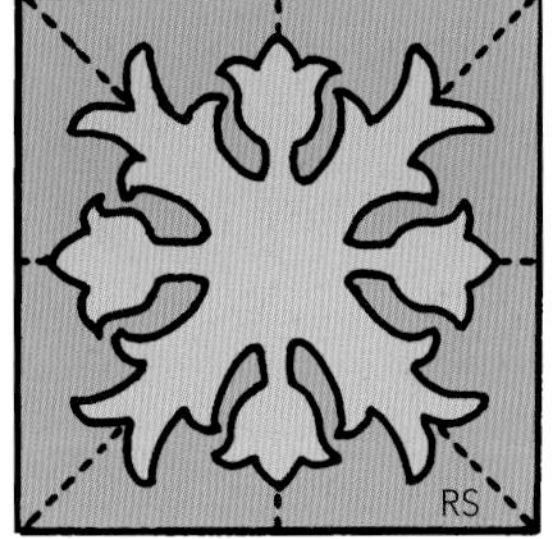

Fig 5d

7 Pin the appliqué to the background fabric in several places, then tack (baste) in place, using ¼in (6mm) long stitches and keeping them about ¼in (6mm) from the edge of the design so that the appliqué is held firmly in place (Fig 6). Press the work.

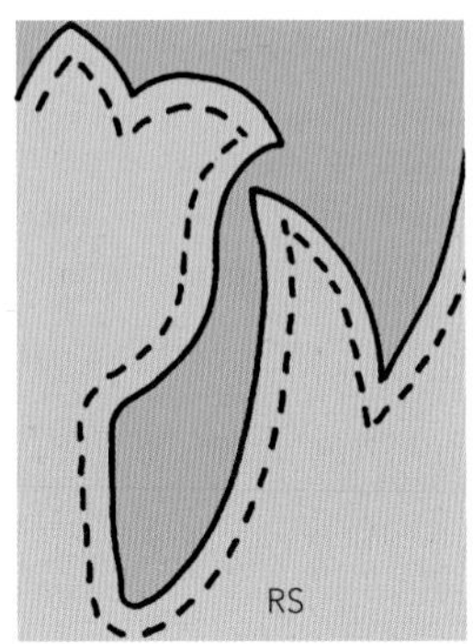

Fig 6

8 Using thread to match the top fabric, turn under and sew the raw edge just ahead of the needle. The turning should be about ⅛in (3mm) and is made by stroking the fabric under with the point of the needle (Fig 7). Sew using small, closely spaced slip stitches.

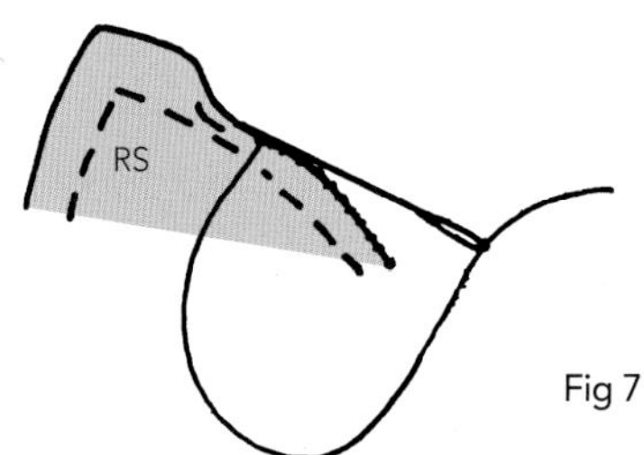

Fig 7

Jeanette Hogarth used several strip borders to frame her quilt before adding a more complex pieced Seminole border and a final edging of Prairie Points. How cleverly she has negotiated the corner of her continuous border designs!

"Some time ago a quilting class was started in our village by Alison Maudlin. Having never quilted before, I joined the class and this sampler quilt is the result. Now I can't stop quilting!" **Jeannette Hogarth**

9 When sewing an outside point of the design, work to within ⅛in (3mm) of the point and make a firm stitch (Fig 8a). Using the point of the needle, stroke down the raw edges of fabric away from the last stitch and tuck under the usual ⅛in (3mm) (Fig 8b). Sew the turned edge and continue.

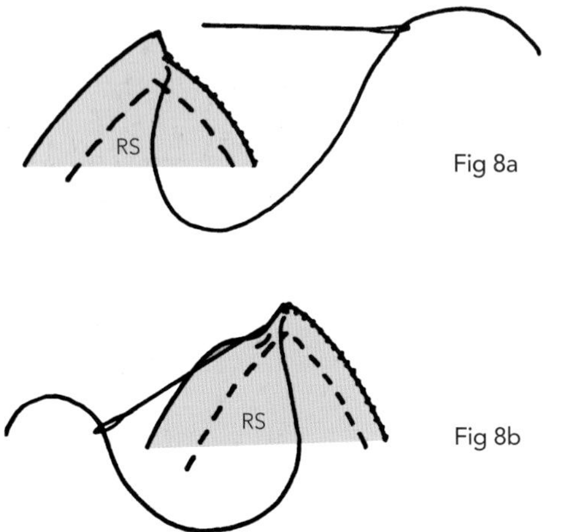

Fig 8a

Fig 8b

10 Do not clip any inner points. Use the needle point to sweep the seam allowance under in a scooping movement. Repeat the movement from side to side until the point becomes rounded and all the seam allowance has been stroked under. Sew the curve with very closely spaced slip stitches (Fig 9).

Fig 9

11 Continue turning under and sewing the edge of the appliqué design until it is completely sewn down. Remove the tacking stitches and press.

12 Turn the block to the reverse side and carefully cut away the background fabric behind the appliqué, leaving a seam allowance of ¼in (6mm) beyond the stitch line (Fig 10) – see Tumbling Blocks page 26 for instructions. This reduces the layers and makes quilting easier.

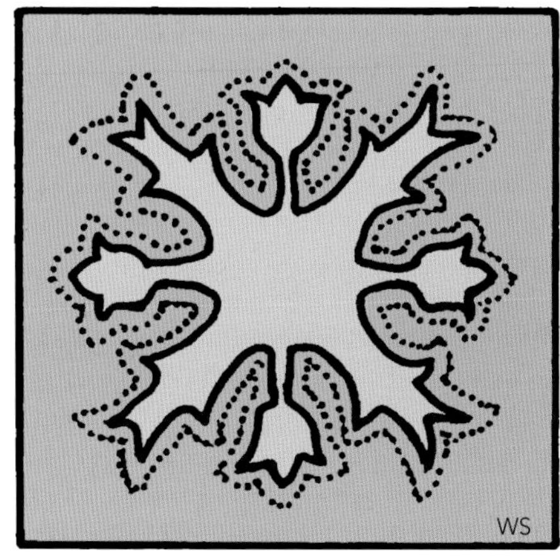

Fig 10

Fig 3 – Template actual size

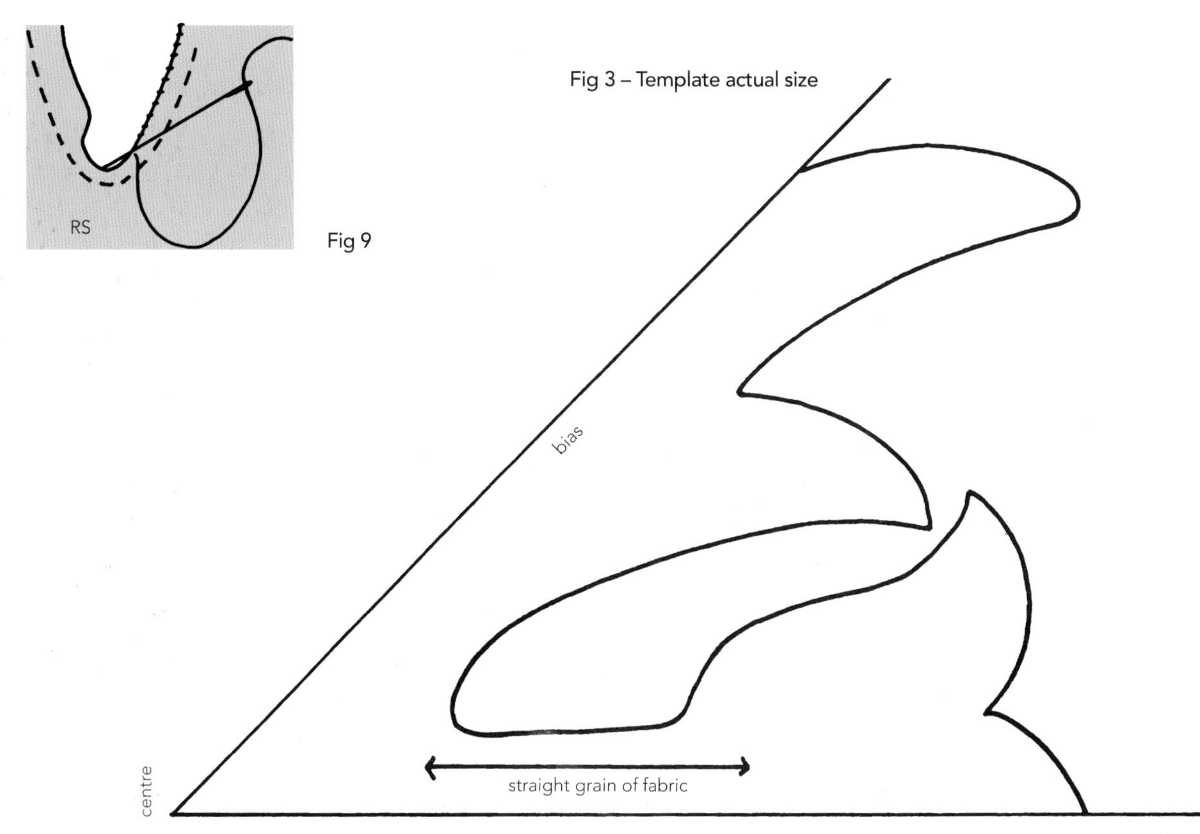

Pieced Patchwork

Honey Bee

This block and the following design, Grape Basket on page 107, have been included to make up the number of blocks needed to complete the sampler quilt. Neither have brand new techniques to be mastered, so I have deliberately kept the instructions fairly basic so you get used to working on your own.

This particular pieced patchwork design can be worked by hand or machine and incorporates some hand appliqué, so uses the skills you should have acquired so far. Honey Bee is one of those classic blocks that could be repeated several times in your sampler quilt if more blocks are needed – a chance to play with colour combinations perhaps.

Colour Choices

Three or more fabrics are used in Honey Bee, so it is a good design for using up scraps. The curved appliqué shapes are meant to represent bees. Presumably the centre Nine-Patch could be a flower or possibly the hive – what does it matter? Just choose the fabrics to suit your quilt, as always, by getting out the blocks you have already completed to see what is needed for balance. This gets easier and easier as there are more completed blocks to relate to. At this stage also, you probably have very little fabric left to choose from, which simplifies the selection process quite a lot!

Construction

This block is usually made by American piecing, using templates and drawing round them. The piecing can then be done by hand or machine. If you wish to use this method, make templates using the sizes given in Fig 1 and proceed as usual for drawing round, cutting and so on.

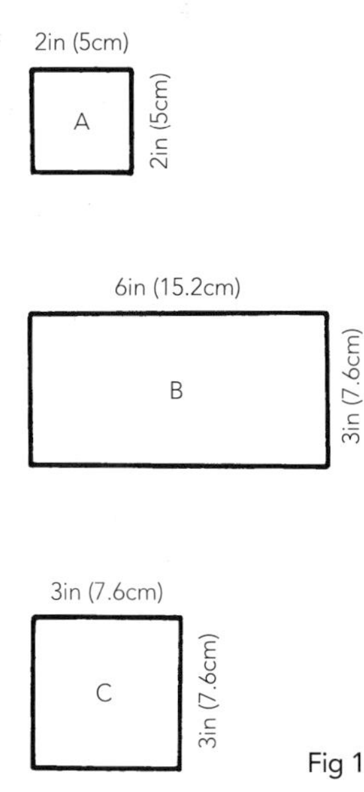

Fig 1

Alternatively, as all the shapes are squares or rectangles, apart from the appliquéd bees, it makes sense to calculate the sizes of the shapes to include the seam allowances, cut with rotary equipment and stitch together with machined ¼in (6mm) seams. This is template-free machined patchwork, like the Trip Around the World block on page 36. To do this you need to look at the *final* measurements of each shape shown in Fig 1. To each measurement add on ½in (1.3cm) to allow for the ¼in (6mm) seam allowance on both sides of the shape (see Fig 2). Shape A is 2½in (6.3cm) square, shape B is 6½ x 3½in (16.5 x 8.9cm) and shape C is 3½in (8.9cm) square.

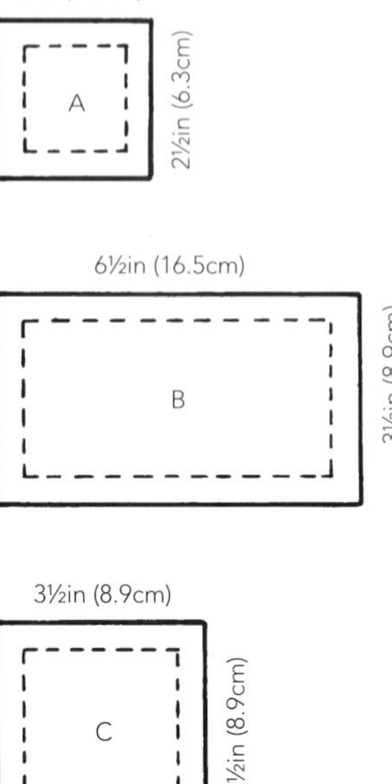

Fig 2

1 Following whichever method of construction you prefer, cut out nine of shape A, five in one fabric, four in another. Cut four of shape B and four of shape C.

2 Assemble the central Nine-Patch square by stitching three rows of three squares each. From the front, press the seams towards the darker fabric (Fig 3a). Join the rows together to make a Nine-Patch square (Fig 3b).

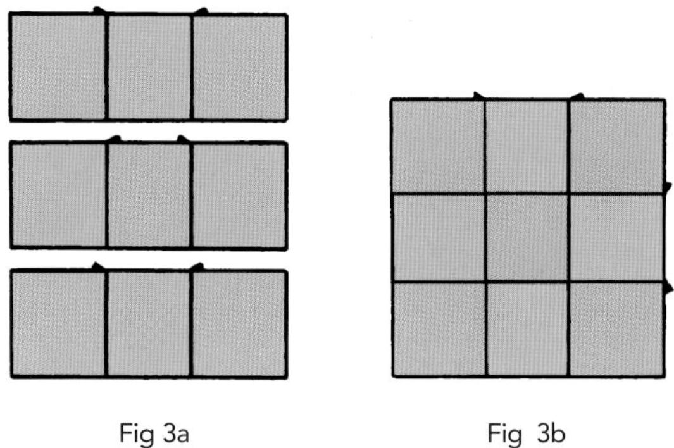
Fig 3a Fig 3b

3 Now, on either side of the Nine-Patch join on the two side rectangles or B shapes (Fig 4).

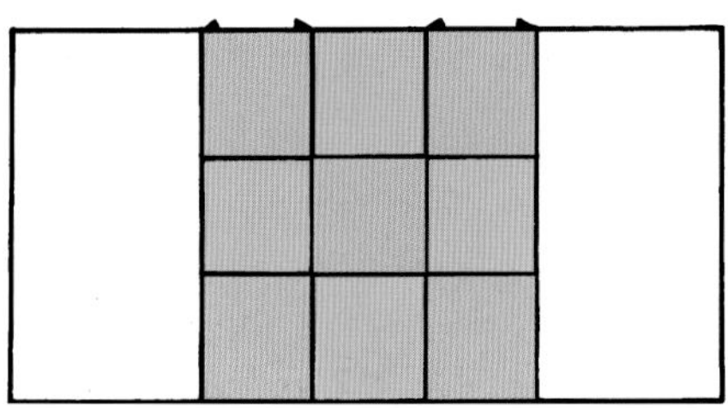
Fig 4

"This was my first ever quilt, which I made for my daughter Jade. We chose the colours because they were bright and happy. My sampler quilt took me one year to make, and along the way there were plenty of discussions on how wonderfully bright it was!" **Davina Wing**

4 Stitch together the top row of shapes C, B and C. From the front press the seams towards shapes C (Fig 5). Repeat this to make the bottom row.

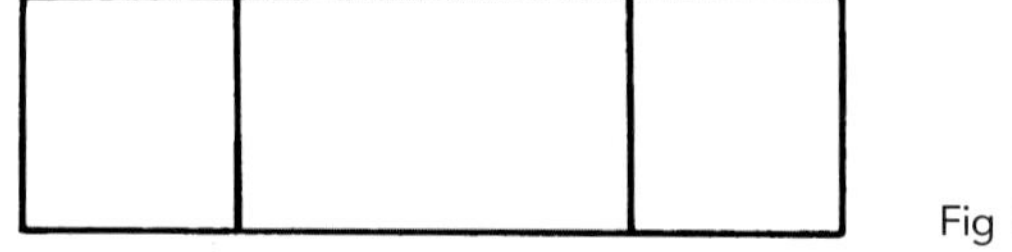

Fig 5

5 Join the three rows together, locking the seams so that they match exactly (Figs 6a and 6b).

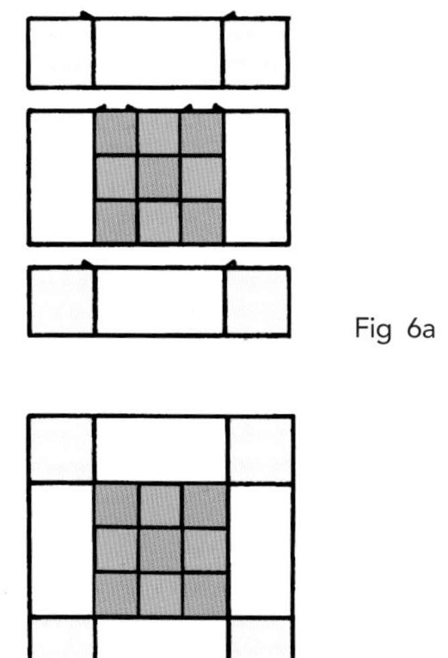

Fig 6a

Fig 6b

6 Shapes D and E in Fig 7 represent the body and wing respectively of the bee. The appliqué can be done using freezer paper or by needle-marking the outlines as in Rose of Sharon on page 83.

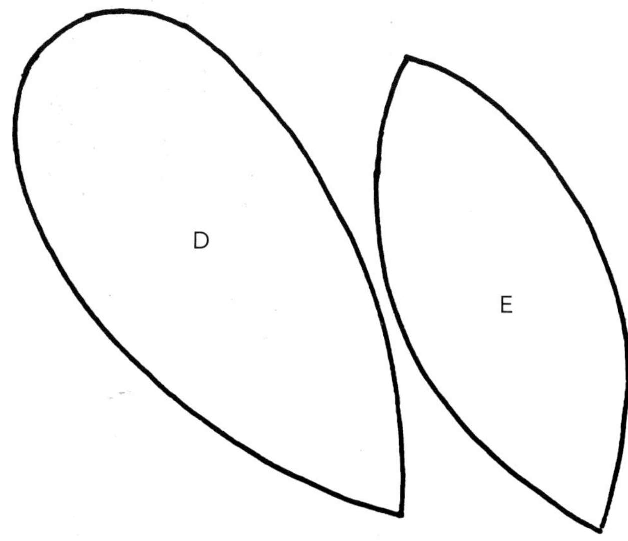

Fig 7 – Templates actual size

Four bee body shapes and eight bee wing shapes are needed. If you are needle-marking, make templates of shapes D and E. Needle-mark on the backs of the chosen fabrics and cut out with a ¼in (6mm) seam allowance. Tack (baste) under the seam allowances, following the needle-marked creases.

If using freezer paper, trace four bee body shapes and eight bee wing shapes on to the smooth side of the freezer paper. Cut out the shapes and iron them, shiny side down, on to the wrong side of the fabrics. Cut out with a ¼in (6mm) seam allowance. Follow the instructions for using freezer paper given in Dresden Plate on page 76. If the folded fabric at the pointed sections of the shapes does not tuck flat and shows from the front of the appliqué, either tuck it under while stitching the appliqué on to the background or secure it with a dab of glue from a glue stick. Provided the glue is water-soluble it will not harm your fabric.

7 Arrange the four body shapes and eight wings on the pieced block (Fig 8) and pin or tack in place. Sew each one on to the background with small slip stitches, using thread to match the appliqué not the background.

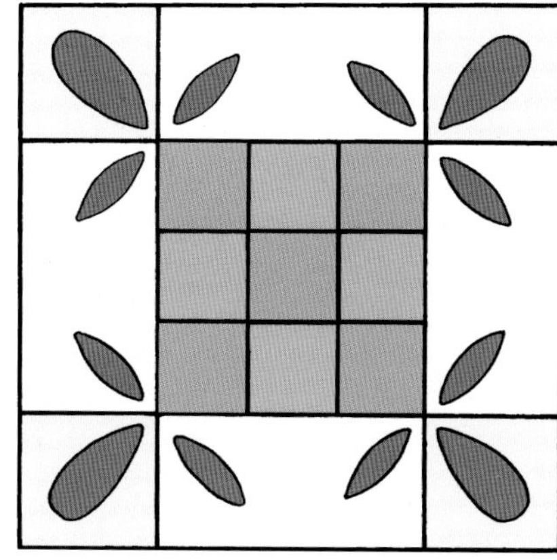

Fig 8

8 Once the appliqué has been completed, the backing fabric can be cut away to reduce the bulk. If it has been traditionally stitched this is a matter of choice, but if freezer paper has been used the back layer has to be cut away so that the paper can be removed.

9 Press the completed block from the front and measure it – it should be 12½in (31.7cm) square. If not, trim or add a border – see page 236 for instructions on trimming the blocks and adding borders.

10 Add the framing sashing strips, following the instructions on page 236.

American Pieced Patchwork

Grape Basket

This is the second of the optional bonus blocks for the sampler quilt. Again there is nothing new in the techniques used to make it, so instructions are fairly basic. Many basket blocks can be found in traditional American patchwork. Some are set as straight baskets, often with appliquéd flowers, others, like Grape Basket, are set on the diagonal, which adds interest to the quilt. This is a small block, 10in (25.4cm) square, so it needs a frame to make it up to the required 12½in (31.7cm) square. The pieces are quite small but not difficult to piece and the resulting block will give richness to the quilt. The simplest way to construct it is with templates and American piecing by hand or machine.

Colour Choices

In this block the 'basket' is set on a background fabric and uses two or more fabrics as preferred. Use Fig 1 as a guide for planning your design – make a tracing and shade it in with coloured pencils if this helps. Remember that an extra frame 1in (2.5cm) wide must be added to the design before the final sashing.

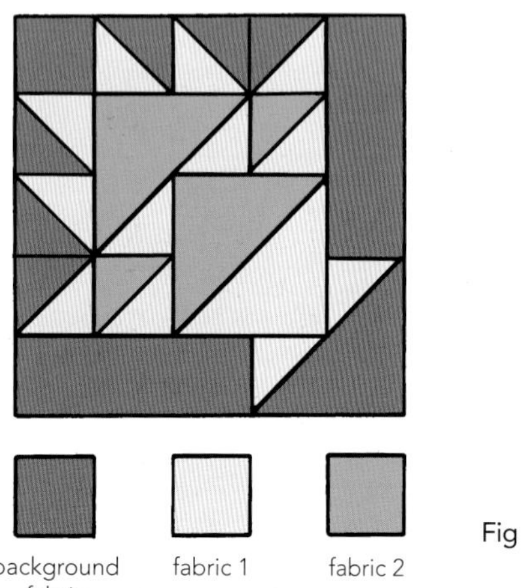

Fig 1

Construction

1 Make templates of the five shapes in Fig 2 overleaf. See page 15 for making templates.

2 On the wrong side of the appropriate fabrics draw around the templates with a sharp marking pencil. Following Fig 1, mark on the background fabric: two of shape A, one of shape B, two of shape C, two of shape D and one of shape E. On fabric 1 mark twelve of shape C and one of shape E. On fabric 2 mark two of shape C and two of shape E. Cut out each shape, adding a ¼in (6mm) seam allowance on all sides.

3 This design is not an obvious Four-Patch or Nine-Patch, so the hardest part is sorting out a sequence for piecing. The main design, separated from the two side and final corner sections, is shown in Fig 3. This main block can then be divided into two halves (Fig 4) and each half in sections, as shown in Figs 5a and 5b.

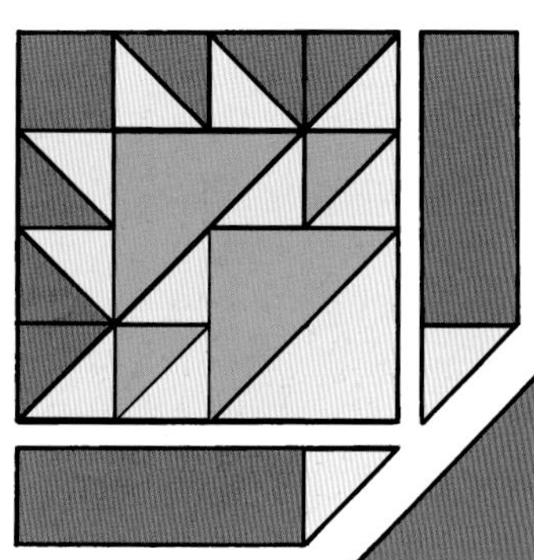

Fig 3

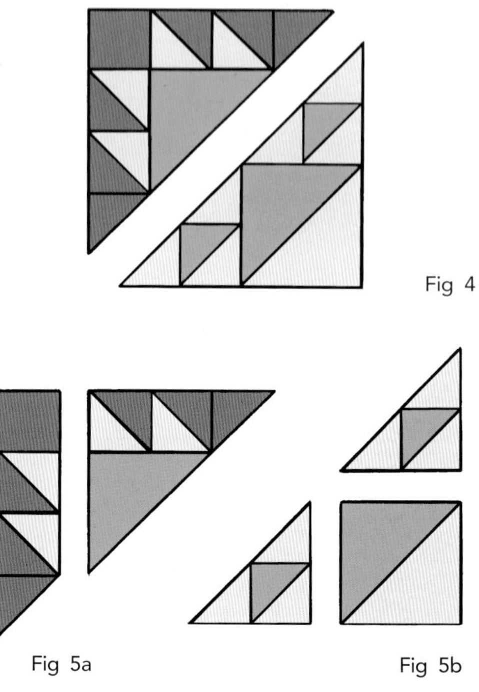

Fig 4

Fig 5a

Fig 5b

4 Now join the two halves to make a square (Fig 4). Assemble the two side sections (Fig 3) and join them to the main design square (Fig 6).

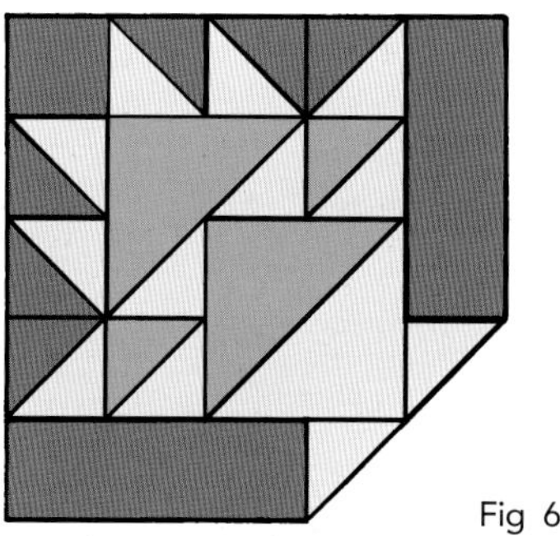

Fig 6

5 Finally, add the last corner to complete the block, so it will appear as shown in Fig 1.

"I started quilting in September 2006, never having done any sewing before, and this was the first quilt I made. I very soon found it to be addictive and always like to have at least one project on the go. The quilt is called 'Amazed' because when it was finished I looked at it and was amazed that I had managed to make it." **Amanda Boundy**

6 The block now needs its extra border. Cut four strips from your chosen fabric, two measuring 1¾ x 10½in (4.4 x 26.7cm) and two 1¾ x 13in (4.4 x 33cm). Follow the instructions for adding an extra border given in Card Trick on page 44.

7 Measure the block – it should be a little larger than 12½ in (31.7cm) square. Trim it to exactly 12½in (31.7cm) square, see page 236 for instructions on trimming the blocks. Add the framing sashing strips, following the instructions on page 236.

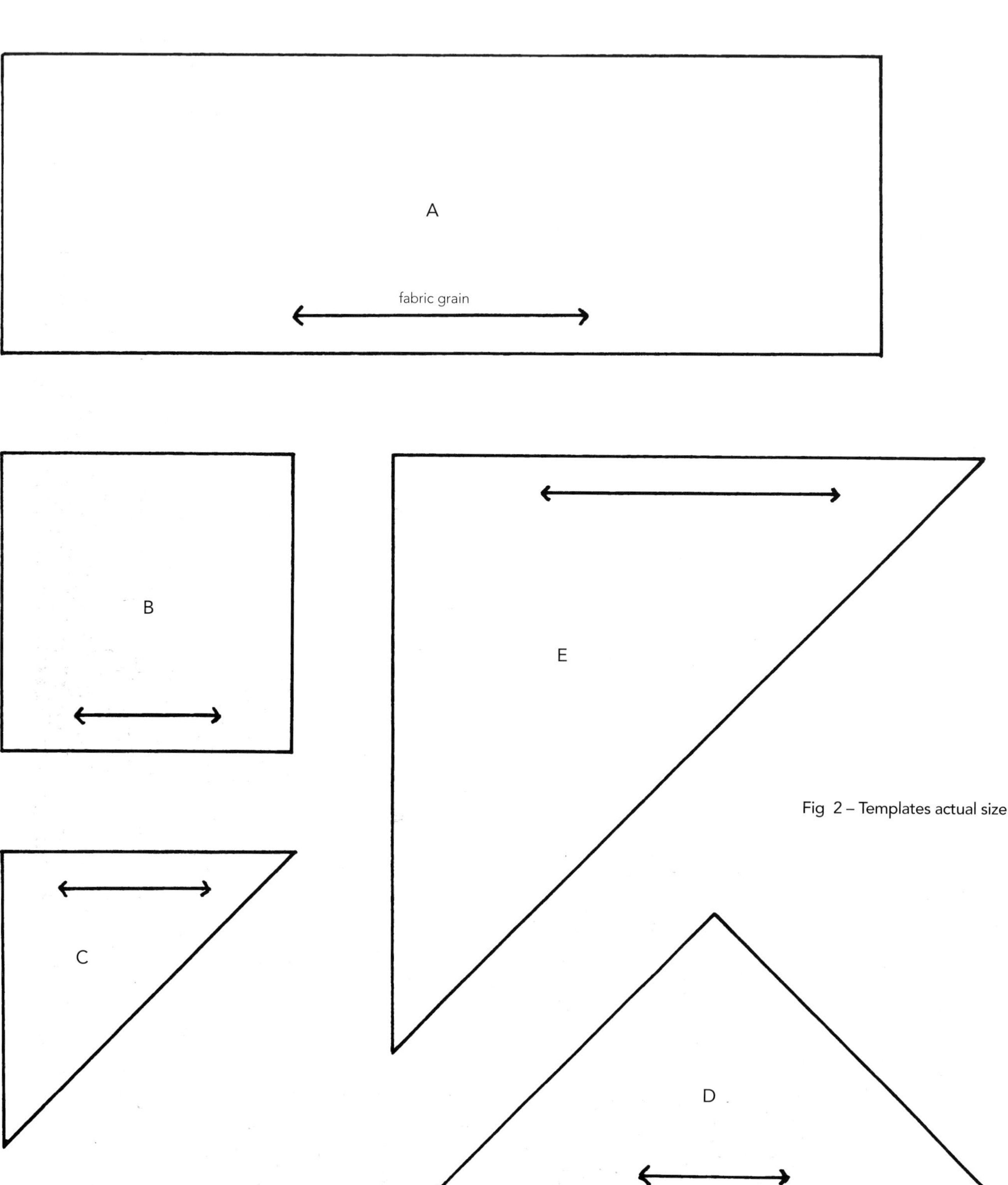

Fig 2 – Templates actual size

English Patchwork

Floor Tile

In this new compilation of both Sampler Quilts I have added a final block for the first half to bring the number of blocks up to twenty. In the original book, there were twenty techniques, one of which was quilting, so everyone had to choose an extra block for themselves if they wished to make a twenty-block quilt – but not any more! I have slipped in a block that Judy Baker-Rogers used in her lovely quilt shown on page 113 and in close-up on page 115. It is a pattern that uses the traditional English Patchwork technique, combining two shapes to make a design often seen on floors in Edwardian houses in England and in a much older form on church floors, each piece separated by narrow lines of cement.

One of the shapes is a small square, the other a variation of the much-loved hexagon, still six-sided but not with regular 60° corners, making it seem stretched out on two sides to make a longer shape (see Fig 1). The method of making is just as for Tumbling Blocks on page 23 but using the two shapes instead of the one diamond.

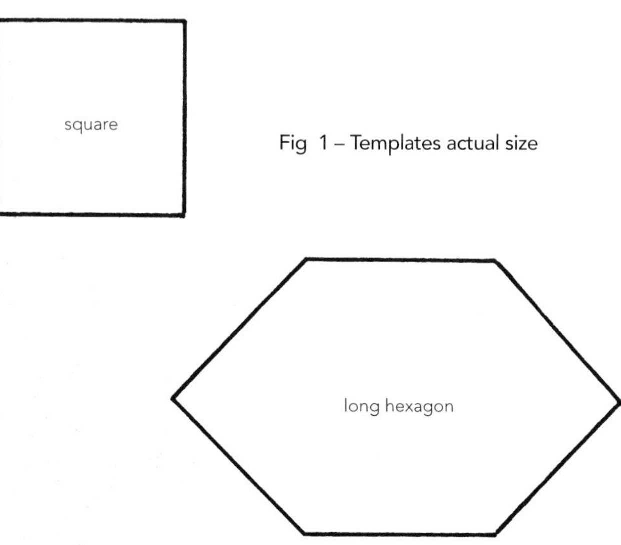

Fig 1 – Templates actual size

Colour Choices

Five fabrics have been used for this design, so here is a chance to use up some of the leftovers from earlier blocks that look good together. Judy used slightly textured fabrics for four of her choices, with the centre four long hexagons in a patterned fabric, which has been carefully cut to make a feature of the rose design on the fabric. This technique, known as 'fussy-cutting' in the United States, is often featured in English Patchwork designs, as the template system makes it easy to cut a shape in exactly the right position to give this effect. If you wish to fussy-cut pieces of your chosen fabrics in this design, make the templates from plastic so that you can see exactly where to position them for the best effect. Once joined together the whole design is placed centrally on a square of background fabric and stitched into place.

Construction

1 Make a template of both the square and the long hexagon by tracing the shapes from Fig 1, cutting them out and sticking them on to card or use template plastic. See page 15 for instructions on making templates.

2 Using a really sharp pencil to keep the shape accurate, draw round the template on to thick paper (the cartridge paper in children's drawing books is ideal). Do not use card as it is too thick. Mark the corners of each shape by continuing the drawn lines to just beyond the template corners so that they cross. This cross marks the exact corner and will make cutting out more accurate (Fig 2).

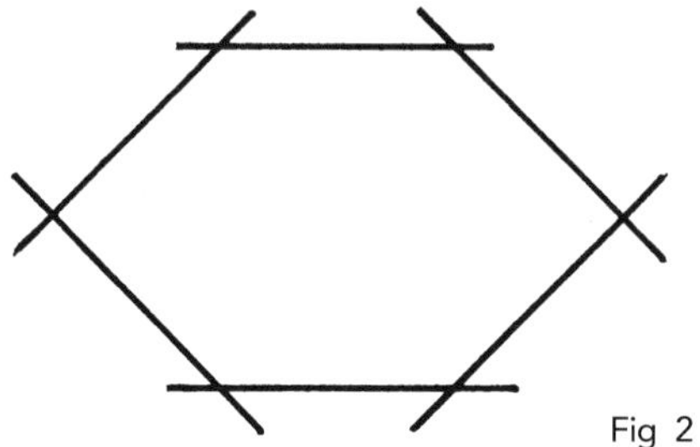

Fig 2

3 Draw and cut out twelve paper squares and twenty paper long hexagons, cutting just inside the drawn lines to prevent the shapes becoming larger than the originals.

4 Decide where each of the chosen fabrics is going to be used in the design and count up how many of each shape will be needed in each fabric. On the wrong side of each fabric, pin the correct number of paper shapes, following the straight grain of the fabric and leaving a ¼in (6mm) gap around each paper, as in Fig 3.

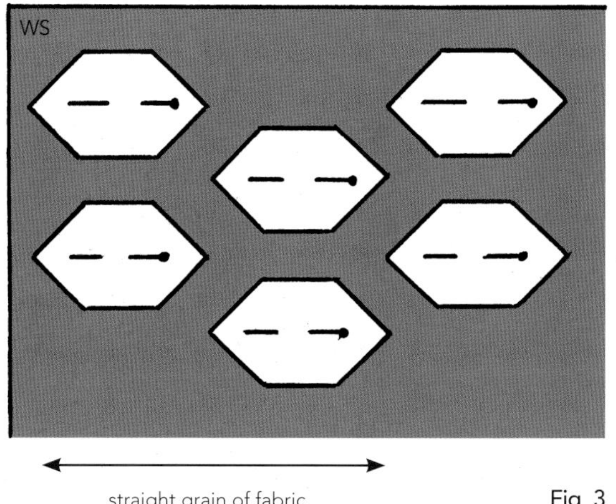

Fig 3

5 Turn back to the instructions for making the Tumbling Blocks design on page 24 and follow step 6 to fold the seam allowances over the papers and tack (baste) them into position.

6 Arrange the pieces into your chosen design and check that you like the effect: now is the time to change your mind and rearrange them if necessary.

"I've called this sampler quilt 'The Awesome Quilt' because of the great learning experience I had in the making of it and in the joy of playing with my favourite colours." **Judy Baker-Rogers**

7 The stitching together of the pieces is very much the same as for Tumbling Blocks, but there is a sequence for the joining together that will make the task easier. First, arrange the four centre long hexagons (marked A in Fig 4a) and stitch them together, following the method given for the Tumbling Blocks (step 7 second paragraph and step 8 on page 24).

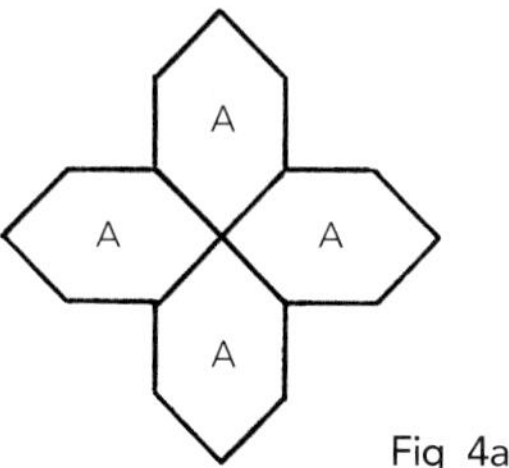

Fig 4a

8 Arrange the next four long hexagons (marked B in Fig 4b) around the centre block. Stitch them to the centre block, sewing a double stitch at each turning corner to strengthen it.

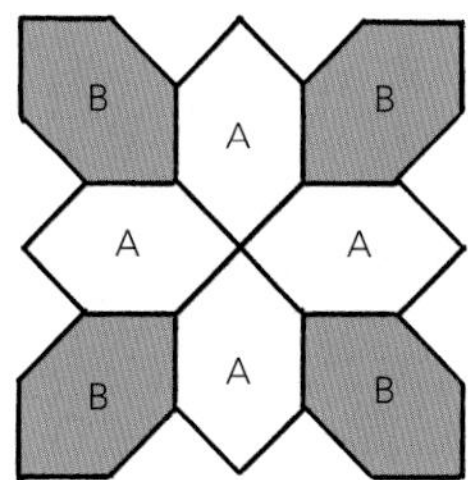

Fig 4b

9 Arrange the eight inner squares (marked C in Fig 4c) around the stitched block. Stitch each square to the block, sewing a double stitch at each turning corner to strengthen it as before.

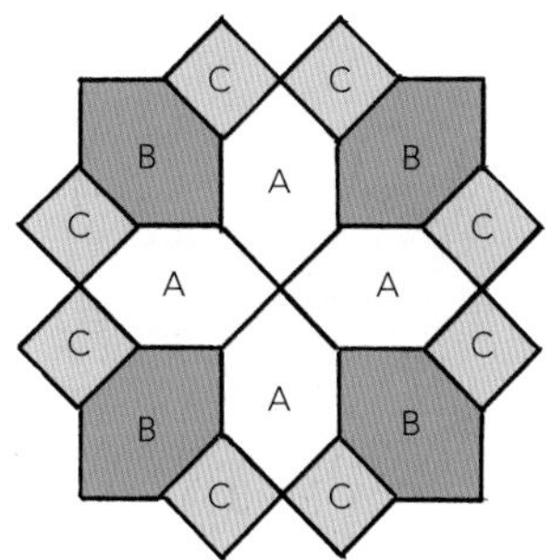

Fig 4c

10 Add the four long hexagons (marked D in Fig 4d) as in the diagram and stitch them to the block. Follow this with the eight outer long hexagons (E) as in Fig 4e and finally the four outer squares (F) as in Fig 4f. This completes the pieced design.

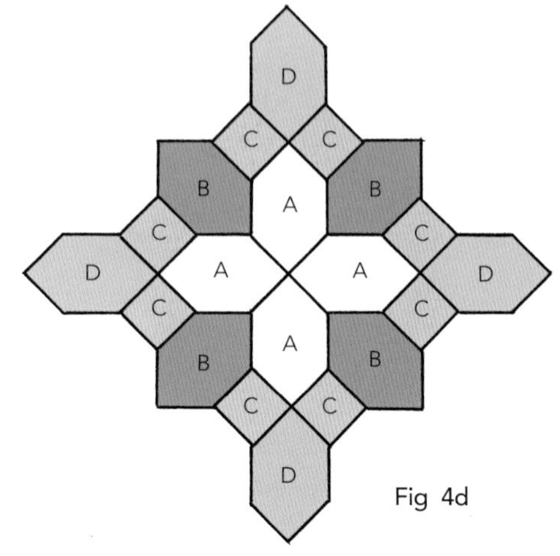

Fig 4d

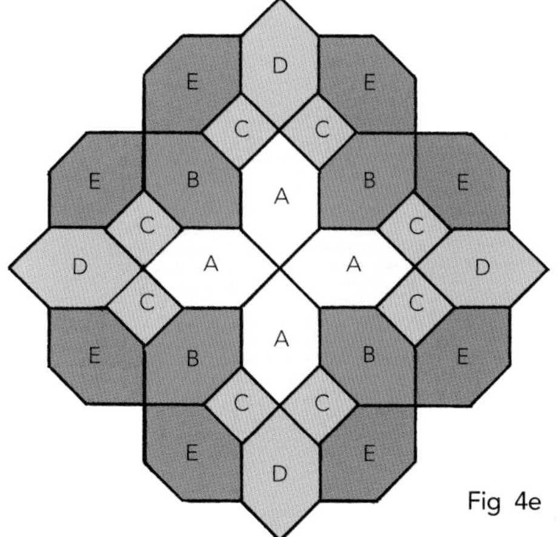

Fig 4e

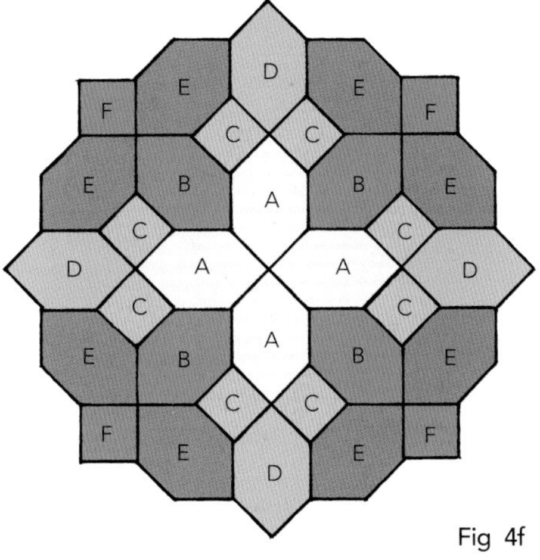

Fig 4f

11 Cut a 13in (33cm) square of fabric for the background. Use the same method described in the Tumbling Blocks instructions page 26 steps 10–15 to remove the papers and arrange and stitch the design on to the background, finally trimming it to an exact 12½in (31.7cm) square. To add the framing sashing strips, see page 236 for instructions.

Variations

The arrangement of squares and long hexagons that Judy used is just one of many that can be devised using different combinations of fabrics. The balance and symmetry of these patterns is very pleasing and could form a splendid quilt by simply being repeated in a formal arrangement.

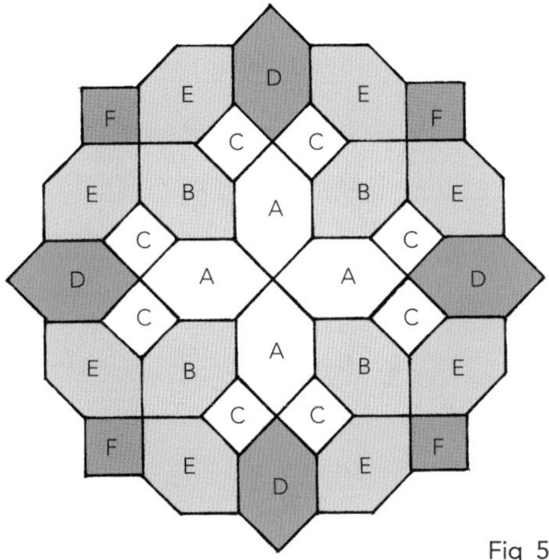

Fig 5

The arrangement shown in Fig 5 uses the same five colours but their positioning gives a lighter centre area, with the stronger colours framing it.

Judy Baker-Rogers' added several borders to frame her quilt, and enriched the wider areas with curvy hand quilting.

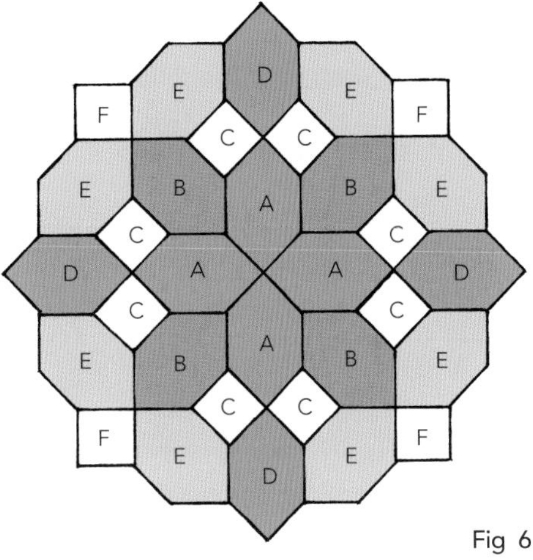

Fig 6

Fig 6 shows an arrangement of five colours, with the darkest colours grouped in the centre and the single light squares used as accents spread evenly across the design.

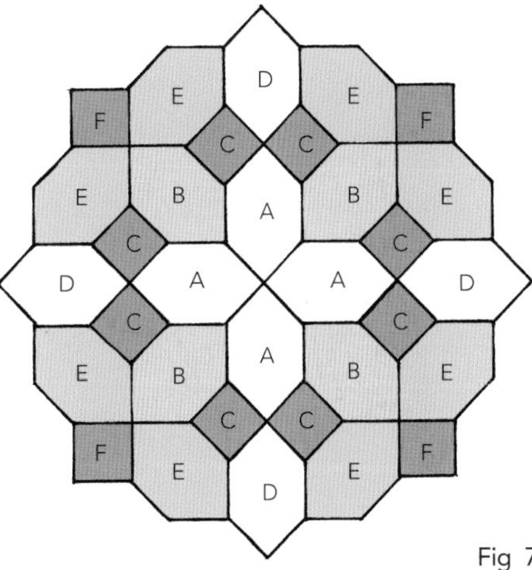

Fig 7

The design in Fig 7 uses just four of the original five colours, omitting the very dark shade, and making a strong centre with the lightest shade.

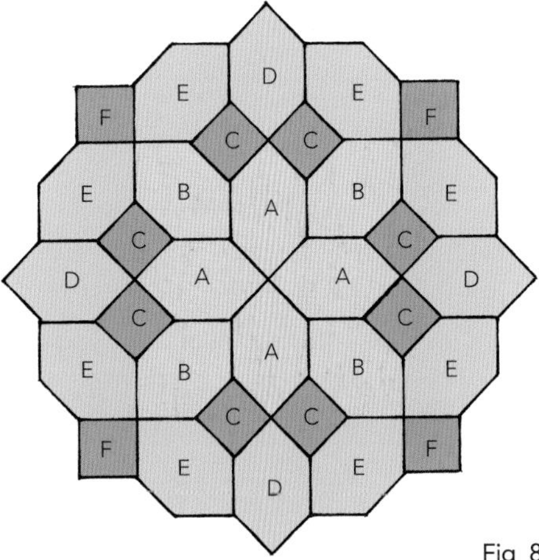

Fig 8

Fig 8 shows exactly the same arrangement of shapes but limiting colours to just three, giving a simpler, bolder look.

Making Blocks 21 to 40

Each block in this section, like the first section, is fully described, with guidance in selecting colours and fabrics, step-by-step instructions, and clear diagrams throughout. Again, the blocks are presented in sequence, so the skills learned in one design are built upon in the following techniques. Many of the blocks in this section are more complex than those of the first part of the book and can be used together to make a really impressive heirloom quilt. They can also be mixed in with the simpler designs from the first section to give variety and balance to the final arrangement. With a total of forty blocks in this *Essential Sampler Quilt Book* there are plenty to choose from!

English Patchwork Hand Piecing

Inner City

Everyone knows the traditional hexagon shape – it's how most people start patchwork and often, alas, where they also stop. The process of cutting fabric and papers and then laboriously stitching the fabric over the papers before joining these to make a design is slow and does not offer much short-term gratification, especially if the colours and arrangements of hexagons have no planned design. This has meant that the recent upsurge of interest in patchwork has tended to bypass the hexagon in favour of quicker and more exciting techniques. Still, the hexagon shape can be used to create wonderful heirloom quilts following the English Patchwork tradition.

The flower-like arrangement of six hexagons placed around a central hexagon, called Grandmother's Flower Garden (Fig 1), is the most popular design and when the colours are controlled and arranged in an overall design on the quilt, the result is pure pleasure.

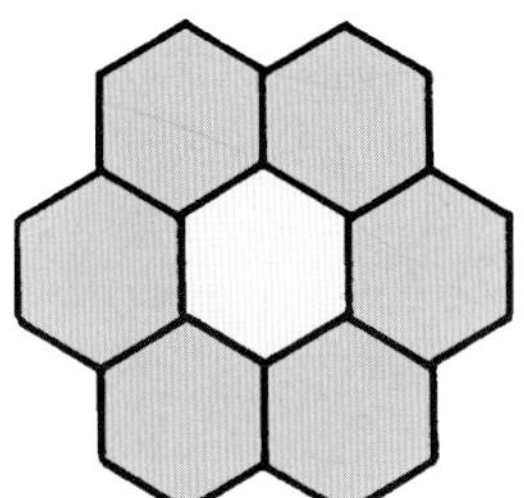

Fig 1

The hexagon can also be used in exciting contemporary designs like this Inner City block. This design is based on a hexagon made in the traditional English patchwork method over paper, but the construction and arrangement are slightly different and result in this elegant three-dimensional design known as Inner City.

Colour Choices

Like Tumbling Blocks, this design has a three-dimensional effect that is achieved by using three fabrics – one light (L), one medium (M) and one dark (D). Arrange the three fabrics next to each other on a surface to check whether there is enough definition between them. It needs to be fairly obvious which fabric is lighter than the others and which is the dark choice. The medium fabric will lie somewhere between these two extremes. Looking through half-closed eyes at the fabrics helps to see the difference in tones. A fourth fabric is needed for the background to the design. Sometimes it helps to leave the decision about the background until the Inner City design is assembled. It is surprising how different it can look when it is reduced to the smaller pieces of the design from the larger pieces of fabric at the start.

Construction

The hexagon used in this block is based on a 120° angle in each corner of the six-sided shape. This is a complex geometric exercise to draw and usually quilters just buy a template in whatever size they can get. However, drawing a hexagon in any size you want is easy if you use isometric paper. This is a type of graph paper printed with lines arranged to make equilateral triangles each with a corner angle of 60°. By drawing along these lines it is a simple matter to draft triangles and hexagons of any size (Fig 2) and create the template needed for this block.

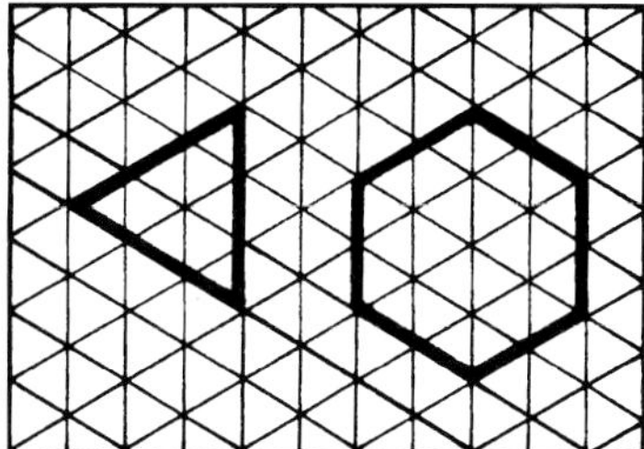

Fig 2

The size of hexagon I have chosen for the block is in a suitable scale for this design. If I were to make a larger piece in the design I am sure I would use a larger hexagon. When in doubt, cut out some hexagons from isometric paper and play with them before making a decision.

1 Make the template by tracing the hexagon shape from Fig 3 below, cutting it out and sticking it on to card, or use template plastic. See page 15 for instructions on making templates.

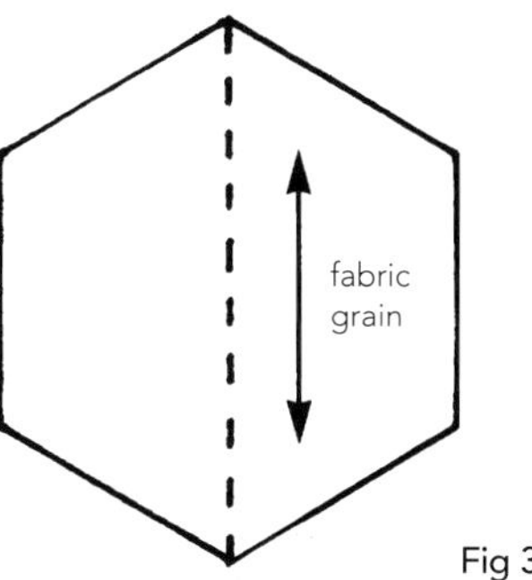

Fig 3

2 This design will keep its position efficiently if the papers are cut from freezer paper (see page 14) rather than from thick paper. If freezer paper is not available, the outer wrapping from packs of photocopying paper is an excellent substitute. Using a really sharp pencil to keep the shape accurate, draw round the template on the non-shiny side of the freezer paper. Mark the corners of the hexagons by continuing the drawn lines to just beyond the template corners so they cross (Fig 4). This cross marks the exact corner and will make cutting out more accurate.

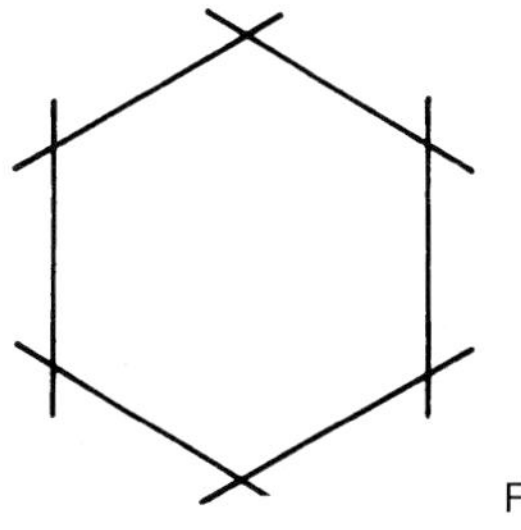

Fig 4

3 Cut out forty-two freezer paper hexagons, cutting just inside the drawn lines to prevent the shape becoming larger than the original hexagon template.

4 From the three fabrics chosen for the design cut two strips of each colour, each measuring 1¼in (3.2cm) wide and 30in (76cm) long. Stitch these together in pairs as shown in Fig 5, stitching a ¼in (6mm) wide seam. Use a much smaller machine stitch than usual to discourage the seams from coming undone when cut. Press the seams open after stitching.

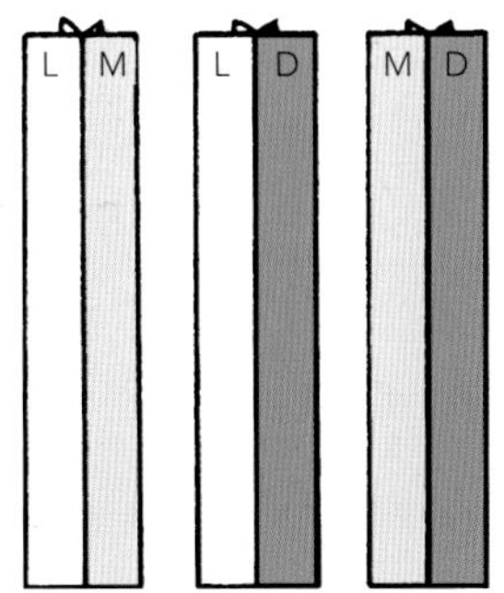

Fig 5

5 Place one joined strip right side down on an ironing pad. Position a freezer paper hexagon shiny side down on the fabric as shown in Fig 6 and press with a dry iron using a wool setting. This will fix the paper in exactly the right position and prevent it from shifting while the fabric is stitched over the paper. Position and press thirteen more hexagon papers on to the reverse of the joined strips leaving ½in (1.3cm) between each paper as in Fig 7. Repeat this with the other two joined strips, positioning fourteen hexagons on each piece.

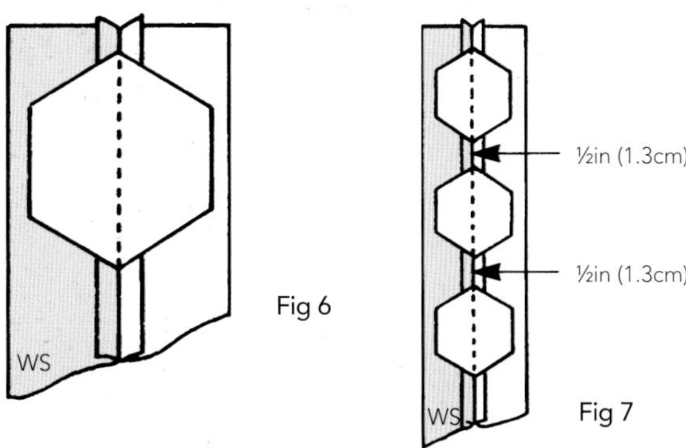

Fig 6

Fig 7

6 Cut around each paper, adding a ¼in (6mm) seam allowance on all sides. This does not have to be carefully measured as it is not critical. However, try to avoid cutting a seam allowance less than ¼in (6mm) as this makes tacking (basting) difficult.

7 Thread a needle with tacking thread (I use either crewel needles or sharps 8 or 9). Begin with a knot and tack fabric to paper by folding the fabric tightly over the paper and stitching it down. Take care when turning corners that include the joining seam that the fabric strips do not pull the machine stitches undone as you turn the fabric over the paper. Finish with a backstitch and cut the thread leaving about ¼in (6mm) for security (Fig 8). Turn the tacked shape over and check that the corners exactly outline the shape of the paper hexagon beneath it (Fig 9).

Fig 8

Fig 9

8 Arrange one hexagon from each joined strip in the desired design (Fig 10). Each group of three hexagons is joined in exactly the same arrangement of light, medium and dark fabrics. There will be fourteen Y-shaped units altogether. Thread a needle with no more than 18in (46cm) of toning thread. If stitching two different coloured fabrics together match the thread to the darker fabric as it is always less obvious than the lighter.

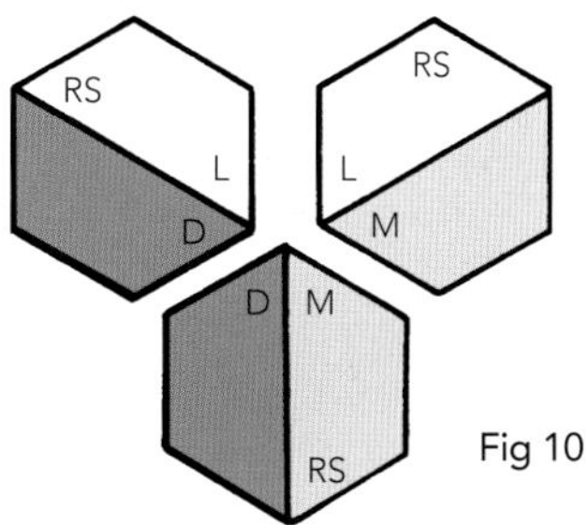

Fig 10

Take two hexagon shapes and place them right sides together, ready to sew. If one edge seems longer than the other, (this happens more often than you would think, so do not blame yourself), place them with the shorter edge on top as you work. As you sew, the top layer stretches, just as it does on a sewing machine, so you can ease the shorter edge to fit the longer. Fix the corner you are working towards with a pin (Fig 11) so that as you stitch the two corners will match exactly.

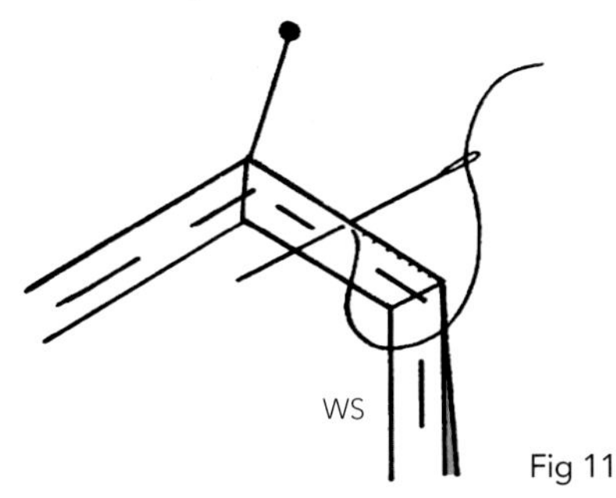

Fig 11

"This quilt was made for my son Will and his wife Sophie for their wedding quilt in May 2009. I chose the Wedgwood colours because the main fabric is like the willow pattern on Will's favourite plate. It took me over a year to make but they haven't had it yet in case it got spoilt before being included in the book." **Lynne Devey**

9 Starting with a double stitch to secure the thread, oversew with small even stitches, making sure that both sets of corners match exactly. The stitches should be about the same distance apart as small machine stitches. If you stitch too closely you can weaken the fabric and make an almost satin stitch effect which will prevent the finished seam from lying flat. Finish the seam with a double stitch and cut the thread, leaving about ¼in (6mm) for safety.

10 Open out the two joined hexagons and attach the third hexagon in the same way, stitching a double stitch at the centre of all three to strengthen the centre (Fig 12).

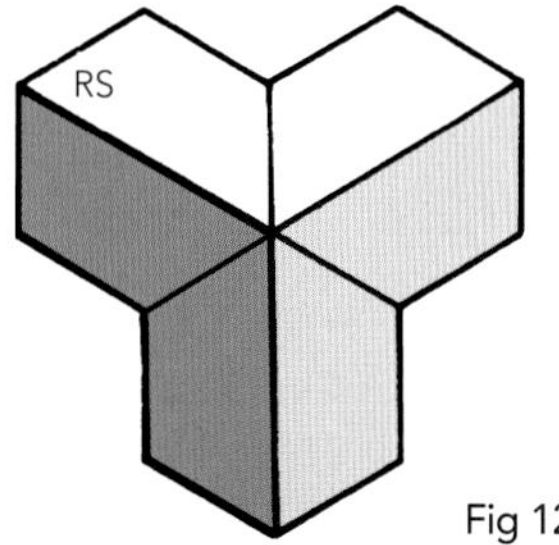

Fig 12

11 Assemble all fourteen Y-shaped units in the same way and join them together in rows as in Fig 13. Join the rows together to make the final design as in Fig 14.

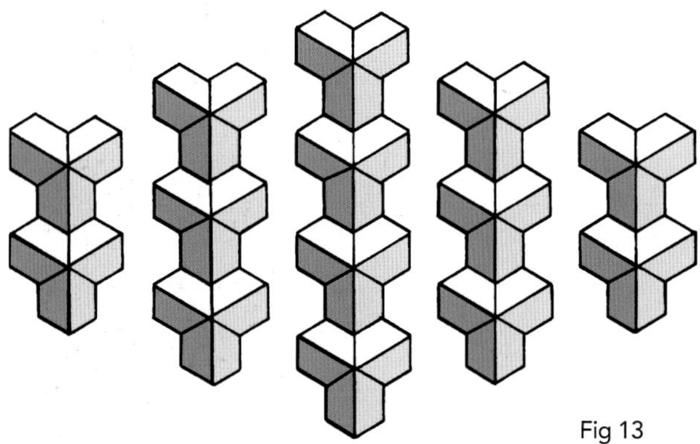

Fig 13

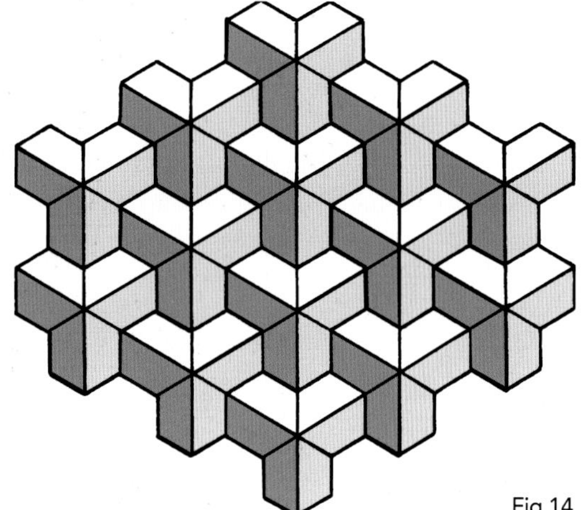

Fig 14

12 Press before removing the freezer papers so outer seam allowances remain turned under. Remove the tacking by undoing the final stitch, pulling firmly on the knot to pull the thread out in one length. Pull the papers off the fabric. Tack around the outer edges of the design to keep the seam allowances in place.

13 Cut a 13½ x 13½in (34.3 x 34.3cm) square of fabric for the background. This can be trimmed after the design is stitched in position to whatever size seems best, probably 13 x 13in (33 x 33cm). When one fabric is stitched to another (known as appliqué) the bottom fabric often draws up slightly to finish up smaller than when you started. By using a 13½ x 13½in (34.3 x 34.3cm) square it can be accurately trimmed to 13in (33cm) once the design has been stitched in place.

14 Place the Inner City design centrally on the background. It helps to fold the square in half from top to bottom and crease lightly. The crease makes a central guideline for positioning the design. Pin or tack the Inner City on to the background square. Using a shade of thread to match the design not the background, sew it on to the background, keeping stitches small and even. Sew a double stitch at each corner to secure it (Fig 15). Be prepared to change the colour of the thread to match each fabric as you stitch around the design.

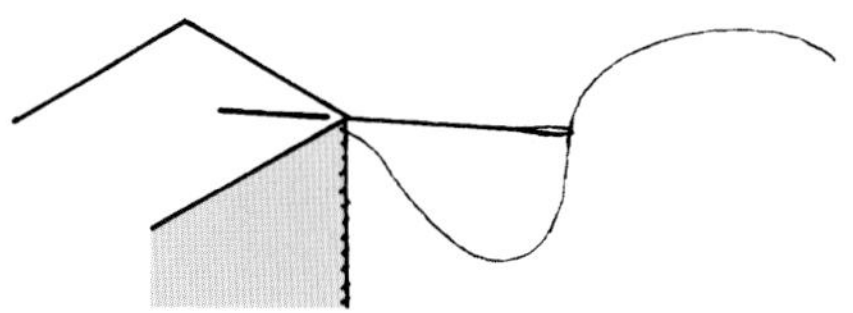

Fig 15

15 Before an appliquéd shape is quilted, its thickness can be reduced by cutting the background fabric away from behind the appliqué. This is not compulsory and if you are nervous about doing this, leave it. However, it does make the whole piece easier to quilt and allows it to lie flatter. Turn the block to the back and, with your fingers, just pull the backing from the appliqué at the centre. Make a small cut in the backing fabric about ¼–½in (6–12mm) inside the line of stitches. Once you have done this, carefully cut away the backing up to ¼in (6mm) from the stitching line of the appliqué, leaving the appliqué itself intact.

16 Trim the finished block to an exact 13in (33cm) square, or to whatever size you feel suits your design. Add the inner framing strips (see page 236) and trim the block to exactly 14in (35.6cm) square. Finally, add the sashing strips (see page 236).

Machine Piecing

Seminole

This attractive form of strip patchwork was begun by the Seminole Native Americans in Florida around the beginning of the nineteenth century. They used plain fabrics in glowing colours to create variations of border designs to use in their blouses, jackets and skirts. It was never a hand technique: the Seminole women used non-electric sewing machines for their complex designs. Now we can use modern machines plus fast and accurate rotary cutting equipment for our own versions of Seminole work. The completed block is complex and rich, and together with the Bargello block (on page 182), contrasts with simpler blocks to make a varied and balanced quilt.

Colour Choices

Two variations of Seminole patchwork are used in the block in the sampler quilt (Fig 1). The centre band is of the classic squares-on-point design and uses three fabrics. The outer two bands are from the same zigzag chevron pattern and use two fabrics alternating in the centre with a third on either side. It would keep the design clearer to use the same three fabrics for each variation. Once these are made, they can be arranged in the block and a decision can then be made about the colour of the dividing fabric strips which also border the block.

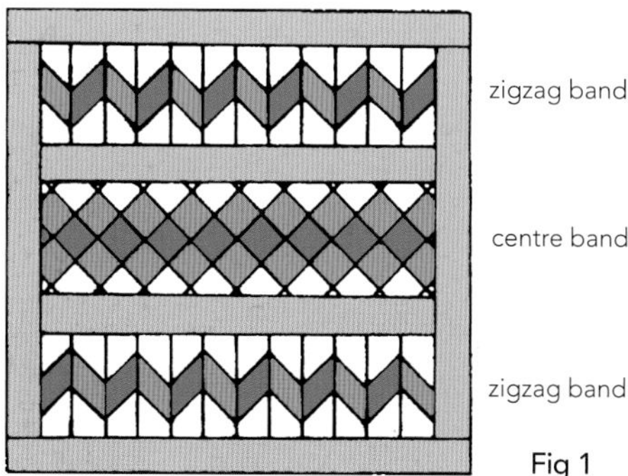

Fig 1

There needs to be some definition between the two fabrics that are used together in the centre of each design band. The third fabric becomes an edging background to the other two, so if you are using certain fabrics throughout as background, these might be suitable here. Take the fabrics and lay them out in order to check that you like the relationship between them – you may want to swap one over with another or even reject one at this stage.

Construction

1 *The centre Seminole band:* having decided on the position of each fabric in the design refer to Fig 2 and cut from fabric A (centre) one strip 1½in (3.8cm) wide and 16in (40.6cm) long. Cut from fabric B two strips 1½in (3.8cm) wide and 16in (40.6cm) long. Cut from fabric C two strips 1¾in (4.5cm) wide and 16in (40.6cm) long. Notice that the strips that are on the outside edges of the band are cut ¼in (6mm) wider than the others.

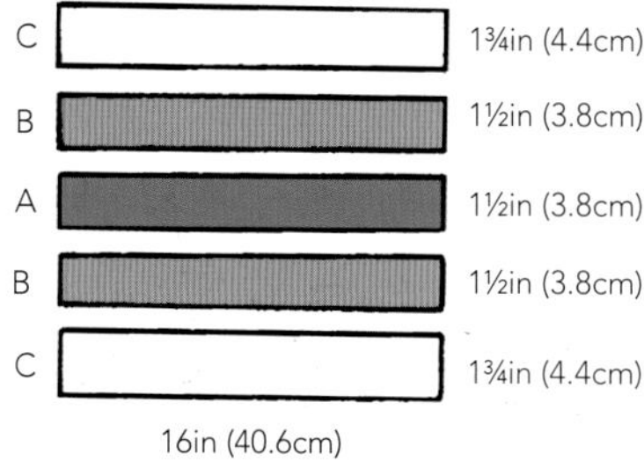

Fig 2

2 Set the stitch length on your sewing machine to about two-thirds the size of the usual dressmaking stitch to prevent the seam from coming undone when the strips are cut across. Choose a thread colour that will not strongly contrast with any of your fabrics, darker rather than lighter. I find that shades of grey or neutral will blend in with most fabric combinations. The seams need to be a scant ¼in (6mm). Use a ¼in (6mm) foot or a strip of masking tape on the machine to help you stitch an accurate seam. Stitch the five strips together, alternating the direction you sew the strips to keep the band straight and not slightly rippled (Fig 3).

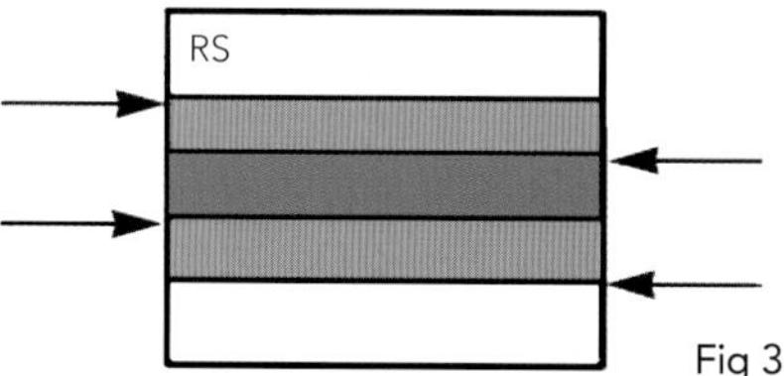

Fig 3

3 Press the band of strips from the front with the seams pressed in the same direction.

4 Take the band and place it horizontally on the cutting board, lining up the top edge with one of the horizontal markings on the board. Place the band with the seams pressed towards the top of the band as this will make it easier to cut. If the band is slightly rippled, do not worry, just pat it as flat as you can and carry on. If five strips of different fabrics lie perfectly flat, this is a miracle.

Using a rotary ruler and cutter, trim one end of the band vertically to straighten it and then cut off a piece 1½in (3.8cm) wide (Fig 4). Continue to cut off similar pieces each 1½in (3.8cm) wide. You should get ten pieces from the band of strips.

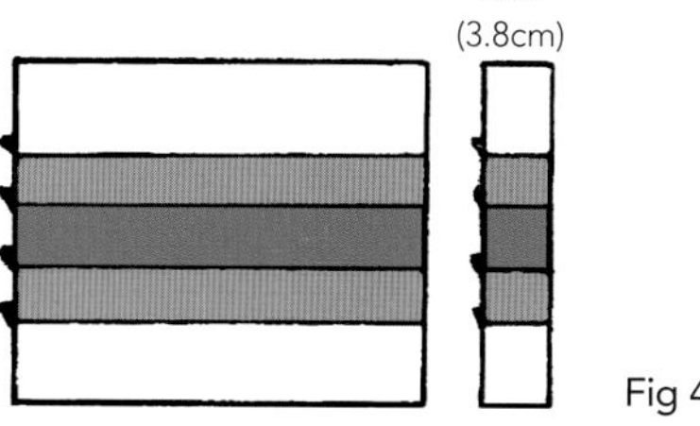

Fig 4

5 Place the ten pieces ready for stitching next to the sewing machine, Take two pieces, place them next to each other, then turn the right-hand piece round 180° so that the seams are now lying in the opposite direction to those of the first piece. This will make it easier to match the seams. Step the second piece *down* so that the seams line up as shown in Fig 5. Flip piece 2 over on to piece 1, right sides facing, and pin the first seam alignment. Pin diagonally, as this will help to keep both sets of seam allowances flat while stitching (Fig 6).

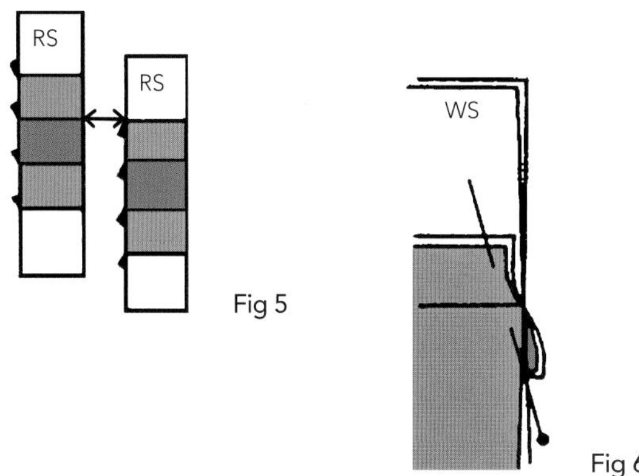

Fig 5

Fig 6

If it worries you to let the other seams lock in naturally as you stitch without pinning them, then pin all three seam junctions before stitching – I stitch as far as the pin at the first seam junction, remove the pin and before continuing to stitch, lock the next set of seams together with a stitch ripper and bold them firmly in place as I stitch. I repeat this for each of the seam junctions as I get to them. If this works for you, don't bother to pin excessively. If you have cut and stitched your strips together accurately, there shouldn't be a problem. If there is a problem, blame the fabric and pin each seam junction before stitching.

6 Open out the two joined pieces and check that the positioning is correct. Pick up piece 3 and turn it so that the pressed seams are lying in the opposite direction to piece 2. Step piece down in the same way as before. Flip it over on to piece 2 and match and pin the first seam alignment. Stitch, matching the three seam junctions carefully either by holding them in place or by pinning. Open the pieces out and check that all is well. If you spot a poorly matched seam junction, leave it until all ten pieces are joined. You may well be able to cut the band of pieces here and so lose the nasty bit. Repeat the process with piece 4, then 5 and so on until all ten pieces are joined.

Chain Stitching

You can save time and thread by stitching the pieces together with chain sewing – stitching each pair together one after the other without taking them off the machine and breaking the thread. If you do this, remember that each pair of pieces must be arranged identically with pressed seams in exactly the same direction each time.

To chain sew, stitch to the very end of the first pair and, without lifting the pressure foot, place the next pair in position and continue to stitch, starting at the top edge of the pieces (Fig 7). Continue to chain sew the pairs until all are joined. Take them off the machine and cut the threads that hold each pair to the next.

Open out two pairs, line up the seams, pin and stitch them together, chaining the second set after them. (The remaining pair has to sit this round out.) Finally, join the three sections together, lining up the seams as before.

7 Press the band from the front, pushing the seams to one side. Use your hand to guide the seams towards one side and try to press each strip from bottom to top along the grain of the fabric rather than across the band, as this can stretch and distort the band (Fig 8).

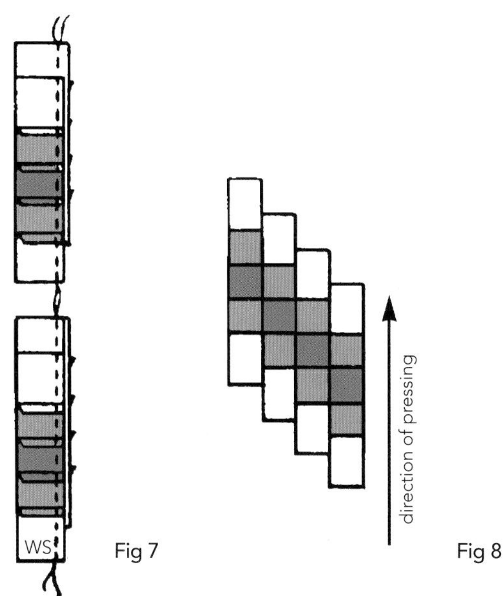

Fig 7

Fig 8

8 At this stage the band of pieces needs to be straightened up at either end (Fig 9). It would, however, be very wasteful to cut off the excess from both ends. There is a cunning way to straighten the band without any waste. Study the band and choose a part where you are not too happy with the matching of the seams. Place the band horizontally on a cutting board, positioning the top points along a horizontal marking on the board (Fig 10 overleaf). Place a rotary ruler vertically on the band at the point where you are unhappy with the seam matching. This cannot be near either end, but anywhere along the band is fine. Position the ruler through the centre of a diamond to keep the design balanced. Cut through the design with a rotary cutter – not a nice moment, but be brave. Remove the left-hand section and place it at the other end of the right-hand section (Fig 11 overleaf). Step the design *downwards* to match the other pieces. Match the seams as before and stitch the two sections together. Press this last seam from the front to one side in the same direction as the other seams. Your band is now straight!

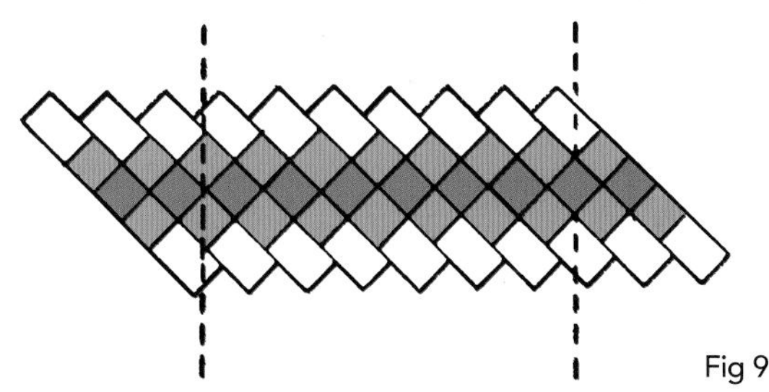

Fig 9

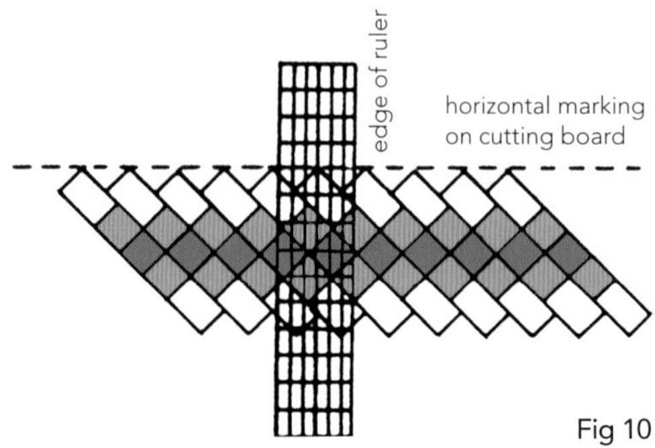

Fig 10

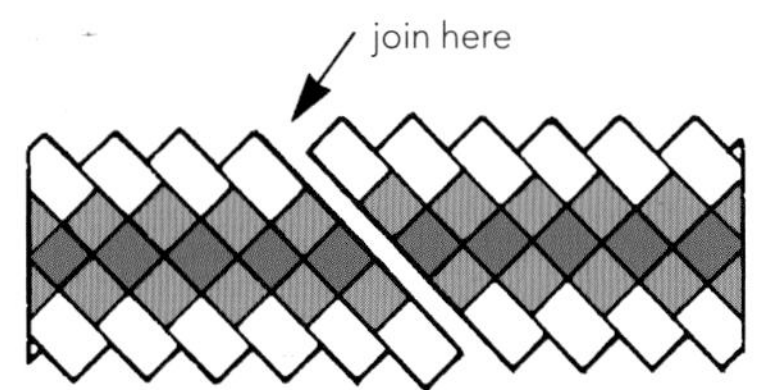

Fig 11

9 The band is very stretchy if you pull it from side to side, so edging strips must be attached to keep it firm. It is probably best to leave this until all three bands of Seminole have been completed before choosing which fabric looks best for the strips.

10 *Making the zigzag bands:* I used the same set of three fabrics for this design as for the centre band, which helps to unify the overall design. Using the zigzag design in two short lengths in this block is quite wasteful as a triangular wedge at each end of the strips is cut off and discarded. However, it is a lovely design and if used in longer lengths as a quilt border would not be wasteful at all.

Cut two sets of strips as in Fig 12, each 1½in (3.8cm) wide and 31in (78.7cm) long. Stitch these together into two bands. Press seams from the front with the seams pressed all in one direction.

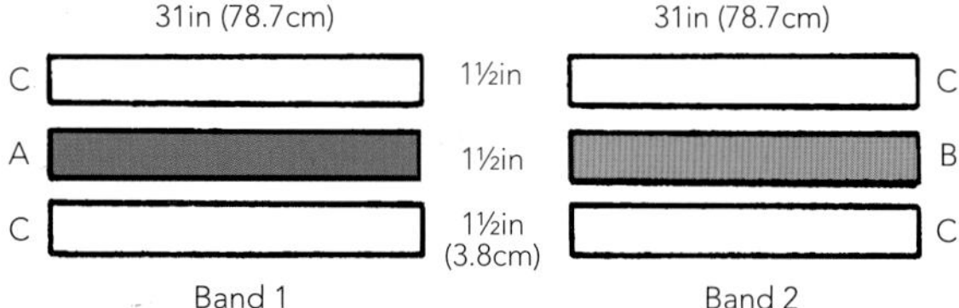

Fig 12

11 Take band 1 and place it horizontally on the cutting board right side *up*. Take band 2 and place it right side *down*, on top of band 1 with the seams lying in the opposite direction to band 1 (Fig 13). Match the edges and seams carefully.

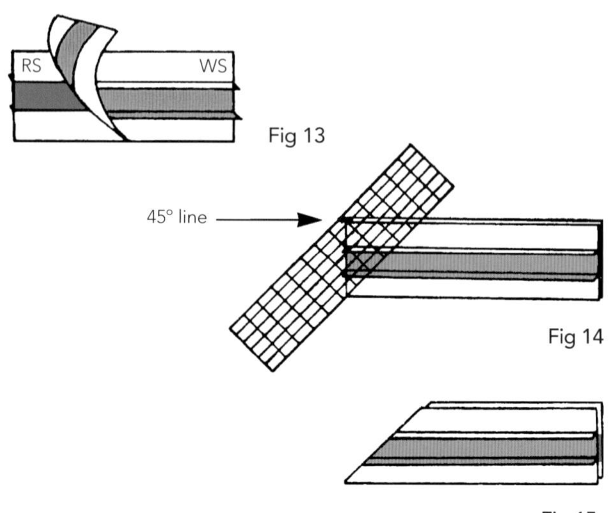

Fig 13

Fig 14

Fig 15

The pieces for the zigzag design are cut at an angle of 45° to the strips. This is easy to do with a rotary ruler using the 45° marked line. Look carefully at your ruler: some are a mass of criss-crossed extra lines, but one or more will be labelled 45°. Place the ruler across the bands of fabric with the 45° line running along the top edges of the fabric as shown in Fig 14. If you can't seem to match your ruler with the diagrams, try another 45° line on the ruler or flip the ruler over and use the wrong side of the 45° line. Cut through both layers of fabric with a rotary cutter along the angled edge of the ruler (Fig 15). Remove the two triangles of fabric.

12 Find the marking on the ruler that is 1½in (3.8cm) from one long edge. Pass the ruler over the slanted cut edges of the fabric until the 1½in (3.8cm) line is exactly on top of the cut edges (Fig 16). Cut along the ruler's edge with a rotary cutter. Lift the ruler and set aside the pair of cut pieces. Repeat the process, cutting a total of twelve pairs of pieces.

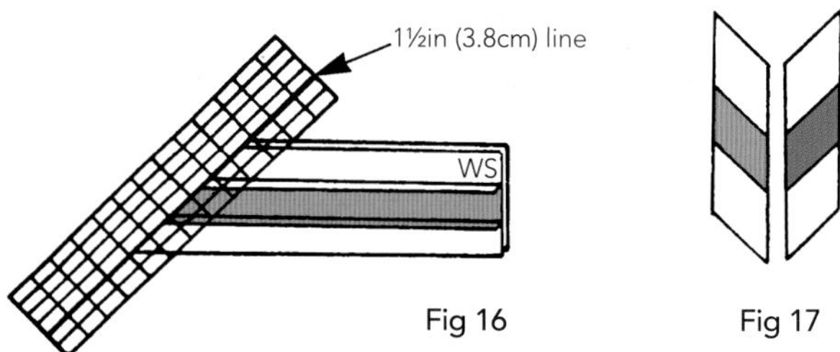

Fig 16

Fig 17

13 Open out the first pair – it should look like Fig 17. Close the pair together again with right sides facing and pin the edges carefully, matching the seams. Stitch this first pair together. Continue to pin and stitch each pair in exactly the same arrangement as the first. This can very easily be done using the chain sewing technique described earlier. Open each zigzag out and press from the front with the seams to one side.

"I wanted to make my first quilt bright and cheerful but still elegant. I found the navy and red rose fabric and built up the colours from there. I loved making it and Lynne's instructions were excellent. It took around five months to complete and was made for our guest room. Another one will need to follow soon!" **Pamela Gunn**

14 Join six zigzags together, pinning and matching seams carefully (Fig 18). Chain sew if possible as it saves so much time and thread. This makes the top band for the block. Join the remaining six zigzags for the bottom band. Press from the front with seams pressed all in one direction.

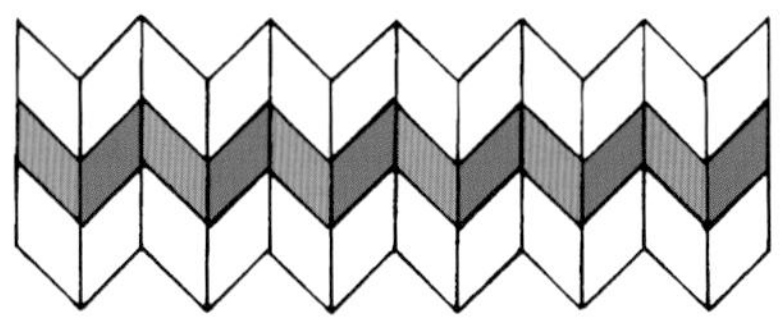

Fig 18

15 *Attaching the edging strips:* arrange the three Seminole bands as shown in Fig 1 (page 124) so that you can choose the fabric that will look best between the bands. I used the same fabric to border the block, but this may not be your choice. At this stage your three bands will not be the same length – probably the centre band will be longer than the two zigzag bands. Trim down the centre band equally from both ends to match the zigzag bands. If the zigzag bands are not exactly the same length as each other, press and ease out the shorter band with a steam iron until it matches the longer band. When you have either cut or stretched the bands so they are all the same length, cut two strips of the edging fabric each 1½in (3.8cm) wide and a length to match the Seminole bands.

16 Place the centre Seminole band horizontally on the cutting board and lay a rotary ruler along the inner seam lines (Fig 19). The band is very flexible and you can move parts of it up and down so that as many inner points as possible can be lined up with the edge of the ruler. Don't expect miracles – not all inner points will be exactly on line, just get as many as possible. Ignore seam allowances that may be showing – it's where the actual stitch lines end that you are lining up the ruler (Fig 20). Draw along the edge of the ruler with a soft pencil.

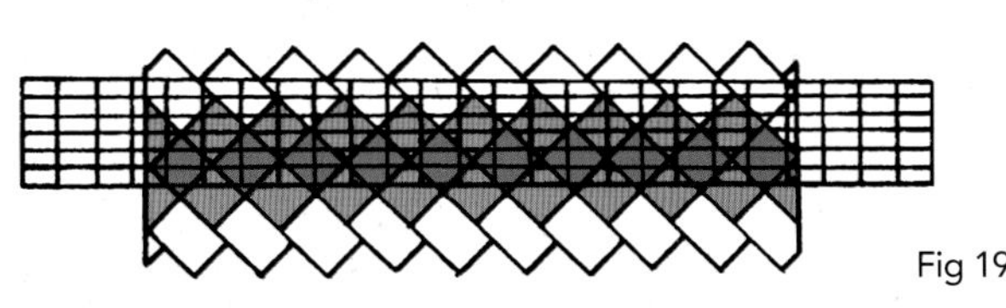

Fig 19

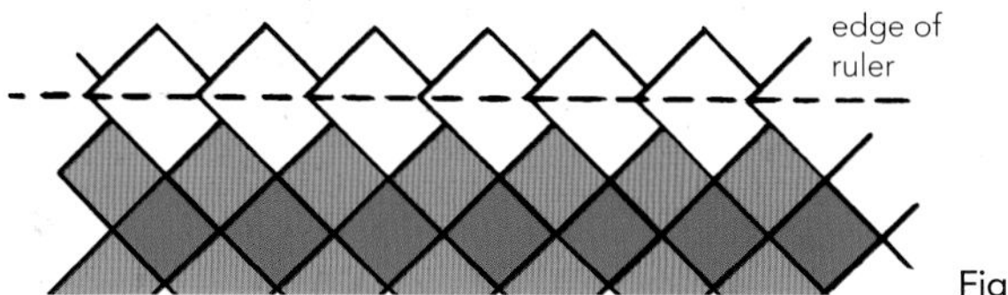

Fig 20

17 Turn the centre Seminole band through 180° and repeat the process. While doing this check that both drawn lines are parallel to each other, so that the width of the finished band will be consistent.

18 Place one edging strip right side *down* on the Seminole band, matching its edge with a drawn line on the band (Fig 21). Pin it in position and stitch with the usual ¼in (6mm) seam. Repeat this with the second strip, pinning it along the second drawn line and stitching it in position. Press back the strips and check that the section of Seminole design is looking evenly balanced between the strips. Once you are happy with it, trim the pointed sections back to within ¼in (6mm) of the seamline.

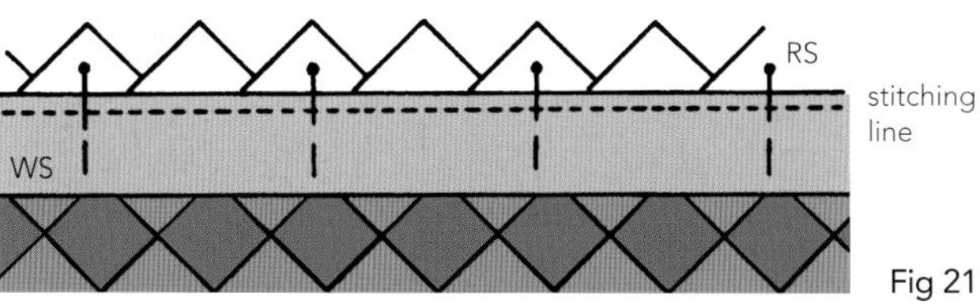

Fig 21

19 Place one zigzag band horizontally on the cutting board. Place a rotary ruler across the band and align the top points of each inner zigzag as much as possible with the line on the ruler that is ½in (1.3cm) from its edge (Fig 22). Cut along the edge of the ruler with a rotary cutter. Repeat this at the other end of the zigzag band. Trim the second zigzag band the same way.

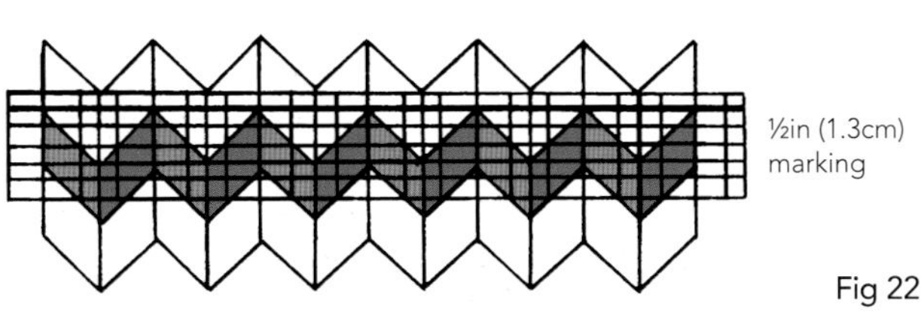

Fig 22

20 Pin and stitch each zigzag band to either side of the centre design, taking care not to stretch the zigzag band while stitching it. Press the seams from the front towards the edging strips.

21 Measure the block from top to bottom and from side to side. Trim down wherever necessary to make it square, or just add wider border strips on the shorter sides. The block needs to finish up exactly 14in (35.6cm) square once the framing strips are added. If the block measures 11in (29.2cm) or more, cut the border strips 2in (5cm) wide and trim the block down afterwards to 14in (35.6cm) square. Finally, add the sashing strips (see page 236).

American Patchwork Hand Piecing

Tangled Star

I first saw this traditional pattern in a calendar designed by an American quilter friend Pepper Cory. Each month featured a different design, all based on stars and all measuring 12in (30.5cm) square. The twelve squares, known as blocks, were combined in a quilt in much the same way as my sampler quilt. I like this block because of the way the interlocking shapes weave over and under each other.

The traditional way to make a patchwork block like this is to draw it out on to graph paper and make templates of the various shapes that make up the design. No seam allowances are included. This is the way that the patchwork blocks that evolved over the years in the United States have all been

made: new designs were drawn out, stuck on to card and then cut into the required templates. The templates were drawn around on the back of the chosen fabrics and the shapes cut out with a seam allowance added to the drawn lines. With intricate designs like this the old way still seems to be the best. It is possible for ace machinists to piece the block by machine, following the drawn lines with machine stitches instead of by hand. However, there are some nasty angles which can present problems to the less experienced machinist so I suggest this block is pieced by hand.

Colour Choices

The essence of the design is a spiky star and a square shape that weave through each other on a background (Fig 1). The tangled shapes are not stitched on to a large background square but every piece is cut to shape and joined with its neighbour to form the complete block. The two fabrics for the star and square need to look good together with the third background fabric. Try folding the fabrics into small shapes and arranging them side by side on the possible background fabric when choosing. An extra colour could be used in the central area to give more depth if desired. You may be planning to use a certain fabric throughout the quilt as the background, in which case your choice of fabrics for the star and square shapes will be controlled by this. Remember that the block will finish up a 12in (30.5cm) square and will need a framing border before the sashing strips, so this extra fabric should also be considered when choices are being made.

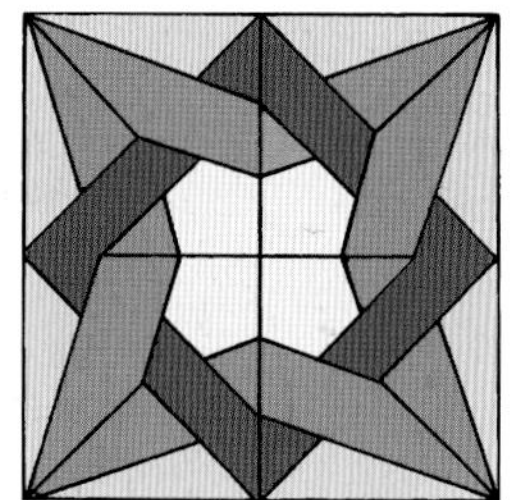

Fig 1

Construction

1 Make card templates by tracing the six shapes from Fig 2 on page 133, cutting them out and sticking them on the card, or use template plastic. Mark the directional arrows – these show how the template should be positioned on the grain or weave of the fabric. Mark the centre corner on template B. When the four quarters of the design have been assembled, this corner of each of the four sections is positioned in the centre of the block.

2 On the wrong side of each fabric draw around the templates accurately using a sharp pencil, matching the direction of the arrows with the fabric grain. The drawn lines mark the sewing lines. Allow at least ½in (1.3cm) between each drawn outline so that seam allowances of ¼in (6mm) can be added to the shape when cutting out.

For the larger star shape you will need four of shape A, four of shape D and four of shape E. For the smaller square shape you will need four of shape C and four of shape A reversed on the fabric. To do this, flip the template over on the fabric making sure that the grainline arrow matches the weave of the fabric.

For the background you will need four of shape B (the centre background shape), four of shape F and four of shape F *reversed* – marked as (R) on Fig 3b.

3 Cut out each shape to include the ¼in (6mm) seam allowance, either by eye or by using a rotary cutter and ruler. The seam allowance is not critical, but it is very helpful if cut accurately as then the edges of the fabrics line up as you match the drawn stitching lines.

4 Arrange the cut pieces on a flat surface or pin them in position on a polystyrene tile or board. Final decisions can be made on the effectiveness of the fabric choices at this stage.

5 This design breaks into four quarters, each identical in design and construction (Fig 3a). Any block that divides in this way is called a Four-Patch. Assemble each quarter in turn as shown in Fig 3b before joining them all together.

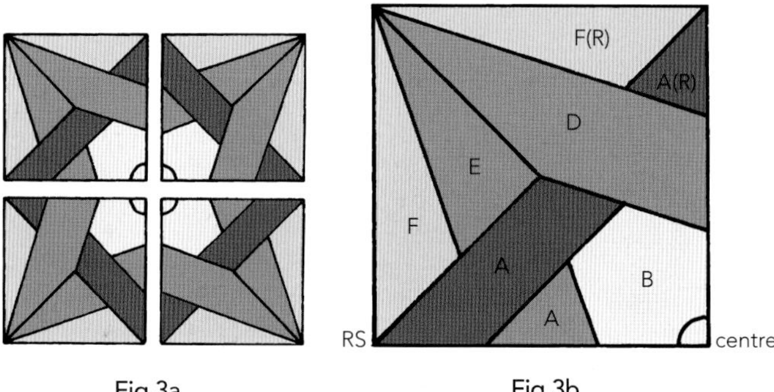

Fig 3a Fig 3b

The order of joining (known as piecing) each quarter section is not immediately obvious. First join piece A to piece B and then attach C (Fig 4). Work with the *right* side of the fabric uppermost when first arranging the pieces as this gives the design shown in Fig 3b: from the back of the fabric the design is reversed, which can be confusing. Place shapes A and B with right sides facing along the two sides to be joined. The pencil marks will be on the outside and must be positioned *exactly* on top of each other as they indicate the sewing lines. Align the starting point of the sewing lines by pushing a pin through both layers of fabric

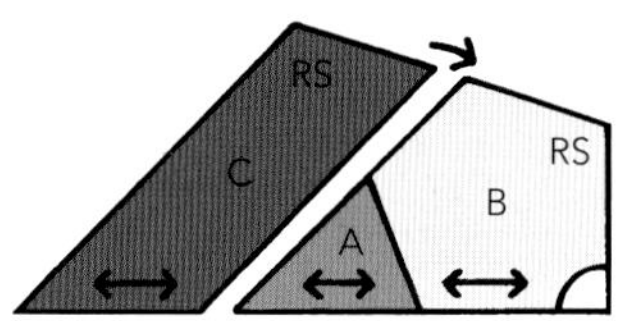

Fig 4

"I'm in one of Lynne's regular groups and started this quilt prior to the publication of The New Sampler Quilt Book, *but alas it was almost two years before it was finished. Nevertheless as it becomes more 'worn and washed' I love it all the more."* **Kathie Levine**

until the head is on the surface of the top fabric. Repeat this to mark the finishing point (Fig 5). Reposition the pins at right angles to the seam. Add more pins along the seamline, matching the marked lines (Fig 6).

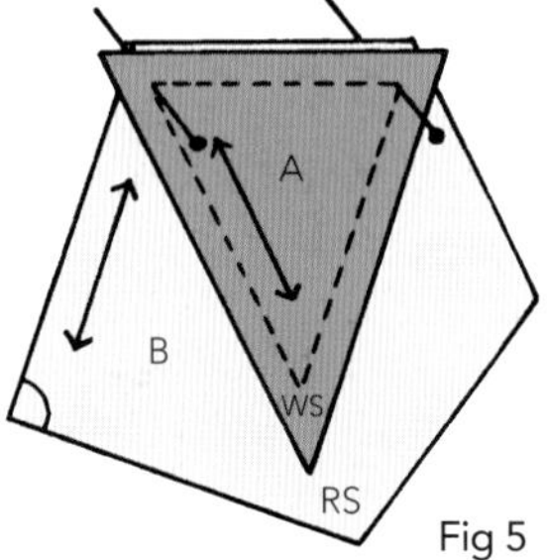

Fig 5

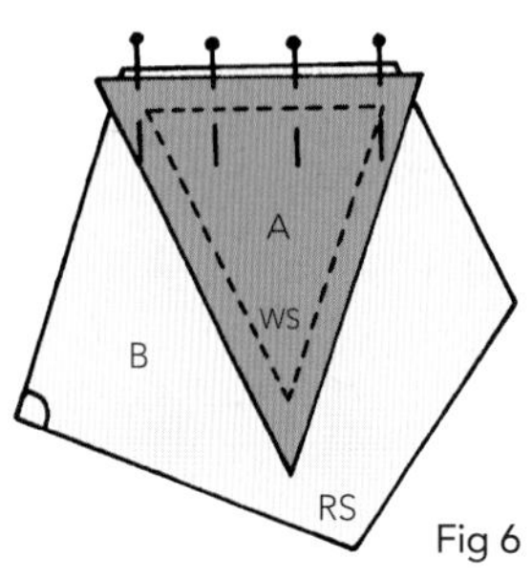

Fig 6

6 Starting with a double stitch, sew along the pencilled line with small running stitches about the same length as machine stitches, loading several stitches on to the needle at a time. Begin each run of stitches with a backstitch to secure the work firmly (Fig 7). Do not sew into the seam allowances – these are left free so that once the block is complete the seams may be pressed to one side. They are never pressed open, as the hand-sewn stitches are not strong enough. Do not press any seams until the whole piece is complete as there is no set rule for which way each seam is to be pressed – just wait until the block is assembled and then press the seams whichever way avoids too much bulk at the back of the work.

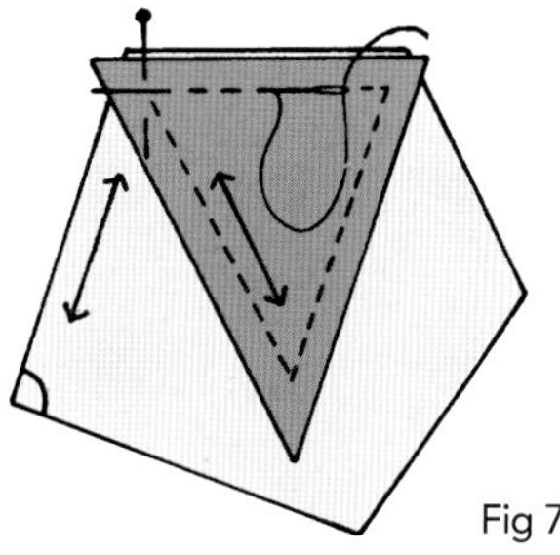
Fig 7

7 Once piece A is joined to B, pin piece C in place on to A and B with right sides facing. When stitching this second seam don't sew over the seam allowances in the middle but sew up to the seam and make a backstitch. Pass the needle through the seam allowances to the other side. Backstitch again and continue sewing (Fig 8). In the same way pin and stitch together pieces E and F (Fig 9).

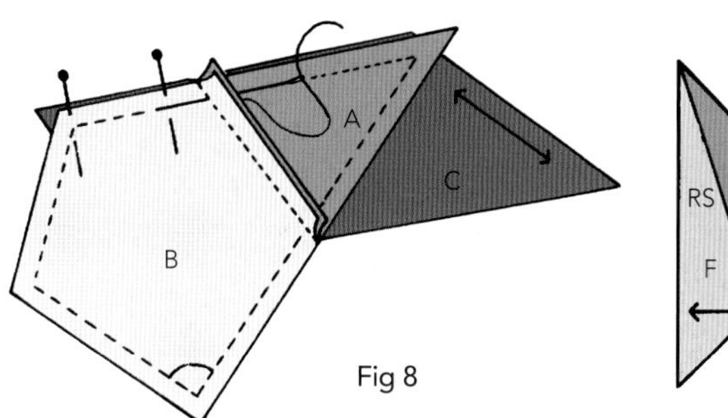

Fig 8

Fig 9

8 Join together the first section (A + B + C) and the second section (E + F) as in Fig 10.

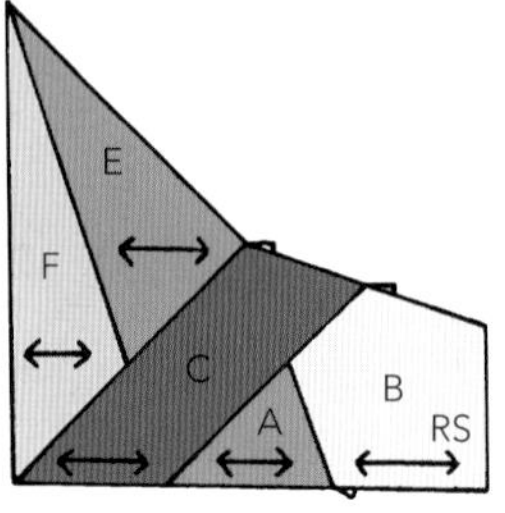

Fig 10

9 Pin and stitch together pieces A (reversed) and F (reversed) as in Fig 11. Pin and stitch piece D to this pair as in Fig 12.

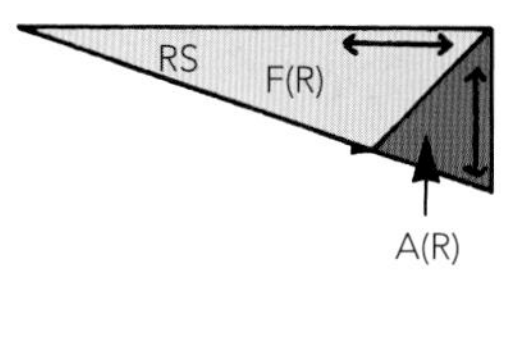

Fig 11

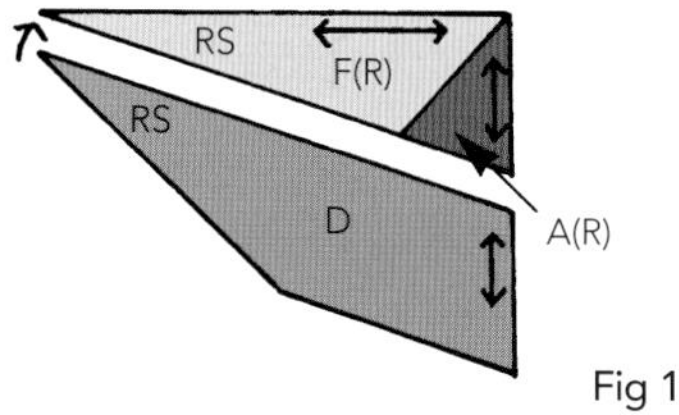

Fig 12

10 Finally, join the two parts of the design together to complete it. Take care to match the stitching lines exactly, especially at the centre of the design where shape D makes a wide angle. This is the part that is so much easier to negotiate by hand rather than by machine. As before, stitch to the junction of seams, make a backstitch to secure it, pass the needle through the seam allowances and make another backstitch before continuing stitching along the seamline. This completed square forms one quarter of the block.

11 Pin and stitch the other three quarters of the block in the same way. Arrange the four sections in the block design (see Fig 1). Stitch the top two sections together, pinning and stitching along the drawn lines as before. Repeat this with the remaining two sections (Fig 13). Finally, stitch the two halves together, matching the centres carefully.

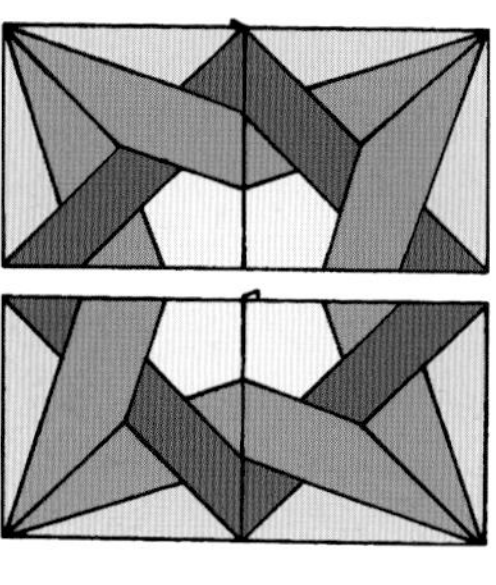
Fig 13

12 Press the completed block lightly, pushing the seams in whichever direction reduces the bulk of the seam allowances. The block should measure 12½ x 12½in (31.7 x 31.7cm).This is a 12in (30.5cm) square block but the extra ¼in (6mm) seam allowances on both sides make it up to 12½in (31.7cm) at this stage.

13 Check that your block measures exactly 12½in (31.7cm) in both directions. If it is slightly smaller, add ¼in (6mm) to the width of the framing strips and after these are added to the block trim the whole thing down to exactly 14in (35.6cm) square. If the block measures more than 12½in (31.7cm) square, add the framing strips and then trim all the sides down to the final measurement of 14in (35.6cm) square. Finally, add the sashing strips (see page 236).

Fig 2 – Actual size templates

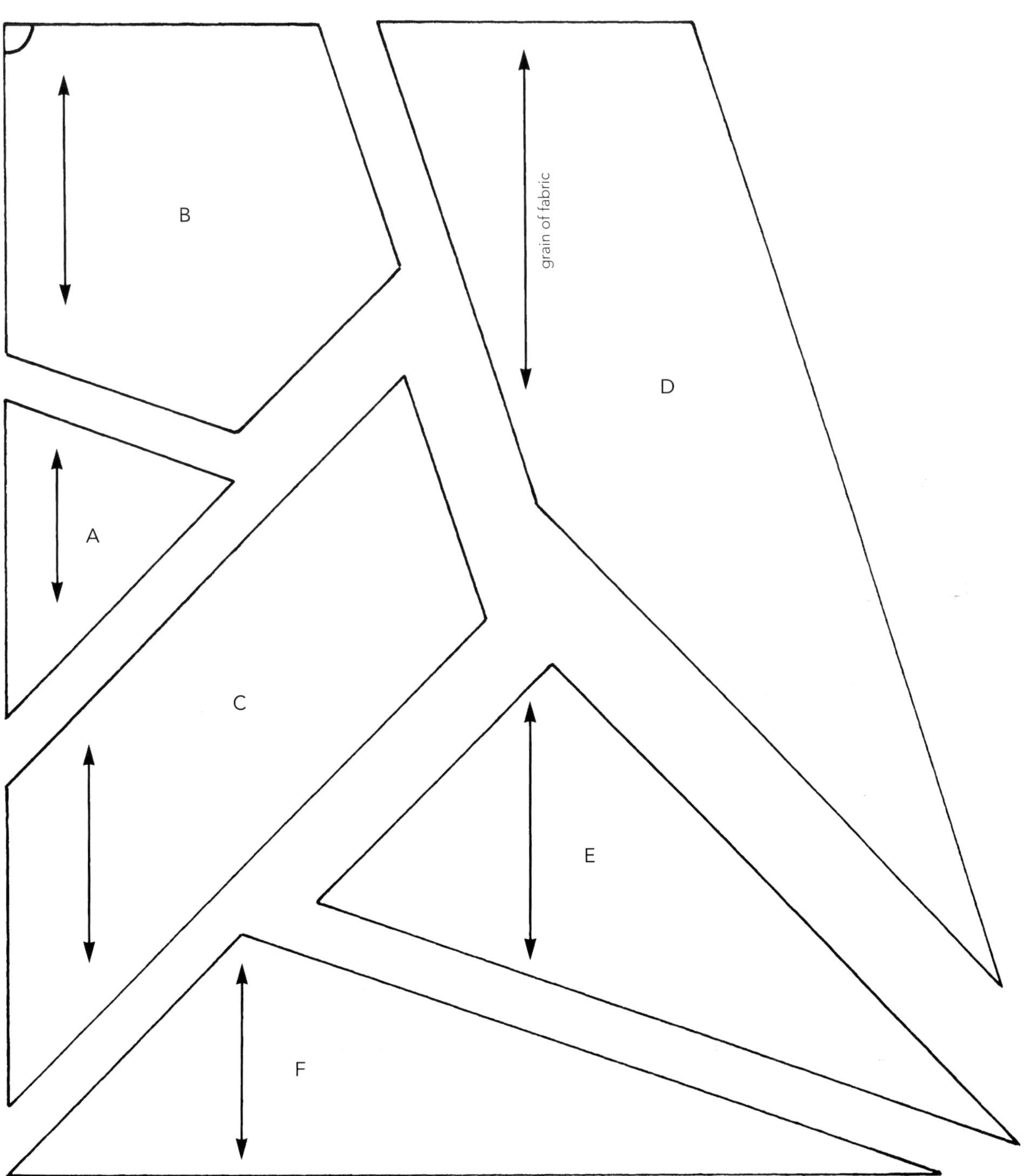

Machine Piecing

Quick Triangles

In the first *Sampler Quilt Book* I included a block that was based on sixteen squares, each of which was divided diagonally into two halves (see Fig 2 opposite). Traditionally these were constructed by drawing round a template, cutting out the shapes to include a ¼in (6mm) seam allowance and piecing them together by hand or machine, following the drawn sewing lines in the American piecing technique. There is a quicker and easier way of mass-producing these squares already pieced, using rotary cutting equipment and a sewing machine. You will still have to join the squares together and match corners accurately but the preliminary cutting and stitching is simplified.

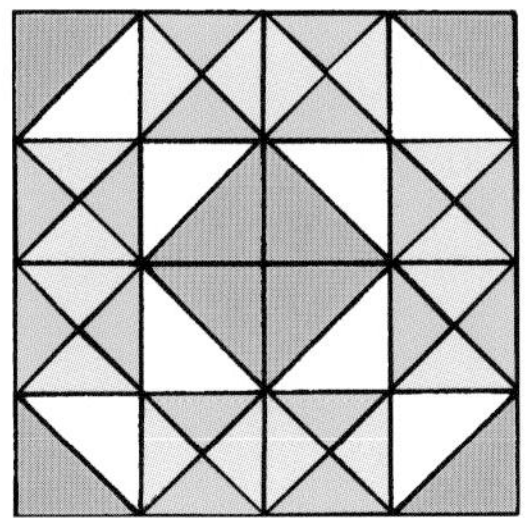

Fig 1

This block (Fig 1) combines eight squares that are divided into two triangles and eight squares divided into four triangles (Fig 3). The technique for making each set of squares is similar but different measurements must be used for each set.

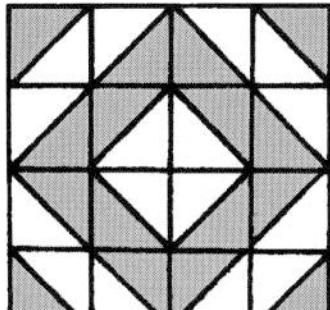

Fig 2

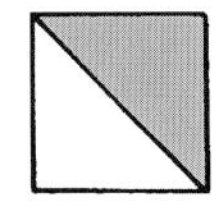

Fig 3

When making half-square triangles for a machined design that uses 3in (7.6cm) squares finished size, an extra ½in (1.3cm) must be added for the seam allowances on either side plus another ⅜in (1cm) to allow for the diagonal seam across the square, making ⅞in (2.2cm) in total. In other words, for a finished 3in (7.6cm) square the starting measurement must be 3⅞in (9.8cm) (Fig 4). The same ⅞in (2.2cm) is always added to any size finished square when using this technique to make half-square triangles.

When making quarter-square triangles there are extra seam allowances to be included in the calculations. In addition to the usual ½in (1.3cm) for the seam allowances on each side there are two diagonal seams across the square. All these seams mean that a total of 1¼in (3.2cm) needs to be added to the finished measurement of the square. So for a 3in (7.6cm) finished square, the starting measurement must be 4¼in (10.8cm) (Fig 5).

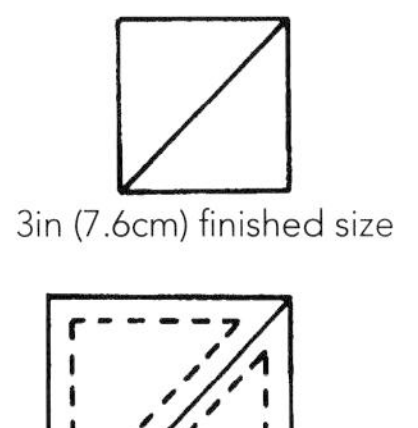

3in (7.6cm) finished size

3⅞in (9.8cm)

Fig 4

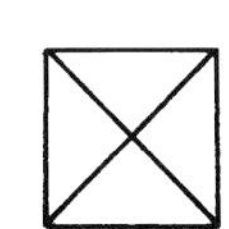

3in (7.6cm) finished size

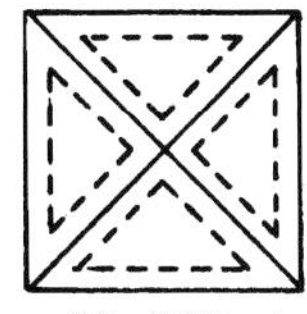

4¼in (10.8cm)

Fig 5

To construct quarter-square triangles using any size finished square, 1¼in (3.2cm) must always be added to the finished square measurement. These are not easy measurements to play with, but need to be used to produce an accurate set of squares.

Colour Choices

The design of triangles shown in Fig 1 uses four fabrics, two combined for the half-square triangles and two more for the quarter-square triangles. In my block I used two very similar cream fabrics with two similar blue fabrics, but you may like to introduce a wider range of shades. The half-square triangles make a large diamond in the centre of the block and also appear as corners, so the strongest of your fabrics may look best here teamed with a background fabric. Once the sixteen squares have been constructed it is possible to play with them and use an arrangement that is different from the one shown in Fig 1 if it suits your fabric better.

Construction

1 *Making the half-square triangles:* from each of the two chosen fabrics cut a piece measuring about 8½ x 8½in (21.6 x 21.6cm). Place them right sides together and press. This will help keep the two layers in place. It greatly helps the precision piecing of the fabrics if they are spray-starched before use, particularly the fabric for the quarter-square triangles. This keeps everything firm while stitching, especially the stretchy bias edges and corners.

2 Place the two layers of fabric on a cutting board. On the top fabric you are going to draw a grid of four squares – two rows of two – each square measuring 3⅞in (9.8cm) (Fig 6). To do this accurately it is better to use the measurements on the ruler rather than those on the cutting board. Find the line or marks on the ruler that are 3⅞in (9.8cm) from one edge. You may find it easier to mark this distance by sticking a small piece of tape at each end of the ruler on the 3⅞in (9.8cm) line. Place the ruler vertically about ¼in (6mm) from the left-hand edge of the fabrics (Fig 7a).

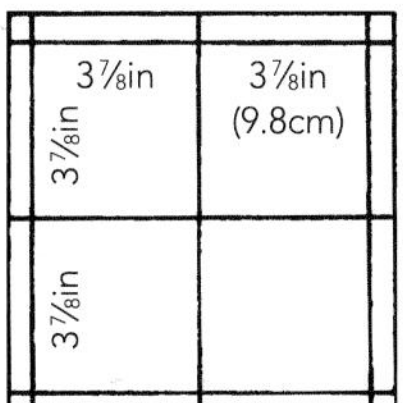

Fig 6

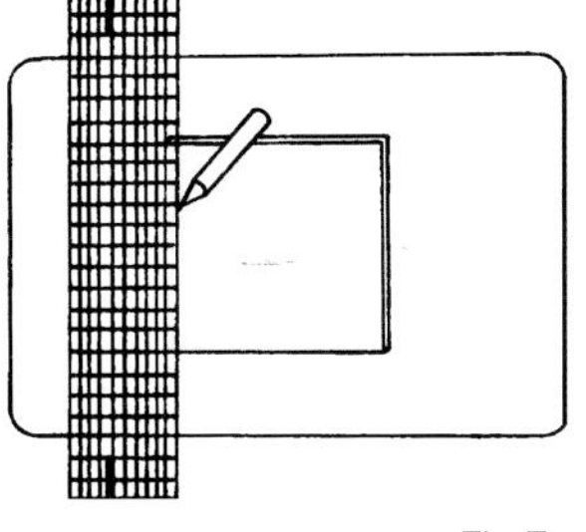

Fig 7a

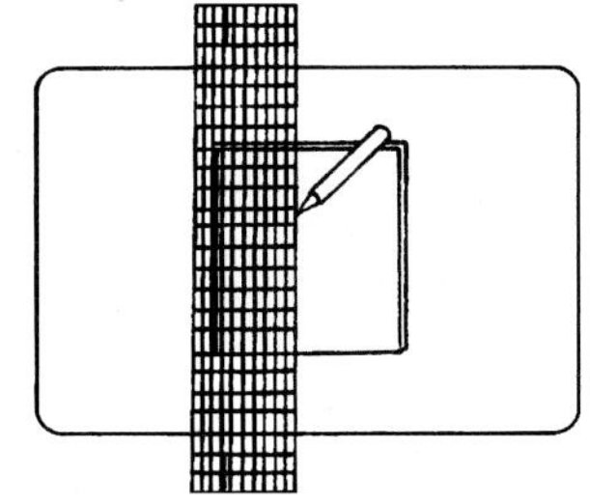

Fig 7b

Using a marking pencil, draw a line from top to bottom on the fabric along the ruler's edge. Move the ruler across the fabric to the right until the marked 3⅞in (9.8cm) line is exactly on top of the drawn line (Fig 7b). Draw a line along the ruler's edge. Once again move the ruler across to the right until the new drawn line lies exactly under the 3⅞in (9.8cm) line on the ruler. Draw a line along the ruler's edge. Left-handed quilters should begin marking from the right-hand side and move the ruler across the fabric to the left.

3 Turn the ruler horizontally and draw a line on the fabric about ¼in (6mm) from the bottom edges (Fig 8a). As before, move the ruler upwards over the fabric until the 3⅞in (9.8cm) line is exactly on top of the drawn line (Fig 8b). Draw a line along the ruler's edge. Repeat this once more to complete the grid of two rows of two squares each.

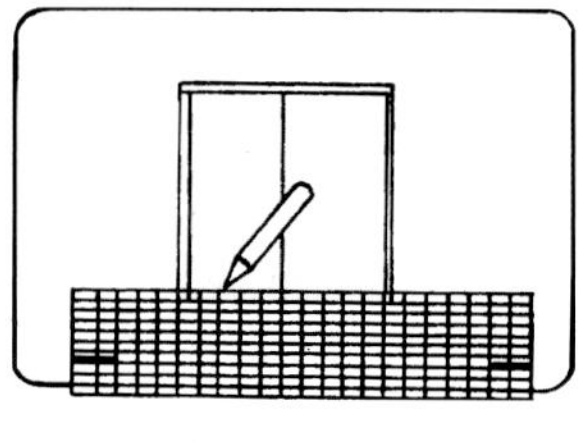

Fig 8a

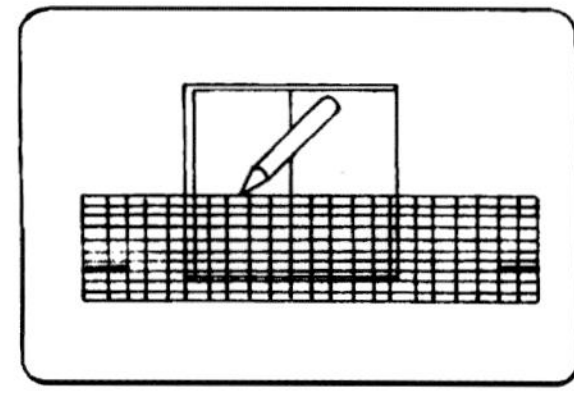

Fig 8b

4 Now draw diagonal lines across each square in one direction only, as shown in Fig 9.

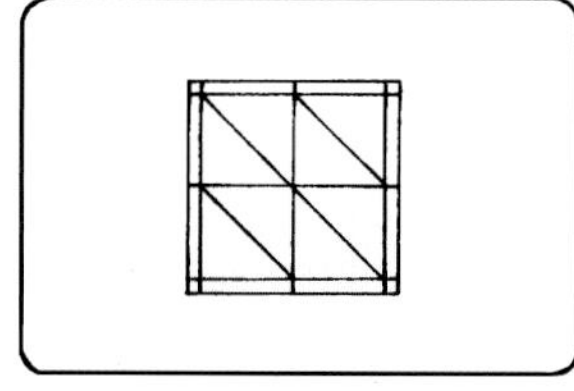

Fig 9

5 Pin the two fabrics together with four to six pins to hold the layers securely while stitching.

6 Machine a line of stitching on *either side* of the drawn diagonal lines at exactly ¼in (6mm) using a slightly smaller stitch than usual (Fig 10). If you have a strip of masking tape stuck to your machine as a stitching guide you will not be able to see it through the layers of fabric, so another way of stitching a ¼in (6mm) seam accurately must be found – try one of the following.

a Use a special ¼in (6mm) foot on the machine.

b If your machine has the facility, move the needle until the distance between it and the side of your usual machine foot is exactly ¼in (6mm).

c Draw in a stitching line ¼in (6mm) away from the diagonal line on both sides, using a different colour marking pencil to avoid confusion.

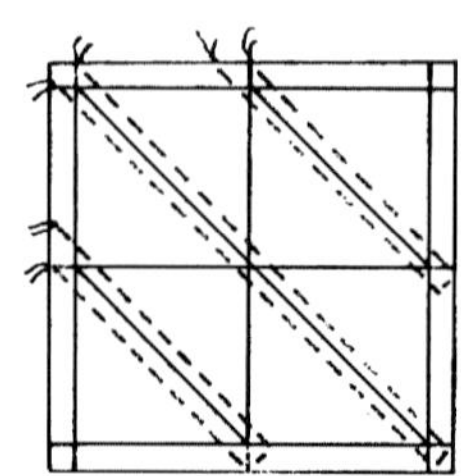

Fig 10

7 Once the pairs of lines have been stitched, take the fabrics from the machine and place them on the cutting board. Remove the pins and using a ruler and cutter, cut along the drawn vertical lines. Without moving the fabric, cut along the drawn horizontal lines. Finally, cut along the drawn diagonal lines (Fig 11). You will find that a miracle has happened and that when you pick up each triangle of fabric it has been stitched to another and you have a pieced square made of two triangles of two different fabrics. Some of the triangles will have a line of stitches across one corner (Fig 12). Loosen these gently by pulling the fabrics apart – they will easily come undone and the threads can be removed.

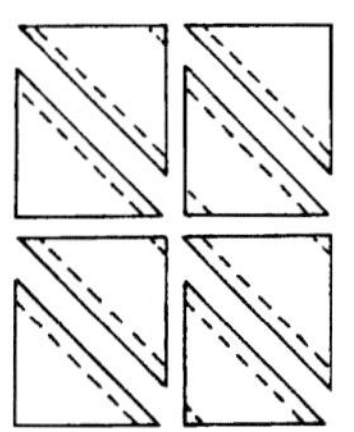

Fig 11

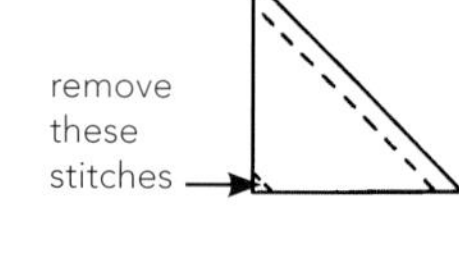

Fig 12

8 Now press each square from the front with the seams pressed towards the darker colour fabric.

9 *Making the quarter-square triangles:* from each of the two chosen fabrics cut a piece measuring 9 x 9in (22.8 x 22.8cm). Place them right sides together and press.

10 Place the two layers of fabric on a cutting board and draw a grid of four squares as before, but this time each square must be 4¼ x 4¼in (10.8 x 10.8cm). You may not need to mark your ruler with tape as it is easier to find the 4¼in (10.8cm) line than it was the 3⅞in (9.8cm) line (Fig 13).

4¼in
4¼in
(10.8cm)
4¼in
4¼in

Fig 13

"I was asked to teach a group of beginners to quilt at my local quilt shop. I chose Lynne's book because of the wonderful patterns, variety of techniques and clear instructions. Seven of us completed our quilts in fourteen weeks and went on to make bigger quilts and cushions to match. For my quilt, I fell in love with the border fabric and chose the others to match." **Juliet Simpson**

11 Draw diagonal lines across each square in *both* directions, as shown in Fig 14.

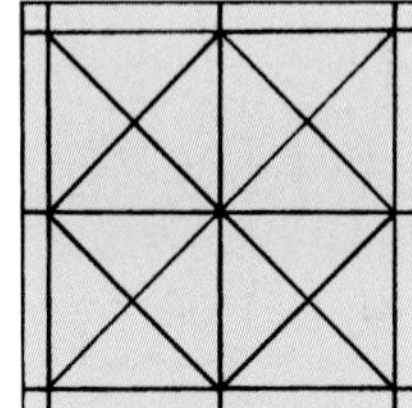

Fig 14

12 Pin the layers together with four to six pins and machine a line of stitching on either side of one set of diagonal lines at a distance of ¼in (6mm) from the line. Leave the other set of diagonal lines unstitched (Fig 15).

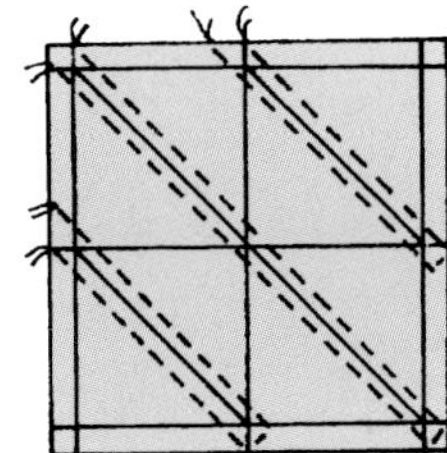

Fig 15

13 Place the fabrics on the cutting board and remove the pins. Using a rotary ruler and cutter, cut along all the drawn vertical lines. Without moving the fabric, cut along the drawn horizontal lines. Take each square and first cut along the *unstitched* drawn diagonal lines (Fig 16). Then cut the drawn lines between the stitched lines (Fig 17).

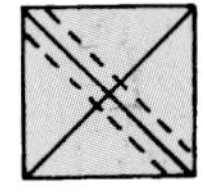

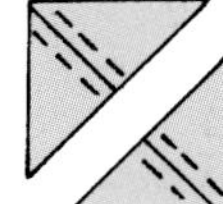

Fig 16

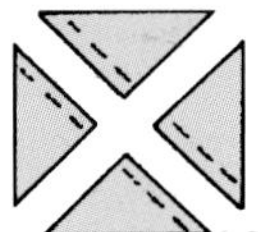

Fig 17

14 Now open out each shape, easing apart any stitched corners. Press the seams towards the darker fabric.

15 The pieced triangles will be in two different arrangements (Fig 18). Separate them into two piles, one for each arrangement. Using one pile only, match the triangular shapes into pairs to make squares. Place them right sides facing and pin the centre matching seams carefully. I pin diagonally so that the seam allowances stay flat while stitching (Fig 19). It is better not to pin the sharp corners together, as these can stretch and get munched up by the machine. The seam you are going to stitch is a stretchy bias diagonal, so handle the fabrics as little as possible. If you have spray-starched your fabric it will be firmer and easier to handle. Don't starch now, as the fabrics will distort and even shrink as you iron them dry. Just remember to try it next time round. Match and pin the second set of triangular shapes to make squares in the same way.

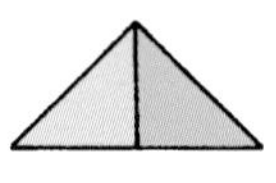

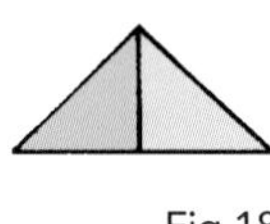

Fig 18

Fig 19

16 Stitch the pairs together, guiding them through the machine with the point of a stitch-ripper or small pair of scissors. Press the seams to one side, pressing from the front of the work.

17 Arrange the sixteen pieced squares in the design shown in Fig 1 on page 135 or try another arrangement if you prefer it. If all the squares do not fit together perfectly, remember that you can swap the squares around as there are eight identical pieces in each set to play with.

18 Sew together the top four squares to make a row. There are several places where two triangles meet in a point. Where this occurs, check that once they are joined the two triangles meet in an arrowhead ¼in (6mm) from the top edges of the fabric (Fig 20). From the front, press all seams on row one in the same direction.

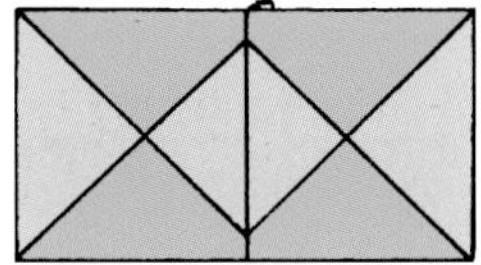

Fig 20

19 Join together the four squares in row two. From the front press the seams in the opposite direction to row one. Join rows one and two, matching seams carefully, especially where two arrowheads meet. Position the tips of the arrowheads exactly on top of each other, checking by peeling the top fabrics back with the pin. When the arrowheads meet, hold them in position firmly and pin. I use long, extra-fine pins so that I can machine stitch over them if necessary. Stitch the seam. Join row three and add it to row two in the same way. Finally, add row four to complete the block. Press the block from the front.

20 Add the inner framing strips (see page 236) and trim the block to an exact 14in (35.6cm) square, then add the sashing strips. See page 236 for adding framing strips and sashing.

Hand Piecing

Celtic Knot

This particular area of patchwork emerged in the early 1980s with the work of Philomena Durcan, a quilter originally from County Sligo in Ireland who was then living in California. She adapted the principle of stained glass patchwork to the Celtic designs of her homeland, using bias strips as the traditional Celtic strapping.

Celtic designs are based on complex interwoven bands, each winding over and under each other, seemingly without end. The medallion design in the Celtic Knot block in this sampler quilt shows all these characteristics. Making the block requires a ¼in (6mm) bias bar, a tool useful for producing the narrow strips needed for Celtic work.

Colour Choices

The Celtic Knot is a central design placed on a background (Fig 1). One fabric is used for the base of the medallion, with the option of a second used in the centre space (not shown in Fig 1). All the lines of the Celtic Knot strapping are made from bias strips which are pinned and stitched on to the medallion fabric. Don't be afraid to use patterned or even striped fabric for the bias strips, as it adds greatly to the richness of the design. If you are doubtful, cut one bias strip of the proposed fabric and lay it across the medallion fabric to get an idea of how they look together.

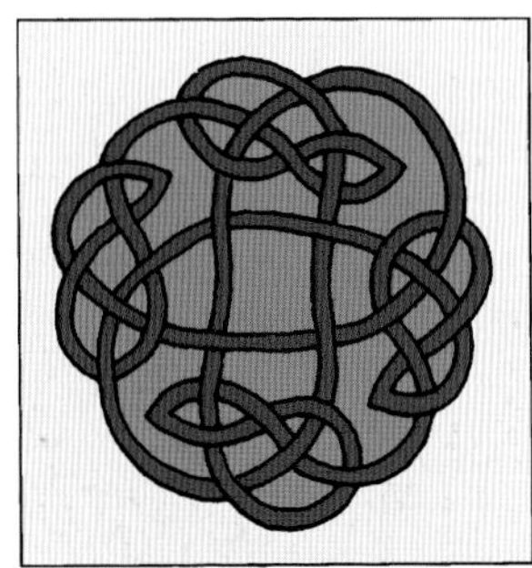

Fig 1

Construction

1 The design drawn in Fig 2 on page 145 is half the Celtic Knot. Trace it on to a large piece of tracing paper, including the centre dotted line. Rotate the tracing paper 180° and complete the knot by tracing the other part of the design, matching the centre dotted lines.

2 From the medallion fabric cut a square 11 x 11in (27.9 x 27.9cm). The knot design must be transferred to the *front* of this square of fabric. Place the fabric over the traced design, matching the grainline arrows on the drawing with the straight grain of the fabric (the direction of the woven threads). Trace it on to the fabric with a sharp marking pencil – use a light box if necessary or dressmaker's carbon paper. Do *not* trace the dotted centre line on to the fabric. Simplify the double lines of the design by drawing only one line midway between the two parallel lines. The over-and-under arrangement can be shown by leaving a gap in the drawn line when it should lie *underneath* a crossing line (Fig 3). By tracing just a central line on to the fabric you avoid the possibility of any drawn lines showing beyond the bias strapping when it is pinned in place.

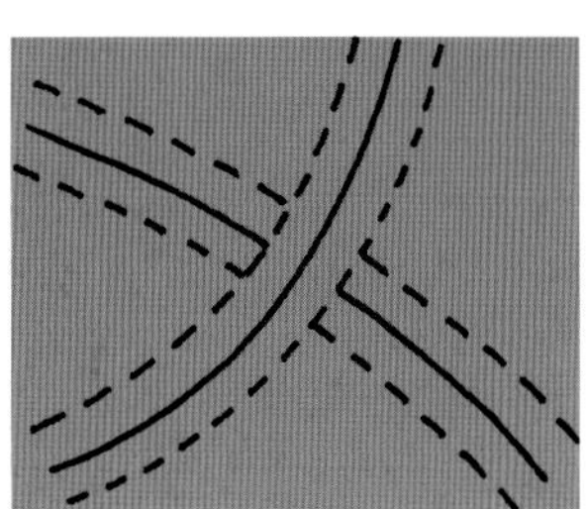

Fig 3

3 Cut around the outer drawn line of the knot design so that the piece of fabric is the same circular shape as the design (Fig 4). Place the cut fabric on top of the traced design with all the drawn lines matching. Fold the fabric back along the centre dotted line and finger press it.

Fig 4

4 Cut a square of fabric 13 x 13in (33 x 33cm) for the background. Fold in half vertically and press lightly. Use the fold as a guide for positioning the cut medallion fabric centrally on it – the folded line on the medallion fabric should be placed on the fold in the background fabric. Pin the trimmed design on to the background in several places, then tack (baste) around the edge using ¼in (6mm) long stitches and keeping them about ½in (1.3cm) from the edge of the design so that the appliqué is held firmly in place (Fig 5).

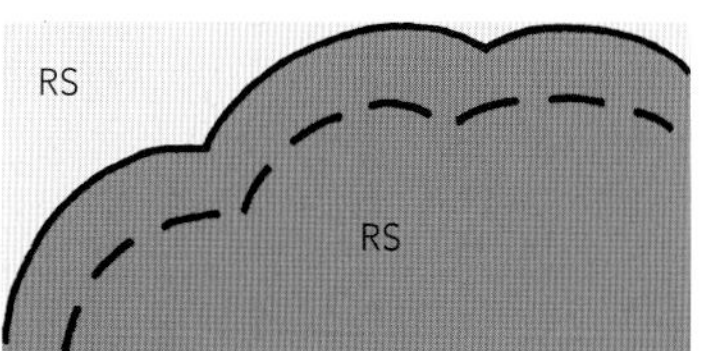

Fig 5

5 If an extra fabric is to be used for the centre area, go back to the original traced design and from it trace just the centre shape on to paper, drawing a single line midway between the two parallel lines of the design as before (Fig 6). Cut this shape out and pin it on to the right side of the fabric chosen for the centre area, matching the grain arrow of the tracing with the straight grain of the fabric. Cut around the shape exactly – no extra seam allowance is needed.

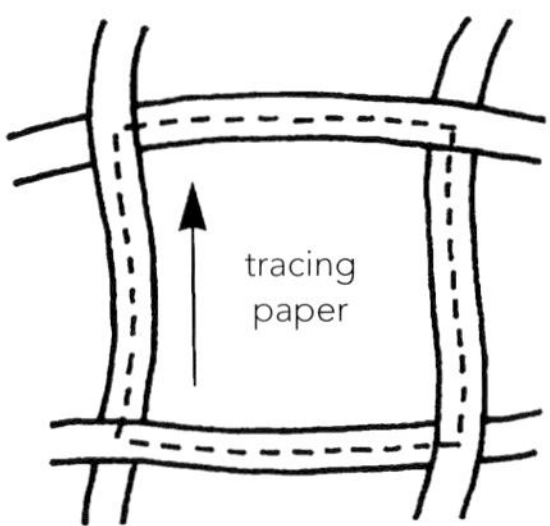

Fig 6

Pin the piece in position in the centre of the design, matching the drawn lines on the tacked fabric with the cut edges of this extra piece. Tack in place (Fig 7).

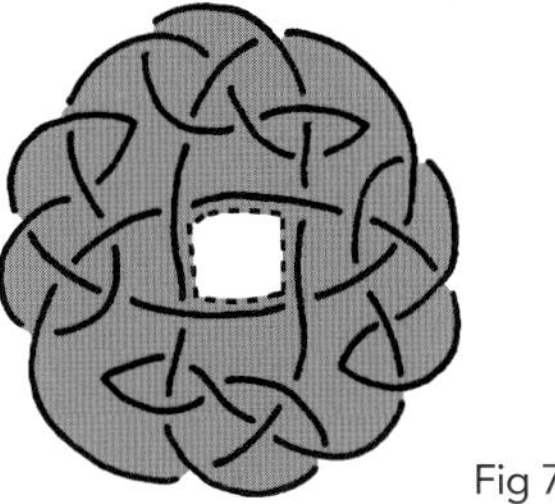

Fig 7

Cutting the strips and making bias tubes: the strips for the Celtic Knot strapping must be cut on the bias of the fabric, i.e., diagonally across the weave. This is because bias-cut strips are very stretchy and can curve around the lines of the design without puckering. For this design 1in (2.5cm) wide bias strips are used. Although about 140in (355cm) of strips are needed for the design they can all be cut from a 14in (35.6cm) square of fabric, as they do not have to be in a continuous length.

6 To cut the strips, place a single layer of fabric across one of the 45° lines on a cutting board, with the grain or weave of the fabric matching the grid on the board. The fabric does not have to be trimmed to an exact 14in (35.6cm) square: an odd rectangular piece will do, as long as its area is at least as much as a 14in (35.6cm) square. Cut along the 45° line with a rotary cutter and ruler (Fig 8). Turn the fabric so that the cut edge is on the left and move the ruler over it until the cut edge lines up with the 1in (2.5cm) marking on the ruler. Cut along the right side of the ruler (Fig 9). Left-handers should cut their strips from the right, not the left. Repeat this across the fabric, cutting 1in (2.5cm) wide strips each time, and also cutting more strips from the small triangle of fabric left after the initial diagonal cut.

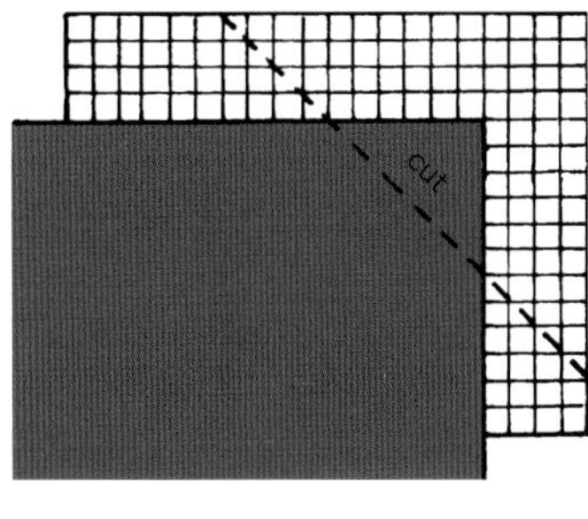

Fig 8

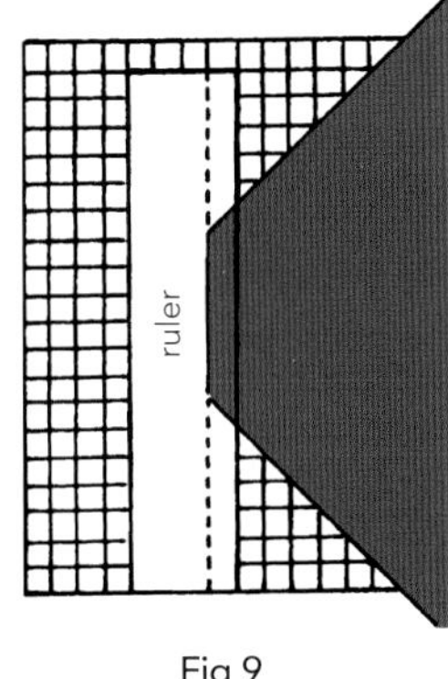

Fig 9

7 To process the bias strips into tubes a bias bar with a width of ¼in (6mm) is needed. With the right side of the fabric facing *outwards*, fold a 1in (2.5cm) wide bias strip of fabric in half lengthways. Using a smaller stitch than usual, machine a ¼in (6mm) seam down the length of the strip to make a tube. The stitched tube will not be pulled inside out – that is why the fabric is folded with the right side on the outside. Make a short sample length of tubing first and slide the bias bar into it. It needs to fit really snugly without any slack (Fig 10a). Once you are happy with the width of the tube, stitch all the bias strips in the same way. Trim the seams to a scant ⅛in (3mm) (Fig 10b). Slide the bar into a tube, twisting the fabric so that both seam and seam allowance lie across one flat side of the bar and cannot be seen from the other side (Fig 10c). Press firmly with an iron and continue to press as you slide the tube off the bar. A steam iron gives a good flat finish to the bias tubes. Press all the fabric tubes in this way. You do not need a continuous length of bias tubing for the design. The raw edges at the end of a tube are hidden under an overlying tube as it passes over it to make the woven design.

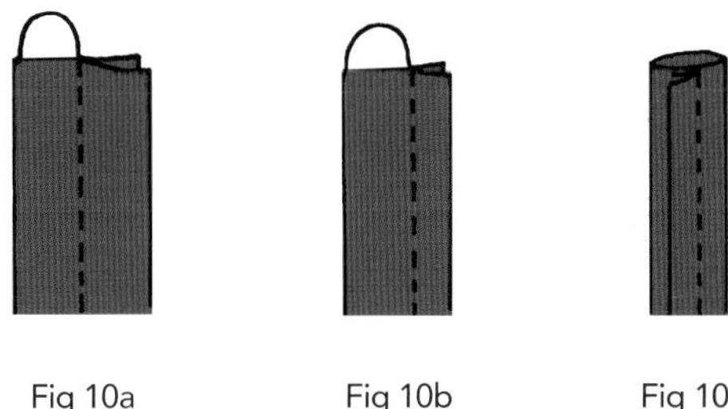

Fig 10a Fig 10b Fig 10c

8 Take a length of pressed bias tubing and trim one end to neaten it. Starting anywhere in the central area of the design, pin the trimmed end of pressed bias tubing at a junction of drawn lines where it will later be concealed beneath an overlying tube. The drawn guideline should lie midway beneath the tube. If an extra fabric has been tacked in place at the centre of the design, its raw edge should also be midway under the bias tubing (Fig 11).

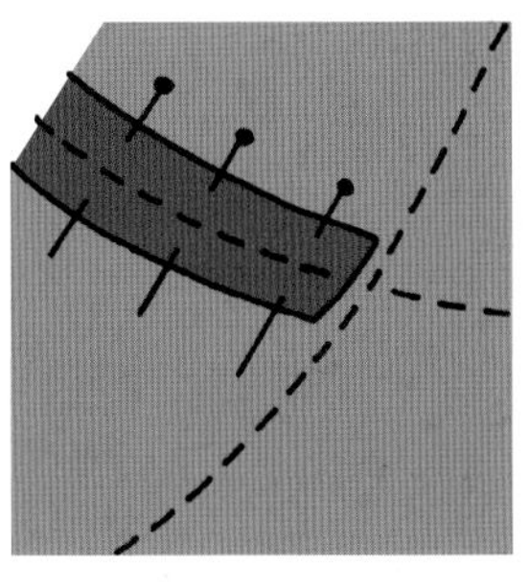

Fig 11

All the lines of this Celtic Knot design are curved, some more than others, so the bias tubing has to be carefully pinned and stitched to follow these curves. Pin and stitch the shorter inside edge of the tubing first. The longer outside edge can then be stretched slightly when sewing to fit the curve (Fig 12). If you fix the longer edge first, the shorter edge will finish up with little pleats in it. Finish each piece of tubing by trimming it so that it ends exactly at a junction where it will be hidden beneath an overlying tube. All starting and ending points are made at these underlying junctions (Fig 13).

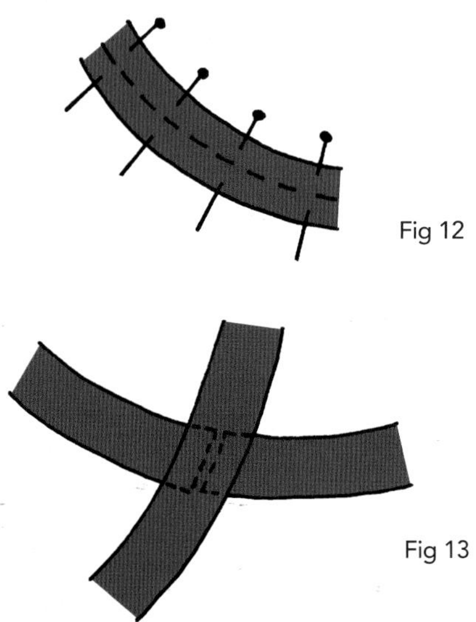

Fig 12

Fig 13

9 *Dealing with the 'overs' and 'unders'*: the Celtic Knot design could be made with one continuous length of pressed tubing weaving over and under itself, but as long as each tube finishes hidden under an underlying tube, the effect is the same. Just pin and stitch each pressed tube as far as it lasts on the design, making sure it finishes hidden as in Fig 13. At a junction of lines where the tubing passes over another, a gap of ¼–½in (6–12mm) must be left in the stitching so that the 'under' tube can be pulled through at a later stage. Once this is in place the gap can then be stitched (Fig 14).

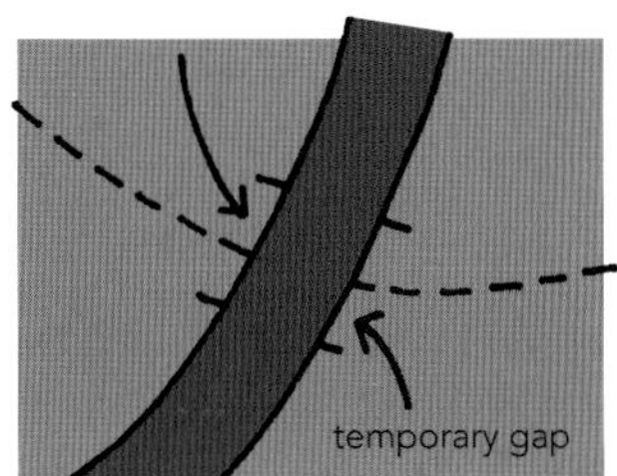

Fig 14

It is all too easy to forget to leave the gaps at each 'over' junction, so I mark them when pinning the tubing in place by pinning a spare length of tubing about 1in (2.5cm) long under the tube in the place to be left unstitched to remind me (Fig 15). Once the danger zone has been passed this piece can then be removed and used in the same way at the next 'over' junction. Do not pin the entire design, only as far as your piece of tubing will cover, finishing with the trimmed end at an 'under' junction.

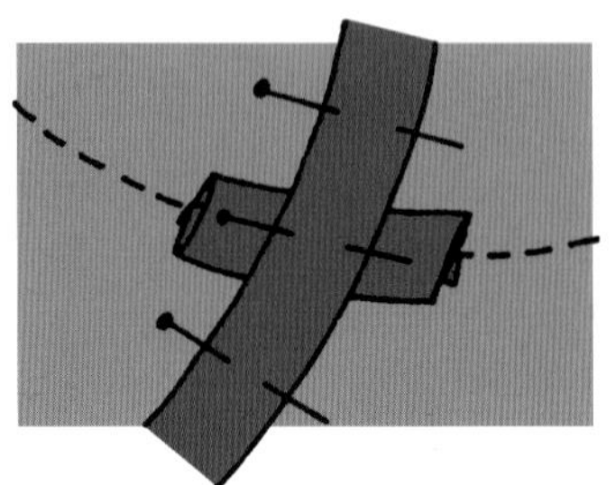

Fig 15

10 Matching the thread to the tube fabric, not the background, sew both sides of the tube in turn to the background with small, even slip stitches, stitching the shorter inner edge first (Fig 16). When you reach a junction where the bias tubing needs to go *under* a section that has already been stitched in place, push the end of the tubing through the gap, using the points of a small pair of scissors to ease it under. Pull the tubing through and use the scissors to smooth the underneath layer flat. Stitch the gap in the top layer of tubing before continuing to pin and stitch the loose piece of tubing.

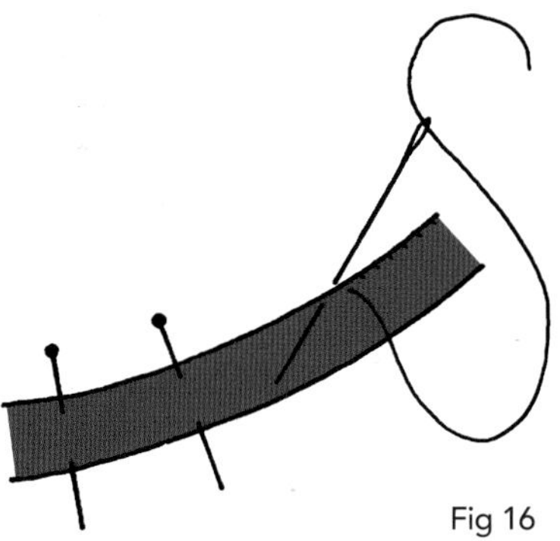

Fig 16

Honor Wood used simple hand quilting close to the bias edging to enhance the Celtic design of the block, while more complex hand quilted feather shapes are used in the surrounding background area.

"Lynne's sampler books and my patchwork teacher Stephanie Pettengell inspired me to realize a long-held ambition: to make and own a quilt. Having not really sewn anything since leaving school in the mid 1960s this was a journey of much learning, pleasure and achievement." **Honor Woods**

This design has four nasty turning points where the bias tubing has to be swung round sharply to make a point (Fig 17). To make the mitred corner, stitch along the pinned inner curve until about ¼in (6mm) from the corner. Position the tube at the far point where it will turn, about ⅛in (3mm) beyond the drawn corner, and catch the edge of the bias tubing with a large pin pushed down into the background fabric (Fig 18). Angle the pin towards you and bring it up through the fabric as shown in Fig 19.

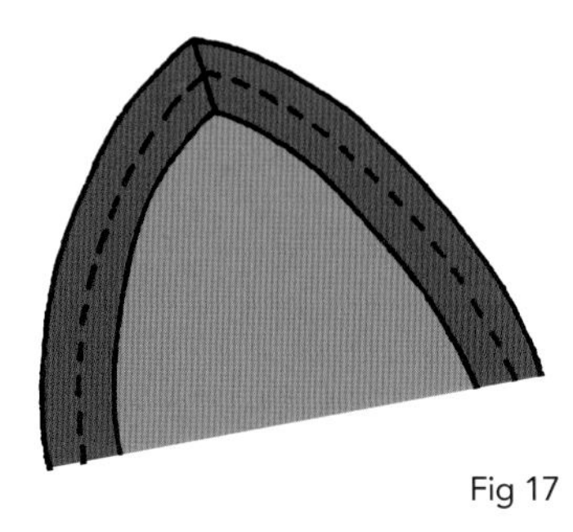

Fig 17

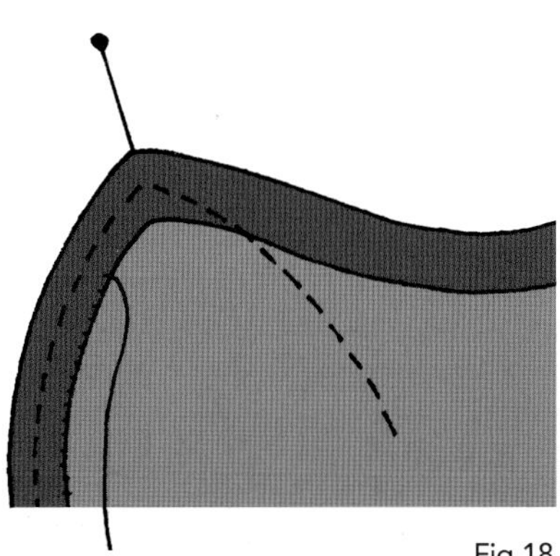

Fig 18

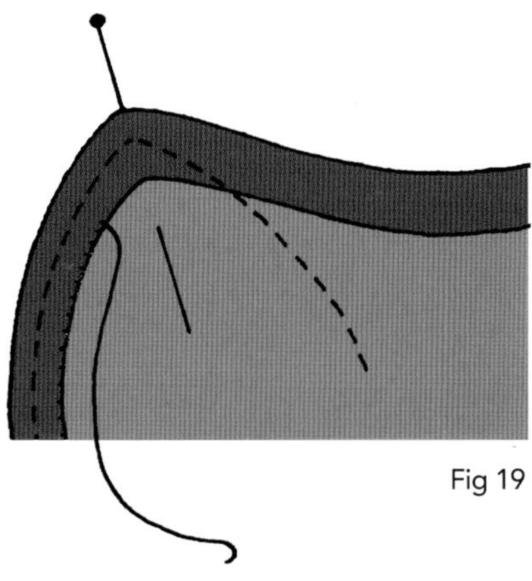

Fig 19

Now pull the tubing sharply into position over the drawn guideline. Use a small pair of scissors to tuck the extra fabric behind the main tubing to form a mitre while holding the tubing firmly in position (Fig 20). When the mitre looks good hold it in position with your thumb. Withdraw the pin slightly and re-pin its point through the mitre to fix it while you sew (Fig 21). Do not stitch the mitre itself, just the edges of the tubing as usual. Continue to pin and stitch the design.

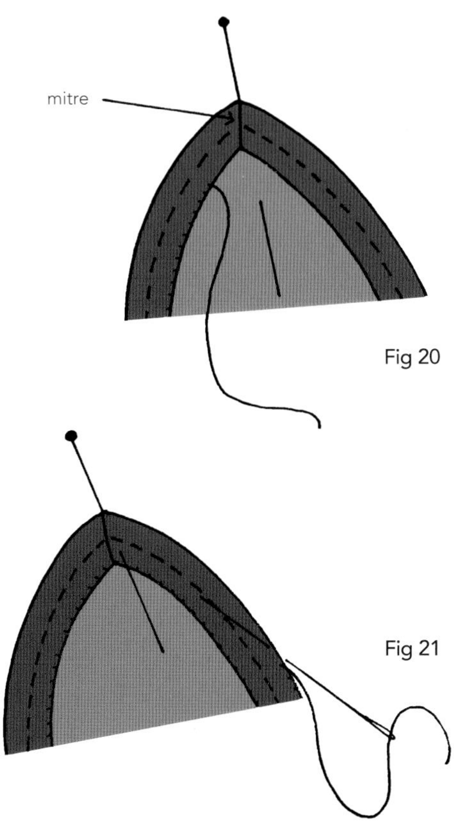

Fig 20

Fig 21

11 Once all the pressed tubing has been stitched into place, the design is complete and the tacking can be removed. The thickness of the block can be reduced by cutting away the background fabric from behind the Celtic Knot. Cut away behind the open areas of the design between the bias tubing. Do not attempt to cut away behind the tubing itself as it is just too narrow to do safely. If you feel too nervous to try any of this, don't worry as it's not compulsory. However, it does make the whole piece easier to quilt, so the choice is yours. To cut the backing away, turn the block to the back and with your fingers pull the background away from the appliqué and make a small cut in the background fabric. Now carefully cut away the backing up to ¼in (6mm) from the stitching lines. Do this in all the open areas of the design.

12 Trim the finished block to an exact 13in (33cm) square, or to whatever size you feel suits your design. Add the inner framing strips and trim the block to exactly 14in (35.6cm) square, then add the sashing strips. See page 236 for adding framing strips and sashing.

Fig 2 – Actual size template

Trace the design, then rotate it 180°
and draw the other half of the design,
matching the centre dotted lines

Machine Piecing

Delectable Mountains

This lovely design is combined with large squares to make the block for the sampler quilt (see Fig 1, opposite). It also makes a striking border for a quilt. I first saw this clever, quick method of making the design in a magazine where it had been devised by Sheila Scawen, a very experienced and talented quilter and teacher. It combines strip patchwork with the quick machined triangles shown in the block on page 134. The Delectable Mountain arrangement of strips does not make a square but a rectangle. The maths involved in devising different sizes for the block is surprisingly tricky because of all the seam allowances to be taken into consideration, so at the end of the instructions for the block

on page 150 I have given some alternative sizings and measurements for future reference for borders.

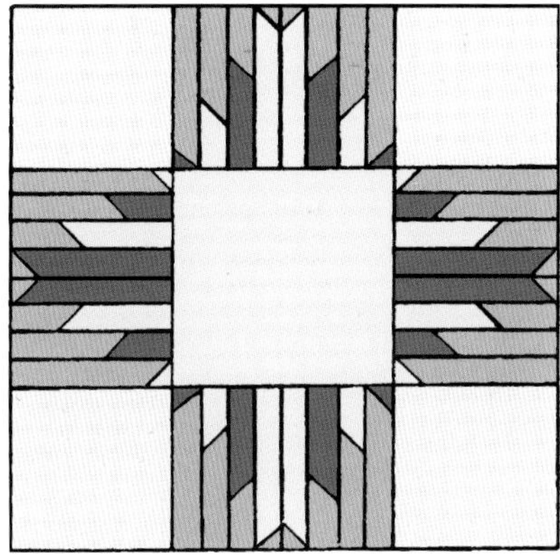
Fig 1

Colour Choices

The saw-toothed edged Delectable Mountains can be made from one fabric plus a background, or from two fabrics combined (Figs 2a and 2b). I used two fabrics for the Delectable Mountains and took one of them for the centre square. You may find it helpful to make the four mountain pieces before deciding on what looks best in the centre and the four corners of the block. The large centre square looks less empty if a patterned fabric is used, or if it is broken up with a quilting design later. Alison Still added an appliqued square on point to give the centre of the block more impact.

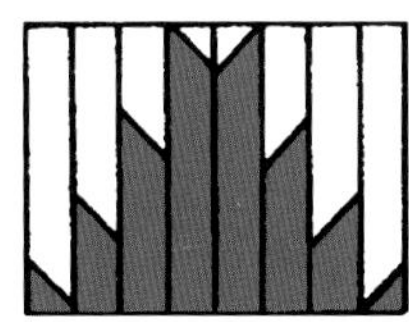
Fig 2a

Fig 2b

Construction

For the design in Fig 2a: if one fabric plus a background fabric are to be used for the design you need to cut four squares of each of the two fabrics, each measuring 4⅞ x 4⅞in (12.4 x 12.4cm).

For the design in Fig 2b: if two fabrics plus a background fabric are to be used for the design you need to cut four squares of the background fabric and two squares of each of the two Delectable Mountain fabrics, each measuring 4⅞ x 4⅞in (12.4 x 12.4cm).

1 Arrange the squares in pairs – one background fabric paired with a mountain fabric. Place the pairs right sides together *exactly* on top of each other. Draw a diagonal line on the top fabric as in Fig 3.

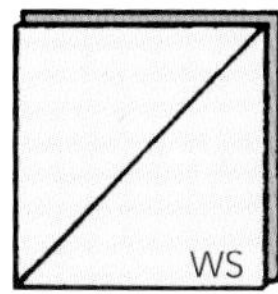

Fig 3

2 Pin the squares together and machine a line of small stitches on *either side* of the drawn line exactly ¼in (6mm) away from the line (Fig 4). This technique was also used to construct the quick machined triangles in the block on page 134.

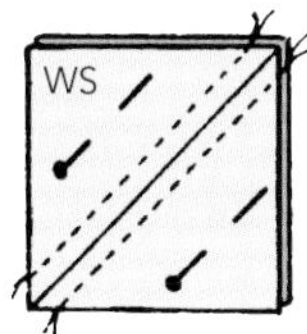

Fig 4

3 Once all four pairs have been stitched, place on the cutting board and using a rotary cutter and ruler cut along the drawn lines so that the squares fall into two halves. Open each half out: each should now form a square divided diagonally into two fabrics (Fig 5). Press each of the eight squares from the front, four with the seam allowances pressed towards the mountain fabric and the other four towards the background fabric.

If you've used *two* fabrics for the mountains, separate the squares into matching pairs of the same combination of fabrics and then press the seams of each pair from the front, with one pressed towards the mountain fabric and the other towards the background fabric.

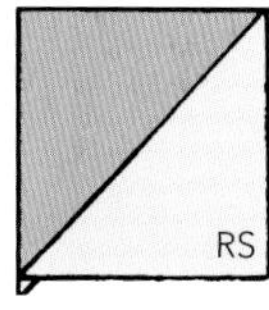

Fig 5

4 Measure each pressed square carefully – it is important they all now measure the same 4½ x 4½in (11.4 x 11.4cm). If a square is too small, press with a steam iron and stretch the square out to get it to the right measurement. If this is not successful, fold the square back into a triangle and re-stitch the seam until the correct sizing is achieved. Squares that are too large can be trimmed down to size, making sure that the diagonal seam still runs from corner to corner of the square.

5 Group the pressed squares in matching pairs (each pair should be made up of the same two fabrics) and place them right sides together, matching the seams and the fabrics. Hopefully the seams of one of the squares will be pressed in the opposite direction to the seams of the other square (Fig 6).

Place the squares on a cutting board, arranging each pair as in Fig 6 with the seams running diagonally from top right corner to bottom left and the mountain fabric in the bottom right-hand half of each square. Check that each pair of squares is lying exactly one on top of the other. Do not pin them as the pins get in the way of the rotary cutter.

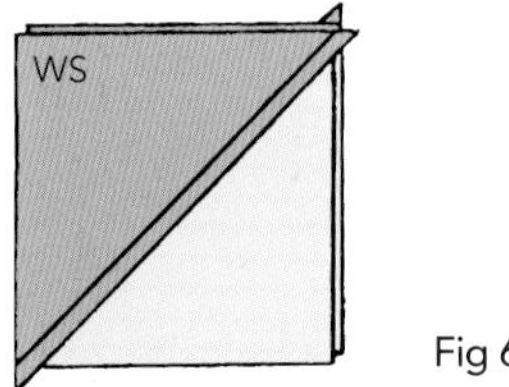

Fig 6

6 Using a rotary cutter and ruler, cut one pair of matched squares into four equal vertical strips, cutting through both layers at once. Each strip should measure 1⅛in (2.8cm) in width (Fig 7).

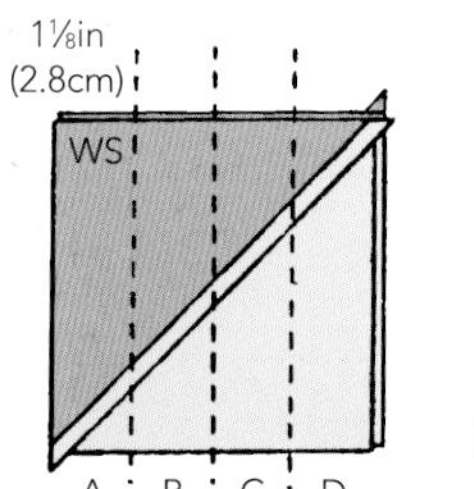

Fig 7

7 Pick up the two layered strips marked D in Fig 7, open them out and place them right side *up* together in the arrangement shown in Fig 8. Pick up the pair of strips marked C in Fig 7. Place the top strip right side *up* to the *left* of strips D. Place the other strip right side *up* to the *right* of strips D (Fig 9). Place strips B and then strips A on either side of strips D and C in the same way, following the arrangement in Fig 10.

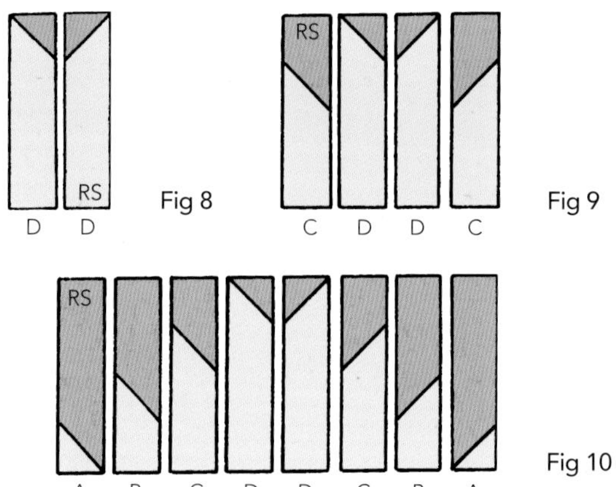

Fig 8

Fig 9

Fig 10

If you've used *two* fabrics for the mountains, repeat the cutting process with a set of squares that use the second mountain fabric. Arrange these strips in the same arrangement as Fig 10 alongside the first set. Exchange the C strips from the first set with the C strips in the second set. Repeat this with the A strips (Fig 11). Stitch together these sets of eight strips before going on to cut the remaining pairs of squares, unless you have a lot of space and a very organized mind.

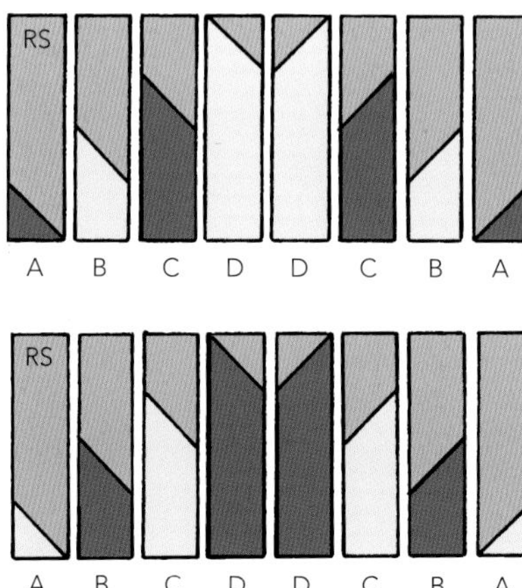

Fig 11

If you've used just one fabric for the mountains, cut and stitch the strips one set at a time for the same reason: if you get the sets mixed up it can take a lot of time and nervous energy to sort them all out again.

8 Stitch together the eight strips, making sure the top and bottom edges match exactly as in Fig 12. Press the centre seam open, as this helps the balanced look of the design. Press the remaining seams away from the centre as in Fig 12.

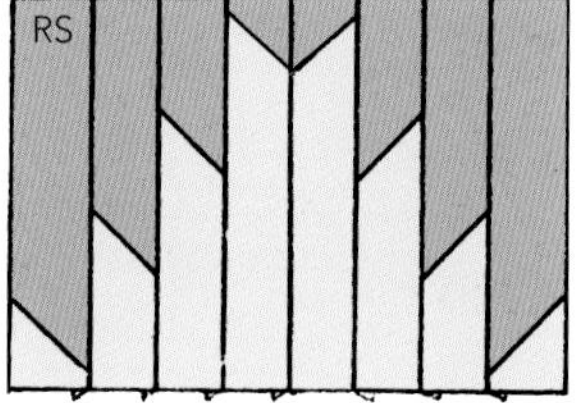

Fig 12

9 Measure the four stitched sets of strips. They should measure 4½ x 5½in (11.4 x 14cm). Don't worry if your measurements do not match these, as long as they are *no larger* than this or the finished block will be too big for the quilt. What is important is that all of the rectangles measure the same as each other. Check the seams and adjust any that are obviously inaccurate. Use a steam iron to help get all four rectangles to the same size. Try to resist the temptation to trim bits off the strips as this can spoil the balanced look of the block.

"For this sampler quilt I used my favourite purple and mauve fabrics and pieced and quilted by hand and machine. I began in 2008, intending to challenge myself with blocks and techniques I had not previously attempted. When I heard of the new book and the possibility of being included in it I became very focussed and all normal life was put on hold! The quilt was completed with a week to spare." **Alison Still**

10 Arrange your fabrics with the completed rectangles of Mountains to finalize your choice for the centre square and corners. If the rectangles measure 4½ x 5½in (11.4 x 14cm) cut a square for the centre measuring 5½ x 5½in (14 x 14cm) and four squares for the corners measuring 4½ x 4½in (11.4 x 11.4cm). If your rectangles do not have these measurements, don't worry – if the centre and corner squares are cut to match your rectangles, the block will fit together nicely. Cut the centre square to match the longer side and the corner squares to match the shorter side of your rectangles (Fig 13).

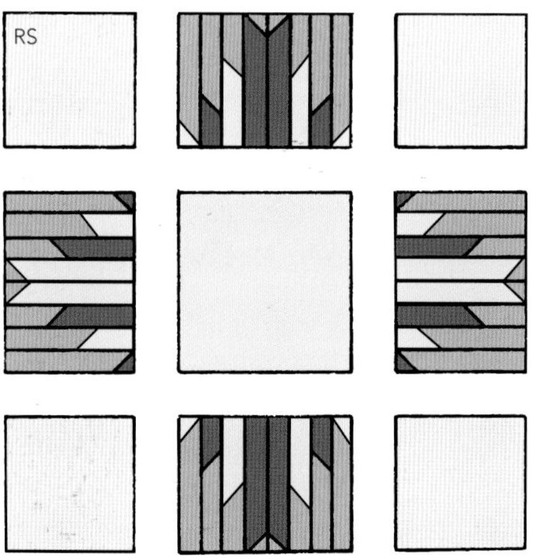

Fig 13

11 Pin and stitch the shapes together in rows (Fig 14). From the front, press the seams towards the squares, away from the pieced rectangles.

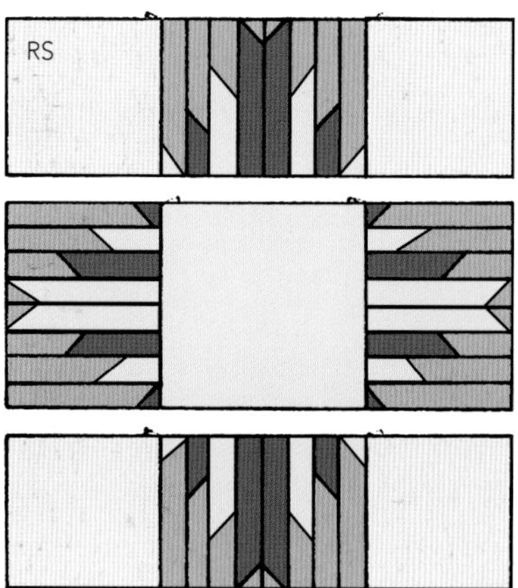

Fig 14

12 Stitch the rows together to make the block, matching seams carefully. Press seams towards the block centre, ironing from the front.

13 The block should now measure 13½ x 13½in (34.3 x 34.3cm). An inner border of strips cut 1¼in (3.2cm) wide can be added and the block then trimmed down exactly to a 14in (35.6cm) square. Finally, add the sashing strips. See page 236 for adding framing strips and sashing.

Some Alternative Sizes for Delectable Mountains

Larger rectangle with final size of 11 x 7in (27.9 x 17.4cm). This can be used together with another mountains rectangle to make a block which, with borders added as in Fig 15, will finish up as a cushion-sized design. The initial squares are cut 8⅜ x 8⅜in (21.3 x 21.3cm). Once stitched and cut into the pieced squares they need to measure 8 x 8in (20.3 x 20.3cm). Cut the squares into four vertical strips as before, each measuring exactly 2in (5cm) wide.

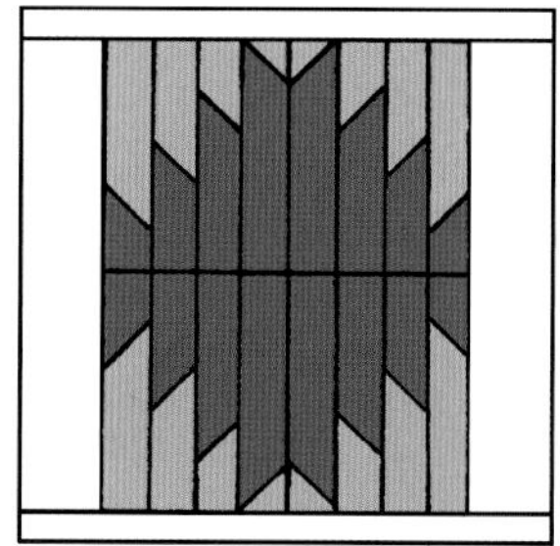

Fig 15

Smaller rectangle with final size of 5½ x 8in (14 x 20.3cm). This is suitable for borders on a quilt (Fig 16). Cut initial squares 6⅜ x 6⅜in (16.2 x 16.2cm). They should measure 6 x 6in (15.2 x 15.2cm) after stitching and cutting into pieced squares. Cut the squares into vertical strips as before, each strip measuring exactly 1½in (3.8cm) in width.

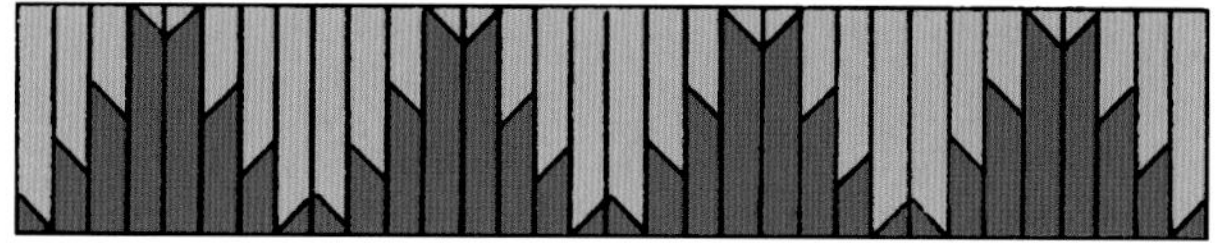

Fig 16

Hand Piecing with Appliqué

Carolina Lily

This is a traditional block that combines pieced patchwork with appliqué, as do so many of the American quilt designs. Although it is a square design it is usually seen in a quilt with the square on point, that is, turned through 45° so that it makes a diamond shape with the corners at the top, bottom and sides. To achieve this effect I have drafted a smaller version of the block than usual, turned it through 45° and added corners so that the final block is square, with the Carolina Lily within it on point (Fig 1 overleaf). This is not an easy block to draft, as it combines long diamonds with triangles and squares. If you wanted a larger version of the block given here, it would be easier to look for

it in a book of block patterns than to spend ages calculating all those tricky measurements. There are many variations of the lily block, some of which have been simplified slightly to make piecing easier. This version combines piecing, stems from Celtic bias strips and appliquéd leaves.

Fig 1

Colour Choices

The lily is made from two fabrics combined in the petals and a third forming each flower base and stem. Any of these three fabrics can be used to make the appliqué leaves. The lilies are set in a background fabric that can also be used as the extra large corners of the block, or another fabric could be chosen for this. I suggest you leave the decision about the corner fabric until the rest of the block is complete, and then you can place the block on the fabrics and see which one looks best.

Construction

1 Make card templates by tracing the seven shapes from Fig 2 on page 157, cutting them out and sticking them on the card, or by using template plastic. Mark the directional arrows, as these show how the templates should be positioned on the grain or weave of the fabric. Also mark the midpoint O on template B. Trim the drawn lines away as you cut each template out to prevent the shapes becoming larger than the originals.

2 On the wrong side of each fabric draw accurately around the templates using a sharp marking pencil and matching the direction of the arrows with the grain of the fabric. The drawn lines mark the stitching lines. Allow at least ½in (1.3cm) between each drawn outline so that the seam allowance or ¼in (6mm) can be added to each shape when cutting out.

To make the four diamonds of the flower lie comfortably together, the grain or weave of the fabric needs special consideration. The diamonds should be arranged as shown in Fig 3a, so half the pieces must be cut as a mirror image. Draw round the diamond template (Fig 2a), matching the grain arrow with the weave of the fabric. Then reverse the template on the fabric and draw round it to make a mirror image (as in Fig 3b). For the lily flowers you will need three of shape A and three of shape A *reversed* from each of the two lily fabrics.

From the third fabric, three of shape B are needed (this fabric will also be used later for the bias stems). Mark the midpoint O in the seam allowance of the B shapes.

From the background fabric you need three of shape C, six of shape D, two of shape E, one of shape F and one of shape G.

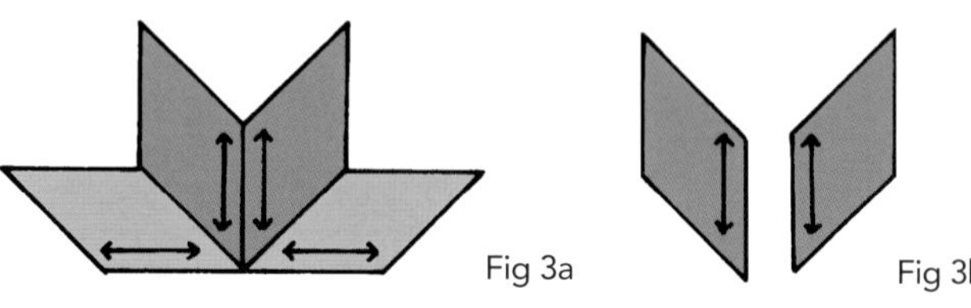

Fig 3a Fig 3b

3 Cut out each shape to include the ¼in (6mm) seam allowance, either by eye or by using a rotary cutter and ruler. The width of the seam allowance is not critical but is very helpful if cut accurately, as then the edges of the fabrics line up as you match the drawn stitching lines. Templates F and G show the position of the bias stems which are appliquéd to the block. The real outline is shown as parallel dotted lines with a stronger line between them. Trace just this middle line on to the *front* of fabric shapes F and G. Use a light box if necessary or dressmaker's carbon paper. The single line will act as a positioning guide for the stems when they are laid on to the block at a later stage.

4 Fig 4 shows the arrangement of pieces to make the block. Follow this carefully and arrange the cut fabric pieces on a flat surface or pin in position on a polystyrene tile or board. Final decisions can be made on the effectiveness of the fabric choices at this stage.

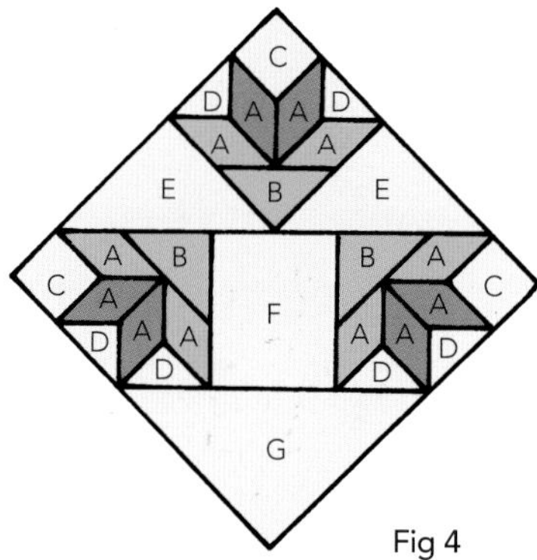

Fig 4

5 Begin by piecing together each lily flower. Arrange the four long diamonds as shown in Fig 3a, taking care to position them so that the centre seam is on the straight grain of the fabric. Place two of the diamonds together with right sides facing along the two sides to be joined. Pin and stitch along the marked lines, following the method used for piecing the Tangled Star block on page 130 (known as American piecing). Stitch from corner to corner of the drawn design without stitching into the seam

allowances. Open out the two diamonds and pin the third diamond to the second, matching the drawn seam lines. Stitch this seam. Pin and stitch the fourth diamond to the lily in the same way. Do not press any seams until the whole block is complete, as there is no set rule for which way each seam is to be pressed. Once it is finished the seams can be pressed whichever way avoids too much bulk at the back of the work.

6 With right sides facing, pin piece B to the joined diamonds, matching the corners and drawn lines as in Fig 5. Position the centre of the four diamonds at the midpoint mark on piece B.

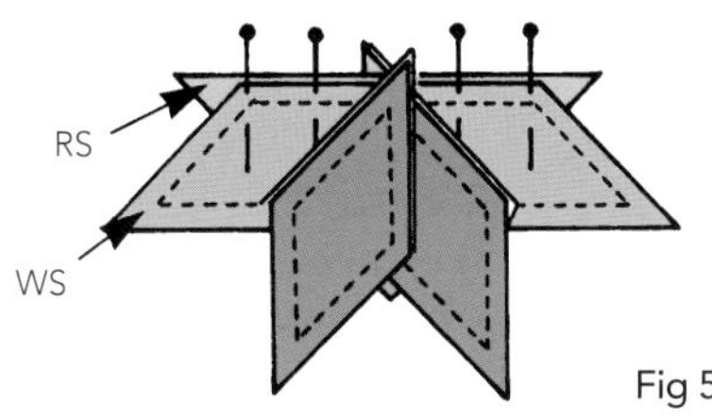

Fig 5

Pin close to the centre cluster of seams but not at the centre junction itself. Begin stitching with the diamond shapes uppermost until approaching the centre junction. Push the seam allowances away from the stitching area and match the marked corner of the stitched diamond to the midpoint on piece B by pushing a pin through both points until the head is on the surface of the diamond fabric. Reposition the pin at right angles to the seam as shown in Fig 6. Stitch up to the seam and make a backstitch. Pass the needle through the corner of the stitched diamond into the corner of the last diamond, bypassing the two middle diamonds (Fig 7). Backstitch to pull all the seams together tightly and continue sewing. Repeat this process with the other two lily flowers.

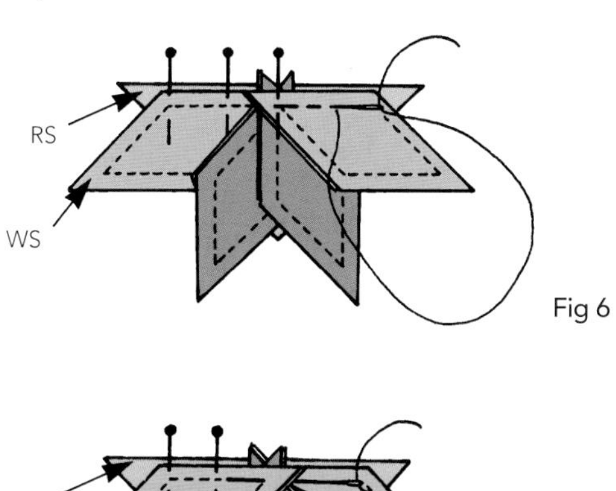

Fig 6

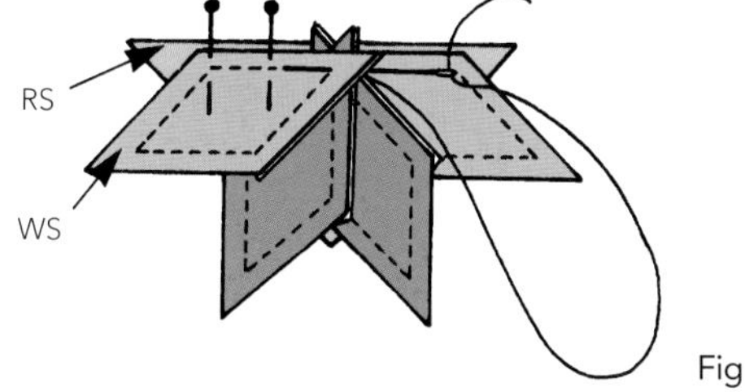

Fig 7

7 Now add to each lily flower one square (C) and two triangles (D). Follow the arrangement in Fig 8a for the centre lily and the arrangements in Figs 8b and 8c for the other two lilies. All three lilies have a different positioning of pieces C and D so follow Figs 8a, 8b and 8c to get this right.

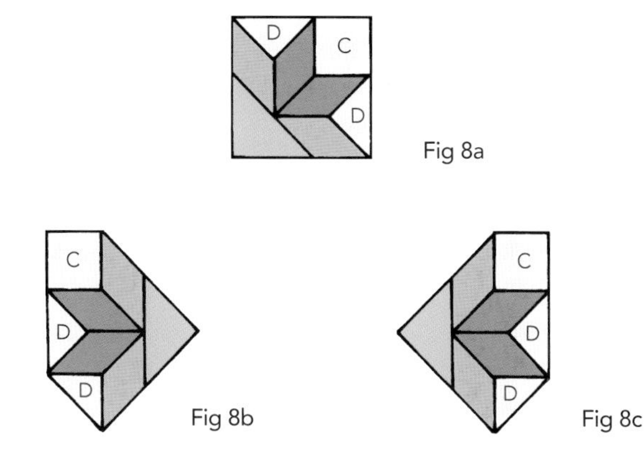

Fig 8a

Fig 8b

Fig 8c

To join shapes C and D to the main lily flower means stitching them into an angle, called setting-in, which is easier by hand than by machine. Beginning with square C, match the corners of the drawn lines of the seam to be stitched with pins in the usual way, working from the outer edge towards the inner corner. Add more pins along the seamline, matching the marked lines (Fig 9). Stitch to the inner corner of the design and make a backstitch (Fig 10). Swing the square round to line up with the edge of the second side of the lily. Match the drawn lines and pin. Push the centre seam allowances to one side, clear of the seam, and stitch along the drawn line as usual (Fig 11). Join the two D triangles to the lily in the same way. Complete each lily unit as in Fig 8a, 8b and 8c.

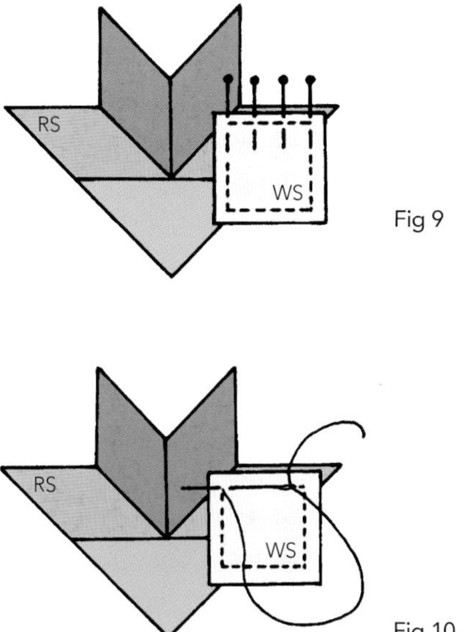

Fig 9

Fig 10

8 The curving stems of this block are made from bias tubes constructed in exactly the same way as in the Celtic Knot block. Three lengths of pressed tube are needed, one 8in (20.3cm) for the centre stem and two 7in (17.8cm) for the side stems, Make and press these, following the instructions for the Celtic Knot block on page 141.

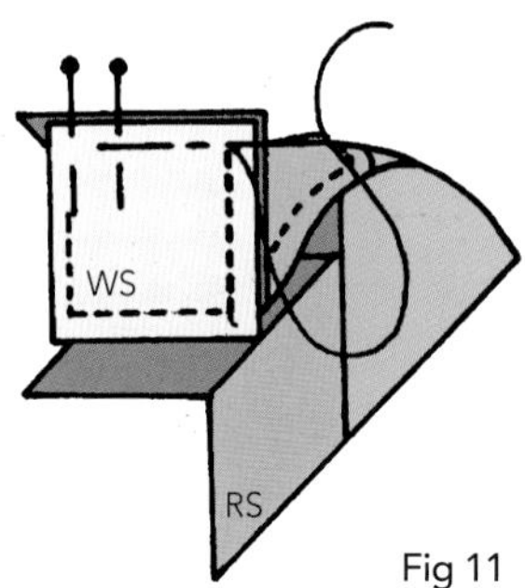

Fig 11

9 The Carolina Lily block is assembled in three sections (Fig 12). Join the two triangles E to the lily shown in Fig 8a. This completes the top section.

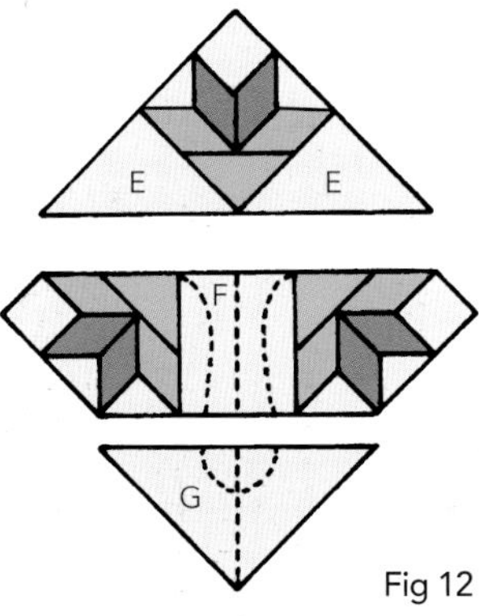

Fig 12

Pin the trimmed ends of the three Celtic tubes on to the *right* side of piece F, over the drawn lines of the stems (Fig 13). The loose ends of the tubes will be stitched on to piece F later once the block is joined together. Pin and stitch the two lilies to the long sides or piece F as in Fig 12, at the same time stitching through the stems where they are pinned on to piece F. You will probably have to stitch with stab stitches at this point because of the thickness of the pinned layers.

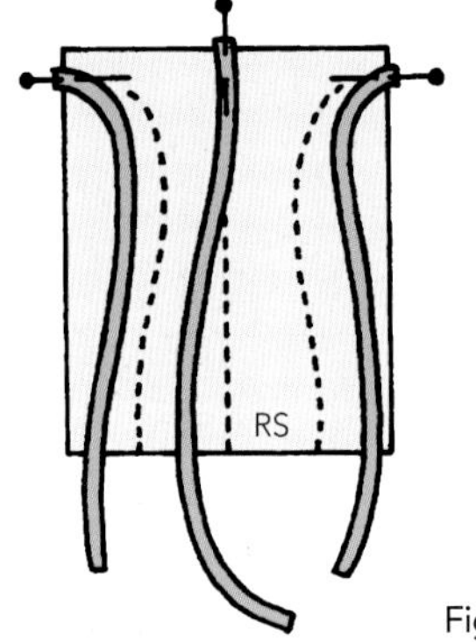

Fig 13

Join the top section to the middle section, matching seams carefully and stitching through the pinned stem in the centre. Now stitch piece C to the centre section of the block to complete it, matching the drawn stem guidelines.

10 Press the block from the front, letting the seams lie in whichever direction avoids too much bulk at the back. They are never pressed open as the hand-sewn stitches are not strong enough.

11 Pin the side stems in position, pinning the inside curves first as described in the instructions for the Celtic Knot block on page 142. Trim each end so that it butts against the centre seamline (Fig 14). Stitch the side stems to the block, using the method detailed for the Celtic Knot block. Because it is better to stitch the shorter side of a curve first, start stitching from the bottom to the point where the curve begins to swing the other way, roughly halfway along (Fig 15). Remove the needle, leaving the length of thread hanging loose, and restart from the other end of the stem, stitching the shorter side of the curve first. Continue to stitch this entire side of the stem. Finish off the stitching at the back as usual. Re-thread the needle with the long loose end of thread and complete the stitching on the remaining side of the stem (Fig 16). The centre stem is then pinned over the drawn line on piece F and stitched in position. It will cover the two raw edges of the side stems. Trim the bottom edge in a V shape to match the edges of the block.

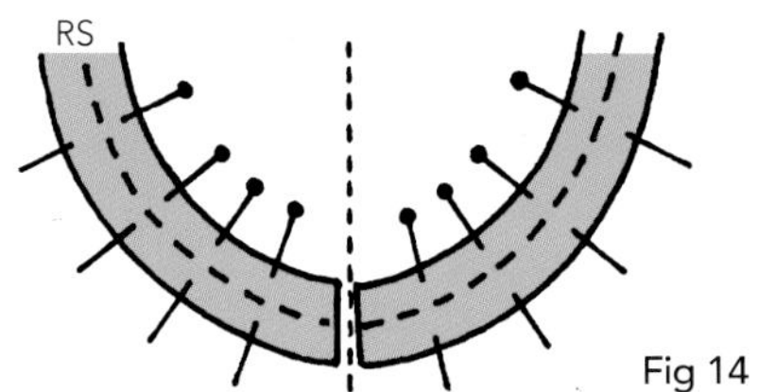

Fig 14

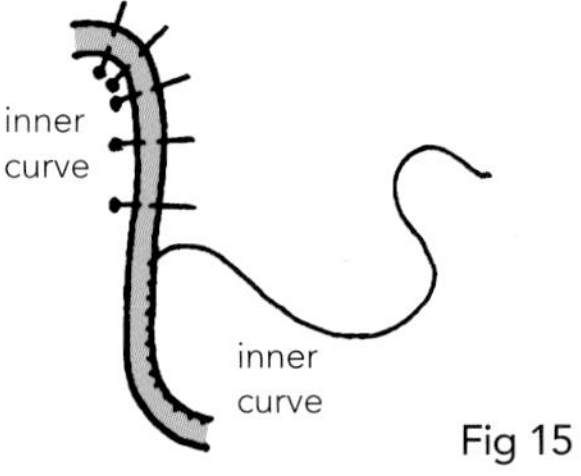

Fig 15

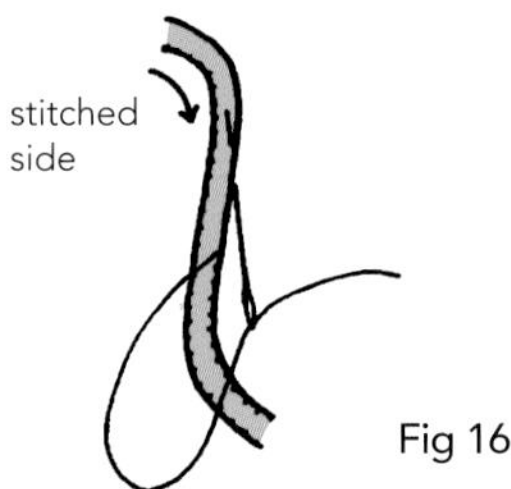

Fig 16

"My son and daughter-in-law chose the fabrics for this, my second sampler quilt. I found it a little difficult working with their colour scheme so added pink to help bring it to life. I agonized over this decision but need not have worried as Tim and Jane love their quilt!" **Barbara Ayre**

12 Trace the leaf shape given in Fig 17 twice on to the smooth side of freezer paper. Cut out the shapes and iron them shiny side down on to the *wrong* side of the chosen fabric. Cut out with a ¼in (6mm) seam allowance. Clip the curve nearly but not quite to the freezer paper. Do not clip near the pointed end of the leaf shape (Fig 18a). Carefully peel off the paper, replacing it in exactly the same position but with the shiny side *upwards* and pin the freezer paper on to the fabric (Fig 18b). I use one or two small pins to stop the paper moving.

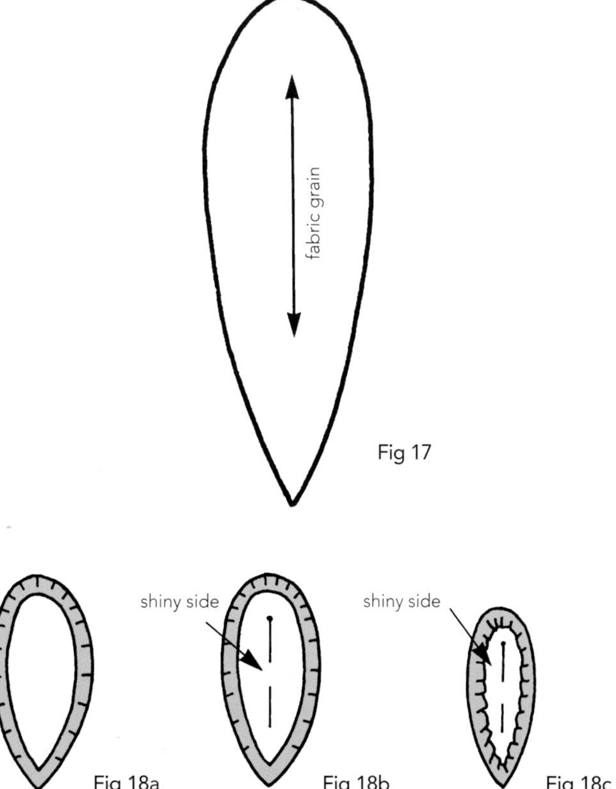

Fig 17

Fig 18a Fig 18b Fig 18c

Use as firm an ironing surface as possible – a thick piece of cardboard with a piece of spare fabric on it to protect the surface is a good emergency board if your usual ironing surface is not firm enough. Set the iron to a wool setting and do not use steam. Using the side of the iron rather than the point, nudge the seam allowance of fabric over on to the freezer paper, easing in the fullness on the curves a little at a time until all the seam allowance is stuck down on the paper (Fig 18c). Take care not to press in any tiny pleats on the outer edge but keep the curve smooth. If there are any areas you are not happy with, peel the fabric back and re-press in the correct position. If the folded fabric at the pointed section of the leaf does not tuck flat and shows from the front of the appliqué, either tuck it under while stitching the appliqué on to the background, or secure it with a dab of glue from a glue stick. Provided the glue is water-soluble it will not harm the fabric. Arrange the two leaves on the block and pin or tack them in place. Sew each one on to the background with small slip stitches, using thread to match the appliqué, not the background. Once the appliqué has been completed, cut the backing fabric away to ¼in (6mm) from the stitching line so the freezer paper can be removed.

13 Press the block. From the fabric to be used for the final large corners surrounding the block (see Fig 1) cut two squares each 7½in (19cm) square. Cut each square in half diagonally (Fig 19).

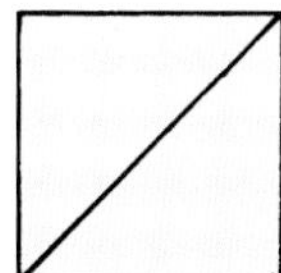

Fig 19

Pin and stitch the long side of one triangle to one side of the block, right sides facing. It should be slightly longer than the square, so balance the extra length equally at either end (Fig 20). Stitch right across the fabric from edge to edge, not just from the corners of the drawn shapes. Press the triangle with seams outwards from the block.

In the same way, pin and stitch a triangle to the opposite side of the block. Press the triangle outwards. Pin and stitch the remaining two triangles to the sides of the block and press outwards.

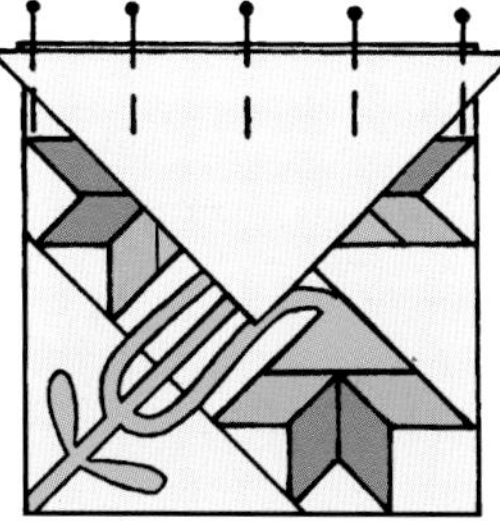

Fig 20

14 Place the completed block on to a cutting board and trim down the sides to ¼in (6mm) beyond the four corners of the Carolina Lily block (Fig 21). The block should now measure about 13in (13cm) square. Cut and add 1¼in (3.2cm) wide framing strips. Once these are stitched in place trim the block down to 14in (35.6cm) square. Finally, add the sashing strips. See page 236 for adding framing strips and sashing.

Fig 21

Fig 2 – Actual size templates

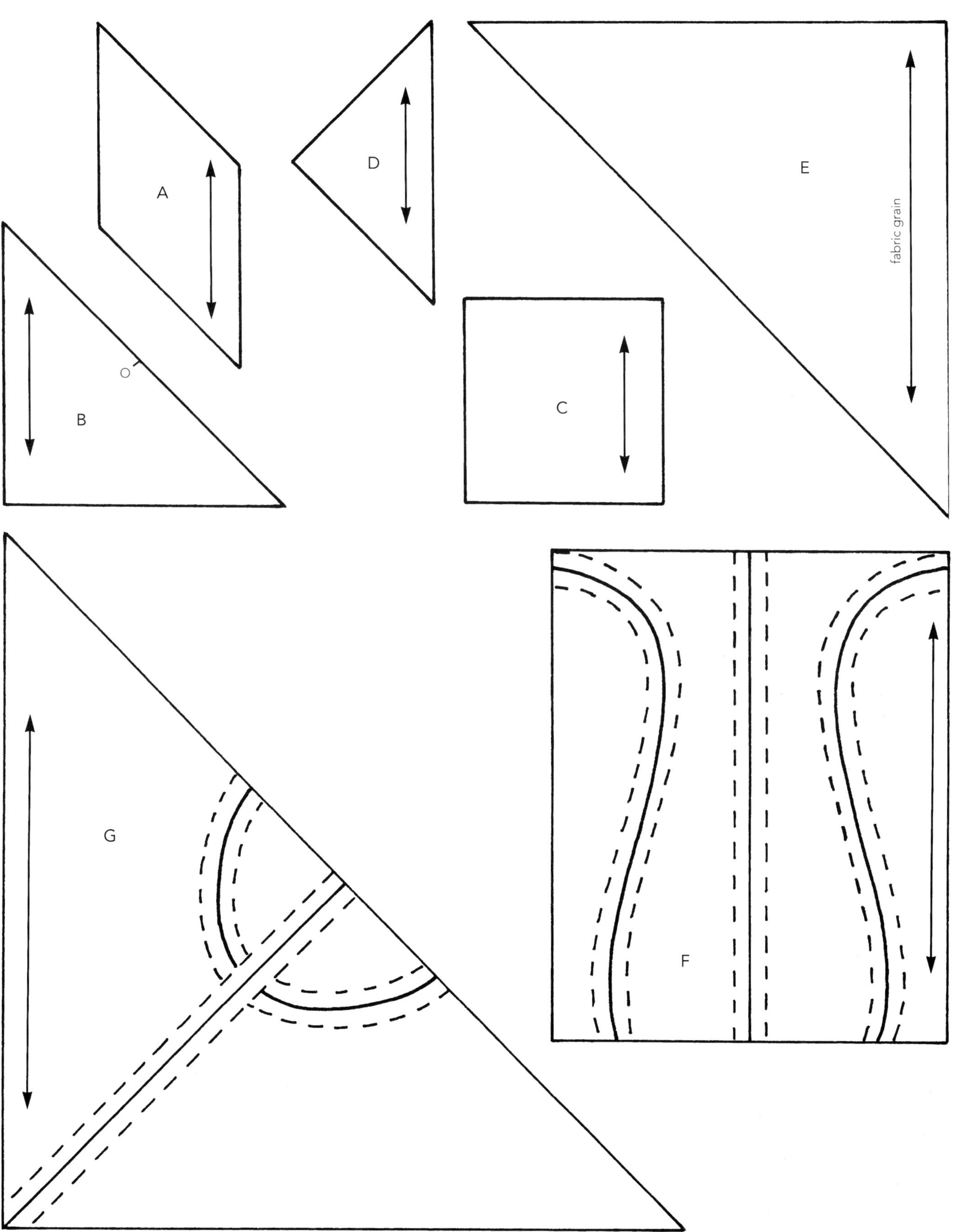

Machine Piecing

Quick Bow Tie

Bow Tie is a traditional patchwork block (see Fig 1 opposite), usually constructed with two templates in the American patchwork tradition, as used in the Tangled Star block. This quick and clever method is based on squares of fabric which are folded and machine stitched to give the bow tie effect. Once you have got the hang of it the blocks can be chain-stitched and mass-produced with amazing and satisfying speed.

Several students have produced wonderful bed quilts using a Bow Tie block based on 3in (7.6cm) squares of fabric, which finishes up as a 5in (12.7cm) block. This size would be too big to use for the sampler quilt, so I have offered two

designs as alternative choices for the block. One uses cut fabric squares measuring 2½in (6.3cm) to make the design of nine Bow Ties shown in Fig 2a below. The other uses 2in (5cm) cut squares of fabric to make a block of sixteen Bow Ties as in Fig 2b and in the block picture, left. This second block is much more fiddly than the first. I suggest that you make just one Bow Tie unit from both designs to try out the technique. If you enjoy working on a small scale, make the second design but if it proves too fiddly for you, choose the larger nine-patch design. Either looks good as the finished block in the quilt.

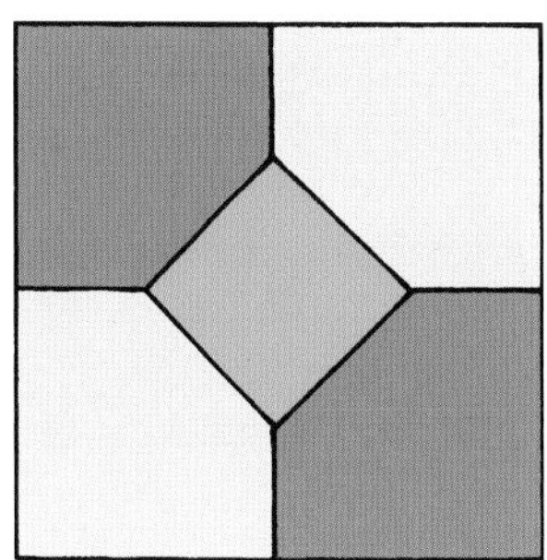

Fig 1

Colour Choices

In the nine-patch design (Fig 2a) each Bow Tie is placed diagonally on a background fabric. It is more interesting if the Bow Ties vary in colour and Fig 3a shows an arrangement of Bow Ties in two colours on a background. Fig 3b shows a design of Bow Ties in one fabric with each knot in a second fabric. More fabrics could be used for the Bow Ties if you prefer that effect. For the more complex design in Fig 2b I used two fabrics for the Bow Ties with one background fabric.

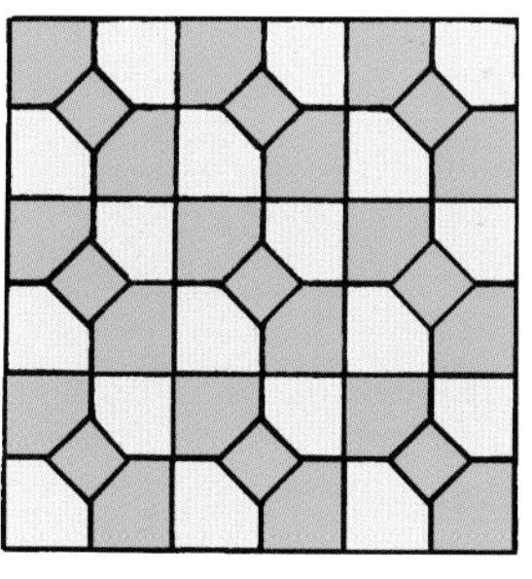

Fig 2a

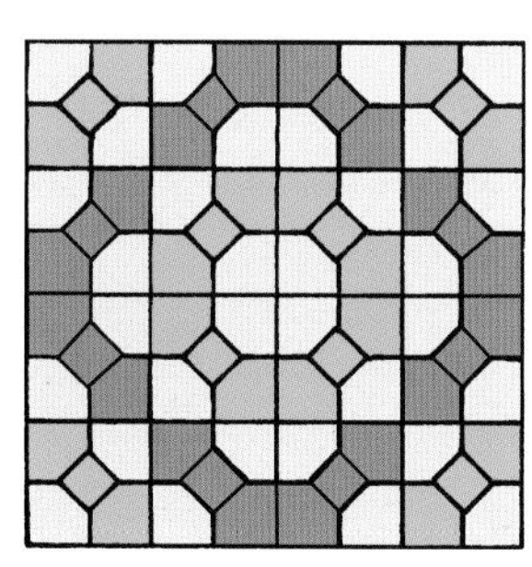

Fig 2b

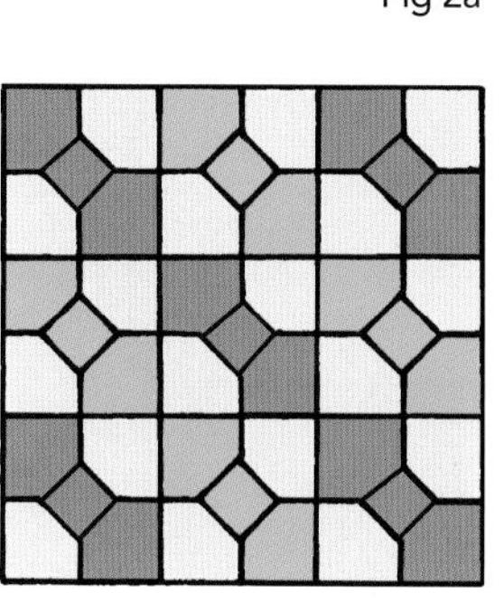

Fig 3a

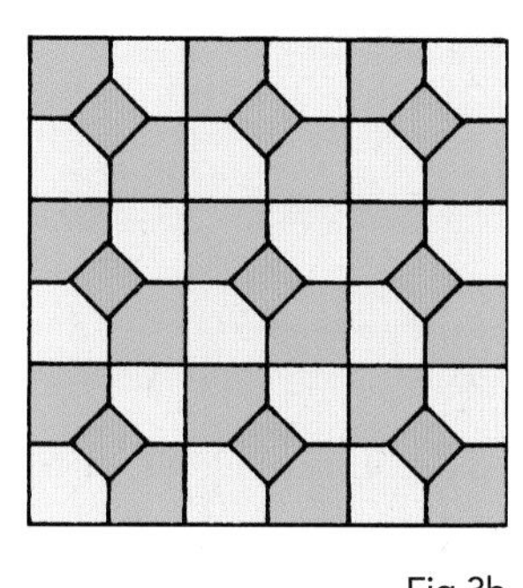

Fig 3b

Construction

The Nine Bow Tie Design

Make up nine Bow Tie units in the method described below, using whichever fabrics suit your plan.

For the design in Fig 3a: cut fifteen squares in one Bow Tie fabric and twelve squares in another bow tie fabric, all measuring 2½ x 2½in (6.3 x 6.3cm). For the background cut eighteen squares each 2½ x 2½in (6.3 x 6.3cm). Assemble five Bow Tie units in one fabric plus background and four Bow Tie units in the second fabric plus background (Fig 4).

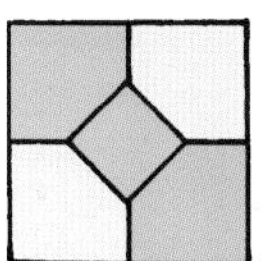

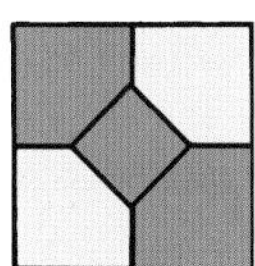

Fig 4

For the design in Fig 3b: cut eighteen squares for the Bow Ties in one fabric and nine squares for the knots in a second fabric, each measuring 2½ x 2½in (6.3 x 6.3cm). For the background cut eighteen squares 2½ x 2½in (6.3 x 6.3cm).

1 Cut three squares of fabric for the Bow Tie itself, each measuring 2½ x 2½in (6.3 x 6.3cm). Cut two squares of fabric for the background, each measuring 2½ x 2½in (6.3 x 6.3cm) (see Fig 5).

bow tie fabric

background fabric

Fig 5

2 Fold one of the bow tie squares in a half with right side *out*. This forms the knot of the bow tie (Fig 6). Place a square of bow tie fabric on a flat surface right side *up*. Place the folded knot strip on top of it with the fold running down the centre from top to bottom and the raw edges to the left (Fig 7).

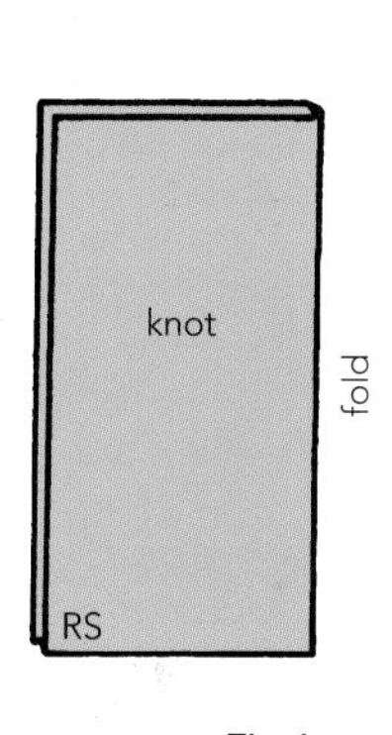

Fig 6

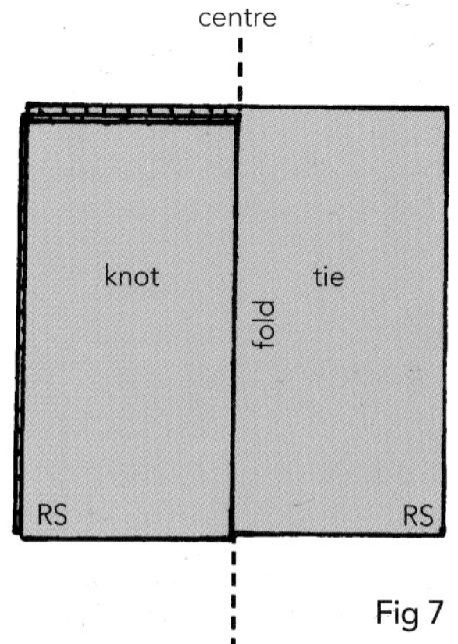

Fig 7

3 Now place a square of background fabric on the top, right side *down*, matching the raw edges of the new square with the raw edges of the underneath layers. You should have a sandwich of the two different fabric squares with their right sides facing and the folded knot rectangle between them (Fig 8).

4 Pin the top edges together (Fig 9). Machine a seam ¼in (6mm) from the top edges through all the layers (Fig 10).

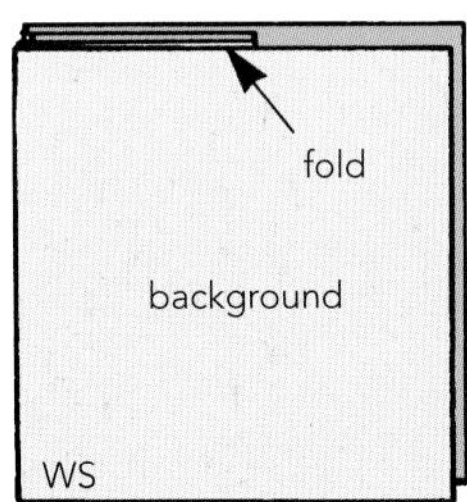

Fig 8

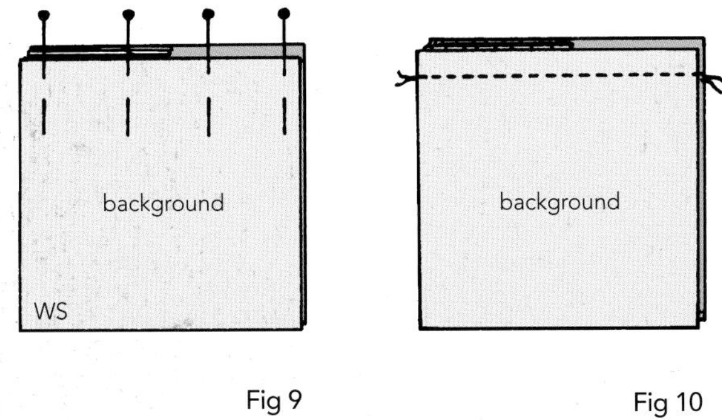

Fig 9

Fig 10

5 Now fold both squares of fabric back from the knot as shown in Fig 11.

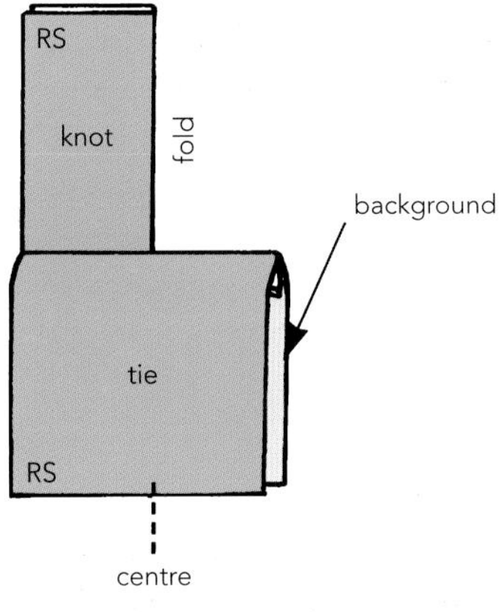

Fig 11

6 Repeat this sequence: Place a square of bow tie fabric on a flat surface with right side up. Place the folded knot strip on it, again with the fold running down the centre from top to bottom and the raw edges to the left (Fig 12).

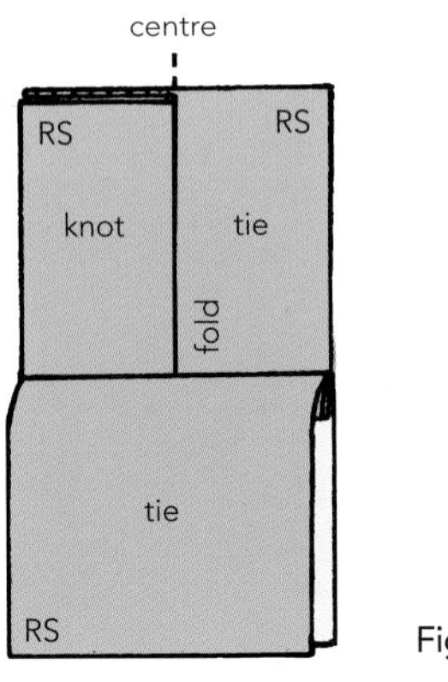

Fig 12

7 Now place the last square of background fabric on the top, right side down, carefully matching the top raw edge with the top raw edges of the other fabrics, as before (Fig 13).

8 Pin along the top edges through all the layers (Fig 14). Stitch a seam ¼in (6mm) from these top edges (Fig 15).

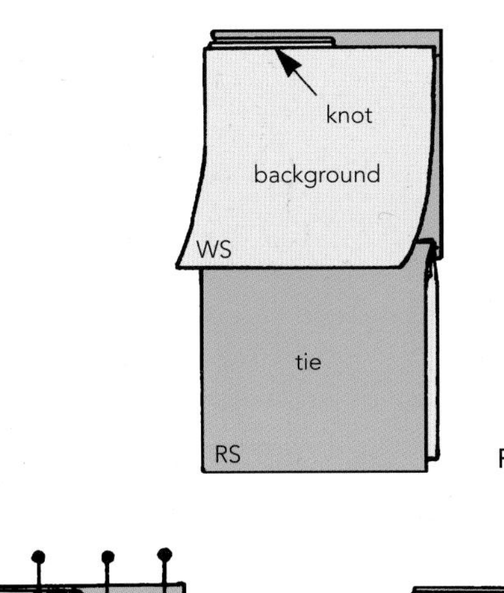

Fig 13

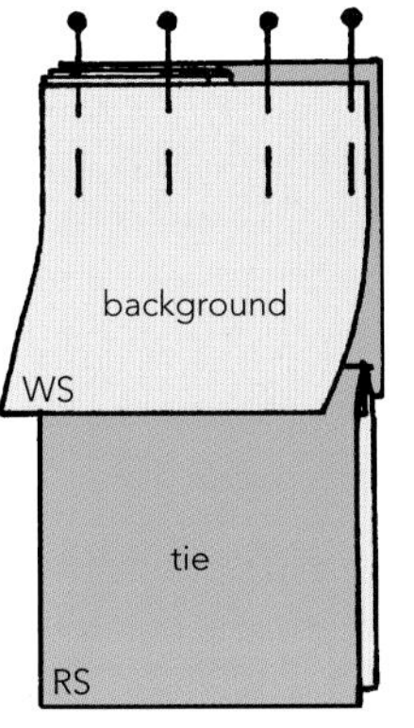

Fig 14

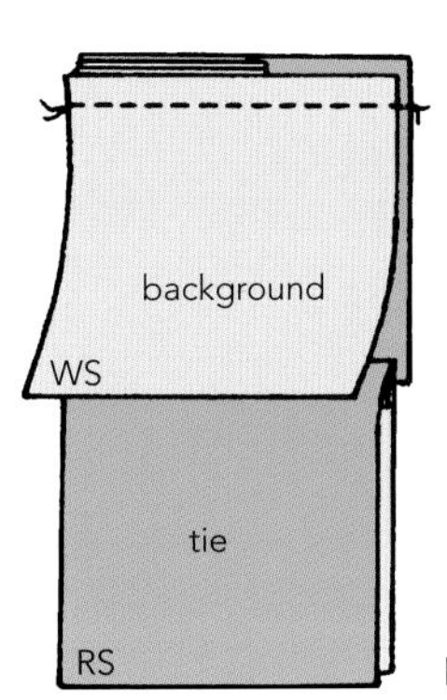

Fig 15

"This is the fourth sampler quilt I've made and, like the others, it went together like a dream – mainly due to Lynne's wonderfully precise instructions. However, it took eighteen months to complete: I live on the Costa del Sol in Spain and for six months of the year it's too hot to quilt!" **Bobbie Turley**

9 Pull the fabric squares back from the knot. It should look rather strange, hopefully as in Fig 16.

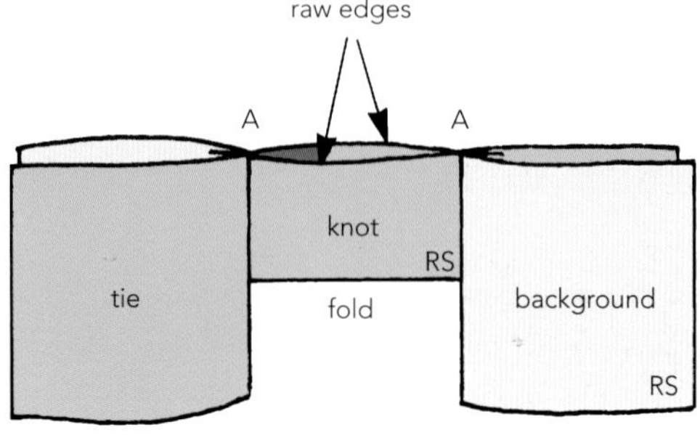

Fig 16

10 Now comes the cunning bit. Separate the two raw edges of the knot strip. Pull them apart and match the two opposite seams, each marked as A in Fig 16 and 17. Finger press the seams at A in opposite directions (Fig 17). Pin the two seams together, matching them carefully (Fig 18).

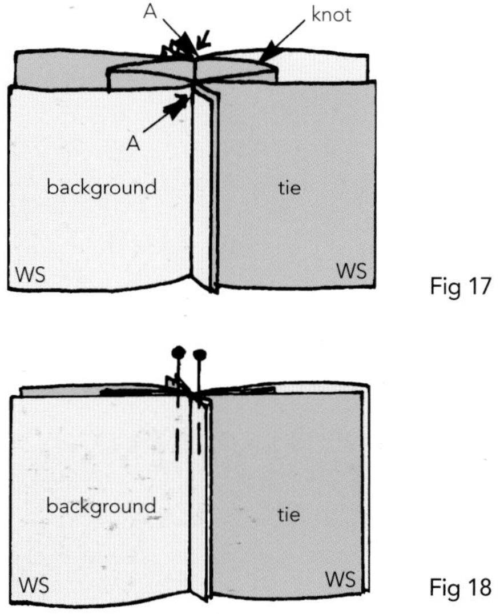

Fig 17

Fig 18

11 Match the top edges of the squares and of the knot that is sandwiched between them, taking care not to catch in any odd folds of fabric. Pin these edges together (Fig 19). Stitch through the layers with a ¼in (6mm) seam (Fig 20).

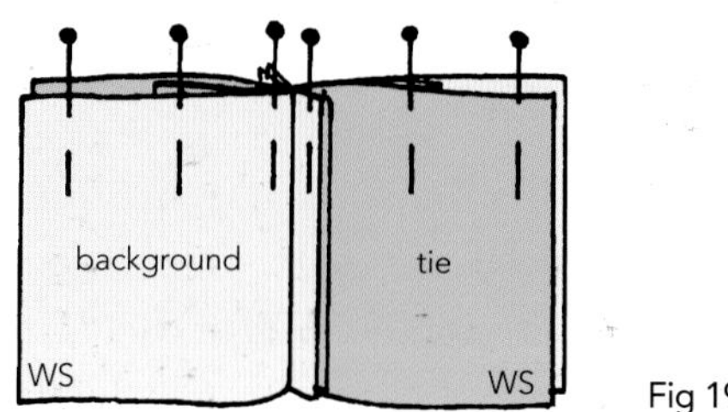

Fig 19

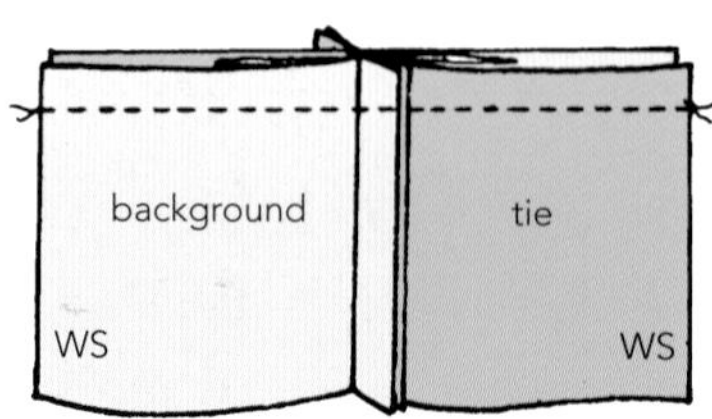

Fig 20

12 Open out the block to reveal the completed Bow Tie with its knot. If there are any little pleats or untidy corners in the knot, check the long stitched edge. There is probably one edge of fabric in all those layers that has dropped lower than the others. Unpick just that section, re-pin and stitch again. Press the Bow Tie block from the front.

13 Assemble the nine Bow Tie units using the same combination for both the design in Fig 3a and 3b: two squares for the tie, one square for the knot and two squares of the background fabric (Fig 21). Press each completed unit and arrange them in the chosen design. Pin and stitch the units into three rows, matching seams carefully. Finally, join the rows to make the block.

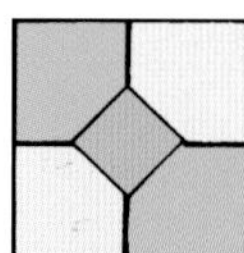

Fig 21

The Sixteen Bow Tie Design

Make up sixteen smaller Bow Tie units in the method described for the units in the Nine Bow Tie design, using whichever fabrics suit your plan.

For the design in Fig 2b: cut twenty-four squares of one bow tie fabric and twenty-four squares of a second bow tie fabric, each 2 x 2in (5 x 5cm). For the background cut thirty-two squares of the chosen fabric, each 2 x 2in (5 x 5cm). Make eight Bow Tie units, using one bow tie fabric plus the background and eight Bow Tie units using the second fabric plus the background. The method for making the smaller 2in (5cm) squares is just as straight-forward as making the latter squares until the pinning and stitching of that final long seam (Fig 20). I find it best to begin in the centre and work out in the opposite direction for the other half. Press the sixteen completed units and arrange them in the design shown in Fig 2b. Pin and stitch the units into four rows, matching seams carefully. Finally, join the rows to complete the block.

14 The finished block, whether you have chosen the nine or sixteen Bow Tie design, should measure about 12½ x 12½in (31.7 x 31.7cm). Add the inner framing strips and trim the block to an exact 14in (35.6cm) square. Finally, add the sashing strips (see page 236).

Hand-Stitched Freezer Paper Appliqué

Clamshell

The Clamshell design is frequently found in antique quilts as pieced shapes or providing a rich overall quilting design. It is usually one of those patterns that people love but avoid because of the high-risk nervous breakdown factor! Template kits for English patchwork have been around for many years, although the problems involved with the joining of the shapes have given it limited popularity. I have always treated the shape as an appliqué, laying down the clamshells in rows on a background fabric and overlapping them row by row (see Fig 2 overleaf). Regular horizontal lines are drawn on the background square to help keep the clamshells level. The limitation of the technique is that

each row overlaps the row above, so the bottom row has to completely cover the background fabric with its points hanging off the bottom. These are trimmed off after the final row is stitched in place.

For the design in this sampler quilt block (Fig 1) I have cheated in that the overlapped rows of clamshells are worked from the top downwards and also from the bottom upwards. The area of raw edges in the centre, where both rows meet, is covered by a row of whole circles appliquéd across both halves of the design. The only way to make sure that everything finishes up in the right place is to draw the design very lightly on the background fabric as a guide to positioning, as with an appliqué design.

Fig 1

Fig 2

Yvonne Romain aimed at making a quilt with a Japanese look. She limited herself to a very tight palette of just three colours – cream, ginger brown and indigo blue – to make her dramatic sampler quilt.

Colour Choices

Several colours or shades can be used for the clamshells, which can be arranged in a variety of patterns on a background fabric (see Figs 3a, 3b, 3c). If you are unsure, try photocopying the design and colouring it in or, better still, make some clamshells in each fabric and then arrange them on the background fabric to see which pattern is the most pleasing. The design is not a large one, so the background fabric is reduced to a smaller square with a wider inner frame added.

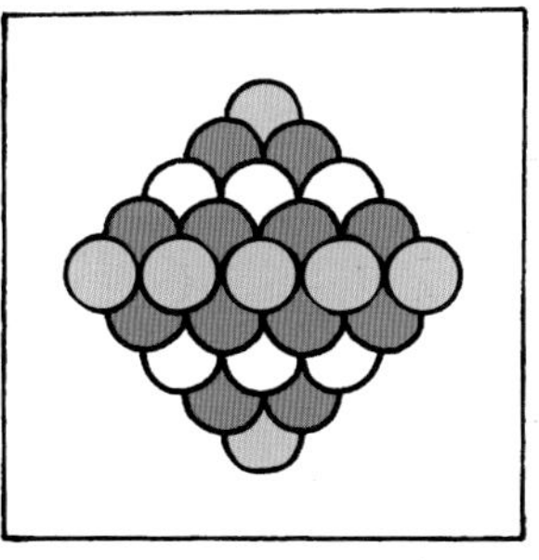

Fig 3a

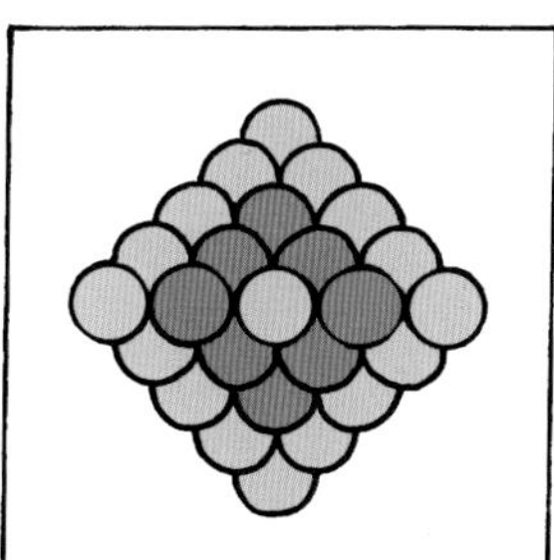

Fig 3b

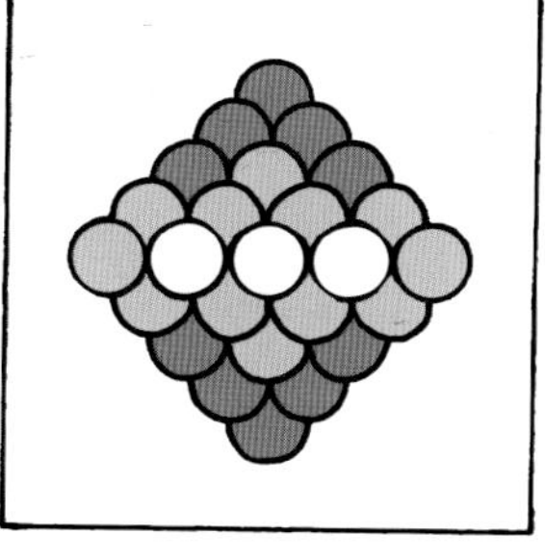

Fig 3c

Construction

1 The template for the clamshell is based on a circle with a 2in (5cm) diameter – see Fig 4a on page 167. The bottom edge (marked with a dotted line in Fig 4a) has had a ¼in (6mm) seam added to make working with the fine point of the clamshells easier. The second template (Fig 4b on page 167) is for the five complete circles that make the middle row of the design.

The technique for this block uses freezer paper as a base for the clamshells and circles. Make the two templates by tracing the shapes from Figs 4a and 4b, cutting them out and sticking them on to card or by using template plastic. Draw round the clamshell template on the non-shiny side of freezer paper using a really sharp pencil to keep the shape accurate. If freezer paper is not available, the outer wrapping from packs of photocopy paper is an excellent substitute. Cut out twenty clamshells from the freezer paper. Draw round the circle template in the same way to make five freezer paper circles and cut these out.

"This quilt took me through a big learning curve technically, and emotionally due to the very sad loss of my parents. Kathy Redmile suggested I think about the colour scheme and who the quilt is for. This made me look at fabrics with a scheme in mind and not just pick up my favourite colours or gorgeous prints and try to make the best of them. Thanks to Lynne's patience I have achieved this minimal-looking quilt." **Yvonne Romain**

2 Iron the twenty freezer paper clamshells shiny side down on the back of the chosen fabrics leaving about ½in (1.3cm) between each clamshell to allow for seam allowances. Match the drawn arrow on the template with the grain of the fabric (Fig 5).

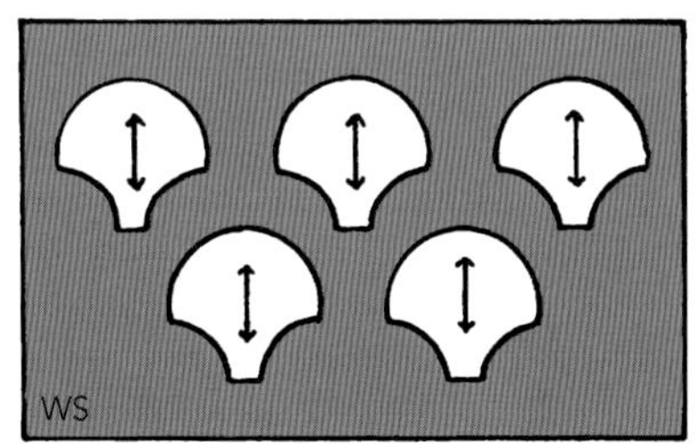

Fig 5

3 Cut out each clamshell adding a ¼in (6mm) seam allowance to the top curved edge only (Fig 6). The bottom two edges already have the seam allowances added to them. The ¼in (6mm) seam allowance around the top edge does not have to be carefully measured but can be cut by eye.

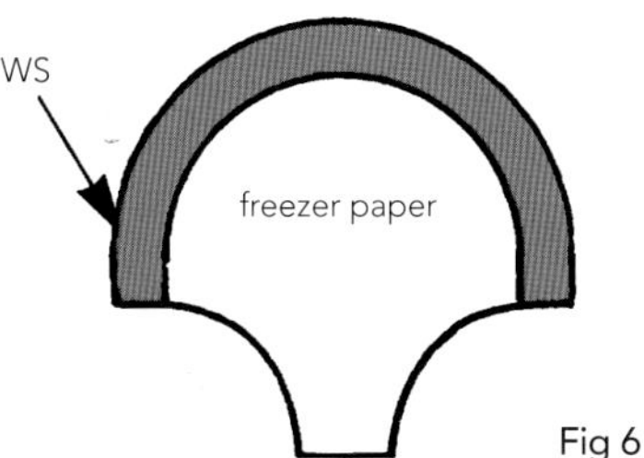

Fig 6

4 Peel the freezer paper off the fabric and replace it shiny side up on the wrong side of the fabric clamshell in exactly the same position, matching the bottom edges of both fabric and paper. Pin the freezer paper on to the fabric (Fig 7). I use two pins to stop the paper moving. Using the side of an iron, nudge the seam allowance of fabric over on to the freezer paper, easing in the fullness a little at a time so that it sticks to the paper. Don't worry too much if the iron touches the surface of the freezer paper. Take care not to press any tiny pleats in the outer edge but keep the curve smooth (Fig 8). If there are any areas you are not happy with, just peel the fabric back and re-press in the correct position.

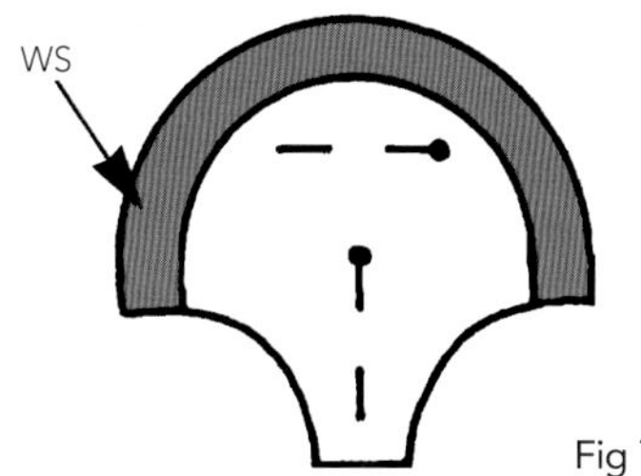

Fig 7

5 Iron the five paper circles shiny side down on the back of the chosen fabrics, leaving about ½in (1.3cm) between each circle to allow for seam allowances. Cut around each circle adding a ¼in (6mm) seam allowance. Peel off the paper and reposition it in exactly the same position but with the shiny side facing upwards. Do not clip the seam allowance but press it over the freezer paper in the same way as the clamshells (Fig 9).

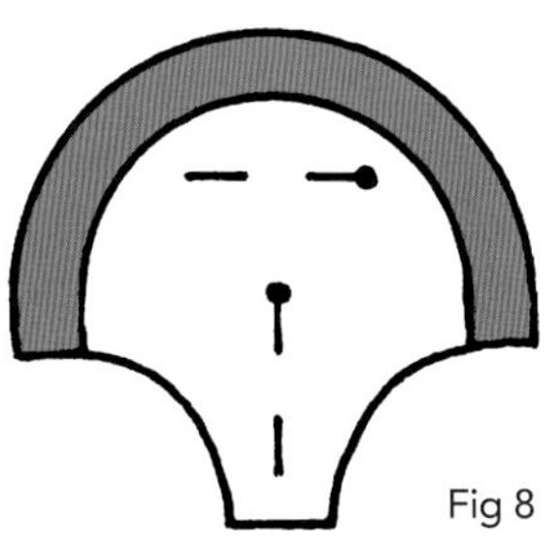
Fig 8

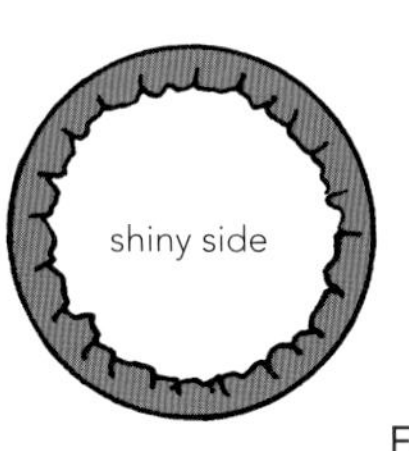

Fig 9

6 Cut a square of background fabric 12 x 12 in (30.5 x 30.5cm). Fold it into quarters and press lightly. Trace the design layout from Fig 10 opposite on to paper, including the dotted centre markings. Place the unfolded fabric square over the drawn design, positioning the fold lines over the dotted lines on the design and matching the centres. This is half the finished design. Draw very lightly with a marking pencil just inside the lines of the design to give an indication of where the clamshells and circles will be positioned. Do not draw exact outlines in case these show around the edges of the appliquéd shapes after stitching. Once the lines are marked on the fabric, turn the background square through 180°, realign the centres and the line of circles and trace the remaining opposite section of the design (as in Fig 1). If the fabric is not fine enough to trace through, use a light box.

7 Arrange the prepared shapes on the background, checking that the design works well. Now is the time to make any changes if needed. The clamshells are arranged and stitched in rows, so the first row is just one clamshell (Fig 11).

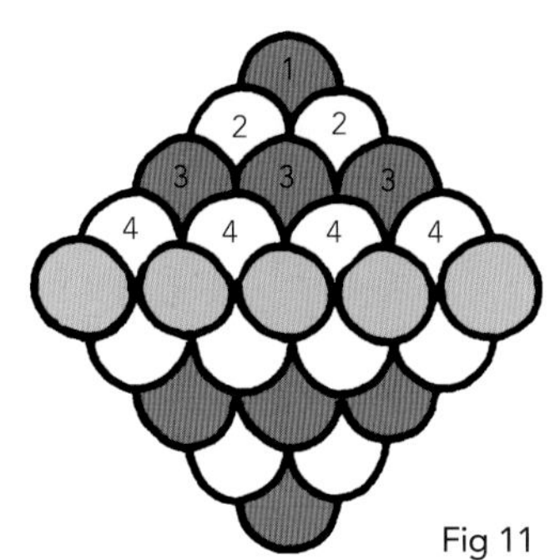

Fig 11

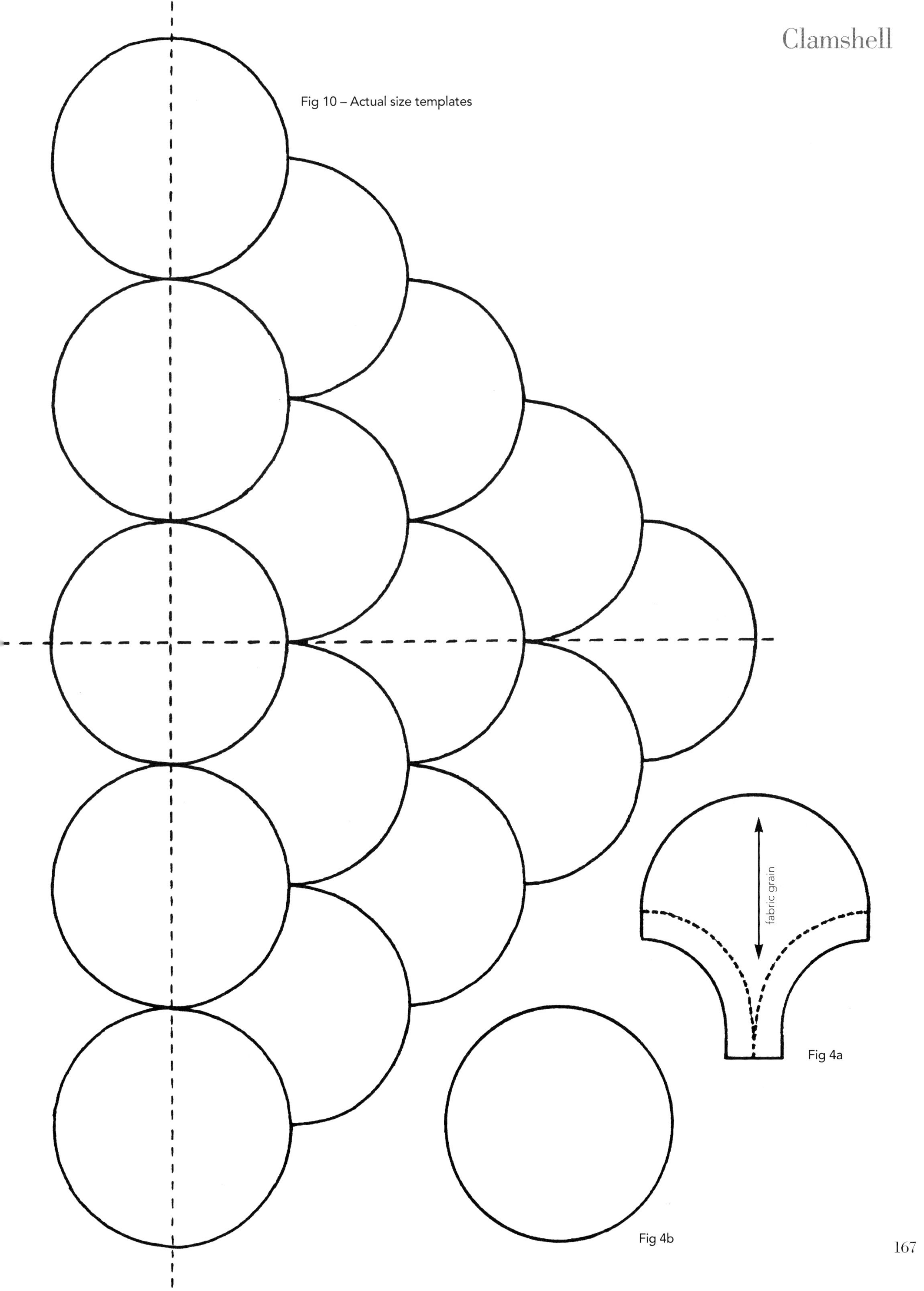

Fig 10 – Actual size templates

Fig 4a

Fig 4b

8 Position the first clamshell on the background fabric and press. This will fix it on the background while you stitch it in place, although you may also want to pin it if you feel it is insecure. Using thread to match the clamshell, not the background, stitch the folded curved edge in position using small, even slip stitches (Fig 12).

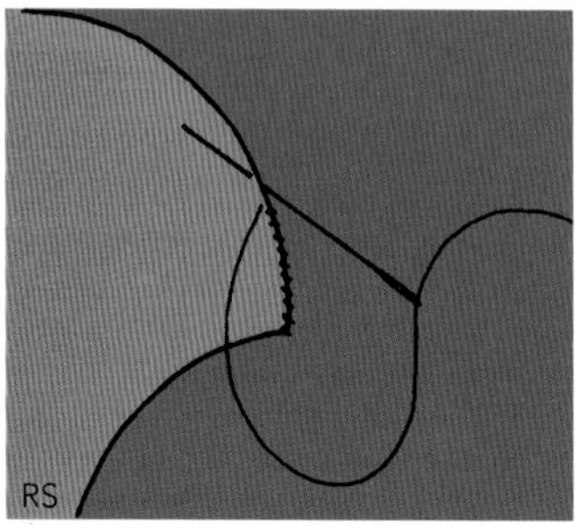

Fig 12

Once the clamshell's top edge is stitched, lift up the bottom edge of the fabric and ease the freezer paper out. Use a pair of scissors with rounded ends slid between the paper and the background fabric to separate them – the paper can then easily be pulled out. Try to remember to remove the paper *before* adding the next row of clamshells. It is very tiresome to remember only after the entire next row has been beautifully stitched in place. You can cut the background fabric away to remove the paper, which has to be done for the centre line of circles, but this is a lot more fiddly than just remembering to remove the papers directly before the clamshells have been stitched down.

9 Arrange the two clamshells that make the second row in position. The outer curves are placed on the drawn lines on the background and should overlap the bottom raw edges of the top clamshell by ¼in (6mm). The two inner corners should meet midway on the stem of the top clamshell with all the bottom edges level as shown in Fig 13. Iron both clamshells to fix their position on the background. Stitch the top curves in place, working right across the row. The stitching does not have to be through all the layers of fabric, just whatever is comfortable depending on the thickness of the fabrics. Once they have been stitched, remove both papers.

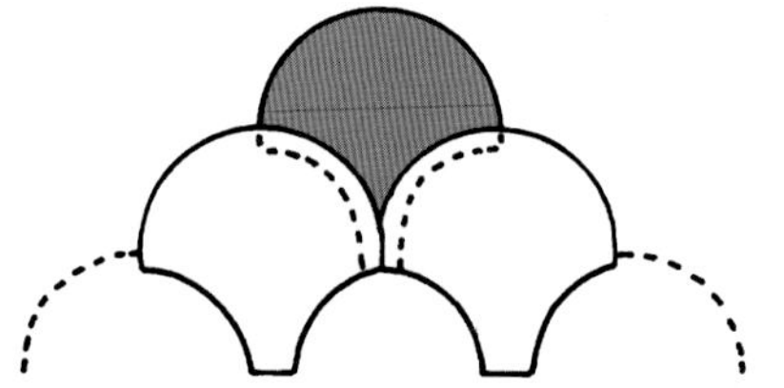
Fig 13

10 Arrange the third row, overlapping the raw edges of the second row by ¼in (6mm), following the drawn lines on the background fabric where they can be seen (Fig 14). Press the row of clamshells with an iron to secure them and stitch along the top curves as before. If the colours of the clamshell fabrics vary in the row, change the thread to match each clamshell as you stitch it. I use a separate needle with each colour thread and use them in turn as I need them.

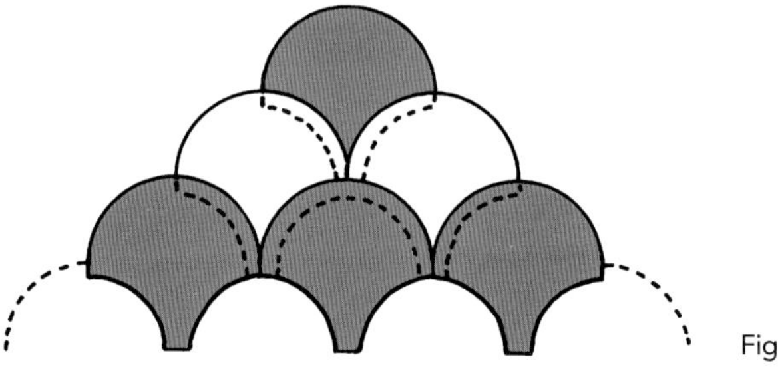
Fig 14

11 Now arrange, press and stitch the fourth row of clamshells in the same way.

12 Leave the centre row of circles. Turn the background fabric round and arrange and stitch the opposite four rows of clamshells in the design, beginning with the top single clamshell and working towards the centre.

13 Position the five pressed circles so that they overlap the raw edges of both halves of the clamshell design, using the drawn lines on the background as a guide where they can be seen. Turn each circle so that the grain of the fabric runs parallel to the grain of the background before pressing them to fix them on to the block. Stitch each circle in place.

14 Turn the block to the back and use the stitch lines as a guide to cut away the backing up to ¼in (6mm) within the stitching lines of the circles, revealing the freezer paper below. Remove the freezer paper from the block (Fig 15).

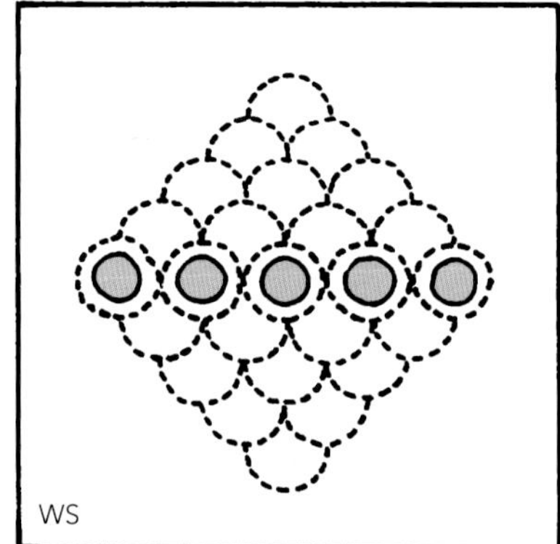

Fig 15

15 Trim the block to an exact 11½in (29.2cm) square. Add the inner framing strips which should be 2in (5cm) wide strips. Trim the block to a 14in (35.6cm) square and add the sashing strips. See page 236 for adding framing strips and sashing.

Machine Piecing

Folded Flying Geese

This folded technique is a close relation of the Bow Tie technique used in another block in this sampler quilt. It uses rotary-cut squares and rectangles which are then folded, layered and stitched to produce the Flying Geese design (see Fig 1 overleaf). The diagonal seams are not stitched but are folded pockets (see Fig 2), which look very effective especially in a small size where piecing would be very fiddly. Folded Flying Geese units can be combined in many different ways but for the sampler quilt I chose to arrange them in a rotating sequence of five units around a central square, which creates great movement to the block. You could experiment with other arrangements if you wish.

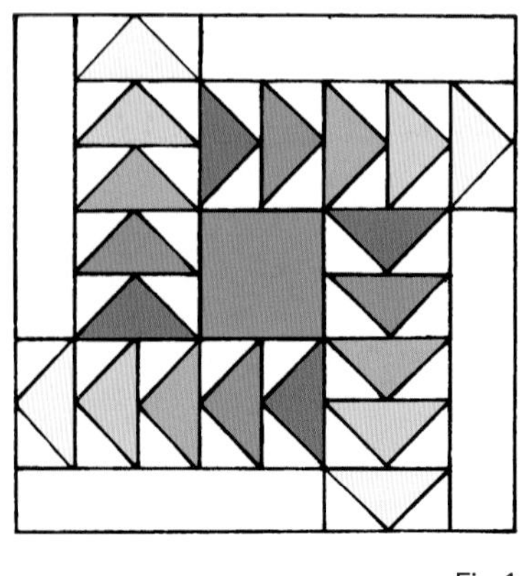
Fig 1

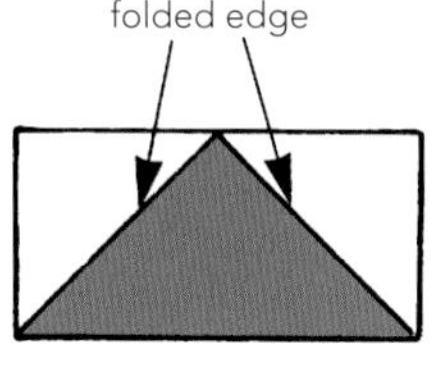

Fig 2

Colour Choices

The design shown in Fig 1 has four lines of Flying Geese, each made up of five units. In my own arrangement (see picture page 2) I used five different fabrics in shades of blue grading from light to dark in the large triangles. This sequence of fabrics was repeated in each row of five Flying Geese. Alternative colour arrangements are shown in Figs 3a and 3b. Fig 3a uses four different fabrics for the larger triangles, one fabric for each row. Fig 3b uses two fabrics for the triangles in opposite rows. The same background fabric has been used for each Flying Geese unit and also for the outer long rectangles. Alternatively, these long rectangles can be of another fabric as in Fig 1. The central square can be a background fabric or a strong colour to make a central focus for the block.

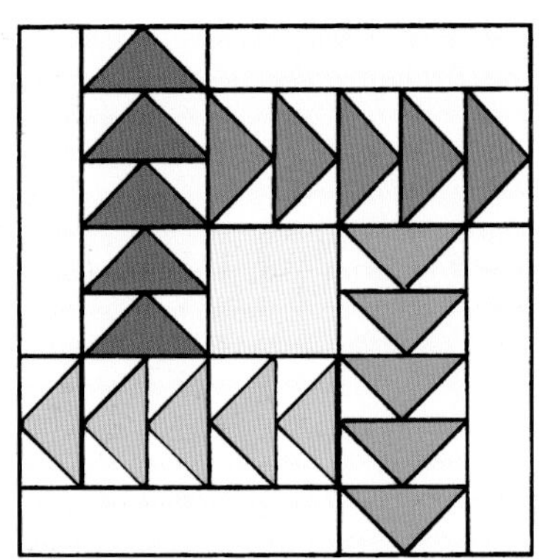
Fig 3a

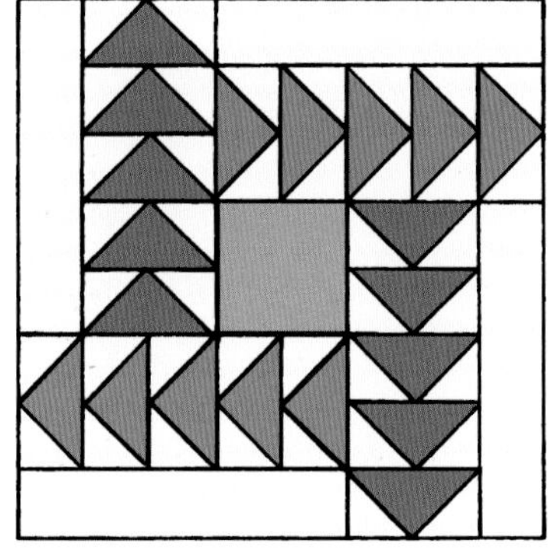
Fig 3b

Construction

Each Flying Geese unit will measure 1½ x 3in (3.9 x 7.6cm) finished size. To make the block, twenty Flying Geese units must be assembled. For each unit you will need one rectangle 2 x 3½in (5 x 8.9cm) for the central triangle (called the 'goose' in the design) and two squares each 2 x 2in (5 x 5cm) for the side triangles (called the 'sky') (Fig 4).

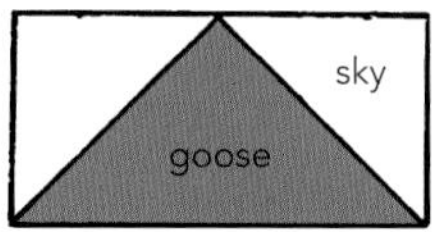

Fig 4

1 From the chosen goose fabric or fabrics, cut a total of twenty rectangles, one for each unit, each measuring 2 x 3½in (5 x 8.9cm). From the chosen sky fabric, which acts as a background, cut forty squares each measuring 2 x 2in (5 x 5cm).

2 Take one goose rectangle and fold it in half with the right side facing *outwards* (Fig 5). Place a square of sky fabric down on a surface right side *up* and place the folded rectangle on the square, matching all the outer raw edges. You will find that the folded edge of the rectangle does not quite reach the edge of the square on the left-hand side (Fig 6).

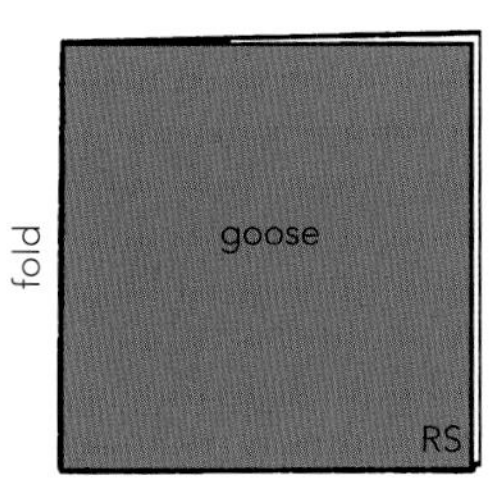

Fig 5

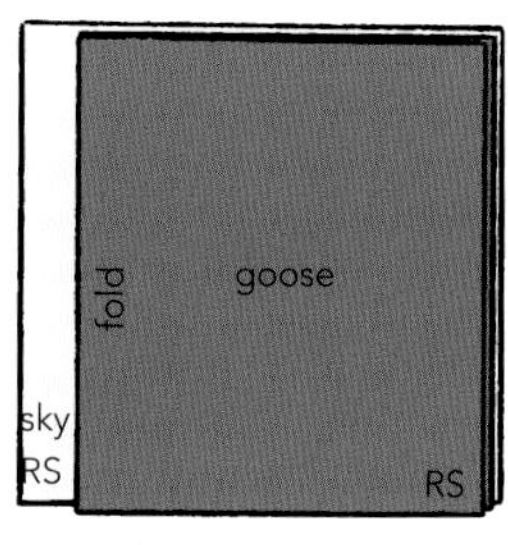

Fig 6

3 Place a second square of sky fabric on the folded rectangle with right side *down*, matching the raw edges of the other sky square exactly (Fig 7), then pin the top edges together (Fig 8). Machine a seam ¼in (6mm) from the top edges through all the layers, including the fold of the rectangle (Fig 9).

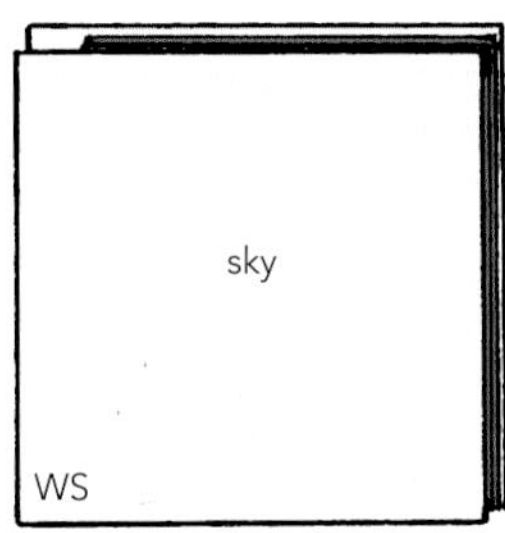

Fig 7

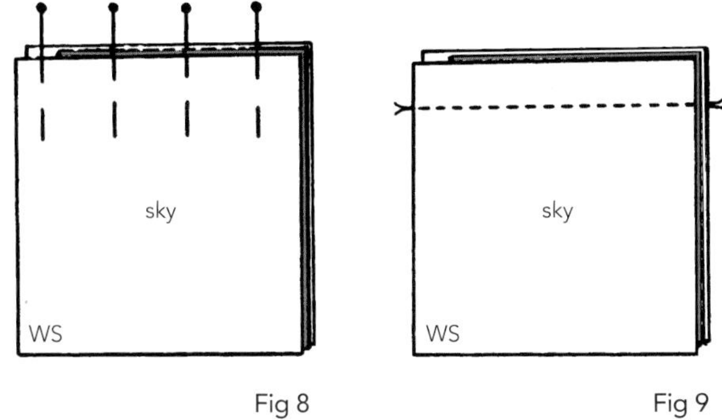

Fig 8 Fig 9

4 Pull the squares of sky fabric back to reveal the centre folded rectangle (Fig 10). Then pull the corner of the rectangle marked A in Fig 10 across to meet the corner of the sky also marked A. Pull the goose corner marked B across to meet the corner of sky marked B (Fig 11). Press the unit, ironing the central seam on the back *open* (Fig 12). Keep the large goose triangle flat on the sky with a couple of pins (Fig 13).

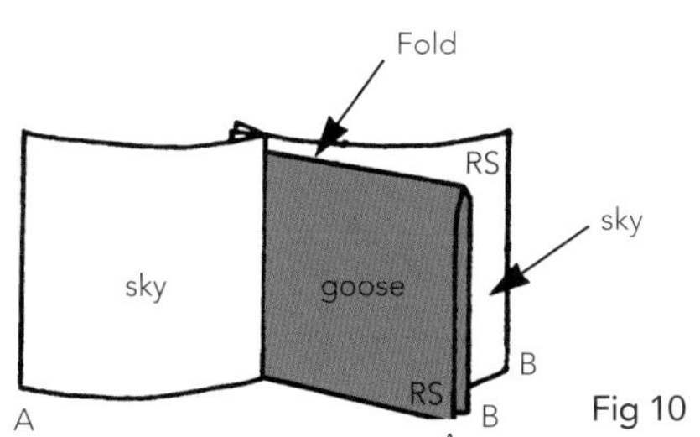

Fig 10

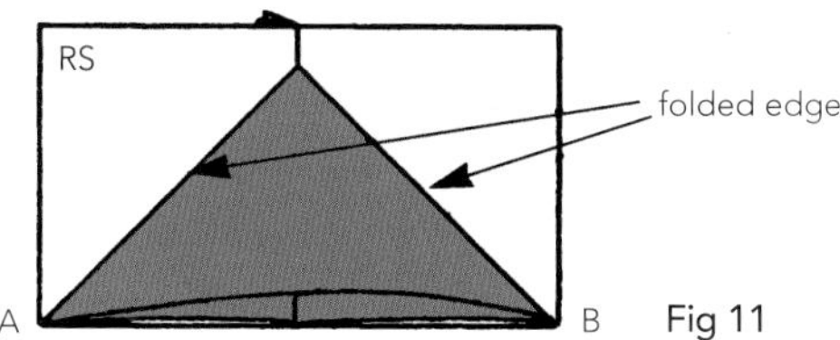

Fig 11

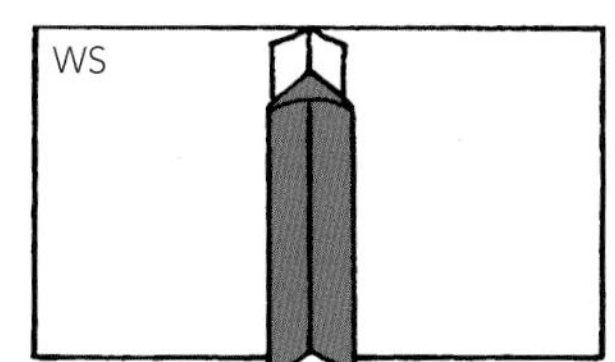

Fig 12

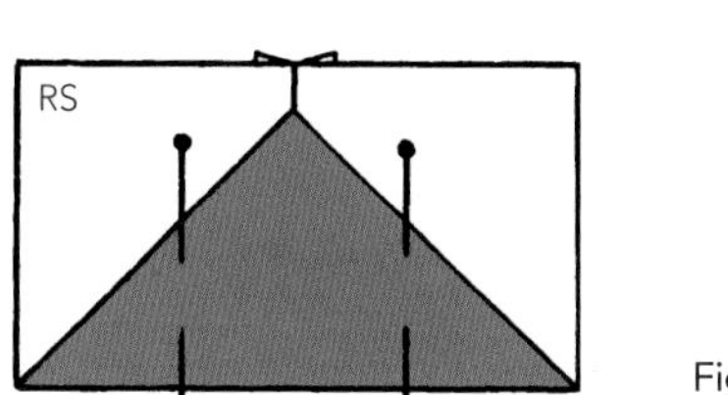

Fig 13

5 Make all twenty Flying Geese units in this way, pressing and pinning each one as described.

6 For the centre square in the block design, cut a square from the chosen fabric measuring 3½ x 3½in (8.9 x 8.9cm). For the side rectangles in the design cut four rectangles from the chosen fabric each measuring 2 x 8in (5 x 20.3cm).

7 Arrange the Flying Geese units in four rows each containing five Flying Geese in the chosen colours (follow either Fig 1, Fig 3a or Fig 3b). Stitch the units into rows with the usual ¼in (6mm) seam. Press the seams of the joined units towards the bottom of the row, ironing from the front of the work (Fig 14).

8 Pin and stitch one long rectangle to the left side of each row of Flying Geese (Fig 15). Press the seam towards the long rectangle.

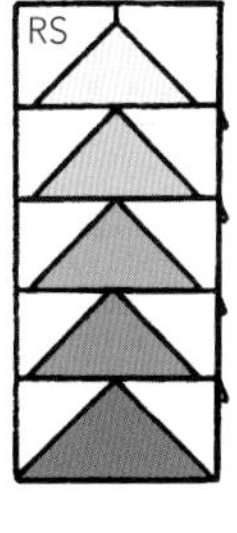

Fig 14

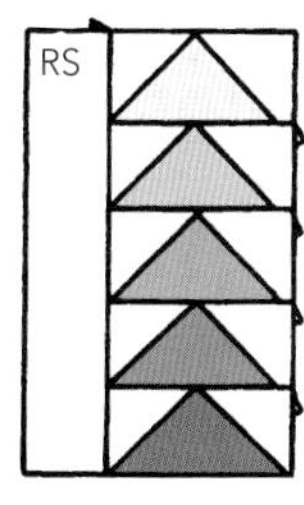

Fig 15

9 Arrange the four pieced sections of the block around the centre square as in Fig 1. To stitch these sections together by machine seems difficult, but there is a clever way of dealing with it. Begin by pinning the centre square to one pieced unit, right sides together, making sure the square is pinned to the *bottom* two Flying Geese units with bottom edges level. The top edge of the centre square should extend ¼in (6mm) above the seam between these two Flying Geese and the other three (Figs 16a and 16b).

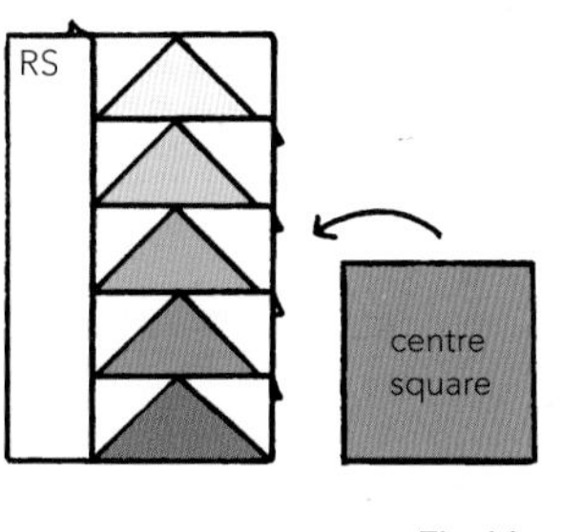

Fig 16a

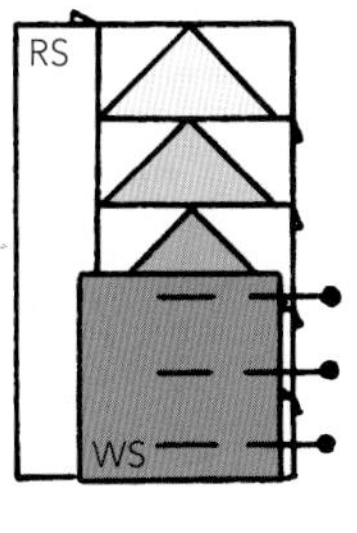

Fig 16b

10 Stitch *part-way* along the pinned seam, leaving the top 1in (2.5cm) *unstitched* (Fig 17). Open the square out away from the pieced section, pressing the seam allowance towards the square (Fig 18).

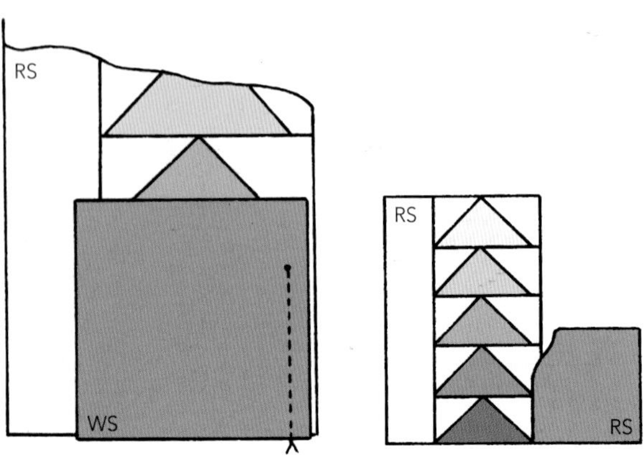

Fig 17 Fig 18

11 Place the section back with the other pieces of the design (Fig 19). Pin and stitch section B to the main part of the block (section A plus the centre square), matching seams carefully. Press the seam towards the centre of the block (Fig 20).

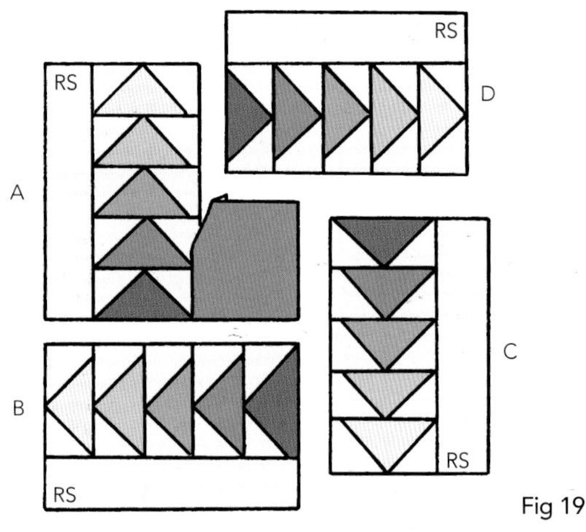

Fig 19

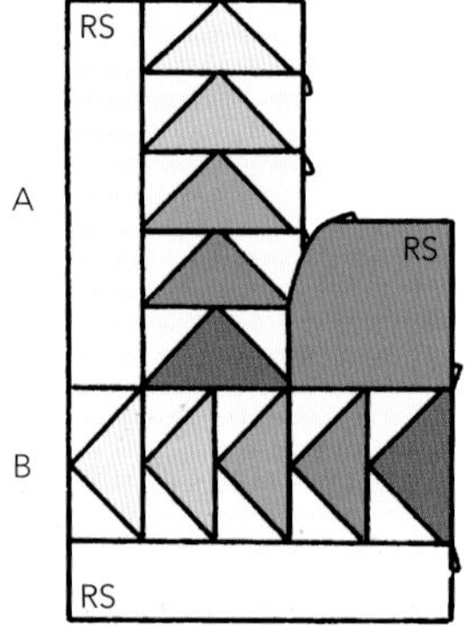

Fig 20

12 In the same way, pin and stitch section C to the main block (Fig 21). Press the seam towards the centre of the block.

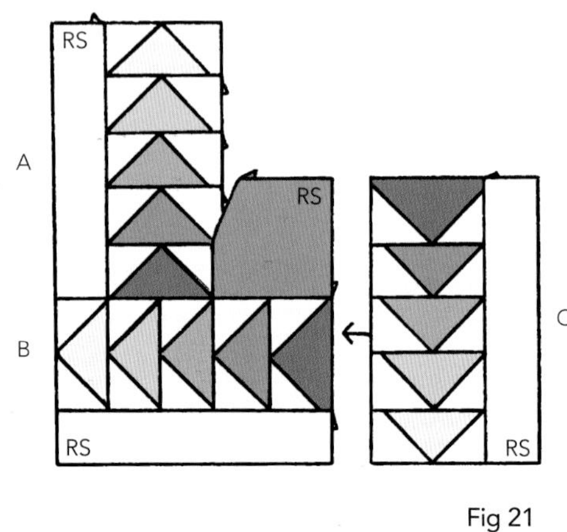

Fig 21

13 Now pin and stitch section D to the main block, as shown in Fig 22.

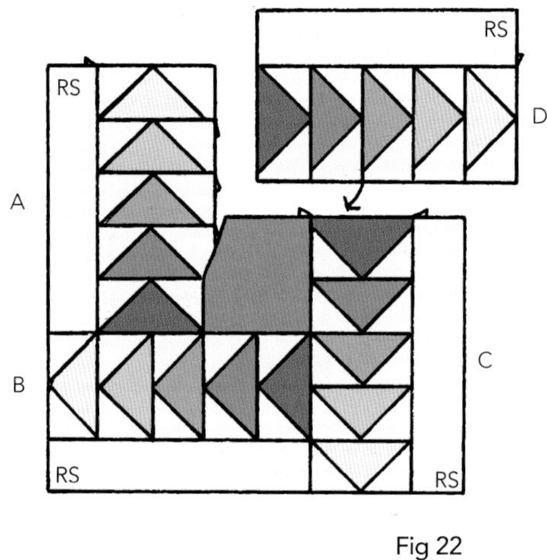

Fig 22

14 Finally, pin and stitch the last seam of the block, continuing the stitches of the original part-stitched seam.

15 Press the block firmly from the front. It should measure 12½ x 12½in (31.7 x 31.7cm), but this is not essential. Add framing strips and trim the block to exactly 14 x 14in (35.6 x 35.6cm). Add sashing strips to complete the block (see page 236 for adding framing strips and sashing).

"When I finished my first sampler quilt I said I wouldn't make another one, but the temptation of going to regular classes with Lynne Edwards at Chelsworth was too much for me so I signed up. The quilt was started in October 1998 and finished in 2006, and I am very pleased with the end result. The quilt was long-arm quilted beautifully by Jan Chandler." **Jane Brooks**

Hand Appliqué

Blanket Stitch Appliqué

In the original *New Sampler Quilt Book*, this design was used for a reverse appliqué block, which over the years I discovered that many quilters did not enjoy, as it calls for very precise needle-turning and stitching. The success of reverse appliqué depends totally on the quality of the fabric: if it tends to fray, the problems created are endless and the quilter swiftly loses the will to live... Meanwhile, over the last ten years I have discovered the joys of hand stitched blanket stitch, using a fusible web such as Bondaweb (called Wonder-Under in the USA) to stick the raw edges of the individual appliqué pieces of fabric on to the background fabric before stitching around the design with blanket stitch.

The fusible web is used to stick only the outer ¼in (6mm) of each appliqué shape to avoid the thick, stiff layers usually associated with fusible work.

I had already used this circular design with its 1930s Art Deco feeling as a sample of blanket stitch appliqué in my teaching (Fig 1) and thought it perfect to drop the tricky reverse appliqué block in the sampler quilt and replace it with the totally addictive blanket stitch technique. I just love the hand stitching aspect, but machinists can, of course, replace this with a machined version if they wish.

Fig 1

Colour Choices

The design is made of a central rose motif with surrounding leaves placed on an inner circle of contrasting fabric, with a decorative ring of appliquéd shapes running around it at a distance. All these are arranged on a square of background fabric. This means one fabric for the rose petals, one fabric for the six leaves, plus a third fabric for the inner background circle – the outer ring of shapes could be made from one of these three, or from another fabric that looks good in the design. For the background fabric I continued my policy of using a neutral cream/beige shade wherever a background appeared in a block in my quilt, but this is not a firm ruling, just my personal choice.

Arrange the fabrics to be used in the design on your background fabric to test their effect before beginning. All the pieces will be cut out and placed in position on the background fabric, starting in the centre and working outwards before anything is stuck down, so it's possible to change your mind about the fabrics at that stage.

Construction

1 Cut a square of fabric for the main background 13½in x 13½in (34.3cm x 34.3cm). Trace the *whole* design on to paper, using the parts of Fig 2 on pages 179 and 181, matching up the dotted lines and referring to Fig 1 if necessary. Mark the appliqué pattern on the *right* side of the background fabric square by tracing the design, using a sharp marking pencil and light box if necessary. The traced lines are a guide for positioning the cut pieces of appliqué fabric, so trace lightly just *inside* the drawn line so that these lines will be hidden when the appliqué shapes are placed over them. If the fabric is too dark for the design to be traced through, use dressmaker's carbon paper and a tracing wheel. (I use an empty fine ballpoint pen to mark the design through the carbon paper.)

2 When using fusible web, the design must be reversed. Fig 3a overleaf shows the centre part of the design reversed ready to be traced with the fusible web. Fig 3b shows the shape for the outer ring reversed ready for the fusible web. Trace the shapes in Fig 3a on to the smooth side of the fusible web. Mark the numbers and grainline arrows on the tracing, keeping these at the very edge of each shape, as the centre part of the fusible web will be removed later. Trace the shape in Fig 3b on to the smooth side of the fusible web twelve times, marking the grainline arrow on each as before.

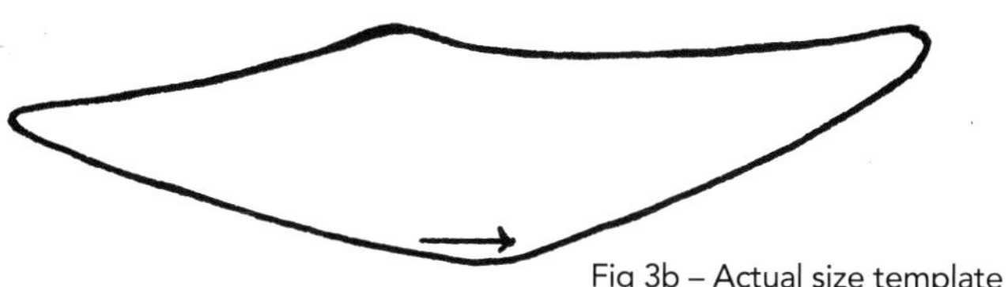

Fig 3b – Actual size template

3 From the traced design, cut out the centre rose pattern in one piece (which includes the numbered shapes 1–7), roughly just beyond the drawn lines to separate it from the rest of the design (Fig 4a). Now carefully cut about ⅛in (3mm) *inside* the drawn lines of shapes 4, 5, 6 and 7 (Fig 4b). Do not attempt to cut away inside pieces 1, 2 and 3 as they are just too small and fiddly.

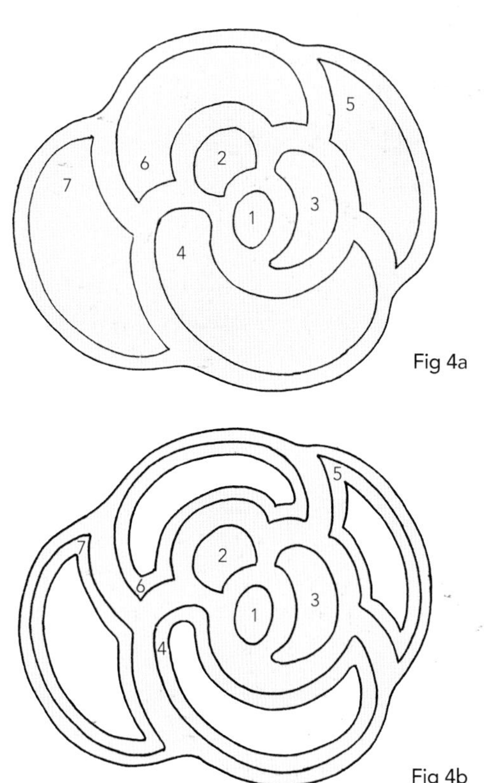

Fig 4a

Fig 4b

Fig 3a – Actual size template

"This was my first big quilt. I learnt so many techniques from sewing each block at Lynne's classes and I am using them in new projects. My materials are centred around the green patterned fabric in the Tangled Star block and I did a mixture of hand and machine sewing and quilting. The large border hangs over each side of the bed. Making this quilt inspired me and quilting has become an addiction!" **Jean Cuthbert**

4 Place this piece of fusible web rough side *down* on the *wrong* side of the fabric chosen for the rose, matching the grainline arrow on piece 3 with the grain or weave of the fabric. Fusible webs like Bondaweb are a disaster if the glue gets transferred by a hot iron to the base of the iron or ironing board, spreading nasty black marks. To avoid this, place non-stick baking parchment on the ironing board before you start and use some between the iron and the fusible web as you stick. Press with a hot iron to stick the fusible web to the fabric.

5 Now cut accurately along the drawn lines through both the fusible web and the fabric to make the seven segments of the rose.

6 From the traced design, cut out roughly each of the six leaves, (numbered 8–13), cutting just beyond the drawn lines as in Fig 5a. Carefully cut away the fusible web about ⅛in (3mm) *inside* each leaf (Fig 5b).

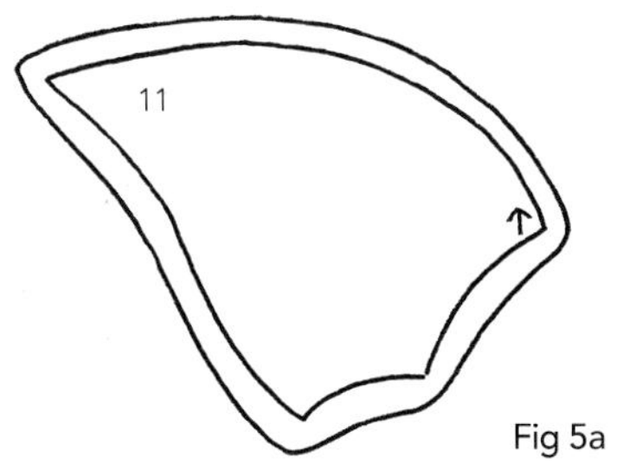

Fig 5a

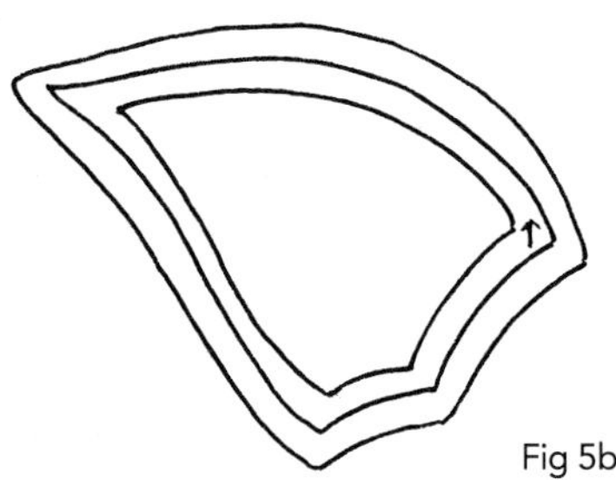
Fig 5b

Fig 2 – Actual size template – top half (see overleaf for bottom half)

This detail from Jean Cuthbert's block shows her effective choice of colour and fabrics, enhanced by the hand blanket stitching and hand quilting between the shapes.

7 Place each leaf shape of fusible web rough side *down* on to the *wrong* side of the chosen fabric, matching the grainline arrows with the grain or weave of the fabric. Press as you did before to stick the fusible web to the fabric. Now, cut accurately along the drawn lines to make the six leaves.

8 Repeat the process described in steps 6–7 with the six segments (numbered 14–19) that make the inner background circle, ironing them to the *wrong* side of the fabric chosen for this part of the design. Do not cut away the fusible web inside pieces 15 and 17 as they are too small.

9 Now repeat the process to make the twelve pieces needed for the outer ring of the design.

10 Remove the backing paper from each of the pieces. Begin with the centre of the design, leaving the outer ring of shapes until later. Arrange the pieces of the rose, the leaves and the inner background circle segments in position on the background fabric, right side *up*, glue side *down*, taking care that each piece covers the drawn outline on the square of background fabric, using the centre part of Fig 1 as a guide. When you are happy with the arrangement, press everything with a hot iron to fix the pieces in place.

11 Now arrange the twelve cut pieces that make the outer ring in position in the same way, matching each piece of fabric with the drawn outline on the background square and making sure that each piece fully covers the drawn line each time. Press with a hot iron to fix the pieces in place.

Stitching the Design by Hand

Use a slightly thicker thread than usual (I like the Gütermann silk thread) and a fine sewing needle like a sharps 9 or 10. Black is often used to outline this type of design, but any choice of colour thread will be fine. You might like to stitch around each fabric in the design with a matching thread or even a variegated thread to add depth.

12 Begin with larger shapes like the leaves and hold the fabric so that the edge of the appliqué shape is running towards you as in Fig 6a. (I am afraid all these stitching instructions are useless for the left-handers. I have found the easiest way for them to re-interpret the directions is to hold the drawn figures up to a mirror and follow the needle and fabric positions from that.) Do not start stitching at the really sharp point of the leaf, but at one of the gentler corners. Make a knot in the thread and bring the needle up from the back of the work in the background fabric, just at the edge of the appliqué fabric (Fig 6a). Keep the edge of the appliqué fabric running towards you and make one stitch at right angles to the edge of the fabric and about ⅛in (3mm) from the edge, bringing the needle back up in the same place you started (Fig 6b).

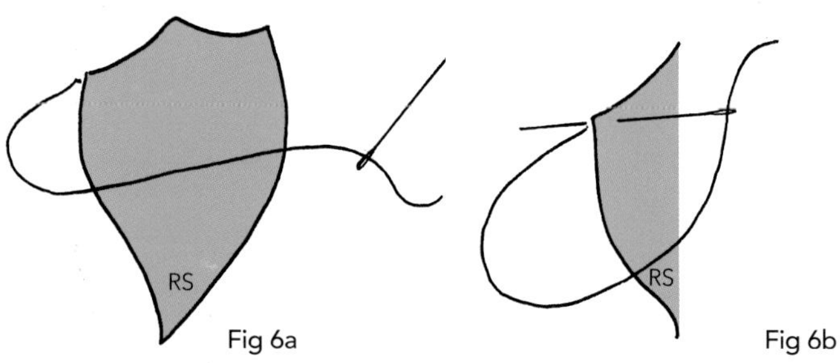

Fig 6a Fig 6b

13 Still keeping the edge of the appliqué running directly towards you, make a wide loop with the thread and insert the needle about ⅛in (3mm) in from the edge of the appliqué fabric as before and at a distance from the first stitch to suit your own taste. Bring the needle out horizontally in the background fabric, just at the edge of the background fabric (Fig 6c). The needle should be at right angles to the edge of the appliqué. Draw the needle through horizontally to the left of the work to tighten the new stitch (Fig 6d).

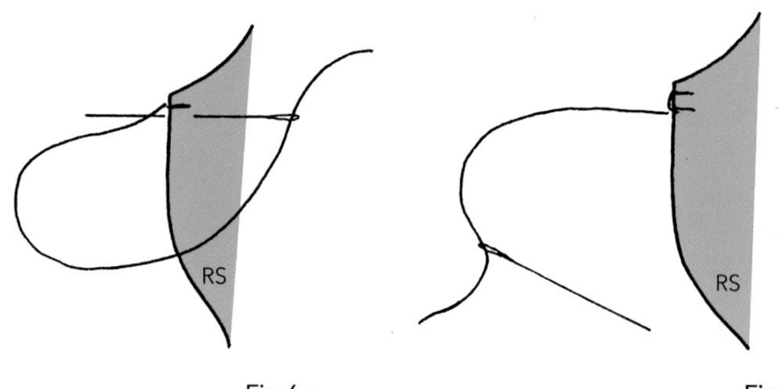

Fig 6c Fig 6d

14 Repeat step 13, turning the work slightly if necessary so that the edge of the appliqué is still running directly towards you. Continue to stitch around the appliqué leaf, keeping the stitches as regular in length and as evenly spaced as possible (Fig 7). To turn sharp corners like the points of the leaves, make one extra tiny stitch on the spot at the corner to keep that long corner stitch in place (Fig 8).

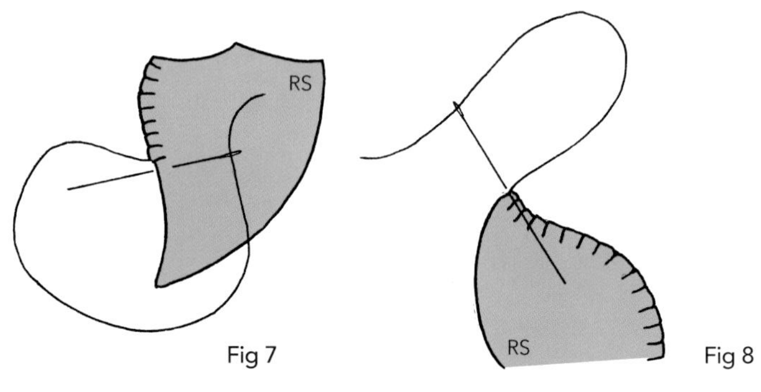

Fig 7 Fig 8

Fig 2 – Actual size template – bottom half

If your stitches do not seem perfect in length and evenness, take heart – my own blanket stitch is nothing like as small and closely spaced as some of my students' but it really doesn't matter. The thickness of the thread and the fabric will dictate the size of stitches to some extent, but also you will soon discover what suits your hand and sewing rhythm to give maximum pleasure in the stitching. Aim at keeping the stitches as even and regular as you can – the size and spacing will vary from person to person.

Stitching the Design by Machine

Many modern sewing machines include a blanket stitch in their selection of decorative stitches and this works well with this design. You need to set up a practice piece and try stitching around it to sort out strategies for getting around corners and negotiating curves. Machines vary in their stitches so you need to get out the manual (oh, that old thing…) and follow any instructions given for using the stitch pattern. My machine has several features that I find invaluable for blanket stitching, including the needle-down function and the knee-lift, so if you have these, try using them while doing your practice pieces. If preferred, a simple zigzag stitch on the machine may be used to stitch around the designs.

As a practice piece draw several leaf shapes on a double thickness of fabric. Stitch around these to get used to stitching curves and going round sharp corners. Then stick some cut leaves on to a background with fusible web and get comfortable with stitching around them before trying out the actual design. The stitch is a pain to unpick, so get it right on a practice piece before you start the block itself.

Once the stitching around each appliquéd shape has been completed by hand or machine, press the block carefully and place it on a cutting board. Trim it down to exactly 13in x 13in (33cm x 33cm). Cut the inner framing strips 1in (2.5cm) wide and attach these (see page 236). Finally, add the sashing strips.

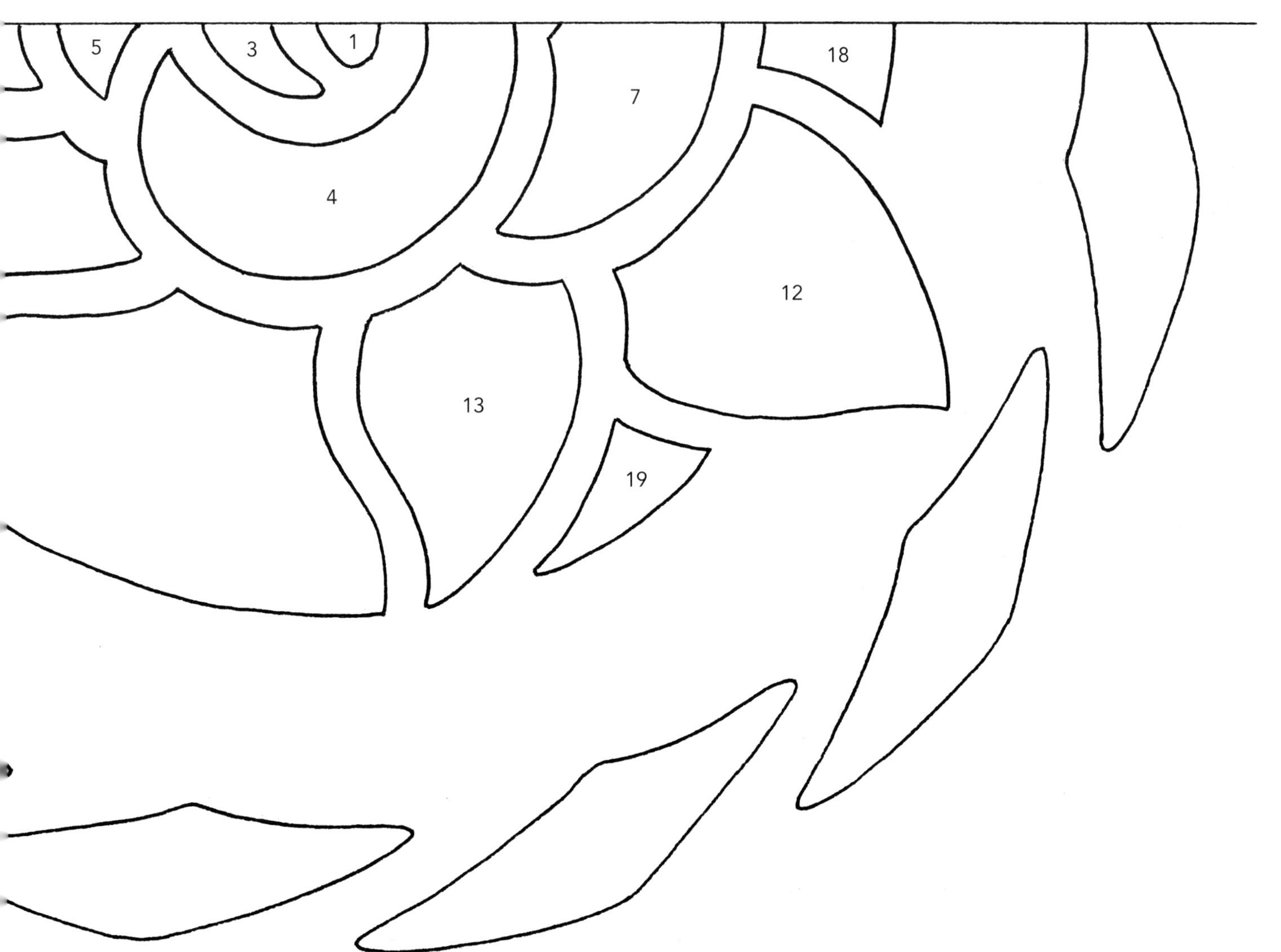

Machine Pieced Strip Patchwork

Bargello

It is only recently that the term bargello has been used in association with patchwork. It has traditionally been the name for Florentine canvas embroidery where parallel vertical straight stitches are worked in many subtle shadings of wool, which rise or fall according to the pattern being followed. Each line of stitches is worked in a different shade from the one before to make curves or flame-like points. The principle of the technique is not unlike Seminole patchwork. Strips of fabric are joined into bands and then cut vertically into pieces of varying widths. Narrow pieces of fabric result in steep curves in the design and wider pieces give gentler slopes (see Fig 1 opposite).

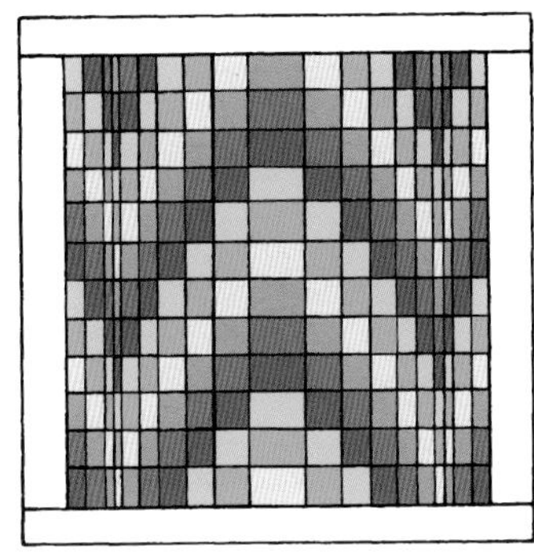
Fig 1

Colour Choices

As the Bargello block needs to be a maximum size of around 13in (33cm) square, it is best to limit the number of fabrics to six. The idea is to shade the fabrics from light to dark. You may like to use just one colour shading, for instance from cream to fawn to ginger to dark brown in the six fabrics. It can be more interesting to use more than one colour, for instance, pale green through to dark forest green to dark grey up to pale silvery grey.

Put out all the fabrics you have to choose from and select any that you think might be useful. Arrange these side by side and overlapping so that you see just a strip of each one, to give an idea of how a small amount relates to its neighbour. Do not limit yourself to six to start with. Once they are arranged you can weed out the less essential. Both prints and plains are fine to use, even very large prints as these become abstract when cut up and add interest to the design. Move the fabrics around until you are happy with the arrangement and aim for gentle shading rather than sharp contrasts.

Construction

1 From each of the six chosen fabrics cut two strips each 1½in (3.8cm) wide and 23in (58.4cm) long. If you cannot get strips as long as 23in (58.4cm), cut four strips that are each 1½in (3.8cm) wide and 13in (33cm) long from each fabric.

2 Arrange the strips in the order that you intend using them. From left-over scraps, cut a small piece from each fabric (about 1in/2.5cm square will do) and stick them vertically on a piece of paper or card. Number each fabric as shown in Fig 2. You will need to refer to this chart as you work.

3 Stitch each set of six strips together in the chosen order. Follow the guidelines for stitching together long strips given for the Seminole block on page 124. You will have two identical bands of strips (or four bands if you are using 13in (33cm) long strips). Do not press these bands yet.

Join the bands together to make one large piece, keeping the colours in the same repeat order (Fig 3). If you are using shorter strips, stitch the bands in pairs to make two pieces. Each will have the same arrangement of strips as shown in Fig 3.

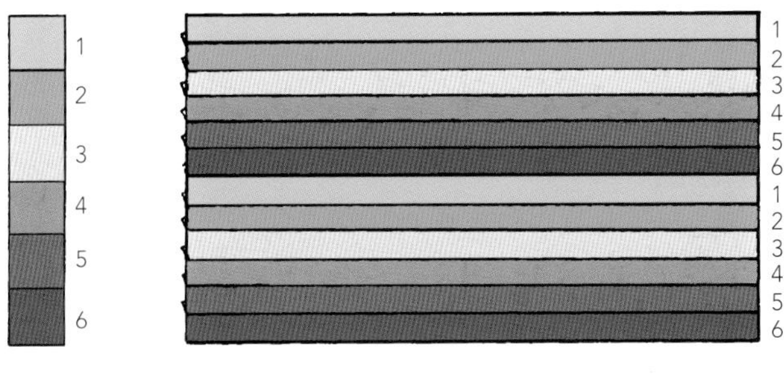

Fig 2

Fig 3

4 Press the seams in alternate directions. Press lightly from the back to establish the directions of the seams and then flip the piece over and press firmly from the front. Make sure the seams are pulled open without folds or the strip widths will not be accurate.

5 Place the piece on a flat surface and with the right side upwards as in Fig 3 bring the bottom strip (fabric 6) up so that it lies on the top strip (fabric 1), with right sides together and the long unstitched edges matching (Fig 4). Check that the piece is lying flat and not twisted, then pin. It does not matter if the side edges do not match – just that both layers of fabric are lying flat. Those using shorter strips will have two shorter tubes each with the same arrangement of strips as in Fig 3.

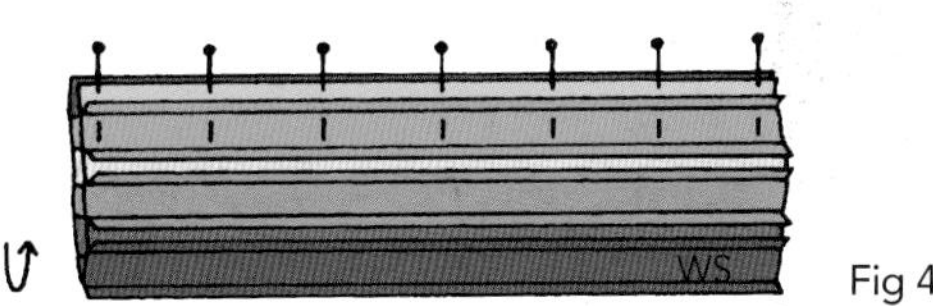

Fig 4

6 Stitch the pinned seam to make a tube. Press the seam in whatever direction fits the alternating arrangement of seams in the rest of the band. Leave the tube with the seams on the outside as in Fig 4.

7 Place the tube of fabrics flat on a cutting board, lining the long top edges up with a horizontal marking on the board. Straighten one end, wasting as little fabric as possible. Now study the cutting chart in Fig 5 overleaf. The first column gives all the information for the first piece to be cut. The top line shows the width of the piece to be cut, which is 1in (2.5cm). Cut the piece as in Fig 6.

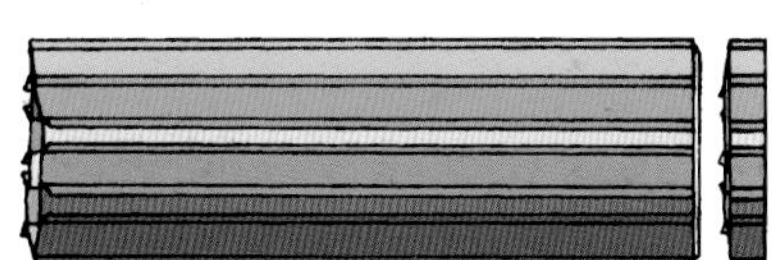
Fig 6

				V						^						V			
WIDTH OF STRIP	1in 2.5 cm	1in 2.5 cm	¾in 1.9 cm	¾in 1.9 cm	1in 2.5 cm	1in 2.5 cm	1¼in 3.2 cm	1¼in 3.2 cm	1½in 3.8 cm	2in 5 cm	1½in 3.8 cm	1¼in 3.2 cm	1¼in 3.2 cm	1in 2.5 cm	1in 2.5 cm	¾in 1.9 cm	¾in 1.9 cm	1in 2.5 cm	1in 2.5 cm
TOP FABRIC	1	6	5	4	5	6	1	2	3	4	3	2	1	6	5	4	5	6	1
BOTTOM FABRIC	6	5	4	3	4	5	6	1	2	3	2	1	6	5	4	3	4	5	6

Fig 5

What you have at this stage is a loop. The two other rows in the chart tell you where the seam must be undone to convert the loop into a Seminole-type piece. For the first piece the top fabric is no. 1 and the bottom is no. 6. They occur twice in the loop, but just locate one pair and ignore the other. Hold fabric 1 in your left hand and fabric 6 in your right and undo the seam that joins them. Pin the piece on a board or lay it out on a clear surface with fabric 1 at the top and fabric 6 at the bottom (Fig 7). Tick the first column on the chart to show that you have dealt with that piece.

Fig 7

8 Cut piece 2, which is also 1in (2.5cm) wide. Find fabrics 6 and 5 next to each other in the loop. Hold fabric 6 in one hand and fabric 5 in the other hand and undo the seam that joins them. Place the second piece next to the first piece with fabric 6 at the top and fabric 5 at the bottom, working from left to right (Fig 8). Tick the second column on the chart once you have done this.

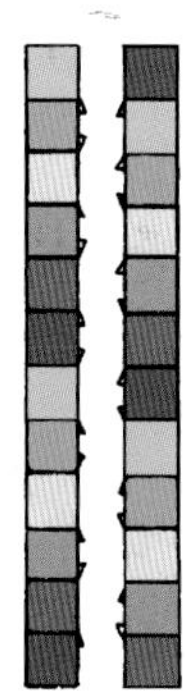

Fig 8

9 Continue to cut each piece in turn, following the width measurements from the chart. The pattern of curves and steps develop as the pieces are unstitched and placed next to each other. The V-shaped symbols on the chart show where the slope comes to a peak or drops to a valley. The slope descends through four pieces and then climbs to a broad peak in the centre of the block. It then descends and rises as a mirror image of the first half (see Fig 1 on previous page).

10 When all the pieces have been cut and arranged begin pinning and stitching them together. The narrower the pieces, the more tricky it is to stitch them, so begin in the centre and work out to one side – that way you will have had some experience of the stitching process before you come to the really narrow pieces. The pinning and stitching is very similar to Seminole patchwork.

To join, place the two strips right sides together and stitch lengthwise, matching seams carefully. The initial pressing of the seams in alternate directions means that the seams will lock together so you can stitch without pinning if you want to. The experience of making the Seminole block will have shown you just how much pinning you need to do. Remember, there are no rules. If you feel you need to pin each junction before you stitch then do so. Take particular care to match seams where there are definite changes in colour as any inaccuracies will show up here. In other areas where the fabrics are more subtly shaded, a mismatched seam will not notice at all. Wait until the whole block is pieced before making a decision to re-stitch a seam, as you may well find that it has merged in with the design and really doesn't stand out at all. Press the seams from the front of the work and to one side before adding each new piece as this makes it easier to handle.

11 Once all the pieces are joined, the block needs to be pressed from the front and placed on a cutting board to check its size. Some of the pieces, especially the very narrow ones, will probably look uneven in width. Use a steam iron to get them pulled out as evenly as possible. Aim to finish up with a reasonably rectangular or square block, never mind the actual measurements. Trim the top and bottom edges to straighten them, but use the steam iron and some judicious pulling to get the sides straight. Measure the block from top to bottom and from side to side. It doubtless won't measure the same, so just add wider framing strips on the shorter sides. Trim the block to an exact 14in (35.6cm) square and then add the sashing strips (see page 236).

"A piece of purple fabric bought at a quilt show started me off on this, my second sampler quilt. The challenge of matching other colours to it added to my obsession for heavily quilted work and put me in 'quilt heaven' for many months. The end result was certainly worth the effort." **Mary Evans**

Machine Foundation Piecing

Pineapple

The Pineapple design is a close relative of Log Cabin, using strips stitched around a centre square. The main difference is that the strips in Pineapple are not just stitched in a square around the centre but also at 45° to the centre, making a more complex eight-sided design (see Fig 1). Traditionally the design has been drawn on to a foundation fabric like calico and the strips stitched to this, using the drawn lines as guidelines. Today, specialist Pineapple rulers make the task easier and quicker, although there is less control over the general accuracy, and joining many blocks together for a quilt often means a good deal of fudging. The Pineapple block in this book is made using a foundation piecing technique.

Fig 1

Colour Choices

The block uses two alternating colours for the strips with a third in the centre and the final corners. A variety of different fabrics in each colour can be used for the strips or just two fabrics throughout the block. The centre can be a contrasting fabric or one that tones more subtly with the two main fabrics. Decisions on the fabric for the corners can be left until that stage in the design is reached when it is easier to make the right choice.

Working with a Foundation

The foundation or base on which the design is drawn and to which the fabrics are stitched can be one that is removed once the block is completed, such as paper or a woven tear-away foundation, or one that is left permanently in place, such as calico.

For the Pineapple block in this quilt it is better to use a foundation that can be removed afterwards so the block has the same thickness and flexibility as the others in the quilt. It helps to be able to see through the foundation, so tracing paper or freezer paper are both excellent, or a woven tear-away foundation which can be purchased from fabric shops.

Stitching along a drawn line on a foundation is easier if an open-front foot is used on the machine so you can see both needle and line as you stitch. Use a larger size 90/14 needle as this makes larger holes in the foundation, making it easier to remove. For the same reason, reduce the stitch length to about 18–20 stitches to the inch. Do a test run on a measured inch on some fabric and count the stitches to find the correct setting for your machine.

Construction

1 Cut a square of foundation such as tracing paper, freezer paper or a tear-away woven foundation measuring 12½ x 12½in (31.7 x 31.7cm). Fold it lightly into four quarters (Fig 3).

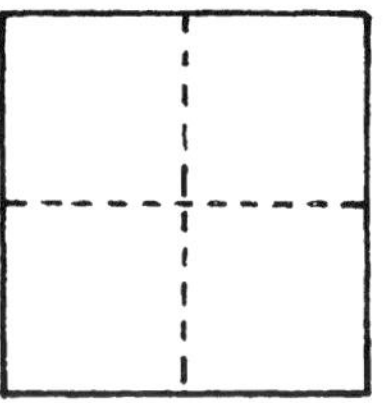

Fig 3

2 Trace the design shown in Fig 2 on to one quarter of the foundation, matching the dotted lines in Fig 2, on page 191, with the folds in the foundation shown in Fig 4 below. Number the lines as in Fig 2. Turn the foundation and position a second quarter over the design in Fig 2, matching the dotted lines and folds as before. Trace the design on to the foundation and add the numbers. Repeat this in the remaining two sections of the foundation to complete the full Pineapple design, as seen in Fig 1.

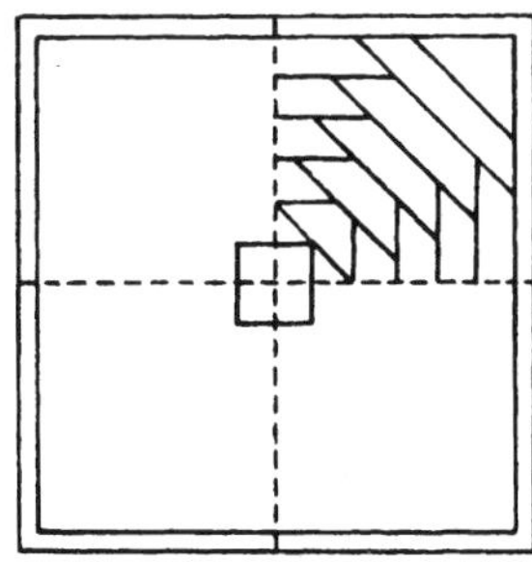

Fig 4

3 From the fabric chosen for the centre square cut a square measuring 2½ x 2½in (6.3 x 6.3cm). From the fabrics chosen for the two main colours, cut strips 1½in (3.8cm) wide. A total of about 110in (280cm) of strip is needed for the strips that run out towards the sides of the block (shown as pale mauve in Fig 1). A total of about 120in (305cm) of strip is needed for the strips that are set at 45° and run towards the corners of the block (shown dark mauve in Fig 1). If you are using several different fabrics, cut them for each round of strips as you go.

4 Place the centre square of fabric right side up on the unmarked side of the foundation (this is the front) over the drawn centre square on the design, so that it overlaps the drawn square by ¼in (6mm) on all sides. If you cannot see too well through the foundation, hold it up against the light on the sewing machine. Pin the square in position (Fig 5).

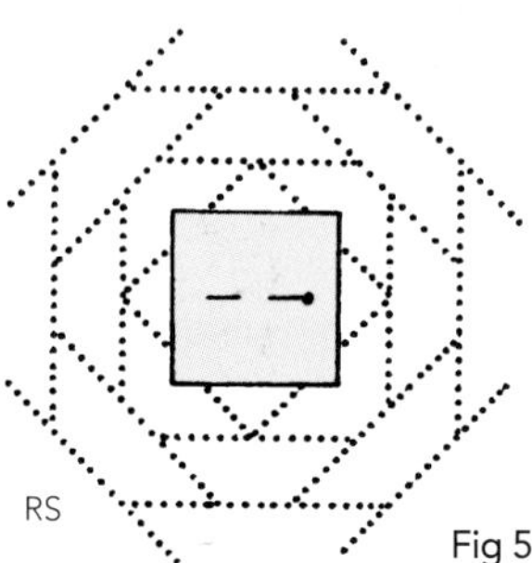

Fig 5

5 To make Round One, from the fabric chosen for the strips shown as pale mauve in Fig 1 cut four pieces each 2½in (6.3cm) long. Place one piece on the pinned square, right sides facing, with the edges matching (Fig 6). Pin in position, keeping the pin well away from the seam allowance where the stitching will be. Turn the foundation over to the drawn side (the back of the block). The numbers show the order of stitching. Stitch along the drawn line marked 1 through both thicknesses of fabric, extending two or three stitches beyond the beginning and end of the drawn line (Fig 7).

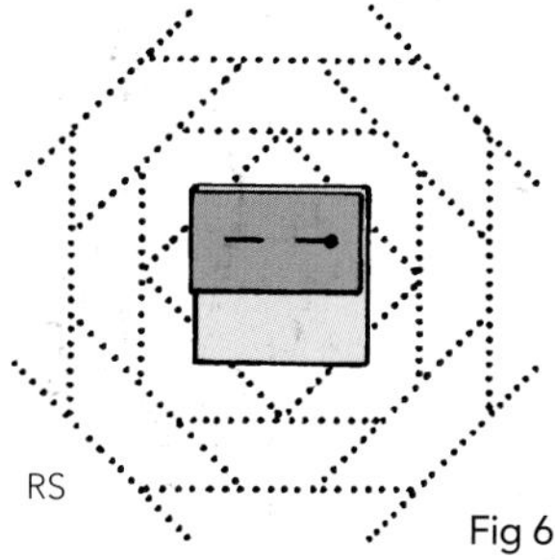

Fig 6

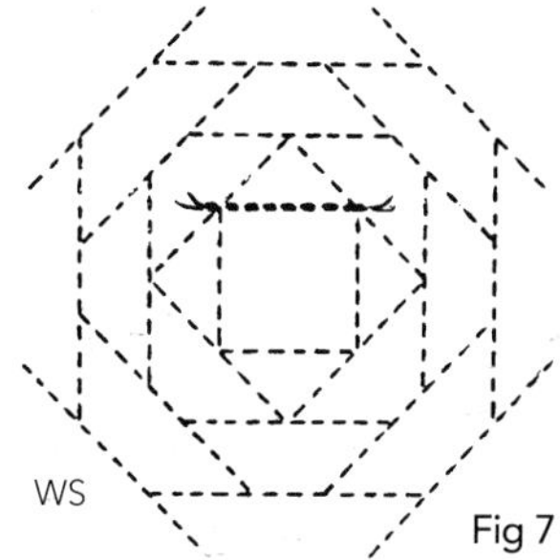

Fig 7

6 Turn to the right side and trim the seam allowance down to a scant ¼in (6mm) by eye with a pair of sharp scissors. Flip the strip over on to the foundation, finger press the seam and press with an iron from the front of the work (Fig 8).

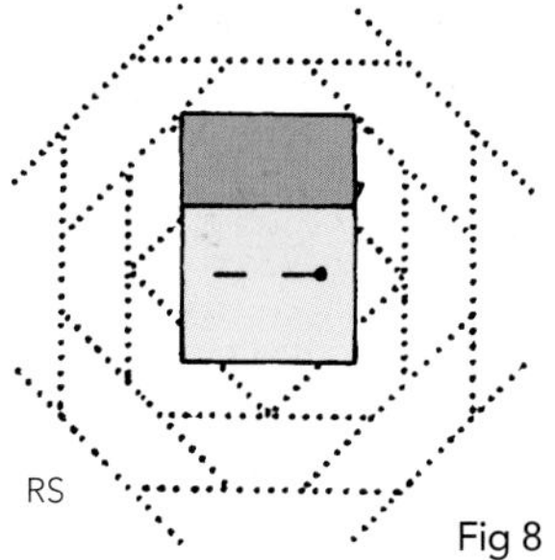

Fig 8

7 Repeat this process with a second piece of fabric on the opposite side of the centre square. Press it over on to the foundation as before (Fig 9).

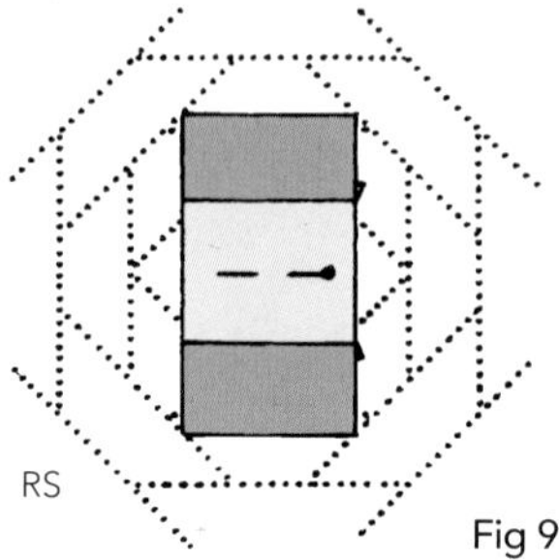

Fig 9

8 In the same way pin and stitch the remaining two pieces to the other sides of the centre square. Press over on to the foundation (Fig 10).

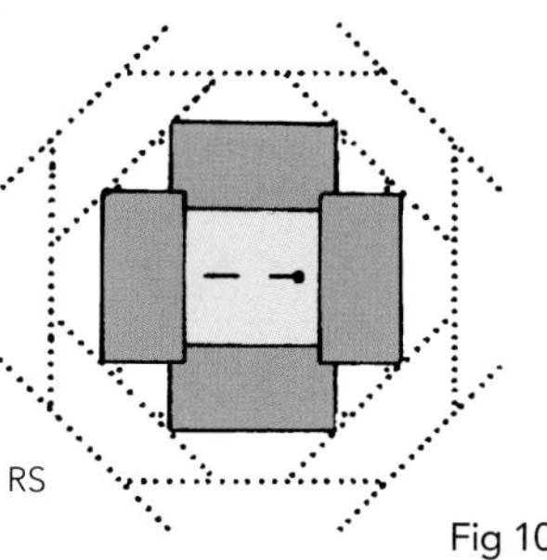

Fig 10

9 Cut four pieces from a strip of the second fabric (the dark mauve strips in Fig 1), each 3½in (8.9cm) long. These will make Round Two of the design. It is not easy to position these strips in the correct place on the front of the block because the line is masked by the fabric already stitched to the foundation. It helps to trim the stitched lengths down at this stage. Turn the foundation to the marked side and place a thin ruler along the next stitching line (marked 2 on the foundation). Pull the foundation back along this line against the edge of the ruler. Do not worry if the foundation pulls away from the stitches at the ends of the seams. Trim the fabric by eye to a scant ¼in (6mm) beyond the folded edge of the foundation (Fig 11). Do this on all four sides on each line marked 2 on the foundation (Fig 12).

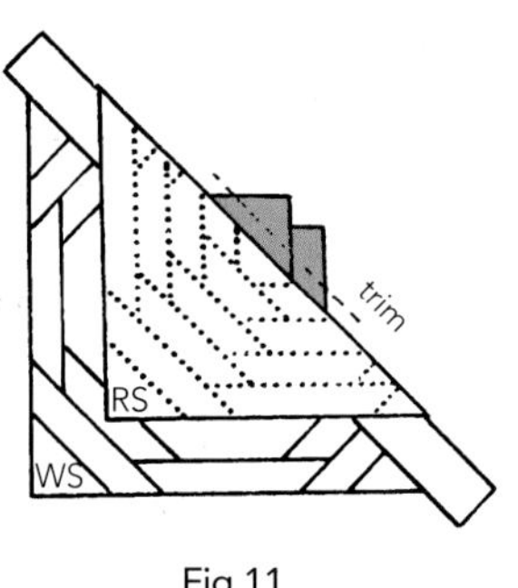

Fig 11

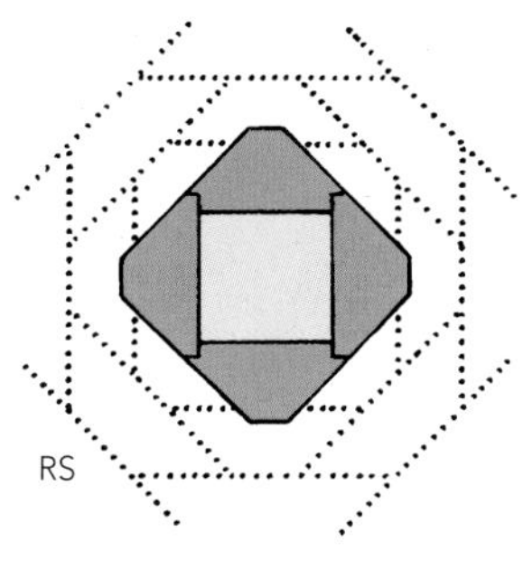

Fig 12

"I chose my favourite colours of purple and turquoise for this sampler quilt. I loved trying out some new blocks and sampling a variety of techniques. Each block was quilted separately and then joined together." **Karen Moore**

10 Position one cut strip of the second fabric on one of the trimmed sides of the block with right sides facing, lining up the edges. Pin in position and turn the foundation over to the marked side. Stitch along the drawn line marked 2 through both layers of fabric, sewing two or three stitches beyond the drawn line at the start and finish. Turn to the right side and flip the fabric over on to the foundation. Press into position with an iron.

Repeat this with a second cut strip on the opposite side of the block and then the other two cut strips, pressing each strip out on to the foundation as they are stitched.

11 Trim the excess fabric from the block by turning the foundation to the drawn side and placing a ruler along each line marked 3. Pull the foundation back against the edge of the ruler and trim the fabric to a scant ¼in (6mm) beyond the folded edge of the foundation (Fig 13).

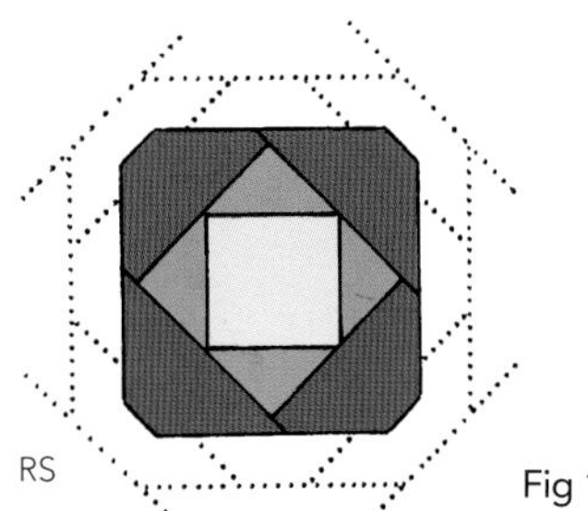

Fig 13

12 From a strip of the first fabric (shown as pale mauve in Fig 1) cut four pieces each 3¾in (9.5cm) long. Pin and stitch them to each side of the block, stitching along the drawn lines marked 3 on the foundation. This makes Round Three of the design. Flip each piece over and press on to the foundation. Use a ruler placed on the lines marked 4 to trim the fabric down as before. You will find that as the block progresses gaps appear between the pieces of fabric along each edge and you may not need to trim the fabric back to be able to position the next round of strips accurately. Just do whatever makes it easiest for you.

13 The next round of strips (Round Four) uses four pieces of the second fabric each 4½in (11.4cm) long. Stitch these to the foundation as before.

14 Continue to build out the block, stitching four strips each time along the marked lines. The *length* of strip used each time is as follows:
Round Five: four strips of fabric 1, each 4½in (11.4cm).
Round Six: four strips of fabric 2, each 5¼in (13.3cm).
Round Seven: four strips of fabric 1, each 5¼in (13.3cm).
Round Eight: four strips of fabric 2, each 6¼in (15.9cm).
Round Nine: four strips of fabric 1, each 6¼in (15.9cm).
Round Ten: four strips of fabric 2, each 7in (17.8cm).

15 For the final corners of the block cut two squares from the chosen fabric each measuring 4¼ x 4¼in (10.8 x 10.8cm). These are slightly larger than necessary, but it is better to have a little extra to trim down in the final size.

Cut each square diagonally to make the four corners. Pin the longest edge of each triangle to the corners of the block, right sides facing, and stitch along the drawn lines marked 11 on the foundation (Fig 14). Press the corners back on to the foundation.

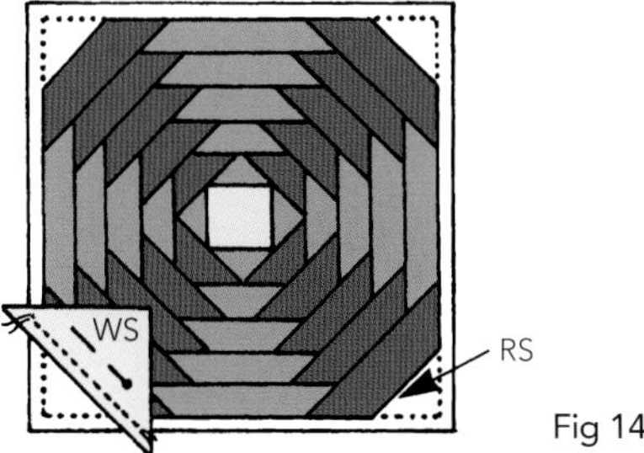

Fig 14

16 Trim the block and foundation to exactly ¼in (6mm) beyond the outer drawn line (Fig 15). This makes a block 12½ x 12½in (31.7 x 31.7cm).

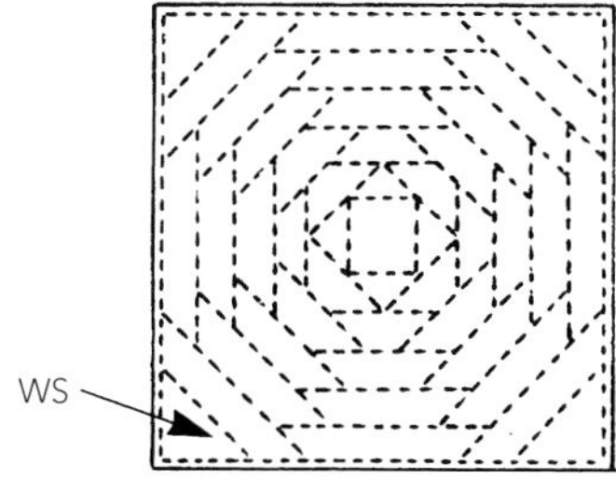

Fig 15

17 It is a good idea to add the framing strips to the block while the foundation is still in place as it adds stability and the stitching line is marked ready for use. Cut framing strips, two measuring 1¼ x 12½in (3.2 x 31.7cm) and two 1¼ x 14in (3.2 x 35.6cm). Pin and stitch the two shorter strips to the sides of the block, stitching along the drawn line on the foundation. Press the seams outwards away from the block, pressing from the front of the work. Pin and stitch the two longer strips to the top and bottom of the block in the same way. Press seams outwards from the front of the block.

18 Turn the block to the back and carefully remove all the paper foundation. Finally, add the sashing strips to the block (see page 236).

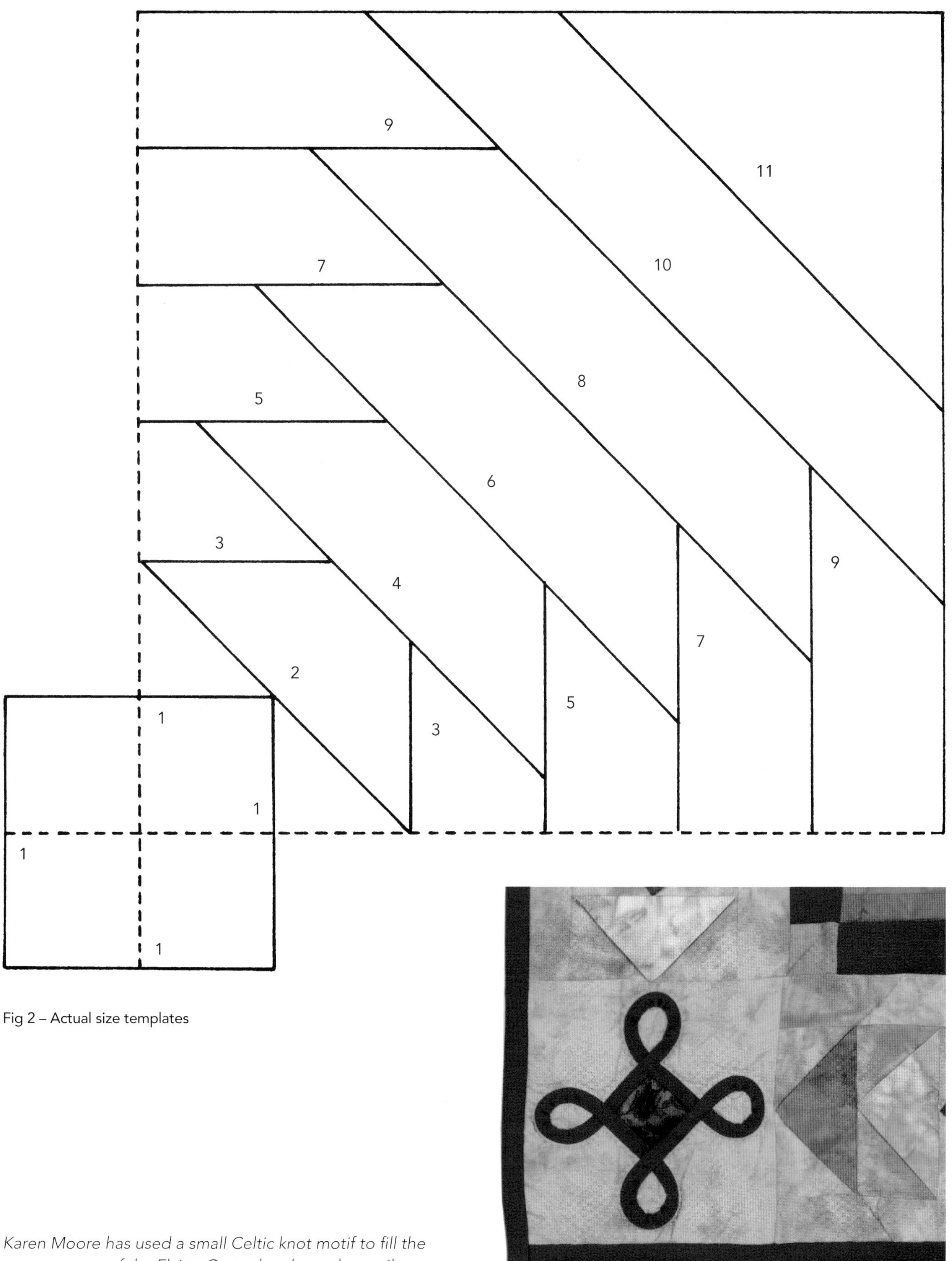

Fig 2 – Actual size templates

Karen Moore has used a small Celtic knot motif to fill the empty corner of the Flying Geese border on her quilt.

Hand or Machine Piecing

Attic Windows

The Attic Windows block has long been a favourite for quilters because of its three-dimensional effect. Each square is made from three pieces that when assembled give an impression of a window with the front window-sill and one side of the frame. When a number of these are joined together the effect becomes that of a large window divided up into smaller panes (see Fig 1) opposite. This illusion is created by using the same fabric throughout for the horizontal window-sills and another fabric for all the side window frames. By making one of these sets of strips in a light fabric and the other in a darker fabric, the three-dimensional effect is enhanced.

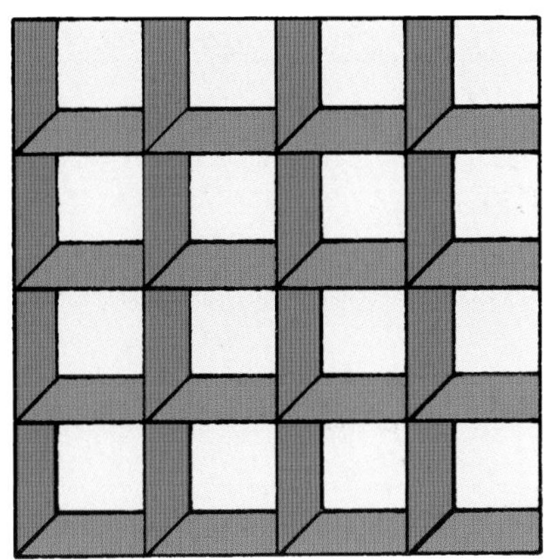

Fig 1

Colour Choices

Although the piecing technique for Attic Windows is straightforward, I have left the block until this later stage in the sequence of techniques because by now you will have had plenty of experience in selecting and balancing fabrics which should help when you start sorting out the choices for this block.

First, choose two fabrics for the window-sills and window frames, one light and one dark. It doesn't matter which you use horizontally for the window-sills and which are used for the vertical window frames, so arrange them together and make your decision by seeing how they look before cutting anything.

The fabric squares used for the windows themselves give an opportunity to create a design that is absolutely unique. A variety of fabrics can be used to paint a picture through the windows: I used varying blues shading from light in one corner to dark in the opposite corner to give the feeling of a night sky. A whole garden scene or townscape could be created by careful selection of sections of fabrics that are cut to size and arranged across the block. You have sixteen windows to play with, four in each row, so there is plenty of scope for enjoying yourself with the design.

If this seems too intimidating then look for windows that create the feeling of depth to accentuate the three-dimensional effect of the block. This may be just one solid fabric or a series of subtly graded shades. Lay out your fabrics and ponder it. Do not rush things: the cutting and piecing are the easy bits, it is the agonizing over the choice of window fabrics that takes the time.

The squares for the windows are 2 x 2in (5 x 5cm) finished size, and it is a good idea to make the template in clear plastic so that you can move it across the fabric and find the most effective sections to cut out and use. This is one design where a pin-board is a great help. Cut out all the separate pieces and pin them in place on the board. Place the board vertically and stand well back so that you can consider the effect. Rearrange or even re-cut pieces if necessary. Once all this agonizing is done, make a note of the final arrangement before you dismantle it to stitch it.

Construction

Templates A and B in Fig 2 are for traditional American piecing. The templates are drawn around on the back of the fabric and the shapes cut out with a ¼in (6mm) seam allowance added on all sides. The drawn lines are the stitching lines and may be stitched by hand or by machine. Template C (Fig 14, page 195) has seam allowances already added and can be used for an alternative machine-pieced method, described on page 195 (step 9).

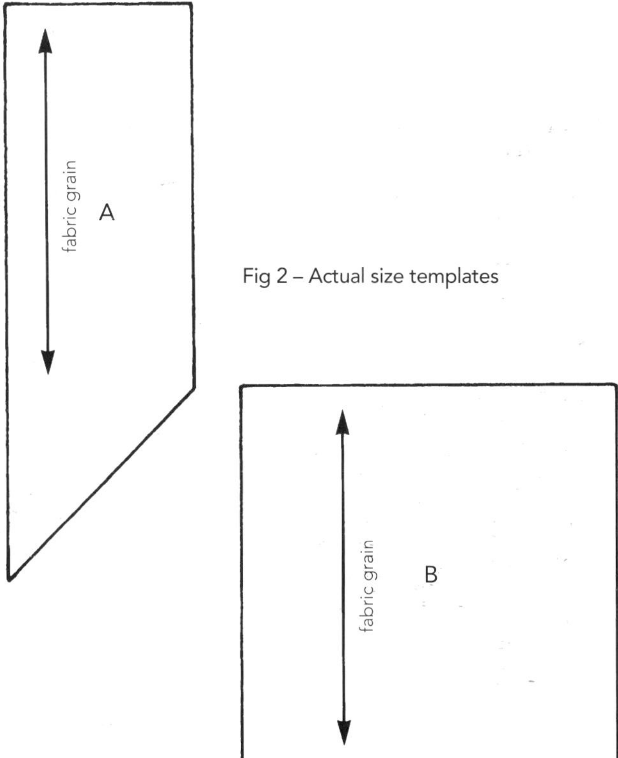

Fig 2 – Actual size templates

Traditional Piecing Method

1 Make the templates, preferably from clear template plastic, by tracing the two shapes from Fig 2. Mark the directional arrows as these show how the templates should be positioned on the grain or weave of the fabric.

2 From the fabric to be used for the window-sills (the horizontal strips in the design) cut a strip measuring 1½ x 52in (3.8 x 132cm). Several shorter strips can be used if you do not have this length in one piece. Use rotary cutting equipment to cut the strips.

From the fabric to be used for the window frames (the vertical strips in the design) cut a similar strip measuring 1½ x 52in (3.8 x 132cm). Again, shorter strips can be used if you do not have this length in one piece.

3 Lay the window-sill strip with *wrong side uppermost* on a cutting board. Draw round template A with a sharp marking pencil sixteen times, leaving a ¼in (6mm) seam allowance at the top and bottom edges and allowing at least ½in (1.3cm) between each drawn outline so that the seam allowance of ¼in (6mm) can be added to each shape when cutting out. Save space by arranging the templates as in Fig 3. Make sure that the template looks *exactly* like that in Fig 3 – do not flip the template over or the design will not work.

Fig 3

4 Cut out each shape to include the ¼in (6mm) seam allowance, either by eye or by using a rotary cutter and ruler. The top and bottom edges are already cut as they are the edges of the fabric strip, so it is just the sides that need to be cut (Fig 4).

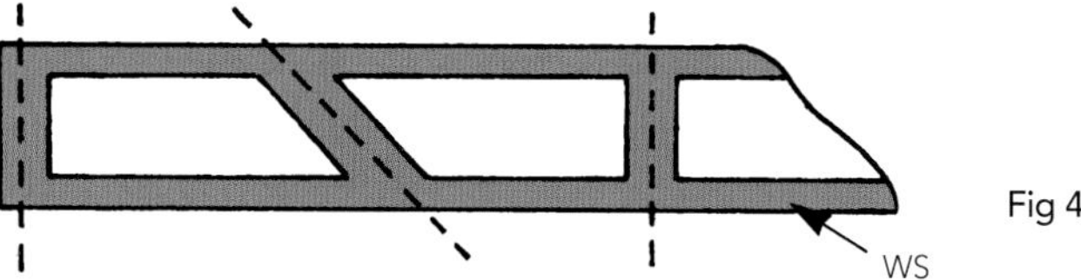

Fig 4

5 Take the cut strip of fabric chosen for the window frames. The same template A must first be *reversed*. Turn it over completely so that the slanted edge is facing the opposite way to when it was used previously. If you do not do this, the piecing of the Attic Window is impossible – you will have the equivalent of two left sleeves!

Using the reversed template A (Fig 5) repeat the process of marking and cutting the strip as for the window-sill pieces. You should finish up with sixteen pieces of one fabric for the window-sills and sixteen pieces of the other fabric for the window frames (Fig 6).

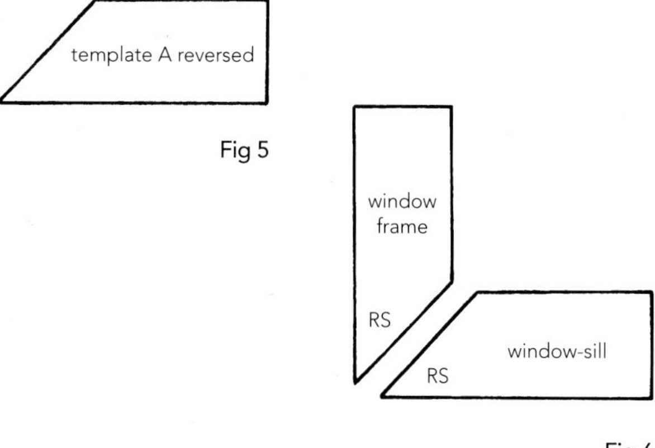

Fig 5

Fig 6

6 If you are choosing specific sections of a piece of fabric for the windows you may need to look and mark on the *right* side of the fabric. To do this make an extra window template in clear plastic that measures 2½ x 2½in (6.3 x 6.3cm) to include the seam allowances. Use this to find the exact part of the design that you want. Draw round it on the *right* side of the fabric and cut out exactly on the drawn line. Turn the square of fabric over and position template B on the *back* of the fabric leaving a ¼in (6mm) seam allowance on all sides. Draw round template B to give the stitching line on the fabric (Fig 7).

If you do *not* need to look at the right side of the fabric when marking and cutting the window squares, use template B only. On the *wrong* side of the chosen fabric draw accurately around the template sixteen times using a sharp marking pencil and matching the direction of the arrow with the grain of the fabric as usual. Allow at least ½in (1.3cm) between each drawn outline so that the seam allowances of ¼in (6mm) can be added to each shape when cutting out (Fig 8). Cut out each square to include the ¼in (6mm) seam allowance.

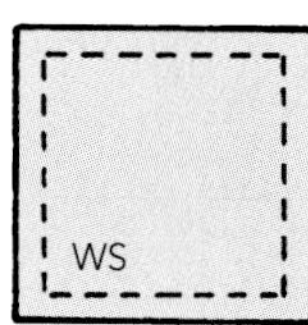

Fig 7

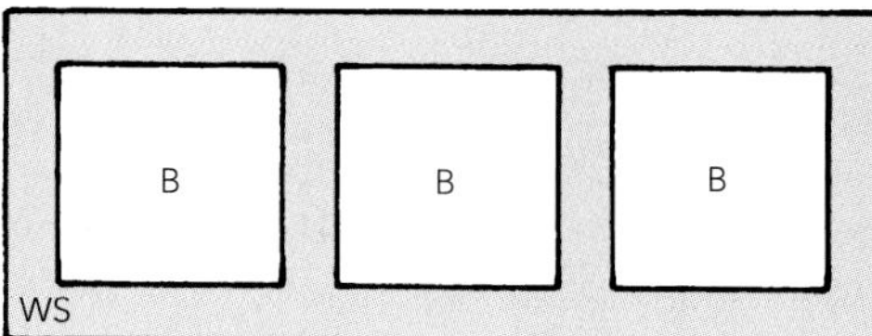

Fig 8

7 Arrange each Attic Window as in Fig 9 and pin them on a board to check the effect of your arrangement.

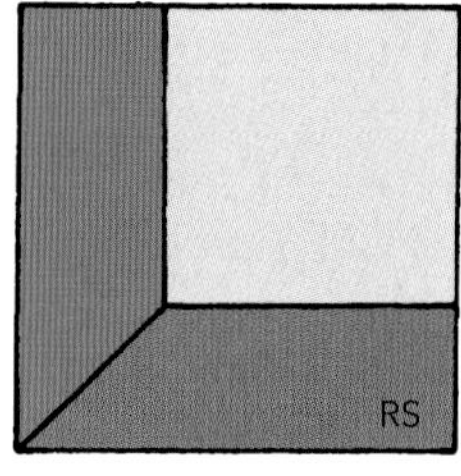

Fig 9

Stitching the Units:

Follow step 8 if stitching the units by hand, or steps 9–13 if stitching by machine.

8 *If stitching the units by hand:* place the window square and one of the side strips right sides together along the two sides to be joined (Fig 10). Pin and stitch along the marked lines, following the method used for piecing the Tangled Star block (page 132), known as American piecing. Do not stitch beyond the marked corners into the seam allowances (Fig 11).

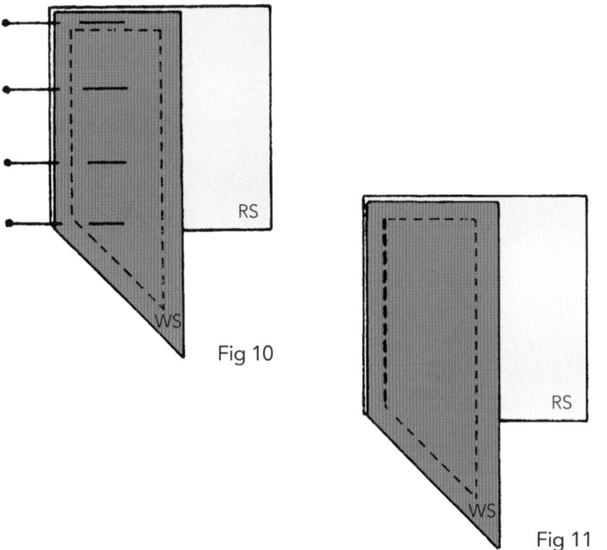

Fig 10

Fig 11

In the same way pin and stitch the other side strip to the square, stitching only to the marked corners of the design (Fig 12). Finally, pin and stitch the last seam, working from the inner corner where the side pieces meet the window square towards the outer corner. Push the seam allowances away from the stitching line and begin by matching the marked corner on both side pieces only, avoiding any fabric of the window square (Fig 13).

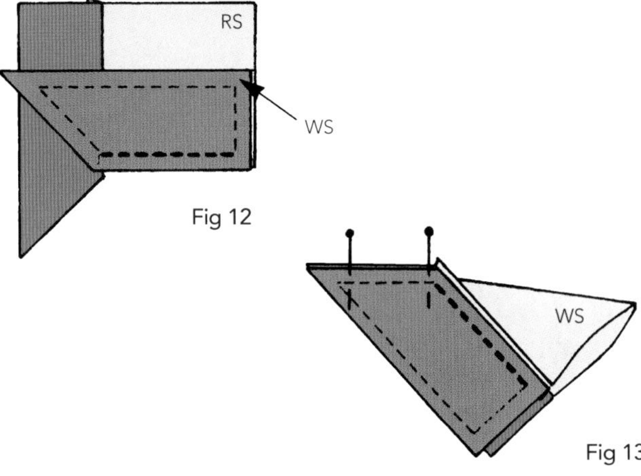

Fig 12

Fig 13

9 *If stitching the block by machine:* you may like to cut the pieces with the seam allowances already added on. Template C in Fig 14 below is for the bottom sill and side frame of the windows with the ¼in (6mm) seam allowance already added.

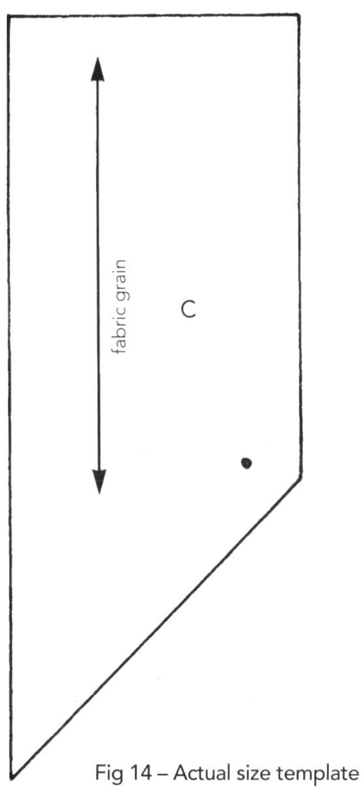

Fig 14 – Actual size template

In this alternative block Juliet Simpson graded the windows in her Attic Windows block from light mauve in the top right corner down to rich red in the bottom left area.

Cut strips as for the hand-piecing technique. Place the template on the wrong side of the strip for the window-sill. The top and bottom edges should match the edges of the fabric strip. Draw along the other two edges of the template (Fig 15).

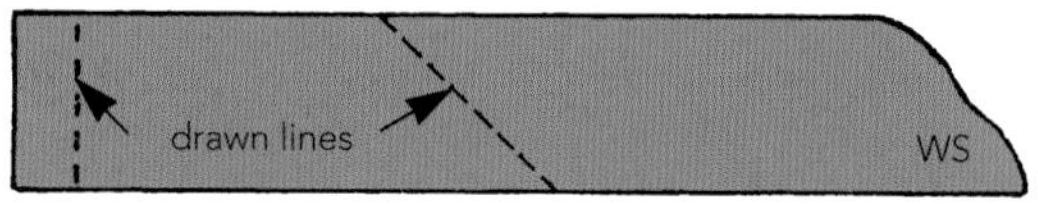

Fig 15

Turn the template round and place it so that the drawn slanted line on the fabric exactly lines up with the slanted edge of the template. Draw along the straight side of the template (Fig 16). Repeat this process along the strip of fabric until sixteen shapes have been marked. Using a rotary cutter and ruler cut exactly along each drawn line to give sixteen window-sill pieces.

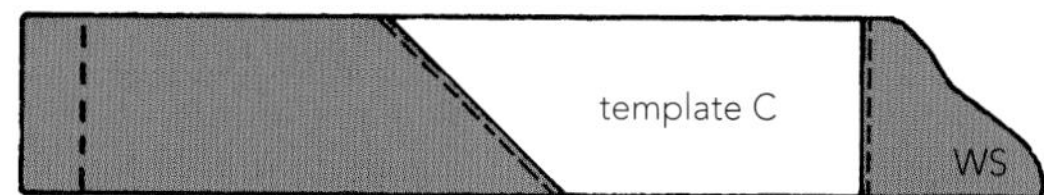

Fig 16

10 Turn template C over and repeat the process on the strip cut for the window frames to give sixteen shapes.

11 For the window, cut sixteen squares of fabric each measuring 2½ x 2½in (6.3 x 6.3cm). You may need to use a plastic template to draw round if you are choosing particular areas of fabric, otherwise cut a strip 2½in (6.3cm) wide and cut squares from it, each measuring 2½ x 2½in (6.3 x 6.3cm).

12 On the *wrong* side of each window square draw a dot at the bottom right corner ¼in (6mm) in from both edges to mark the stitching corner. Do the same at the inner stitching corner on each side strip (Fig 17).

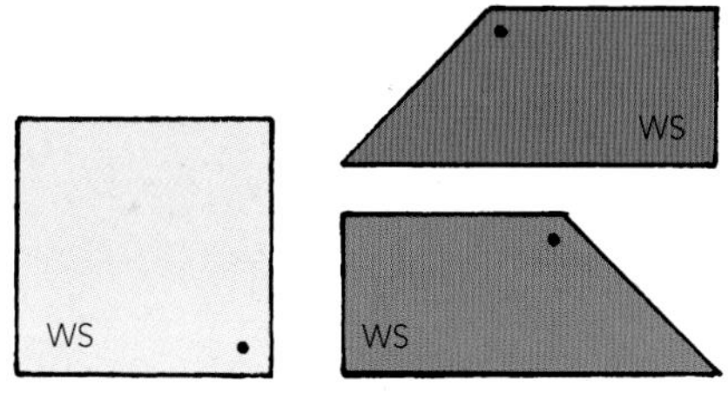

Fig 17

13 Pin and stitch one side strip as shown in Fig 18, matching the marked dots and stitching a ¼in (6mm) seam. Do not stitch beyond the marked dots into the seam allowance. In the same way pin and stitch the other side strip (Fig 19). Finally, pin and stitch the last seam, stitching from the marked dots towards the outer corner (Fig 20). Push all the seam allowances and window fabric away from the seam so that they are not caught in the stitching. This seam is on the bias, so try not to pull and stretch it as you stitch.

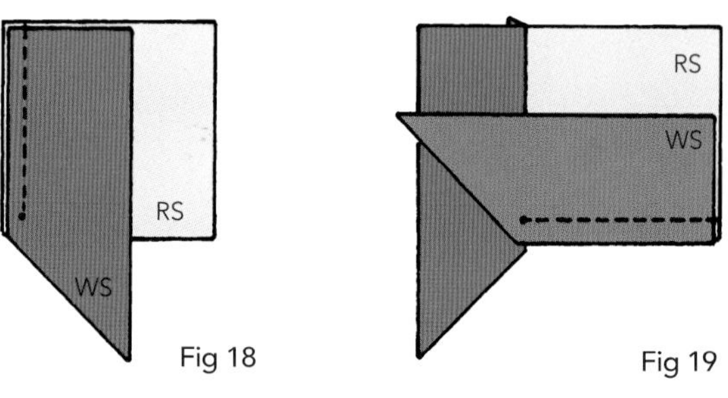

Fig 18

Fig 19

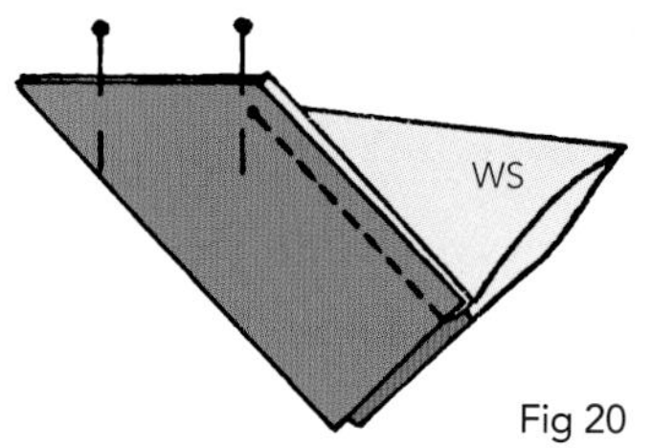

Fig 20

14 Assemble all the sixteen units in your chosen method. Press each unit from the front, pressing the seam allowances away from the window square and diagonal seam allowances to one side.

15 Place the stitched and pressed units in the chosen arrangement. Join the units into horizontal rows, pinning and matching the seams and stitching either by hand or by machine.

If sewing by hand, leave the seam allowances unstitched and press only after the whole block has been assembled. If stitching by machine, press the seams from the front, ironing the seams of row one in one direction, those of row two the opposite way and so on. Join the rows together, matching the seams carefully. Press the completed block from the front of the work.

16 The block should now measure 12½ x 12½in (31.7 x 31.7cm). Add the inner framing strips of a cut width of 1¼in (3.2cm) to bring the block up to 14 x 14in (35.6 x 35.6cm). Finally, add the sashing strips. See page 236 for adding framing strips and sashing.

"A visit to Australia, just before I started this quilt, inspired the colours I used. I loved the earth pigments used by the traditional Aboriginal artists." **Sue Fitzgerald**

Machine Foundation Piecing

Monkey Wrench

When I first began teaching the original Sampler Quilt course I included the block Monkey Wrench (see Fig 1 opposite), but ceased to use it after a while as it seemed too simple a design and slightly out of scale with the other blocks in the quilt. Later I realised that it needed to be used as a repeat design with four smaller versions put together to make one block so that the circular movement of the colours could be seen (Fig 2). This block has great potential for a design used throughout a larger quilt where the curling and uncurling shapes can be exploited. The design used here is quite small. Larger versions may be made by just enlarging the foundation design on page 203.

Fig 1

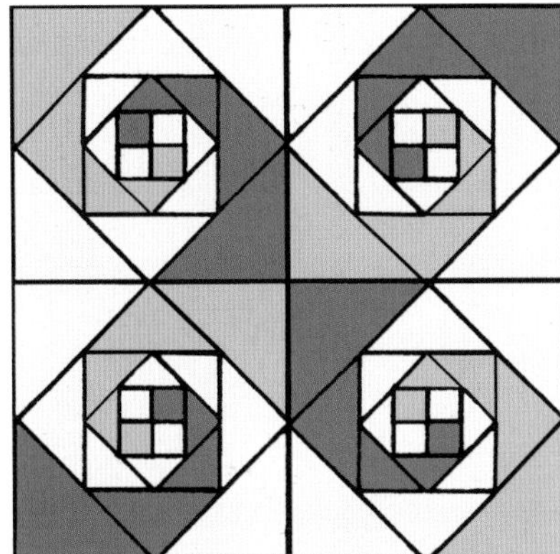

Fig 2

Because each Monkey Wrench block measures only 6 x 6in (15.2 x 15.2cm), it is most accurately and successfully pieced using the foundation technique, where the design is traced on to paper, Vilene, a woven tear-away foundation or even calico. The fabric pieces are placed on to the unmarked side of the foundation and stitched in place along the lines marked on the back of the foundation. This makes the piecing very accurate and keeps the block stable as you work. Once the four blocks are completed they will all measure exactly the same size and can be joined together without the usual 'easing and adjusting' that is part and parcel of quilt-making.

I have described foundation piecing as a machine technique, but it can just as easily be stitched by hand if you prefer. A firm foundation that will stay permanently behind the block, such as calico or a fine Vilene, is best for hand-work, as pulling paper away from hand stitching can strain the stitches.

Colour Choices

The Monkey Wrench block (Fig 1) consists of four curving shapes that spiral out from the centre. Just two fabrics can be used in the opposite spirals as in Fig 1 or three fabrics as in Fig 3. For my quilt (see page 2) I used two of my blue fabrics for opposing spirals with the other two in a background fabric.

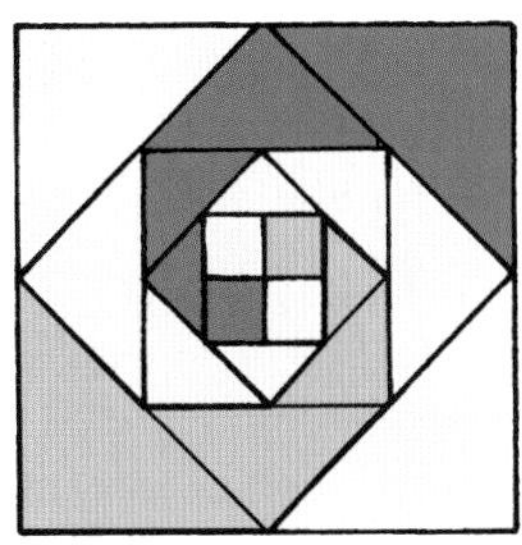

Fig 3

Working with a Foundation

Two types of foundation can be used for this work: one that is removed after the block has been completed, like paper, tracing paper or a woven tear-away foundation; or one that is left behind the block to give it stability, like Vilene or calico. Using a permanent foundation does eliminate the tedious task of pulling all the paper from the block once it is finished but will make the block thicker and heavier, especially if calico is used. I prefer a fine Vilene which can be left in position without adding thickness and is also virtually transparent, a great help when piecing.

For the Monkey Wrench block in this book I would recommend a foundation that can be removed afterwards so that the block has the same weight and flexibility as the others in the quilt. It does help to be able to see through the foundation, so tracing paper or freezer paper are both excellent, or you can buy a woven tear-away foundation from fabric shops.

Using the Fabrics

Most projects using foundation piecing are very vague about the fabric – 'cut pieces larger than you need' is often all the advice they give. Because this block is repeated four times and also because most of the pieces are right-angled triangles I have estimated generously the size of triangles needed to cover each piece and given specific measurements to be cut. This will not only save on fabric but will also get you used to working on a foundation reasonably painlessly.

Preparing for Sewing

To make it easier to stitch exactly on the drawn line on the foundation, an open-front foot is needed for this technique, so that you get a good view of both the line and the needle. The ¼in foot for most machines does this job nicely, or you can cut the centre part out of a plastic foot. I used a hacksaw from a child's toolbox to do this with great success. Change the needle in your machine from the usual 80/12 to a larger 90/14 – this makes larger holes in the paper so that it can be removed more easily. The stitch length should be set even smaller than usual, approximately 18–20 stitches to the inch, for the same reason. Do a test run on a measured inch on some fabric and count the stitches so you will know the correct setting for your own machine.

Construction

1 Cut four pieces of foundation such as tracing paper, freezer paper or a tear-away woven foundation, each measuring 7 x 7in (17.8 x 17.8cm). Trace the Monkey Wrench block, shown in Fig 4 on page 203, carefully on to each foundation, using a ruler and sharp pencil, keeping all the lines as accurate as possible. Also trace the numbers shown on the block.

2 If *three* fabrics are being used for the block (two fabrics plus a background) as in Fig 3, measure and cut one set of the following squares from each fabric, *plus* an extra set in the background fabric as it is being used twice in the design:
two squares 2¼ x 2¼in (5.7 x 5.7cm);
two squares 2¾ x 2¾in (7 x 7cm);
two squares 3½ x 3½in (8.9 x 8.9cm);
two squares 4½ x 4½in (11.4 x 11.4cm).

If only *two* fabrics are being used as in Fig 1 cut *two* sets of squares (four squares of each size) from each fabric.

3 Cut all the squares in half diagonally to make triangles (Fig 5). Sort these into piles of each size and colour ready to use.

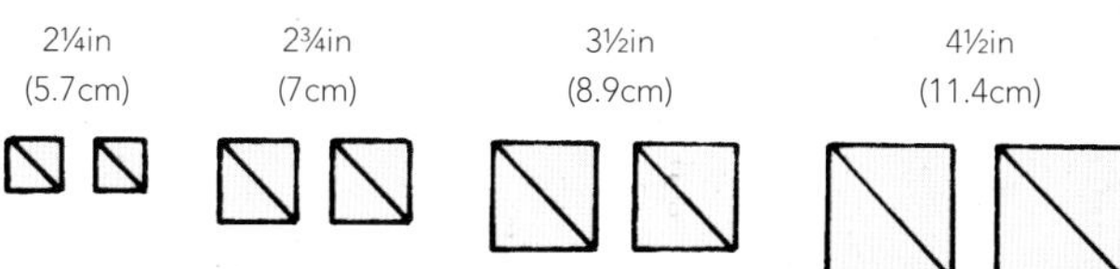

Fig 5

4 The four-patch in the centre of each block is constructed separately and placed on the foundation. If *three* fabrics are being used, cut one strip from each main fabric and two strips from the background fabric. Each strip should measure 1¼ x 6in (3.2 x 15.2cm). Stitch the strips into pairs (Fig 6). Press the seams towards the darker fabrics.

If only *two* fabrics are being used, cut two strips of each fabric, then stitch the strips into pairs and press as above (see Fig 6).

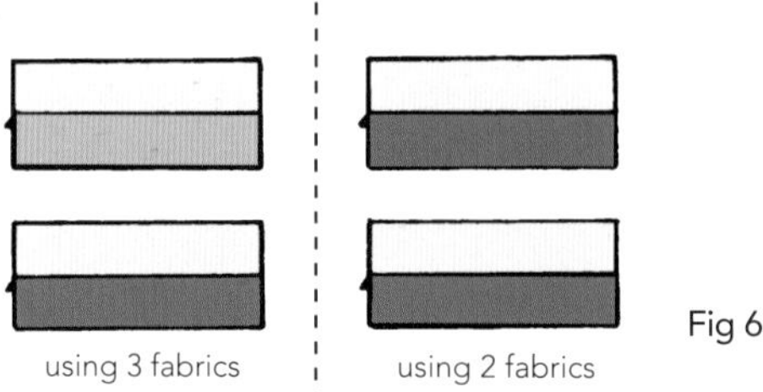

Fig 6

5 From each band of strips cut off four pieces, each 1¼in (3.2cm) wide (Fig 7). Take one piece from the first band and one piece from the second. Turn the second piece through 180° (Fig 8) and place the two pieces right sides facing, matching the centre seam. Pin and stitch the two pieces together (Fig 9).

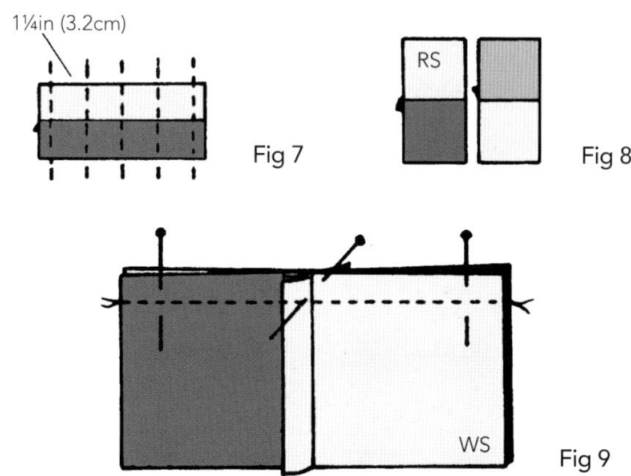

Fig 7

Fig 8

Fig 9

Repeat this with all four pairs, making sure that each pair is pinned in *exactly* the same arrangement as the others, or your four-patches will not finish up the same (Fig 10). Press each four-patch.

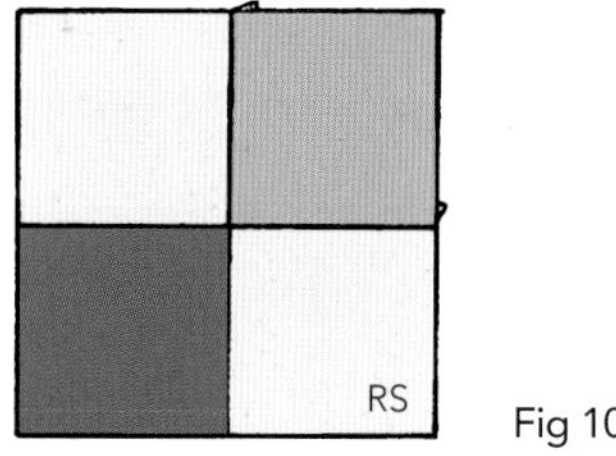

Fig 10

6 Place one four-patch right side *up* in the centre of the unmarked side of the foundation (Fig 11a). Hold it in position and turn the foundation over. Adjust the position of the four-patch so that the seamlines are lying exactly underneath the drawn four-patch on the foundation and the centres are matched. Pin in position. If you cannot see too well through the foundation, hold it up against the light on the sewing machine. The fabric four-patch should show beyond the marked lines by about ¼in (6mm) on all

"With this quilt I decided to only use three colours and to complement the limited colour range with quilting that was, for me, more adventurous by moving away from quilting in the ditch or ¼in. I also found that the hand-sewn blocks were surprisingly more satisfying than I expected." **Jean Williams**

sides (Fig 11b). It helps me to think of the foundation as the curtain on the stage of a theatre: the marked side is the back of the stage curtain, but to see the front of the stage you have to go round to the other side. The fabric you lay on to the other side should also face outwards towards the audience with its back to the foundation.

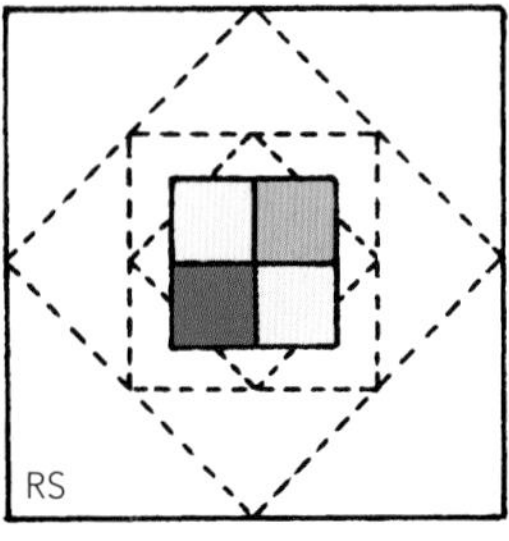

Fig 11a

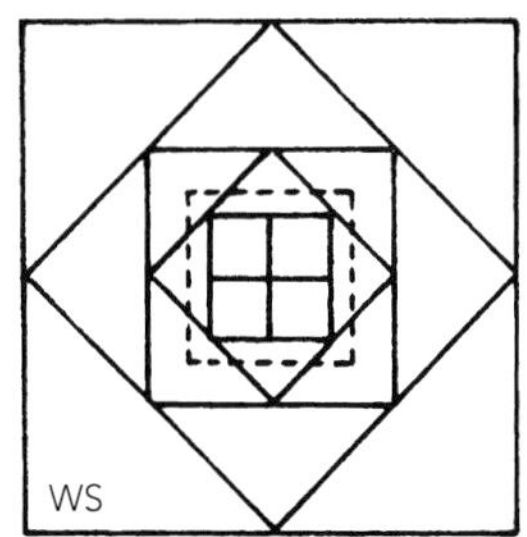

Fig 11b

7 Do not stitch anything at this stage. Look at your pinned four-patch and take the smallest triangle cut from the background fabric. Place it in position right side facing *outwards* on the unmarked side of the foundation – never mind the raw edges (Fig 12). The long bias edge should be next to the four-patch. Flip the triangle over on to the four-patch with right sides facing and the edges matching (Fig 13). Pin the triangle in position and turn the whole thing over so that the marked side of the foundation is uppermost.

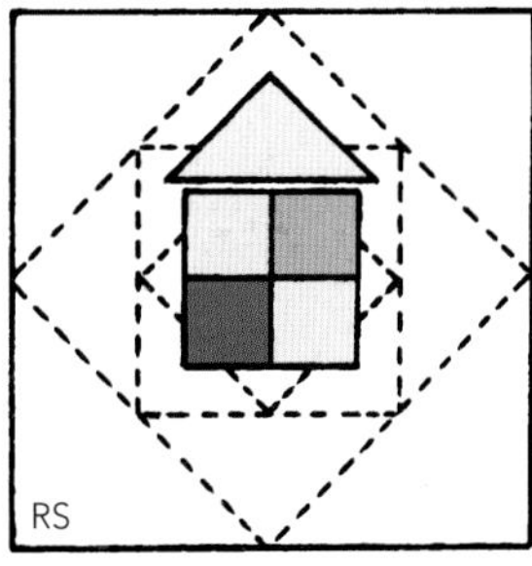

Fig 12

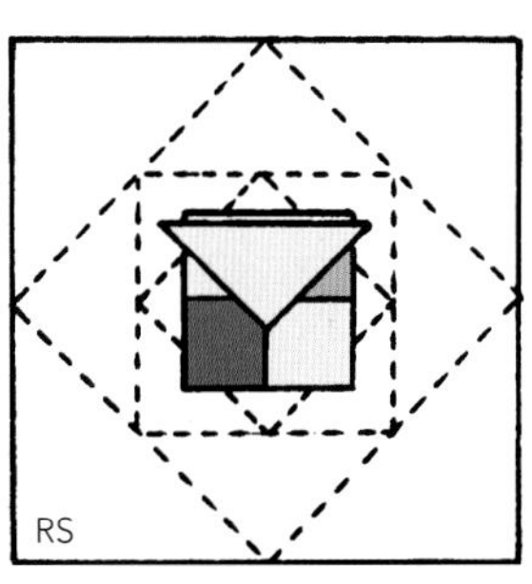

Fig 13

8 Stitch along the marked seamline between pieces 1 and 2, extending two or three stitches beyond the beginning and the end of the drawn line (Fig 14).

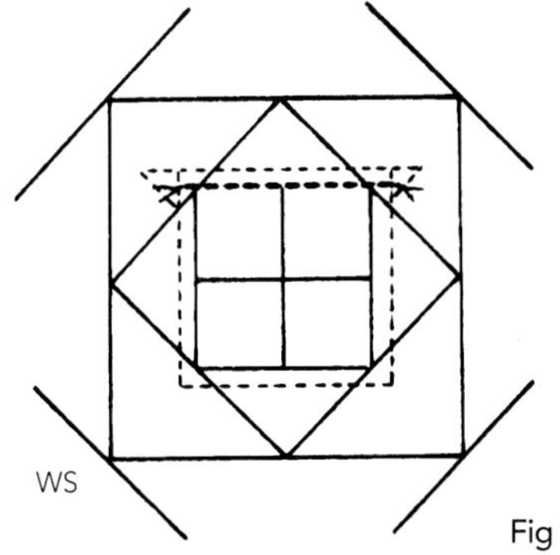

Fig 14

Turn to the right side and trim the seam allowance down to a scant ¼in (6mm) by eye with a pair of sharp scissors. Flip the triangle over on to the foundation, finger press the seam and then press from the front with an iron (Fig 15).

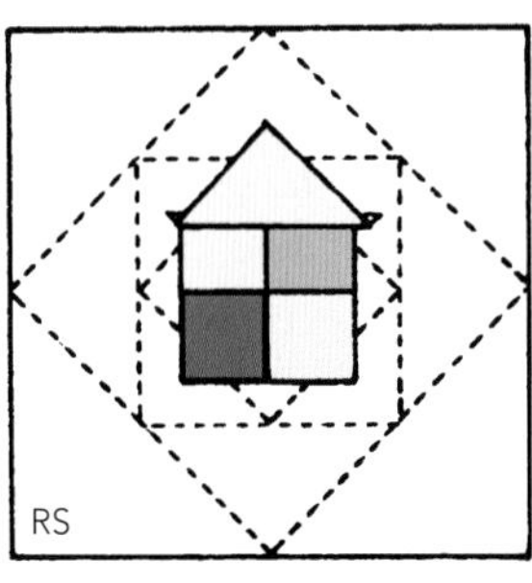

Fig 15

9 Repeat this process for piece 3, marked on the foundation on the opposite side of the four-patch, using the smallest triangle of background fabric as before. Stitch along the seam between pieces 1 and 3. Press over on to the foundation as before (Fig 16).

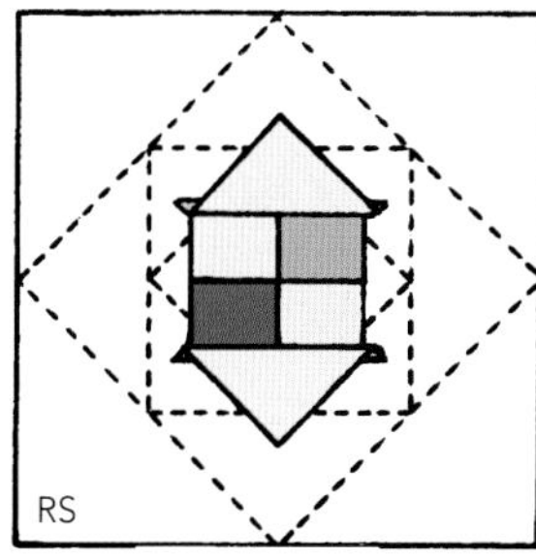

Fig 16

10 Add the triangle for the piece marked 4 on the foundation in the fabric to match the bottom left-hand square of the four-patch seen from the front of the work. Use the smallest triangle (Fig 17).

Add the triangle for piece 5 in the fabric to match the top right-hand square of the four-patch seen from the front of the work. Use the smallest triangle. Press each triangle over on to the foundation after stitching and trimming the seam. This completes Round One of the block (Fig 18).

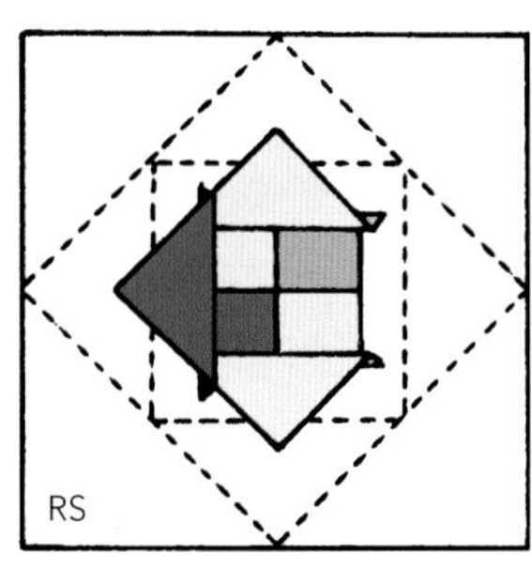

Fig 17

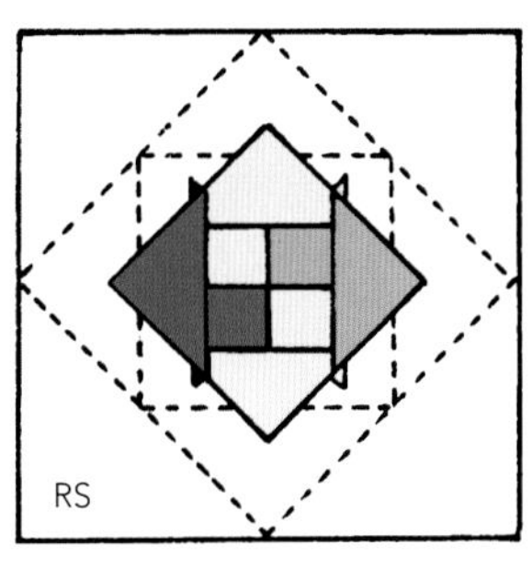

Fig 18

11 Round Two is four more triangles, slightly larger and stitched on in the same way as the first set. The colours are spiralling clockwise, so check with the diagram in Fig 19 as you first lay a triangle in position right side facing *outwards* on the unmarked side of the foundation to make sure that the colour is correct. Then flip the triangle over on to the block fabric with right sides facing and the long edges matching.

Pin or hold the piece in place and turn everything over to the marked side of the foundation. Stitch the seam and trim the seam allowance to a scant ¼in (6mm). Flip the triangle over on to the foundation and press it in place.

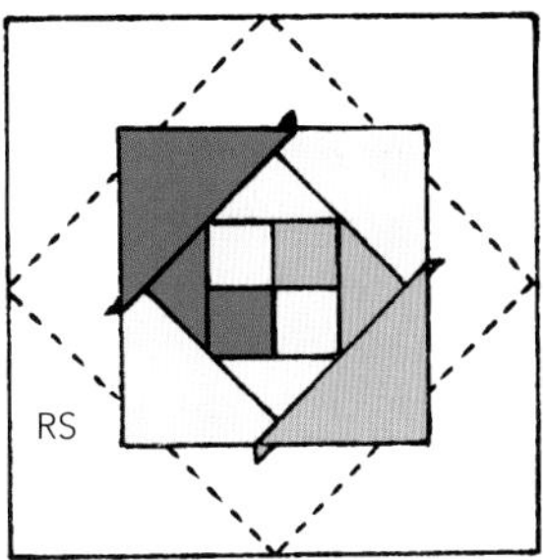

Fig 19

Fig 4 – Actual size template

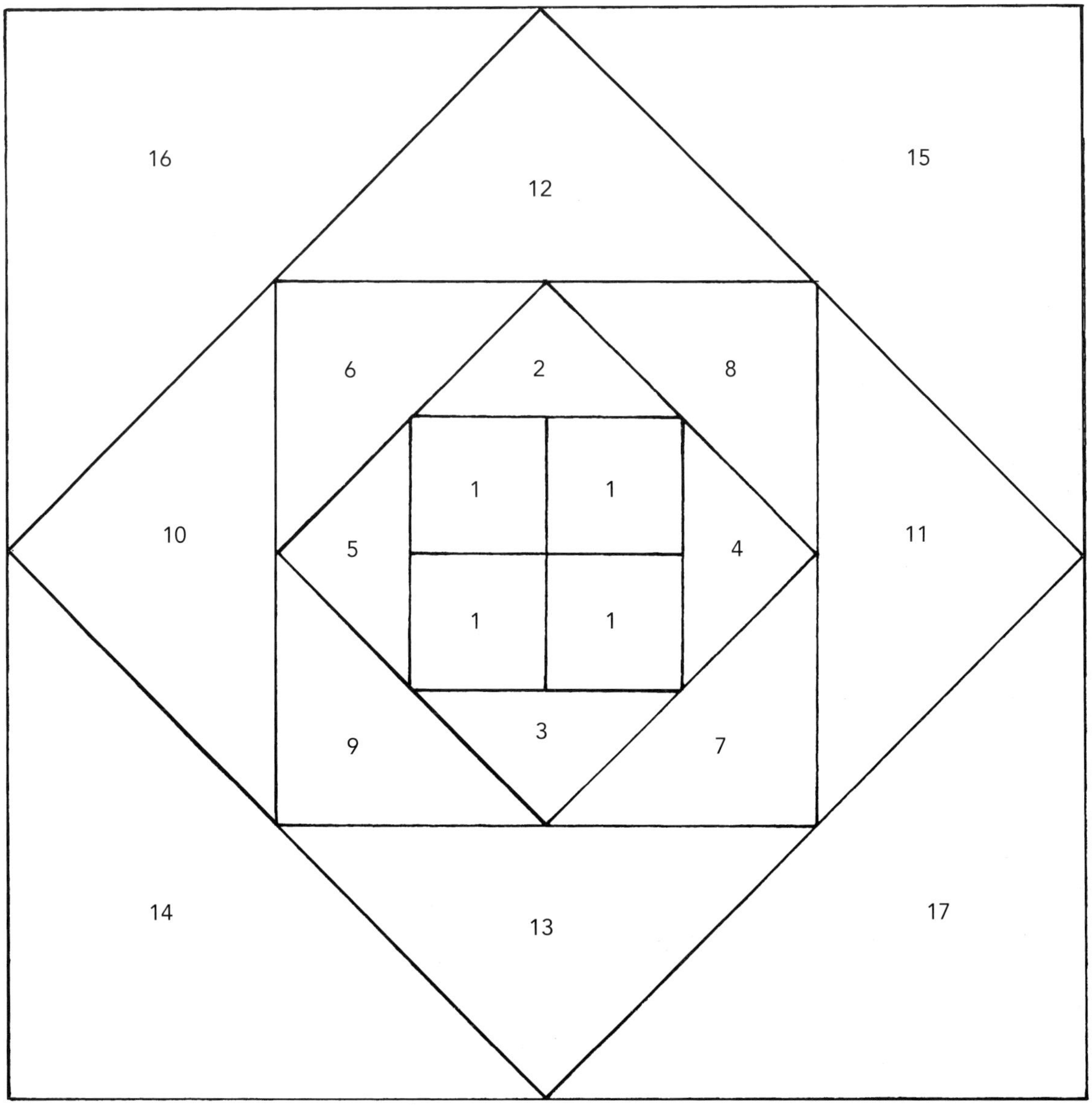

12 Round Three repeats the sequence with the next size of triangles. Round Four makes the final four corners of the block (Fig 20). Continue to add the triangles, following the sequence numbers marked on the foundation piece with the largest triangles on the last corners. Press the completed block from the front. Do not trim any of the outer edges at this stage.

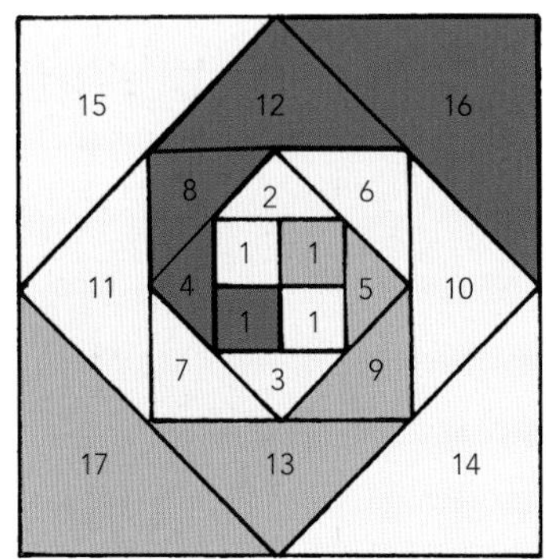

Fig 20

13 Make the other three Monkey Wrench blocks in the same way as the first, using the marked foundation squares and the four-patches and triangles in exactly the same arrangement. Always check that the spirals of colour are moving clockwise as you go along. It is amazingly easy to get careless as you work on block four and think that you can remember which way the spirals go and find you have a beautifully executed but incorrect spiral on the final block. Press the blocks from the front.

14 Take each block in turn and place it foundation side *up* on the cutting board. Using a rotary cutter and ruler, trim the edges to an exact ¼in (6mm) beyond the drawn block (Fig 21).

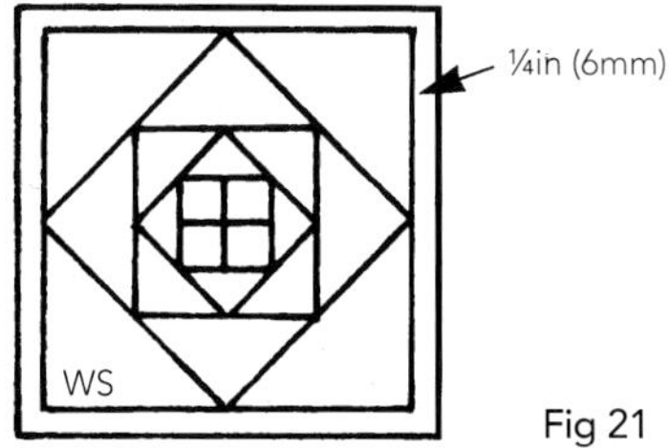

Fig 21

15 Arrange the four blocks in any way that you think most effective. Then take the top two blocks and place them right sides together. Match the drawn lines that mark the edges of the block on the foundation by pushing pins through each marked corner, in the same way as American pieced patchwork lines are matched. Take extra care to match the points in the design that are found at the centre of the two sides being joined (Fig 22). Stitch along the marked lines on the foundation, stitching beyond the lines right from one side of the squares to the other (Fig 23). Press the seam from the front in the opposite direction to the first pair. Take the two bottom blocks and stitch them together in the same way as the top pair.

Now pin and stitch the two sets of blocks together, matching seams carefully and stitching along the marked lines on the foundations. Press the final long seam to one side, or open it if it makes the design look more balanced.

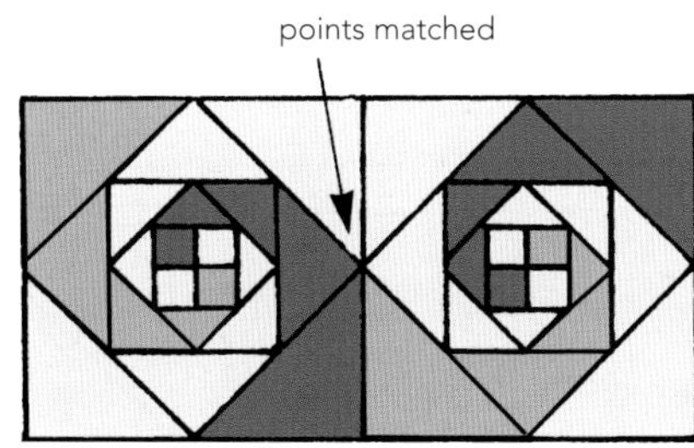

Fig 22

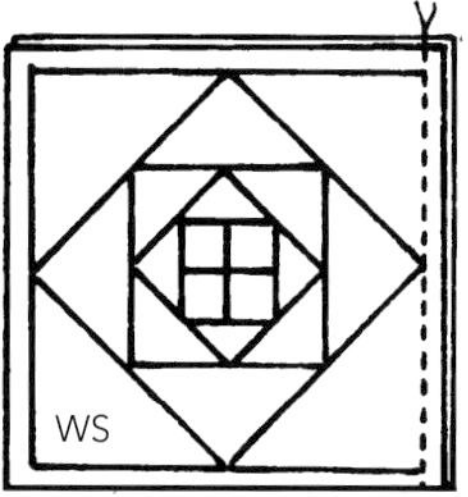

Fig 23

16 It is a good idea to add the framing strips to the block while the foundation is still in place as it adds stability and the stitching line is marked ready for use. Cut framing strips, two measuring 1¼ x 12½in (3.2 x 31.7cm) and two measuring 1¼ x 14in (3.2 x 35.6cm). Pin and stitch the two shorter strips to the sides of the block, stitching along the drawn line on the foundation. Press the seams outwards away from the block, pressing from the front of the work. Pin and stitch the two longer strips to the top and bottom of the block in the same way. Press seams outwards from the front of the block.

17 Now turn the block to the back and carefully remove all the paper foundation. Finally, add the sashing strips to the block (see page 236 for instructions).

Hand or Machine Piecing

Corner-to-Corner Curve

The traditional curved block is the Drunkard's Path, based on a square divided into two curved pieces, one of which is a quarter circle or quadrant with a radius of about two-thirds the size of the square (Fig 2 overleaf). Around 1980 a more subtle curved design was introduced by American quilter Joyce Schotzhauer, which became known as the Curved Two-Patch (Fig 3). The curve was not a quarter-circle but a gentler curve from corner to corner across the square. This block was repeated and combined to make non-traditional designs often of flowers and leaves. For the block in this sampler quilt I used the deeper quarter-circle curve which I find more effective in a restricted area.

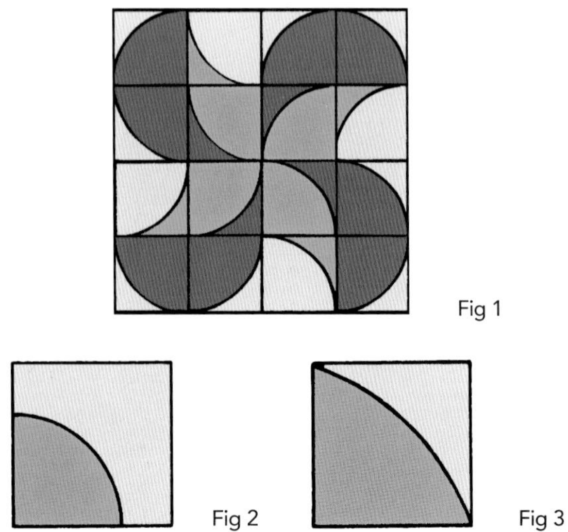

Fig 1

Fig 2

Fig 3

Colour Choices

One design for the block is shown in Fig 1 above and four more in Figs 4a, b, c and d below. Like the traditional Drunkard's Path, all the designs are based on sixteen squares, four in each row. All use three fabrics, one of which can be a background fabric. The completed block has a finished measurement of 12 x 12in (30.5 x 30.5cm), and an inner frame of ¾in (1.9cm) finished width will be needed around the block before the sashing strips, so this extra colour should be considered when choices are being made. Study your chosen design and decide which fabric is to go where. You may find it easier to make a rough sketch or tracing of the block and colour it so that you can count how many of each shape you need to cut from each fabric.

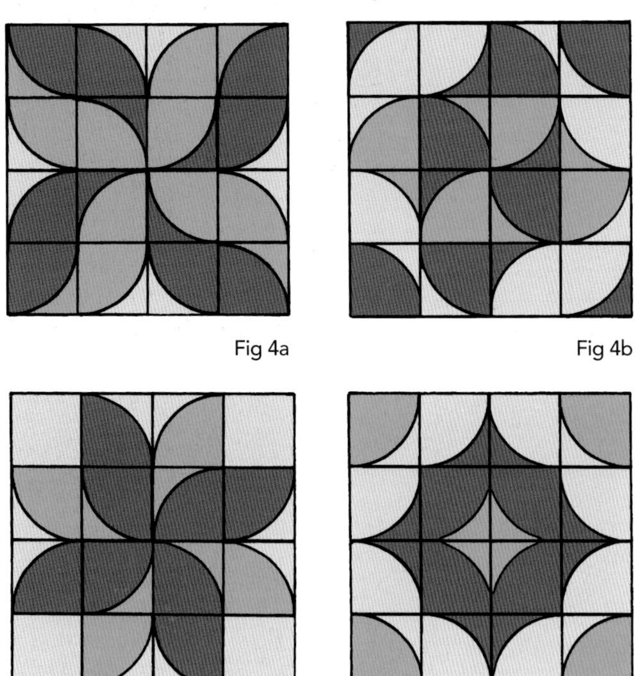

Fig 4a

Fig 4b

Fig 4c

Fig 4d

Construction

1 Templates for the two shapes in the design are given in Fig 5 on page 209. The outer solid line is the cutting line and *includes* the ¼in (6mm) seam allowance. If you want to stitch the block by machine, make card or plastic templates by tracing in the usual way, marking the directional arrows but ignoring the dotted stitching lines shown on each template.

If you want to hand stitch in the American piecing method, you should make templates *without* the seam allowances, but this presents a problem as the sharp corners on the dotted inner lines on piece B taper away to such a long, fine point that it is almost impossible to make a template from it and to draw round it accurately. One solution is to make the templates with the seam allowances added and just judge the ¼in (6mm) seam allowance by eye as you stitch. If this is not easy for you to do accurately (I find it really hard), then make the same templates as for machine piecing. Mark on them only the *curved* dotted stitching lines and the directional arrows (Fig 6). Do *not* cut along the dotted lines. Draw the curved dotted lines on the template and then ignore them for the moment. They will be used later when adding stitching lines.

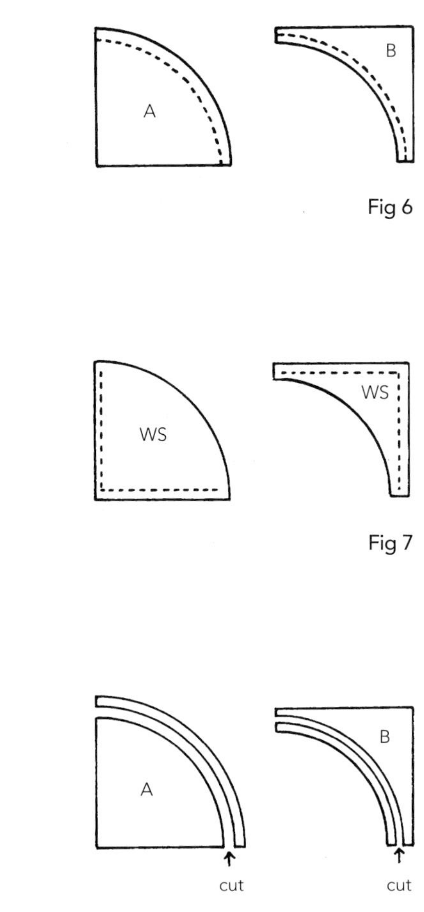

Fig 6

Fig 7

Fig 8

"I challenged myself to make a king-size sampler quilt using predominantly red and cream fabrics. So with the help of Lynne's book my sampler quilt was born, and after several years of enjoyable work, it is ready to go on our bed." **Jill Harford**

2 Whichever way you intend to stitch the block, the first drawing and cutting stage is the same. On the wrong side of each chosen fabric draw accurately around the templates using a sharp marking pencil and matching the direction of the arrows with the weave or grain of the fabric. Unlike American piecing, the drawn line is the *cutting* line, so you do not have to allow extra space for seam allowances. Just position the drawn shapes as close as possible to save fabric.

3 Cut out each drawn shape exactly on the drawn line. A rotary cutter and ruler can be used for the straight edges if preferred, but a pair of scissors is probably best for the curved edges.

4 If you are a hand stitcher and need to mark the stitching line, a ruler and sharp marking pencil can be used for the straight sides to mark the ¼in (6mm) seam allowance. Mark these lines on the *wrong* side of each cut fabric shape (Fig 7). To mark the stitching line on the *curved* edge, first trim each template along the dotted stitching line marked on its *curved* edge only (Fig 8). Only do this once you have cut out all the shapes for the design using the complete templates from Fig 5.

Place the trimmed template A on to the *wrong* side of one of the cut quarter-circles of fabric, lining up the two straight edges on the template with the cut straight edges of the fabric (Fig 9). Draw along the curved edge of the template to make the curved stitching line on the fabric (Fig 10).

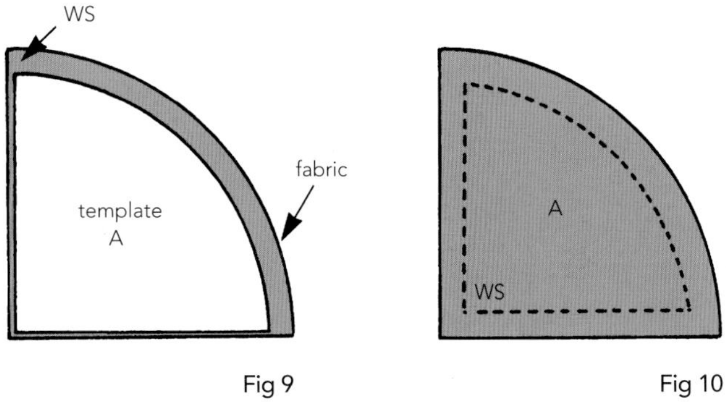

Fig 9

Fig 10

Mark the curved stitching line on each cut quarter-circle shape of the design in the same way. Use the trimmed template B to mark the curved stitching line on all the smaller cut shapes (Fig 11).

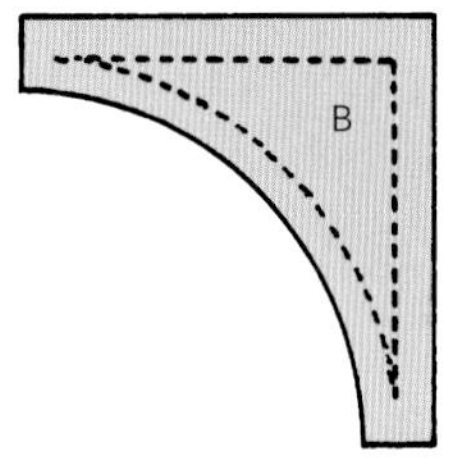

Fig 11

5 Arrange the cut pieces in your chosen design on a flat surface or pin them in position on a polystyrene tile or board. Changes can be made at this stage before any stitching is done.

6 Take the two shapes A and B that make up one of the sixteen squares in the design and fold each one in half along its curved edge, pinching it firmly to mark the centre of the curve with a crease. Do *not* clip any curved edges. With right sides *facing* and the smaller piece B on top, match the centre creases. The edges of both fabrics should be level with each other. Pin as in Fig 12.

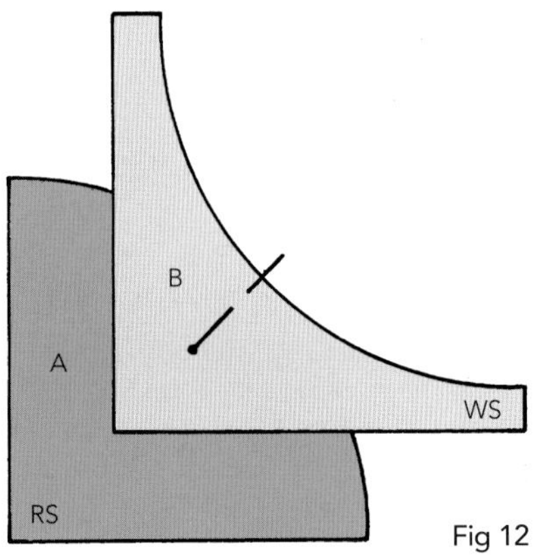

Fig 12

7 Swing each corner of shape B round and pin in position at the corners of shape A, lining up the edges of both fabrics (Fig 13). If the seam is to be machined, no more pins are necessary.

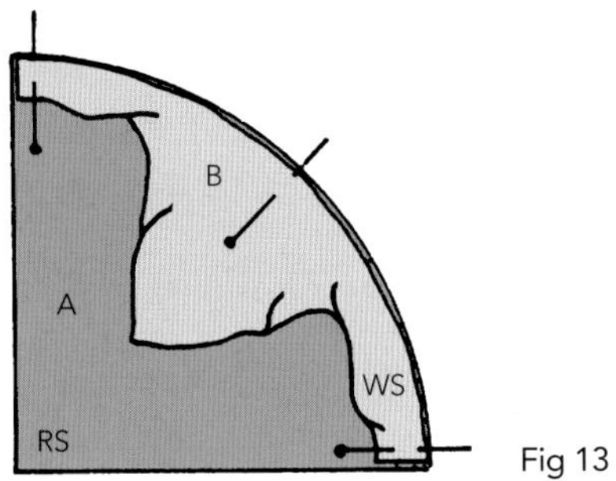

Fig 13

8 Place the pinned fabrics with the smaller piece B uppermost on the machine and stitch an exact ¼in (6mm) seam from pinned corner to pinned corner. The trick is to use the point of a stitch-ripper or a long pin to pull the two edges into alignment no more than ½in (1.3cm) ahead of the needle as you stitch. The top fabric will stretch easily, as the curve is cut on the bias. It will probably take a couple of tries to get a perfect result, but once you are used to stretching the fabric a little at a time, the resulting curves

are accurate and very quickly achieved. The stitched ¼in (6mm) seam should begin and finish midway on the narrow ends of shape B to keep the completed square an accurate shape (Fig 14).

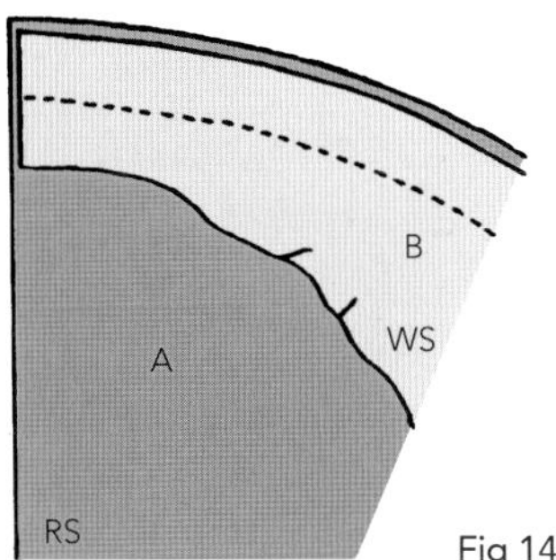

Fig 14

9 If stitching by hand, add more pins to the original three if you wish, stretching the top fabric shape B over your hand to ease it to fit against shape A. Line up the edges of the fabric and begin to stitch from the marked corner of the design, following the drawn stitching line on the top fabric shape B. Check that your stitches are also running through the marked line drawn on the underneath fabric shape A. If the two edges of the fabrics are always exactly matched, this should not be a problem. Stitch with small running stitches and the occasional backstitch in the American hand-piecing technique.

10 Once all sixteen seams are stitched, press the squares from the front with the seams pressed towards the smaller shape B (Fig 15). Arrange the squares in your chosen design.

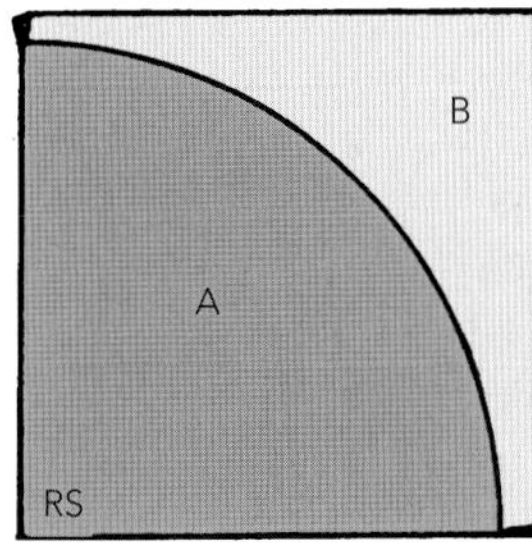

Fig 15

11 Join the squares into horizontal rows, pinning and matching the seams and stitching either by hand or by machine. If stitching by machine, press the seams from the front, ironing the seams of row one in one direction, those in row two the opposite way and so on. Join the rows together, matching the seams carefully. Press the completed block from the front of the work.

12 The block should measure 12½ x 12½in (31.7 x 31.7cm). Add the inner framing strips of a cut width of 1¼in (3.2cm) to bring the block up to 14 x 14in (35.6 x 35.6cm). Finally, add the sashing strips (see page 236 for instructions).

Fig 5 – Actual size templates

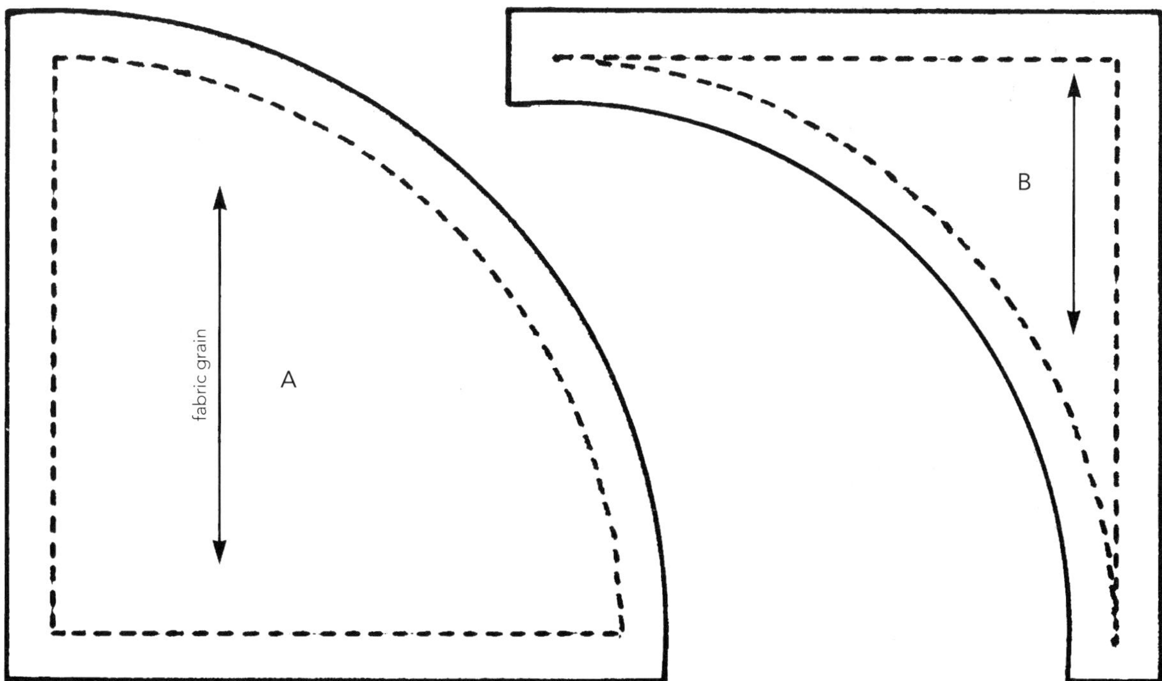

Freezer Paper Machine Piecing

Mariner's Compass

Mariner's Compass is a traditional pieced patchwork block but many quilters find it daunting because of the exact piecing necessary to achieve such fine points. It is now made painless and accurate through foundation piecing on freezer paper and a sixteen-point compass is included in this sampler quilt (see Fig 1 opposite). Once you have made this, it is possible to piece other larger or more complex compasses. I have seen some stunning quilts where the centre is a huge Mariner's Compass, surrounded by a series of framing borders varying in width and complexity. Hand-workers can use the technique easily to piece the block by hand.

Colour Choices

Two fabrics are used for the points of the compass, one for the longer set of points, which alternates with the shorter set made from the second fabric. The compass is set into a circular background and then placed within another background fabric to make the square block. These two background areas can be of the same fabric, so that the compass floats in the block, or of two different fabrics. Towards the centre of the block are small triangular pieces which look best in a contrasting fabric to the main compass. The centre circle is added last of all, so it is probably best to leave that choice of fabric until the rest of the block is assembled when it is easier to judge what looks best.

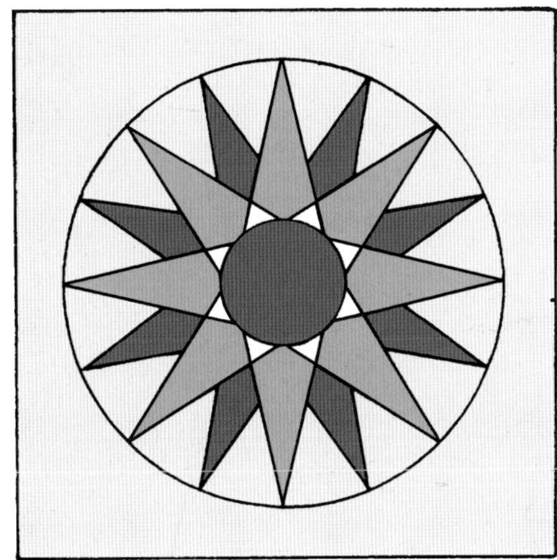

Fig 1

Construction

1 Fig 2 on page 215 shows one quarter of the compass design. Take a square of freezer paper measuring 13 x 13in (33 x 33cm) and fold the paper into four quarters (Fig 3). Unfold it and trace the quarter compass from Fig 2 four times on the freezer paper using the folded lines on the paper as a guide to positioning each section (Fig 4). Number each piece in the order shown in Fig 5.

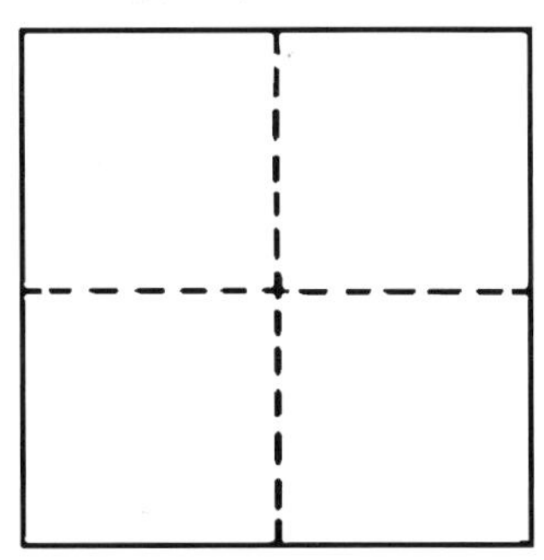

Fig 3

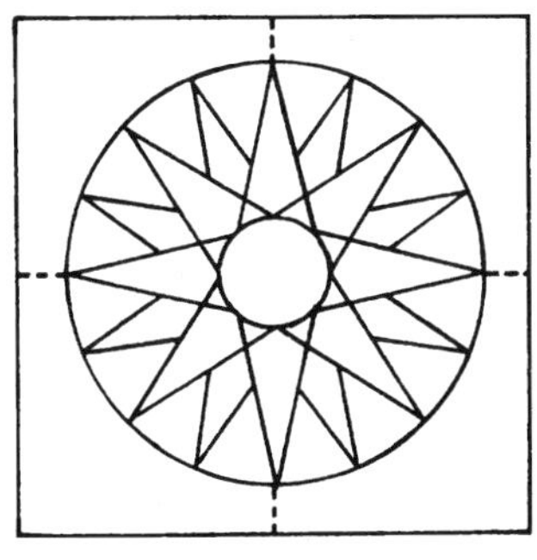

Fig 4

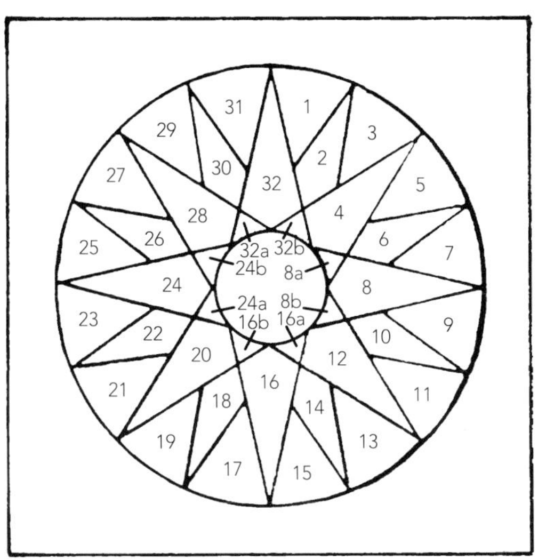

Fig 5

2 From the fabric chosen for the final background square (not the inner background to the compass), cut a square 13½ x 13½in (34.3 x 34.3cm). Press lightly with an iron into four quarters. Cut out the circular design from the freezer paper in one piece but do not start cutting it up into little pieces yet!

3 Place the circle of freezer paper shiny side *down* on to the *wrong* side of the square of background fabric using the fold lines in the fabric to help position the circle exactly in the centre. Press with an iron (wool setting, no steam) to stick the freezer paper on to the fabric. Draw round the paper circle with a fabric-marking pencil, also marking where the compass points touch the edge of the circle. Remove the paper circle (Fig 6). This fabric square will not be needed until the compass is completed.

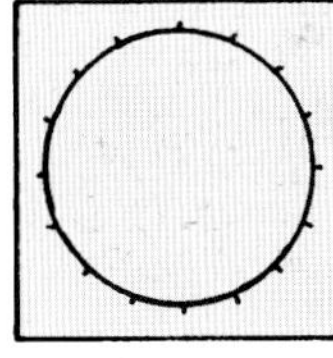

Fig 6

4 From the paper compass cut out the wedge shape made from pieces 1–2–3 (Fig 7). In the same way cut out the seven similar wedge shapes (pieces 5–6–7, 9–10–11, 13–14–15, 17–18–19, 21–22–23, 25–26–27, 29–30–31), leaving the longer points still joined to the centre.

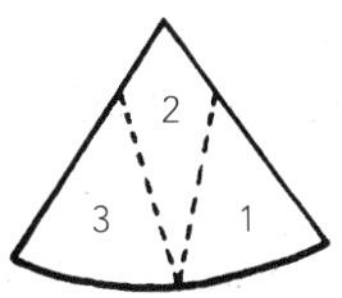

Fig 7

5 *Piecing the wedge sections:* it is easier here to use templates for the fabric that is to be cut and pieced on to the freezer paper. Make card templates by tracing shapes A and B from Fig 8 or use template plastic, marking the grainline arrows. Shape A has been drawn to include an exact ¼in (6mm) seam allowance, while shape B includes a more generous seam allowance of ½in (1.3cm) as this makes it easier to piece.

fabric grain

A

includes ¼in (6mm) seam allowance

Fig 8 – Templates actual size

B

includes ½in (1.3cm) seam allowance

6 From template A cut eight shapes from the fabric chosen for the smaller compass points. No extra seam allowance is needed, so the cutting can be done more quickly by folding the fabric into four layers, drawing round the template on the top layer and cutting several shapes at once with a rotary cutter. In the same way use template B to cut sixteen shapes from the inner background fabric.

7 Take the freezer paper wedge with 1–2–3 written on it. Place it shiny side *down* with the central area on the *wrong* side of a cut piece of fabric from template A (Fig 9a). Use an iron to press the paper on to the fabric. Pin a cut piece of fabric from template B (the inner background fabric) right sides together with fabric A, matching the long edges. Make sure the curved edge is positioned as in Fig 9b.

Turn the paper over and stitch along the drawn line (Fig 9c). Press fabric B out on to the freezer paper (Fig 9d). Take a second cut piece of fabric B and repeat the process on the remaining section of the paper wedge (Fig 9e overleaf). Trim the fabric edges down to ¼in (6mm) on all sides, using a ruler for the straight edges and trimming the bottom curve by eye (Fig 10 overleaf).

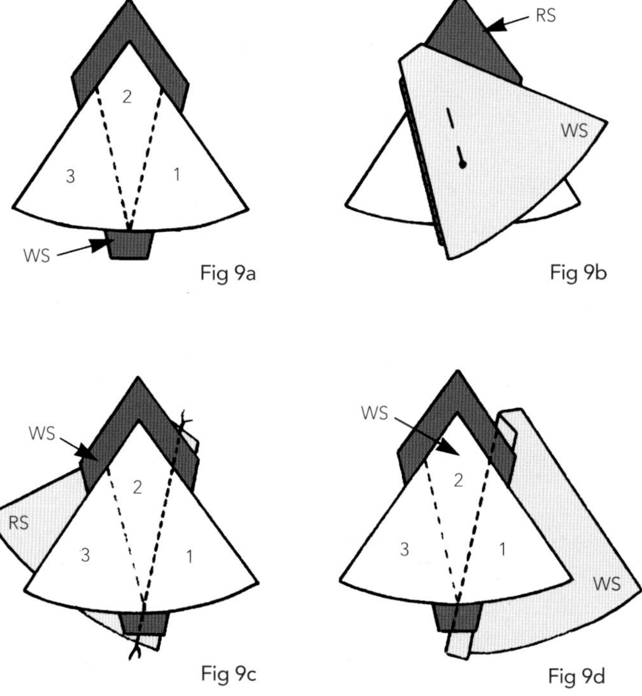

Fig 9a

Fig 9b

Fig 9c

Fig 9d

"When my daughter asked for her quilt to be purple I wasn't confident that I could do it justice, but enjoyed the challenge. It is quilted as a whole piece and my daughter's favourite block is the Celtic Knot."

Annette Chamley

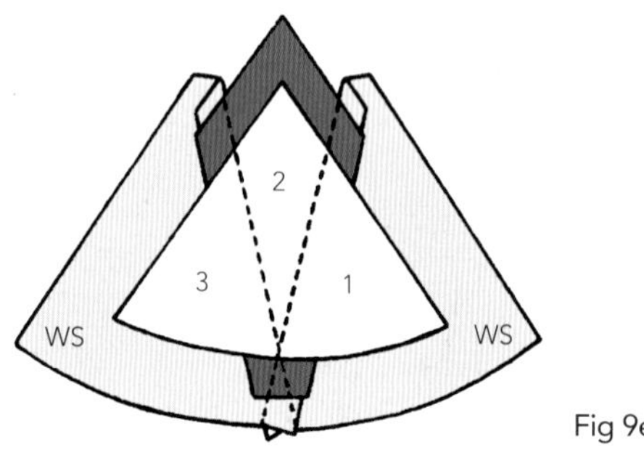

Fig 9e

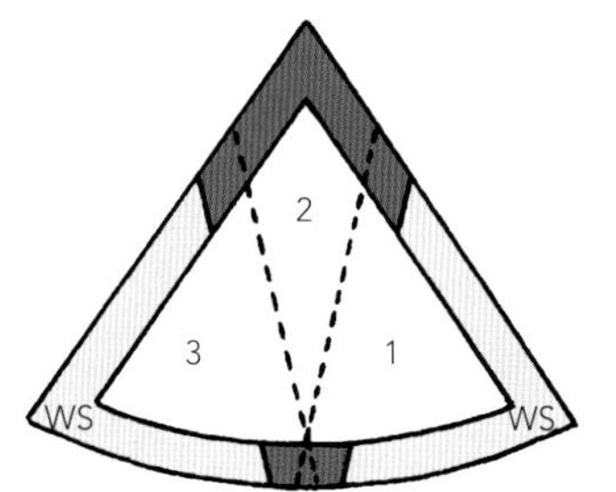

Fig 10

8 From the freezer paper compass, cut points 4, 12, 20 and 28. Press these shiny side *down* on to the *back* of the fabric chosen for the longer points, leaving at least ½in (1.3cm) between each shape and placing them so that the grain of the fabric lies along the centre of each shape (Fig 11).

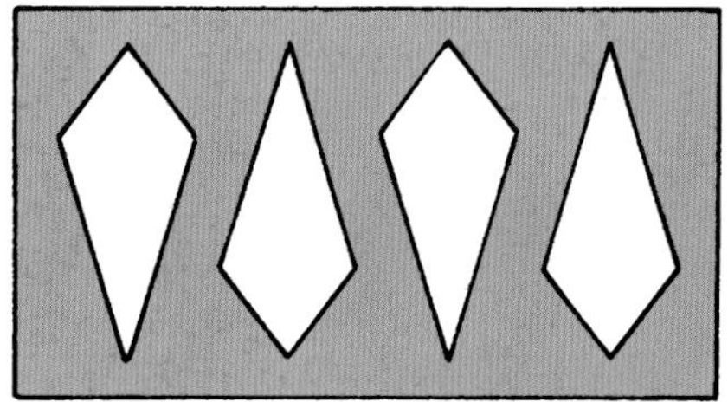

Fig 11

Cut out each piece with a ¼in (6mm) seam allowance on all sides, using a rotary cutter and ruler for accuracy (Fig 12). The edge of the paper marks the stitching line. It is useful to draw lines with a sharp marking pencil at the corners of each shape. This marks the exact corners in case the freezer paper peels back while being handled (Fig 13).

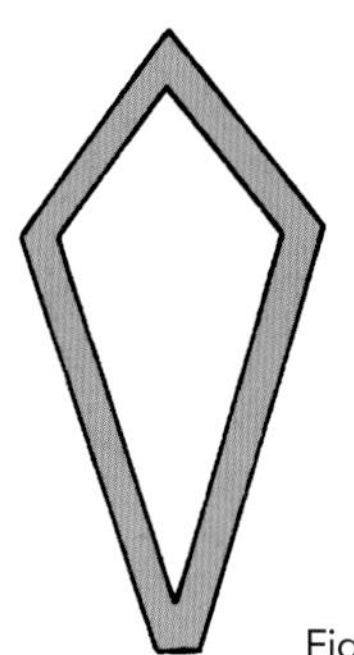

Fig 12

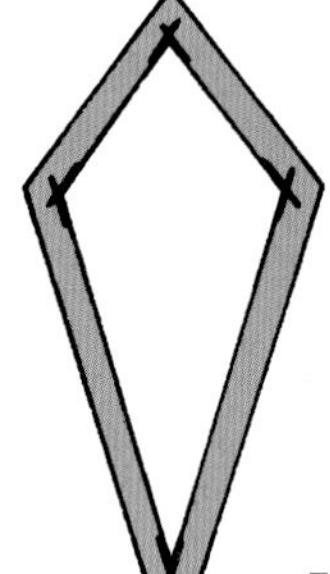

Fig 13

9 Cut the remaining four points 8, 16, 24 and 32 from the centre circle, including with them the small triangular shapes a and b (Fig 14). Iron each paper shape on to the back of the chosen fabric, leaving at least ½in (1.3cm) between each shape. Pull back each of the a and b points and fold them back on the drawn line. Now cut around the paper shapes adding a ¼in (6mm) seam allowance (Fig 15).

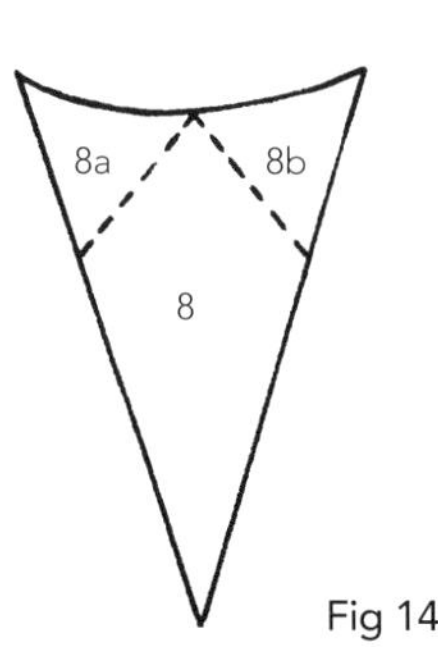

Fig 14

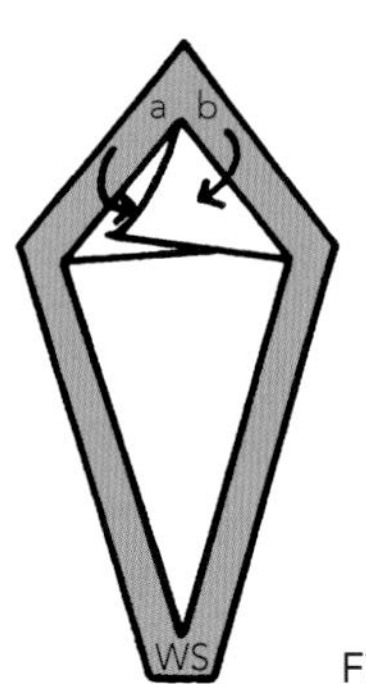

Fig 15

10 From the fabric chosen for the a and b triangles cut eight squares, each measuring 1½ x 1½in (3.9 x 3.9cm). Take piece number 8, unfold the paper points a and b and iron them *down* on to the fabric as before. Turn the piece over so that the fabric side is uppermost. Place a fabric square right side down on to piece 8, matching edges as in Fig 16. Hold it in position while you turn everything over. Stitch along the drawn line (Fig 17). Press the square of fabric out on to the freezer paper (Fig 18).

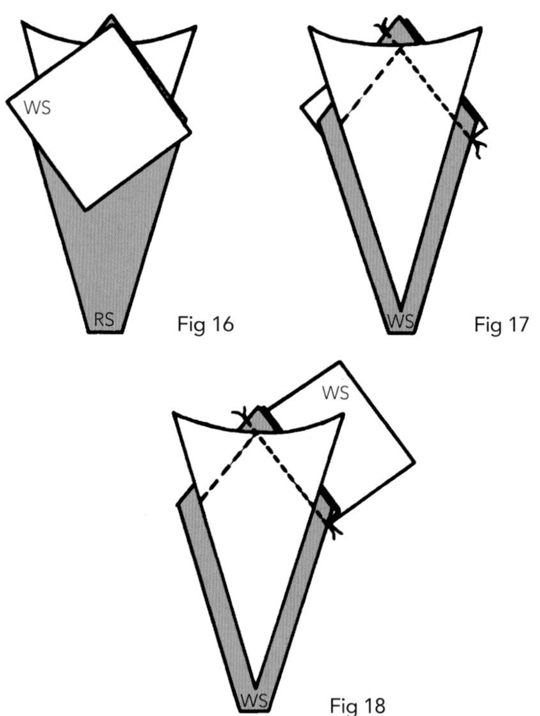

Fig 16

Fig 17

Fig 18

11 In the same way stitch a second square to the other side of piece 8. Press the square out on to the freezer paper (Fig 19). Trim squares a and b to match the paper shape, adding a ¼in (6mm) seam allowance (Fig 20). Repeat this process with pieces 16, 24 and 32.

12 Mark the corners of the freezer paper on the fabric in case the paper lifts off when handled. If it does come loose, iron it down again.

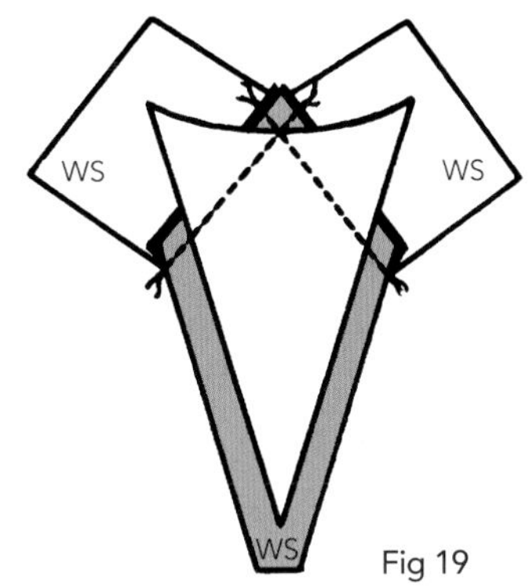

Fig 19

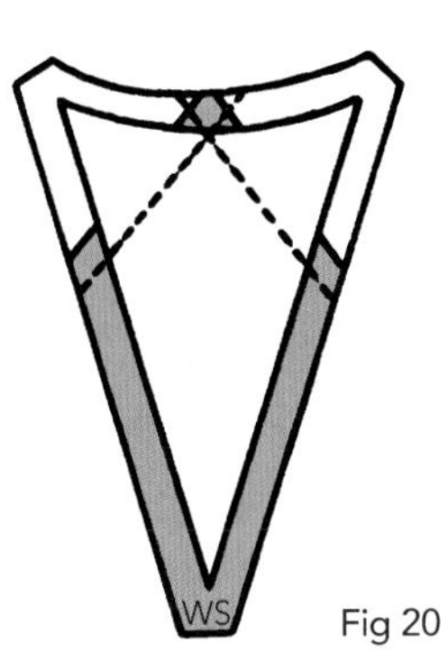

Fig 20

Fig 2 – Actual size templates

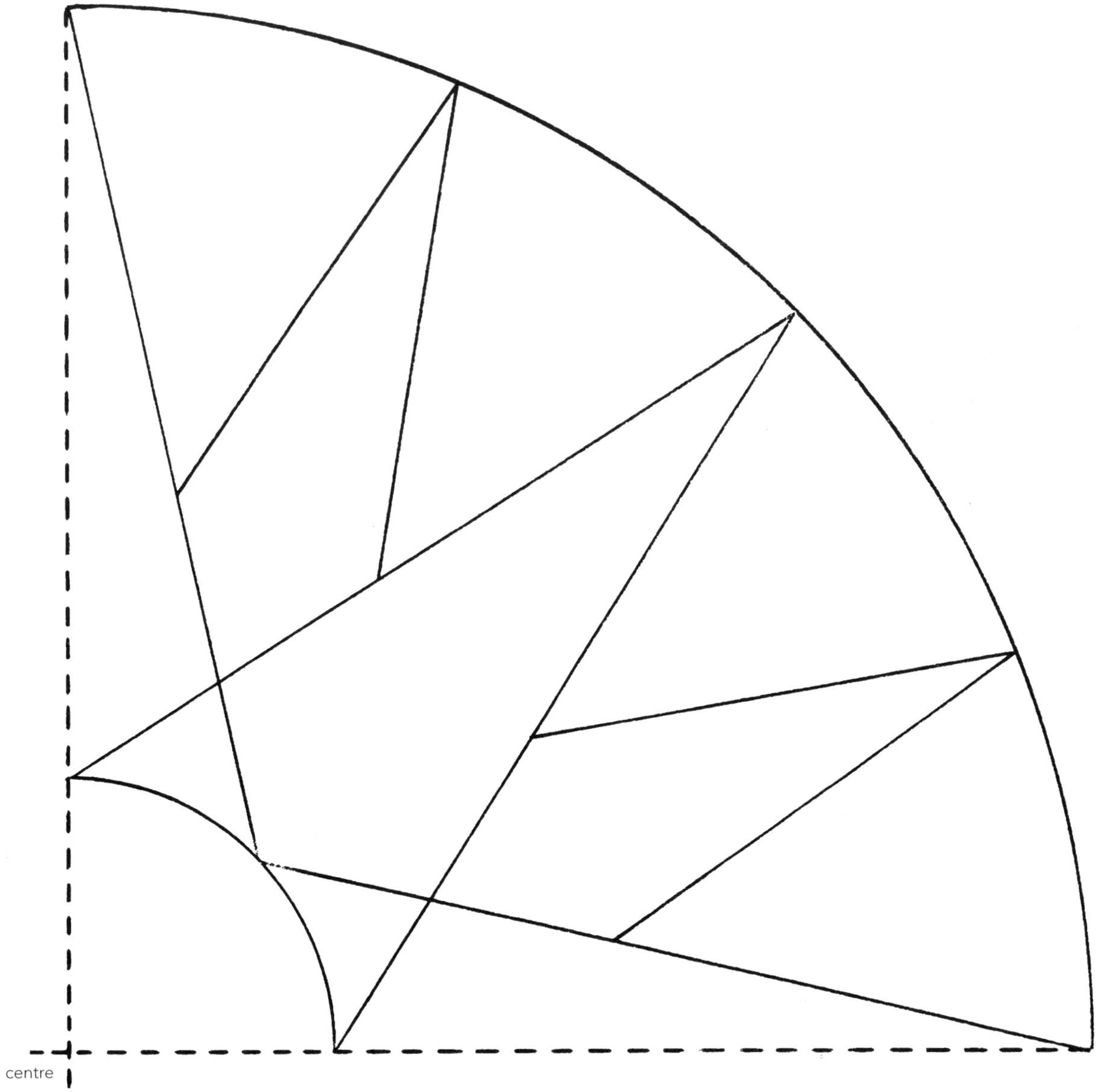

centre

13 *Assembling the compass:* arrange the compass design, paper sides uppermost with the numbered pieces lying consecutively as in the original plan. Pin wedge 1–2–3 and piece 4 together with right sides facing. Match the corners of the freezer paper with a pin at either end of the seam and line up the edges of the fabric. Sew along the edges of the freezer paper including the seam allowance at either end (Fig 21). Press the seam towards the wedge shape. If any freezer paper has been caught in the underneath seam, ease it out carefully. If it is caught really badly, unpick that small section and re-stitch it.

Pin and stitch wedge 5–6–7 to the compass and then the long point 8–8a–8b, matching corners and intersecting seams carefully and pressing seams away from the long points each time (Fig 22).

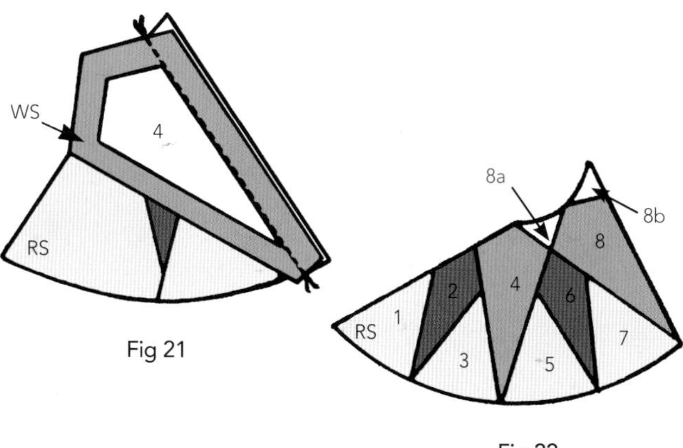

Fig 21

Fig 22

Piece the compass in four sections (Fig 23) and finally join the sections together. Mark the outer curved stitching line by drawing along the curved edge of the freezer paper, then remove all the paper from the block.

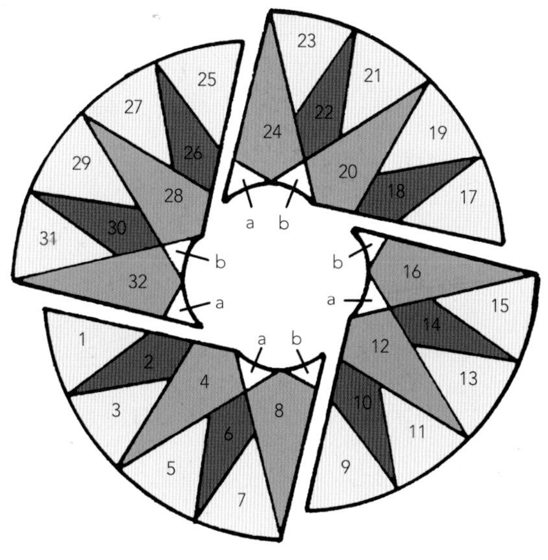

Fig 23

14 *Adding the centre circle:* iron the freezer paper circle (the remaining piece) to the *back* of the fabric chosen for the centre. Cut out the fabric with a ¼in (6mm) seam allowance. Peel the freezer paper from the fabric and reverse it, pinning it on to the back of the fabric circle with shiny side *upwards* (Fig 24). Use the nose of the iron to nudge the seam allowance evenly over the paper (Fig 25). Pin the centre in position on the assembled compass with the grain of the circle horizontal to the compass and appliqué it into place. Remove the freezer paper from the back after stitching.

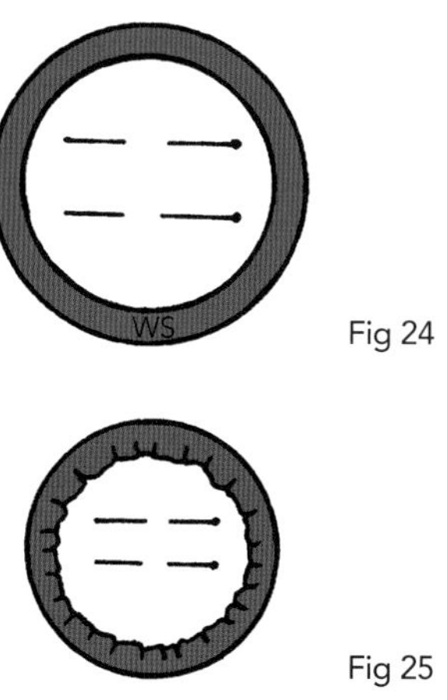

Fig 24

Fig 25

15 *Attaching the outer background section:* take the marked square of background fabric (prepared previously in steps 2 and 3) and cut away the centre part, leaving a ¼in (6mm) seam allowance in the inner section. Clip the curve to within ⅛in (3mm) of the drawn line (Fig 26). With right sides facing, pin the background circle to the compass, matching the marks on the drawn circle with the points on the compass. Check that the compass is positioned with the north-south axis vertical in the background square before stitching along the marked seamline to set the compass in its background frame. Press the block from the front with the final seam pressed towards the outer frame.

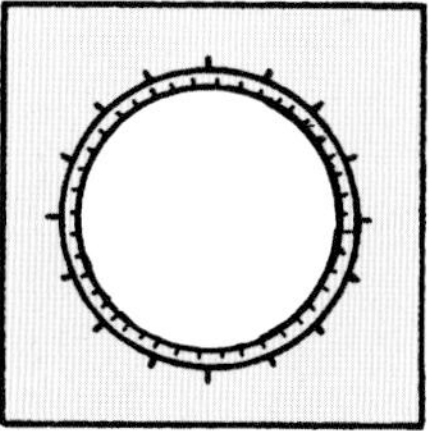

Fig 26

16 Add the inner framing strips to bring the block up to exactly 14 x 14in (35.6 x 35.6cm), then add the sashing strips. See page 236 for framing and sashing.

Hand Stitching

Celtic Appliqué

The design used in the block of Celtic Knot patchwork in this sampler quilt was made by outlining the fabric pieces with ¼in (6mm) bias strips. Similar bias strips were used in the Carolina Lily block on page 151 for the curvy stems. In this block an appliqué design of a lily is outlined with narrow bias strips ⅛in (3mm) wide (see Fig 1 overleaf), a technique originated by Philomena Durcan, the leading exponent of Celtic patchwork.

This technique does not follow the Celtic principle of bias strips weaving over and under each other. Instead the fabric pieces of the lily and leaves are tacked in position on to a background and then outlined with the bias strips, which are

laid on in sequence so that the raw ends of one strip are covered by another strip positioned later in the sequence. The edges of the appliqué do not have to be neatened as they are covered by the bias strips. Working out the order of pinning and stitching the bias strips is the key to this technique, just as it is with traditional hand appliqué blocks.

Fig 1

Colour Choices

The lily design is set on a background fabric, so if you are using one fabric throughout as a background on your quilt you will need it here. The lily is cut from one piece of fabric and the four leaves from another. Realism does not have to play a part here: your flower and leaves can be from any shades that you are using in your quilt. The outlining narrow bias strips can be made from two fabrics – one to outline the petals of the flower, and another around the leaves and for the stems and tendrils. Alternatively, one fabric can be used throughout for all the edgings to keep the design simpler.

Construction

1 Cut a square of fabric for the background measuring 12½ x 12½in (31.7 x 31.7cm).

2 Mark the lily and leaf design from the two sections of Fig 2 (on pages 220–221) very lightly on the *right* side of the background fabric, using a sharp marking pencil and a light box if necessary. If the fabric is too dark for the design to be traced through, use dressmaker's carbon paper and a tracing wheel. (I use an empty fine ballpoint pen to mark the design through the carbon paper.)

3 In the same way trace the lily flower on to the *right* side of the chosen fabric. Match the grain or weave of the lily fabric with the arrows marked on the lily in Fig 2. Cut the drawn flower shape out around its outer edge (Fig 3). Place it in position over the drawn lily shape on the background fabric, then pin and tack the lily in place.

Fig 3

4 In the same way, trace each of the four leaves on to the *front* of the chosen fabric. Match the grain of the fabric with the arrows on the leaf shapes in Fig 2. Cut out each leaf and pin in position over the drawn outlines on the background fabric. Tack (baste) each leaf in place.

5 *Making the bias tubing:* the bias strips needed to make the narrow ⅛in (3mm) wide bias edging can all be cut from a 12in (30.5cm) square of fabric, assuming you are going to use one fabric throughout. If you want to use several different fabrics, cut and stitch the bias tubes from each fabric as you need them.

The bias strips must be cut ¾in (1.9cm) in width. First cut the 12in (30.5cm) square of fabric to be used for the bias edging in half diagonally (Fig 4). Take one of the cut triangles of fabric and turn it on the cutting board so that the cut diagonal edge is to the left and move the ruler over it until the cut edge lines up with the ¾in (1.9cm) marking on the ruler (Fig 5). Cut along the right side of the ruler. (Left-handers should turn the fabric and cut from the right, not the left.) Cut seven strips from the triangle of fabric. Repeat this with the other triangle, cutting fourteen strips in total. Before folding and stitching the cut strips, use a short sample length of strip cut from the left-over fabric first to get the sizing right.

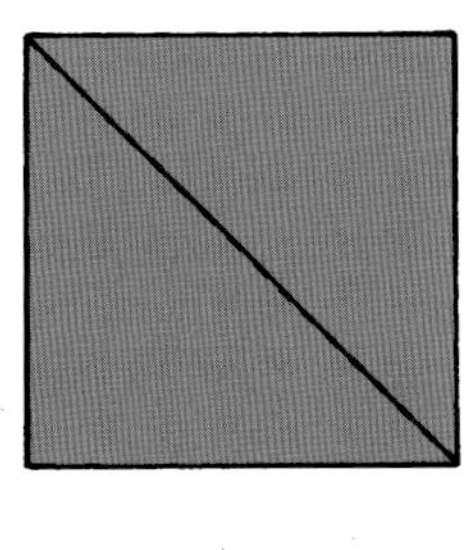

Fig 4

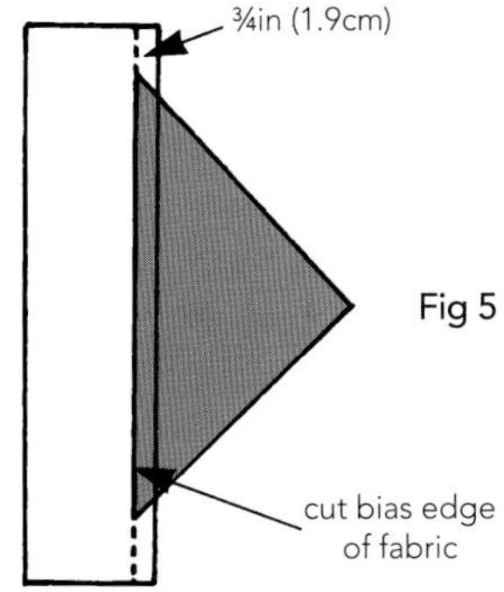

Fig 5

6 Take the strip and fold in half lengthways with the right side *outside*. Don't pull the strip to make the edges match or it will stretch and become narrower. Using a smaller stitch than usual, machine stitch a seam by eye *midway* down the folded strip (Fig 6). This makes a tube that is a generous ⅛in (3mm) in width, which you will find much easier to slide the bias bar through. Check that the bar will just slip into the tube – it needs to fit snugly without any slack (Fig 7a).

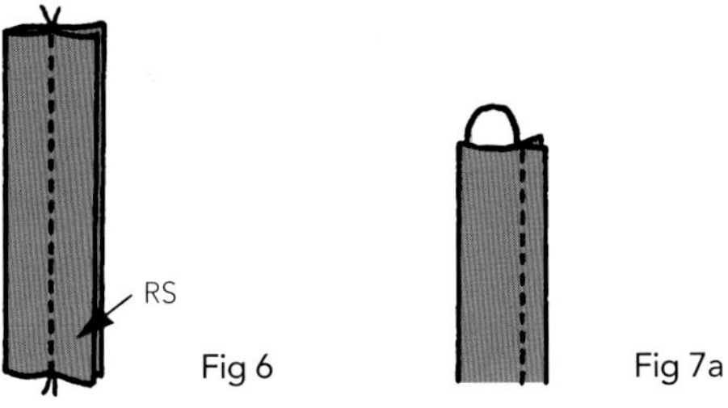

Fig 6

Fig 7a

"I loved this range of fabrics the moment I saw it and knew that I had to have it for this, my second sampler quilt. I made all the blocks at Lynne's classes and completing the quilt was great therapy for me." **Alison Maudlin**

Fig 2 – Actual size template

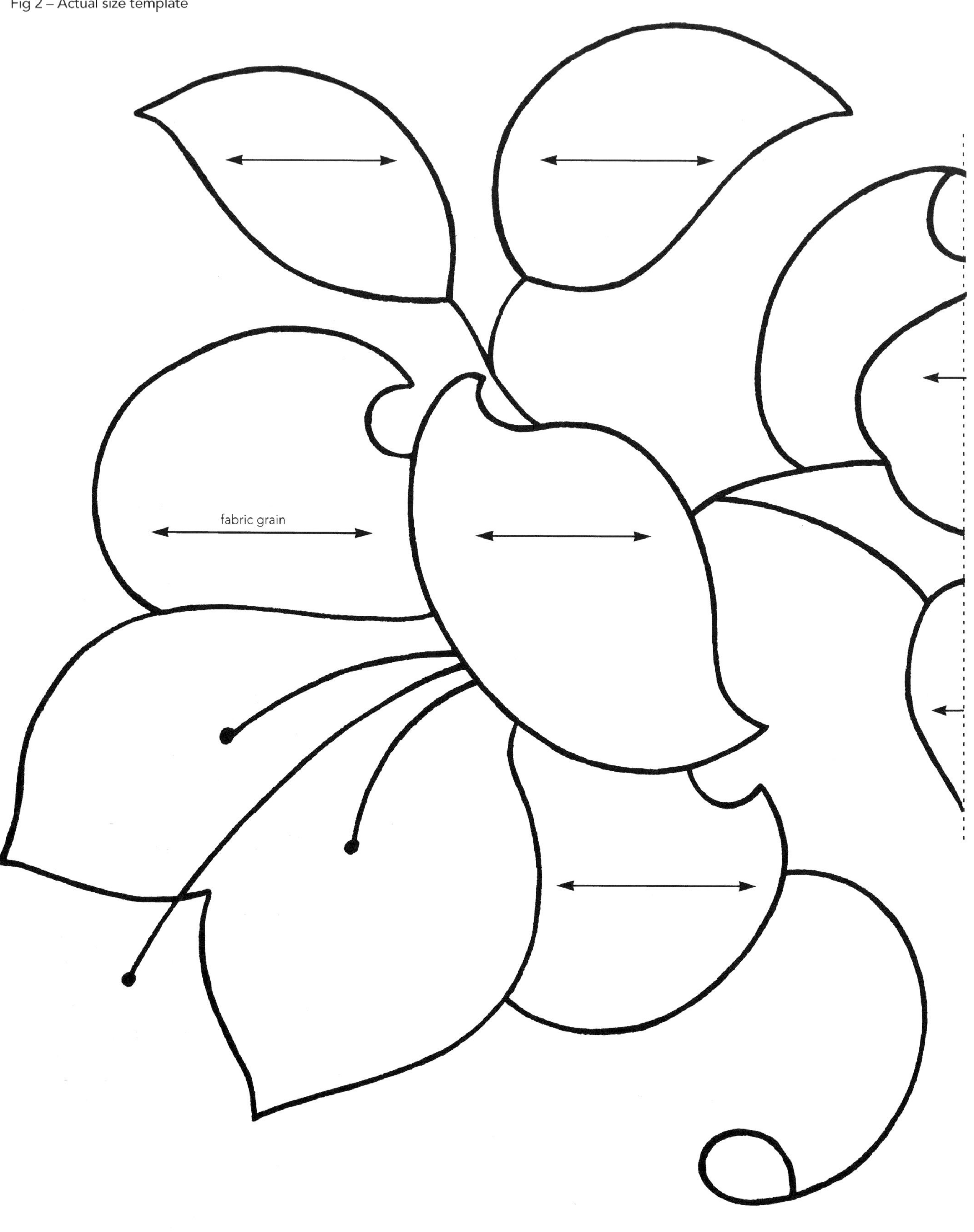

7 Trim the seams very close to the stitching without cutting the stitches. Slide the bar into the tube, twisting the fabric so that both seam and seam allowance lie across one flat side of the bar and cannot be seen from the other side (Fig 7b). With the bar in place, press the seam allowance to one side, using a steam iron for added firmness. Slide the tube gradually off the bar, pressing firmly as you go. Stitch and press all the cut bias strips in this way.

Fig 7b

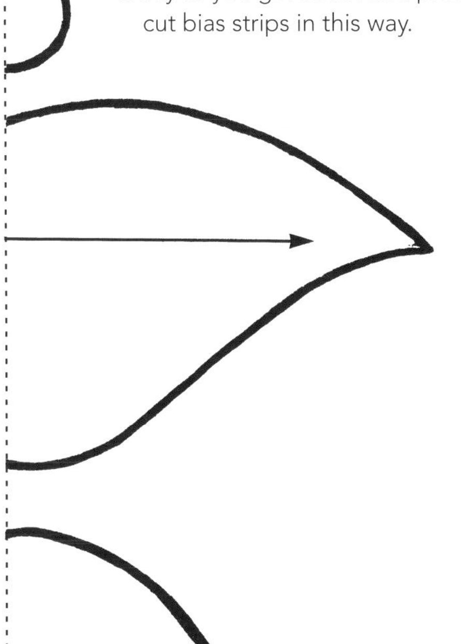

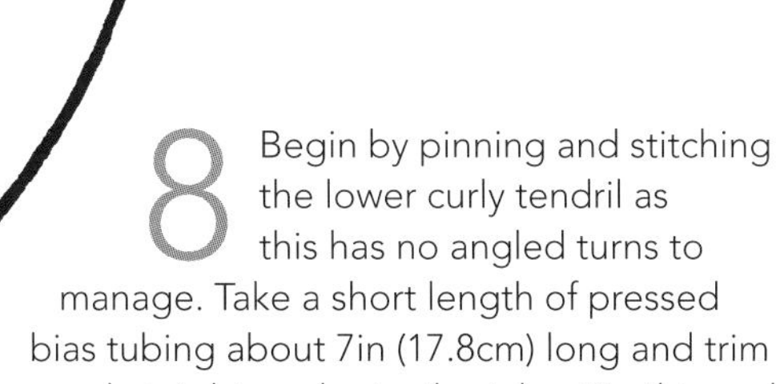

8 Begin by pinning and stitching the lower curly tendril as this has no angled turns to manage. Take a short length of pressed bias tubing about 7in (17.8cm) long and trim one end at right angles to the tube. Pin this end on to the background fabric over the drawn line of the tendril where it meets the lily petal. The drawn line should lie midway underneath the bias tube. Leave the raw end of the tube extending ⅛in (3mm) beyond the start of the tendril so that it can be hidden under the bias stem later (Fig 8). Pin the bias tube over the drawn line of the tendril, positioning the shorter inside edge first and stretching it slightly on the curves so that there are no tiny puckers along that edge. The longer outside edge has to stretch a little more to fit the curve but as it is cut on the bias this is not a problem (Fig 9).

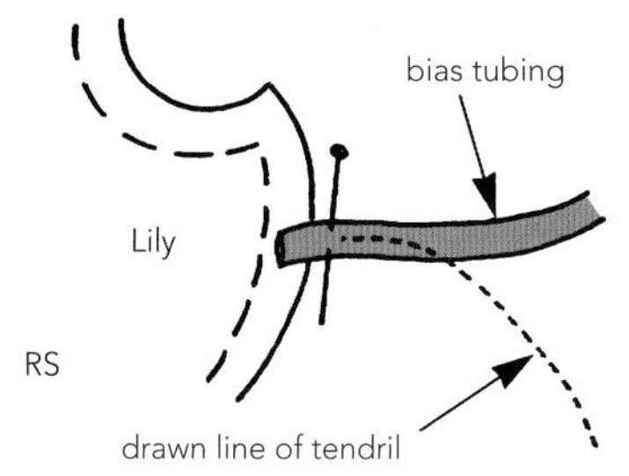

Fig 8

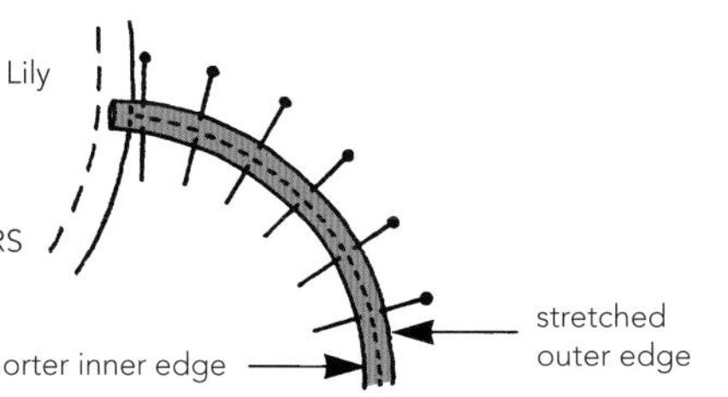

Fig 9

Pin about every ½in (1.3cm) at right angles to the bias tubing. You could pin the entire tendril in place before stitching or just pin a short distance ahead of the stitching as you work. Always stitch the shorter inside edge first. You probably won't need any pins to hold the outer edge in position once the inside edge has been stitched in place. The curled end of the tendril needs to be stretched around and pinned so that its raw end is trapped underneath the pinned tendril (Fig 10). This end is held in place when the tendril is stitched over it.

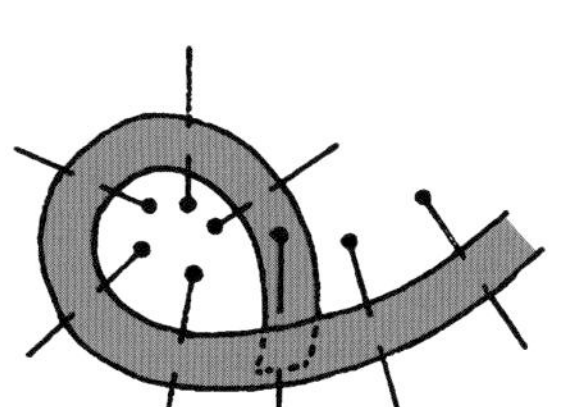
Fig 10

9 Pin and stitch the other tendril in the same way, leaving an extra ⅛in (3mm) where it meets the stem of the adjacent leaf.

10 Each of the two pairs of leaves has the right-hand leaf joining the main stem of the left-hand leaf. Edge the right-hand leaf first. Take a piece of pressed bias tube about 12in (30.5cm) in length. Pin and stitch it in position around the leaf with the inner edge lying on the leaf itself and with the outer edge *just* on the background fabric. This means that nearly all the pressed tube is positioned over the leaf and when stitched in place secures the raw edge of the leaf safely under it (see Fig 11 overleaf).

Pin and stitch the bias tube in the direction shown in Fig 12 overleaf, stitching the shorter inner edges first. Leave an extra ⅛in (3mm) beyond the starting point so that it can be covered later by the bias tubing on the other side of the leaf. Turning the sharp corner at the top of the leaf is not as difficult as it looks. Pin and stitch the inner edge of the bias tube to within ¼in (6mm) of the turning point. Use a large pin to catch the outer edge of the tube at its turning point. Pin this into the fabric as shown in Fig 13. Pull the bias tube sharply round so that it lies in position on the edge of the leaf, tucking under the fold of fabric at the sharp corner with the needle until it makes a mitre. Pull back the large pin and reposition the point to hold the mitred fold in place (Fig 14).

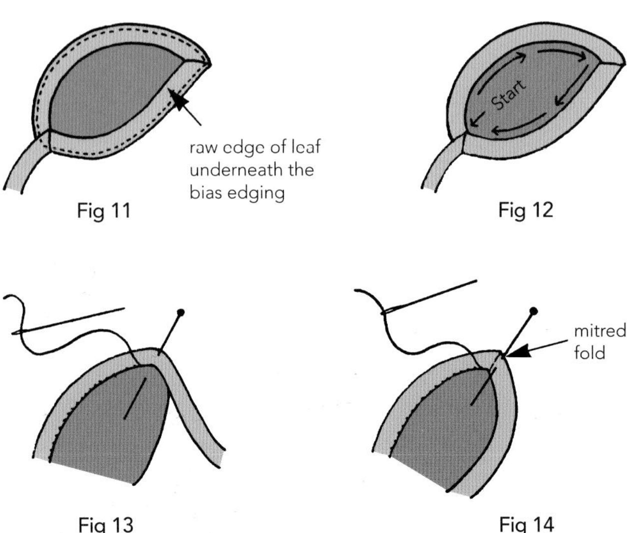

Fig 11 Fig 12

Fig 13 Fig 14

Continue to pin and stitch the bias tube on to the second side of the leaf. Do not stitch the mitre itself (Fig 15). At the base of the leaf, twist the bias tube to cover the raw end of the stitched tube, using a pin as before to mitre the angle and continue with the tube to pin and stitch the stem (Fig 16). Once the inner edges are stitched, sew the outer edges of the tube in place. Leave an extra ⅛in (3mm) of tubing where it joins the main stem – this will eventually be covered by the main stem.

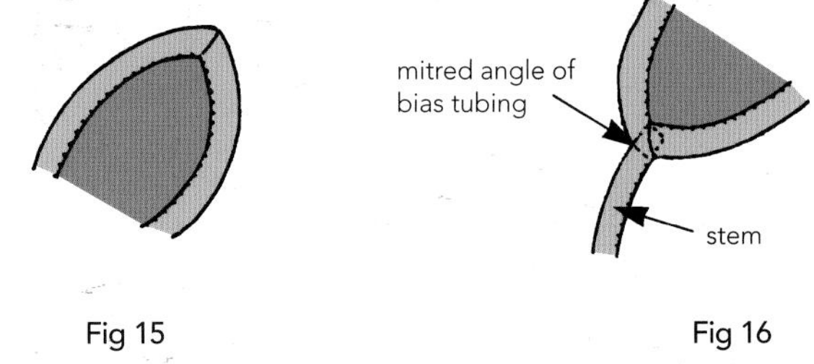

Fig 15 Fig 16

11 Cut a piece of bias tubing about 12in (30.5cm) in length and pin and stitch it around the second leaf in the same way. Its stem should cover the raw edges of the side stems and finish at the lily petal. Trim the end to ⅛in (3mm) beyond the edge of the petal. This end will eventually be covered by the bias edging around the petal itself.

12 Following the same process, edge the other pair of leaves in the same way.

13 Pin and stitch a 7in (17.8cm) length of bias tubing around each of the two side petals marked 1 and 2 in Fig 17, mitring sharp corners and leaving an extra ⅛in (3mm) at either end as before.

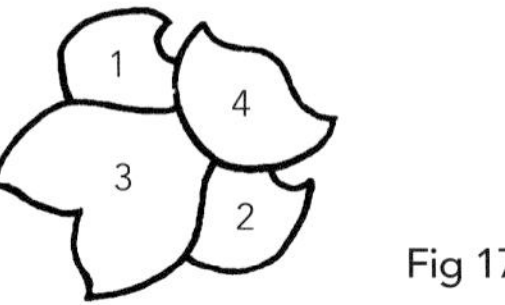

Fig 17

14 Pin and stitch a length of bias tubing about 12in (30.5cm) long around the centre petal marked 3 in Fig 17, covering the raw ends of side petals 1 and 2. Leave an extra ⅛in (3mm) at either end as before.

15 The three stamens are made from three lengths of bias tubing, one about 5in (12.7cm) long and the other two about 3in (7.6cm) long. The stamen end is made by tying a knot in the tubing about ½in (1.3cm) from one end (Fig 18a). Bring the end across the knot (Fig 18b) and tuck it behind the knot (Fig 18c). Secure the end to the back of the knot with a few stitches. The knotted stamen can then be pinned in position, pinning from the knotted end and trimming the other end to leave an extra ⅛in (3mm) where the stamen meets the petal. Stitch the stamen, inner curve first. Knot and stitch all three stamens in this way.

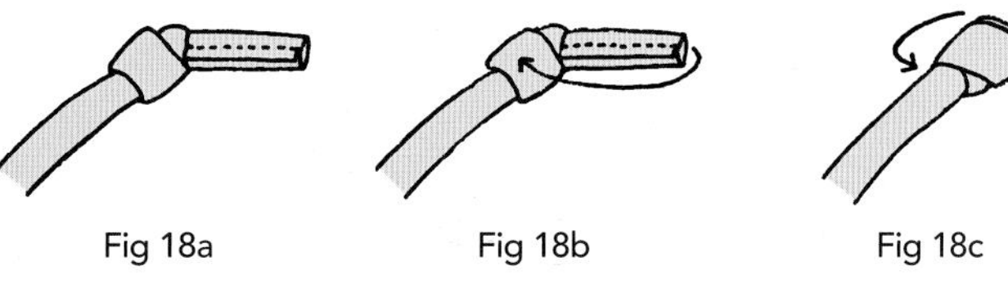

Fig 18a Fig 18b Fig 18c

16 Finally, pin and stitch petal 4 (see Fig 17 above), beginning at a sharp corner so that the raw ends can be tucked under without it being too obvious.

17 Trim the completed block to an exact 12 x 12in (30.5 x 30.5cm) square. Cut two strips for the inner frame each measuring 1½ x 12in (3.8 x 30.5cm) and two measuring 1½ x 14in (3.8 x 35.6cm). Pin and stitch the two shorter strips to the either side of the block. Press the seams outwards away from the block, pressing from the front of the work. Pin and stitch the two longer strips to the top and bottom of the block. Press seams outwards, pressing from the front as before. Finally, add the sashing strips to the block (see page 236 for instructions).

Machine Foundation Piecing

Electric Fan

This block has an Art Deco feel to it and fits in well with the other blocks in this sampler quilt (see Fig 1 overleaf). Four pieced rectangles are arranged around a centre square with the centre circle appliquéd on to the block once piecing is completed (Fig 2). The circle can be omitted if preferred. Each of the four rectangles is made up of two larger curved shapes with a pieced curved strip between them. If this section is pieced on a foundation, the block can be assembled without too much heartache. Other tricky pieced designs like Double Wedding Ring could be tackled using this method of foundation piecing – it makes the combining of so many small pieces less daunting.

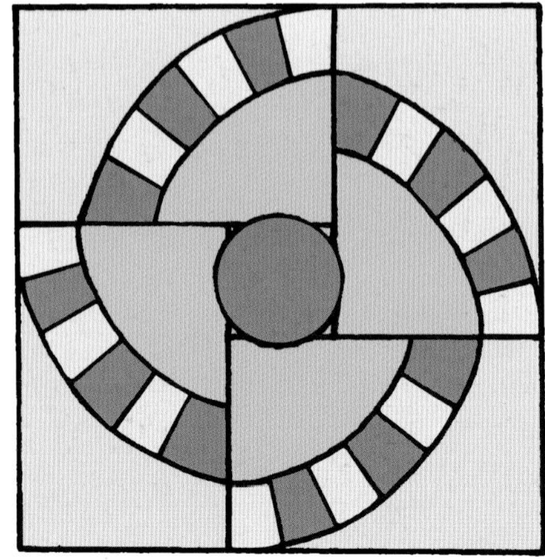

Fig 1

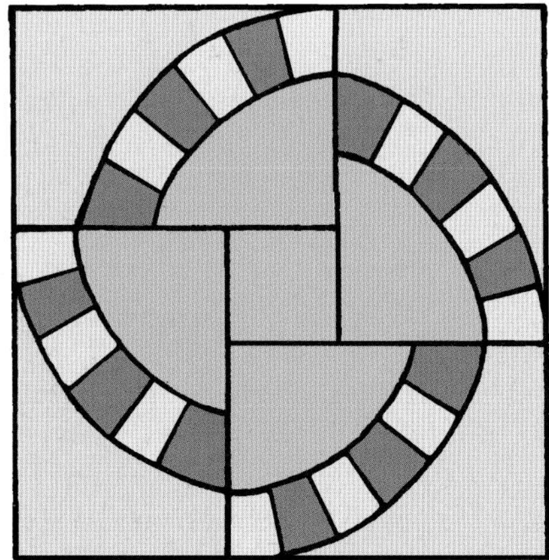

Fig 2

Colour Choices

The Electric Fan is set on a background fabric in the four corners of the block. The main central part of the fan is made from one fabric, with another two fabrics used alternately to form the pieced outer edge of the fan. A completely different fabric can be chosen for the centre circle or one already used in the pieced fan edge. I am inclined to leave that decision until the rest of the block has been assembled.

Construction

1 Make card templates of shapes A and B from Fig 3 on page 229 by tracing them, cutting them out and sticking them on to card, or use template plastic. Mark the directional arrows, as these show how the template should be positioned on the grain or weave of the fabric. The stitching line is shown as a dotted line within the templates. Mark the templates so that you know which way up to use them, as they are *not* reversible.

2 Shape C *only* is to be pieced using the foundation-piecing method. Choose a foundation that can be removed once the piecing is complete, such as tracing paper, freezer paper or a woven tear-away foundation. Trace shape C four times on to your chosen foundation, tracing all the drawn lines and numbers (Fig 4). No space needs to be left between each drawn shape. Cut round each shape C, cutting exactly on the outer drawn line.

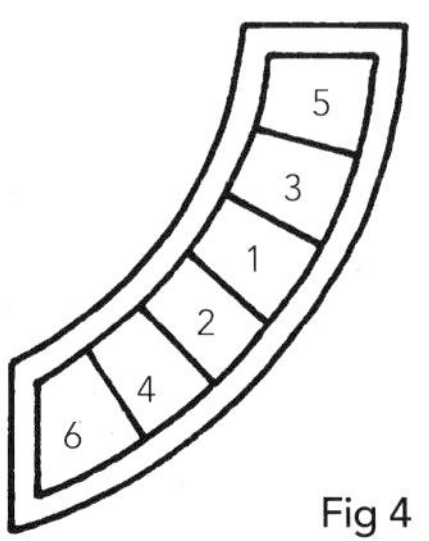

Fig 4

3 On the *wrong* side of the fabric chosen for the central area of the block, draw round template A four times. Check that this template is used *right side up*. Don't flip it over, or the design will not fit together properly. Match the fabric grain with the directional arrow on the template. Cut out each shape exactly on the drawn line (seam allowances are included in the template). In addition, from this fabric cut a square measuring 3 x 3in (7.6 x 7.6cm) for the square that will be pieced into the centre of the block.

4 On the *wrong* side of the background fabric to be used in the corners of the block draw round template B four times. Match the grain of the fabric to the drawn arrow on the template. Cut out the four shapes exactly on the drawn line. Use the template *right side up* – do not flip it over or the design will not fit together.

5 *Foundation piecing the curved strip:* from each of the two fabrics to be used, cut a strip measuring 2½ x 26in (6.3 x 66cm) (two shorter lengths will be fine if you haven't got a 26in (66cm) length in the chosen fabric).

From each strip cut eight pieces 2in (5cm) wide and four pieces 2½in (6.3cm) wide. You should finish up with two sets of pieces as shown in Fig 5. The larger pieces are to be used for the end sections on each strip as they are bigger than the middle four pieces.

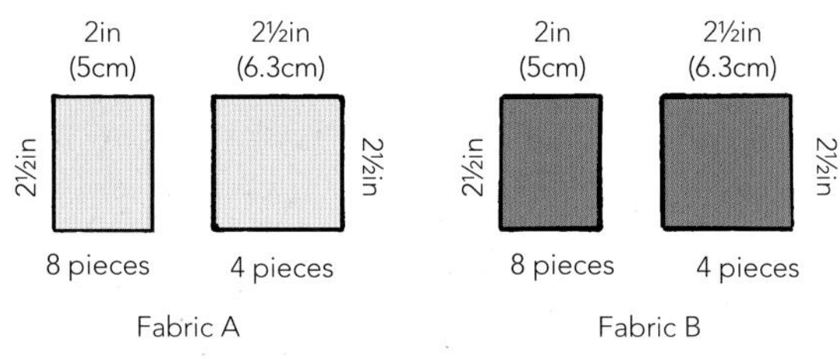

Fig 5

6 Follow the general instructions for foundation piecing given on page 187 to set your machine up ready for stitching. Place a rectangle of one of the chosen fabrics 2½ x 2in (6.3 x 5cm) *right side up* on the unmarked side of the foundation over the section marked 1 on Fig 6. The longer side should stretch from one edge of the foundation strip to the other. Hold it in position and turn the foundation over to the marked side. Adjust the position of the fabric so that there is at least ¼in (6mm) beyond the marked lines on all sides. If you can't see too well through the foundation, hold it up against the light on the sewing machine. Pin in position.

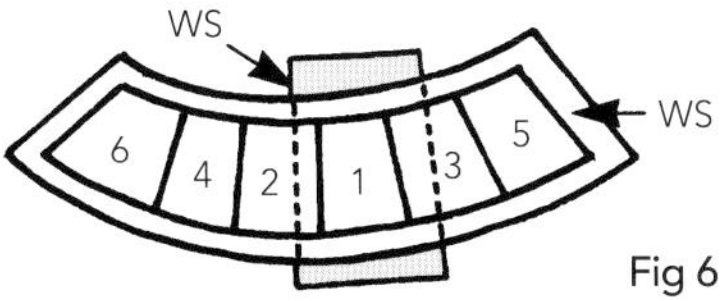

Fig 6

The sections on the foundation are wedge-shaped so the amount of fabric extending beyond the drawn lines will not be a regular ¼in (6mm). I find it helpful to correct this before adding each new piece of fabric as it makes the positioning easier. To do this, fold back and crease the foundation on to the marked back along the line between sections 1 and 2 (Fig 7). I use a thin plastic 6in (15cm) ruler placed along the drawn line to help me. Fold back the foundation against the edge of the ruler to get an accurate crease. Trim the fabric beyond this creased edge by eye to ¼in (6mm). Unfold the foundation so that it lies flat again.

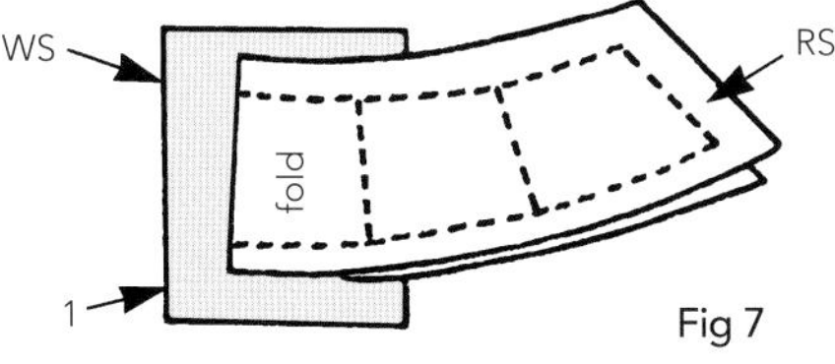

Fig 7

7 Take a rectangle of the second fabric 2½ x 2in (6.3 x 5cm) and place it right side *up* in the correct position over section 2 on the unmarked side of the foundation. You can see where to position it by looking through from the marked side of the foundation. Flip the rectangle of fabric over on to the original pinned fabric with right sides facing. Line up the fabric edges at the seam to be stitched and pin if necessary (Fig 8). If you would prefer just to hold the pieces in place, then do so.

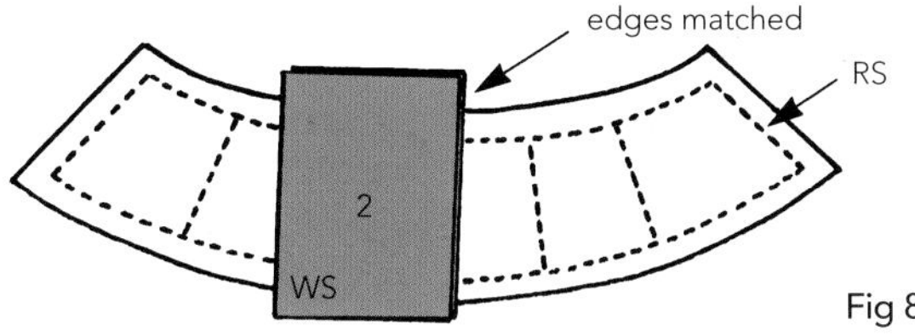

Fig 8

8 Turn the foundation over so that the marked side is uppermost and place it on the machine. Stitch along the line between sections 1 and 2, extending right across the foundation at the beginning and end of the drawn line (Fig 9). Flip over piece 2 and iron it flat in position over section 2 on the foundation (Fig 10).

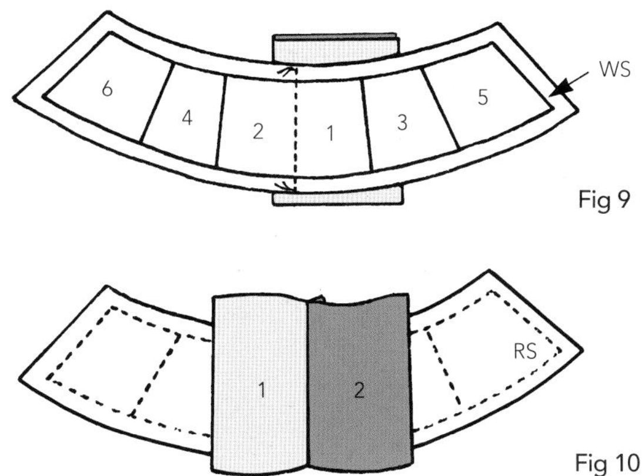

Fig 9

Fig 10

9 Use the thin ruler to fold back and crease the foundation on to the marked back along the seam between section 1 and section 3. Trim the fabric beyond the creased edge by eye to ¼in (6mm) as before. Unfold the foundation so that it lies flat again.

10 Place a rectangle of the second fabric 2½ x 2in (6.3 x 5cm) right side up in the correct position over section 3 on the unmarked side of the foundation. Flip the fabric rectangle over on to the original fabric piece 1, right sides facing. Line up the fabric edges at the seam to be stitched. Pin or hold the fabric in position and turn the foundation over to the marked side. Stitch along the seam between sections 1 and 3, extending right across the foundation at the beginning and end of the drawn line. Flip over piece 3 and iron it flat in position over section 3 on the foundation (Fig 11).

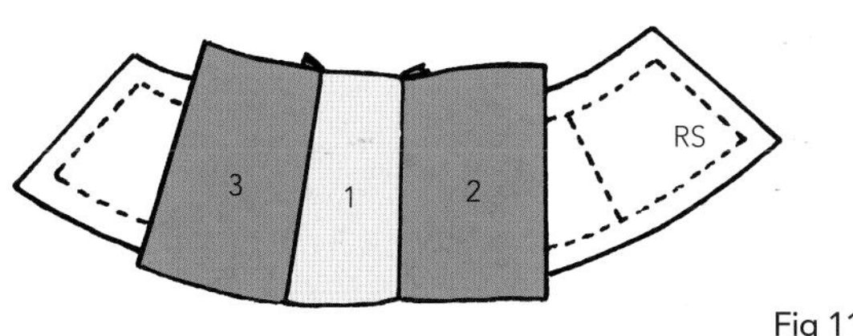

Fig 11

11 Continue to position and stitch each piece of fabric in place on the foundation, following the numbers. Trim the existing seam allowance each time before adding the new piece of fabric by folding the foundation back on the seamline to be stitched and trimming the fabric. Alternate the fabrics as you add each piece on the foundation. Use the larger fabric squares, 2½ x 2½in (6.3 x 6.3cm), for the end sections as these are slightly wider than the rest.

12 Press the completed curved strip now and then trim the fabric to match the *outer* edges of the foundation.

13 In the same way, stitch the fabric rectangles and squares on to the other three foundation strips. Make sure the colours are used in the same alternating arrangement each time. Trim the fabric edges to match the *outer* edges of the foundation.

14 Now remove the foundation, taking particular care not to undo the stitches at either end of the stitched seams.

15 *Assembling the block:* the four rectangular sections can now be pieced, each one as shown in Fig 12. Fold the curved edge of shape A in half to find the centre. Do the same with shape C. Pin the curved edge of shape A to the shorter curved edge of shape C, matching the centres and corners. I find it easiest to pin and stitch with shape C on top. Like all curved seams, it may need quite a few pins placed at right angles to the seam. Clip the curved seam allowance of piece C if necessary to help fit the pieces together. Stitch the usual ¼in (6mm) seam. Press the seam allowance towards the pieced strip.

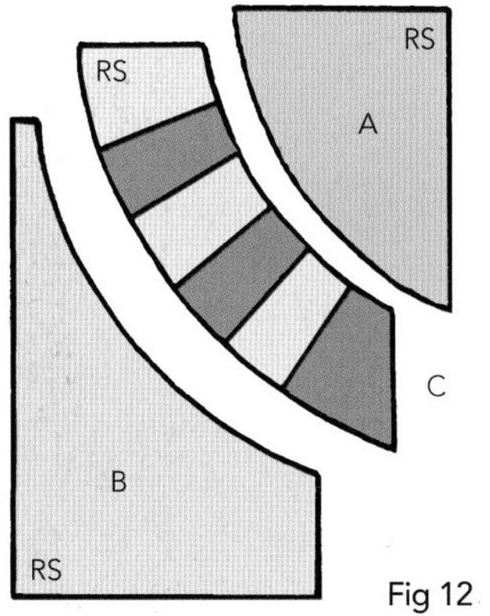

Fig 12

16 In the same way pin and stitch the large piece B to the pieced strip, working with piece B on the top, stretching it slightly to fit where necessary. Press the seam allowance towards piece B. Make all four rectangles in the same way.

17 Now arrange the rectangles together with the 3 x 3in (7.6 x 7.6cm) square cut for the centre of the block (Fig 13). They are assembled in the same way as the Folded Flying Geese in that block.

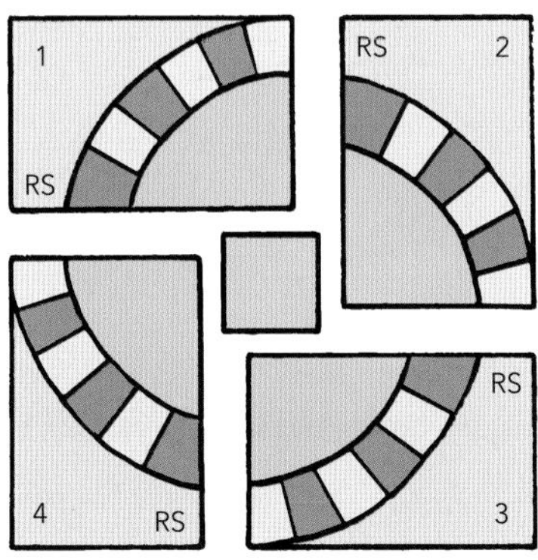

Fig 13

18 Stitch the centre square to unit 1, stitching about *halfway* along the seam only (Fig 14). Open the square out away from unit 1, pressing the seam allowance towards unit 1. Pin and stitch unit 2 to the side of unit 1 and the centre square (Fig 15). Press the seam towards unit 2.

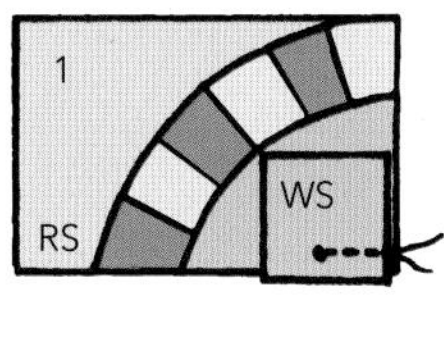

Fig 14

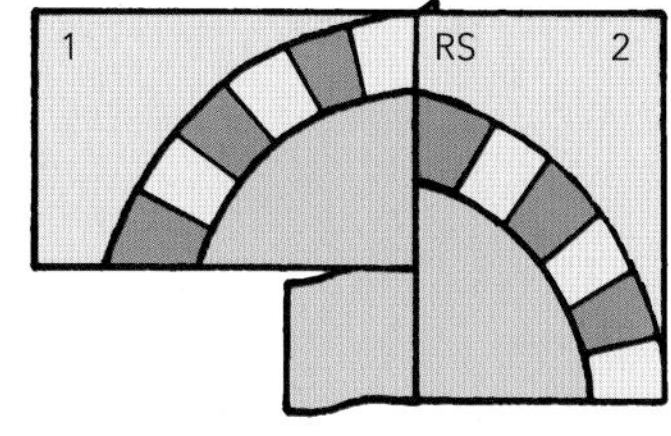

Fig 15

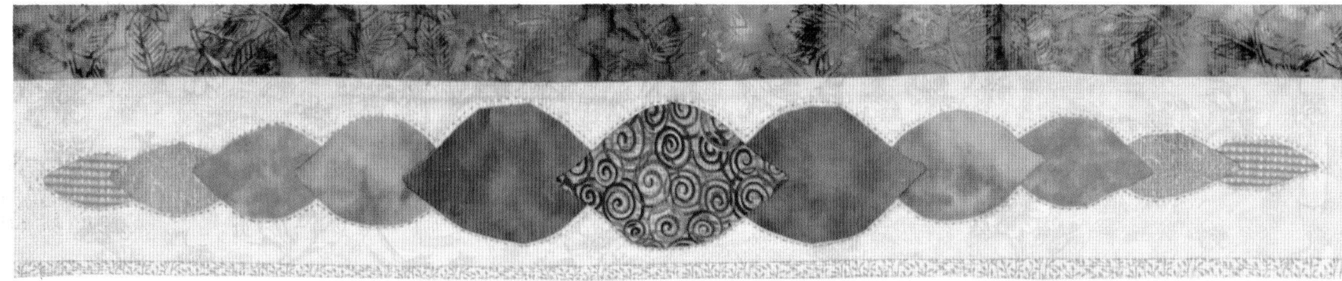

Brenda Day has used an interesting appliqué design in the border of her sampler quilt, made with a selection of the fabrics used in the blocks.

"The best thing about making this quilt was that each block felt like starting a new quilt – exciting and non-repetitive. The mauve and green colours reminded me of a grapevine, hence the title of my quilt, 'Vineyard Sampler'." **Brenda Day**

Pin and stitch unit 3 to the bottom of unit 2 and the centre square (Fig 16). Press the seam towards unit 3.

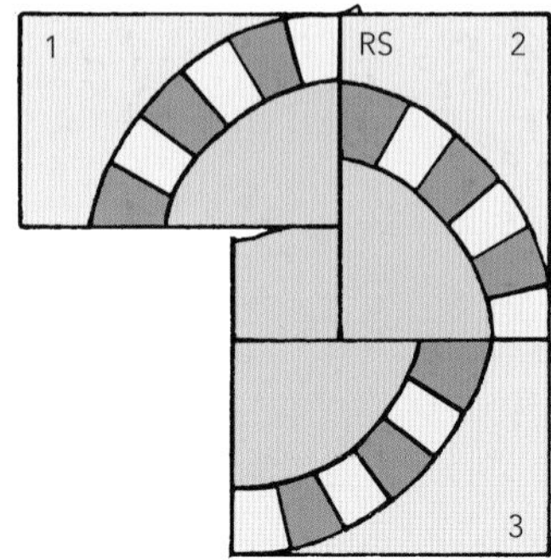

Fig 16

Pin and stitch unit 4 to the side of unit 3 and the centre square (Fig 17). Press the seam towards unit 4. Finally, stitch the seam to join the top of unit 4 and the square to unit 1. Press the seam towards unit 1.

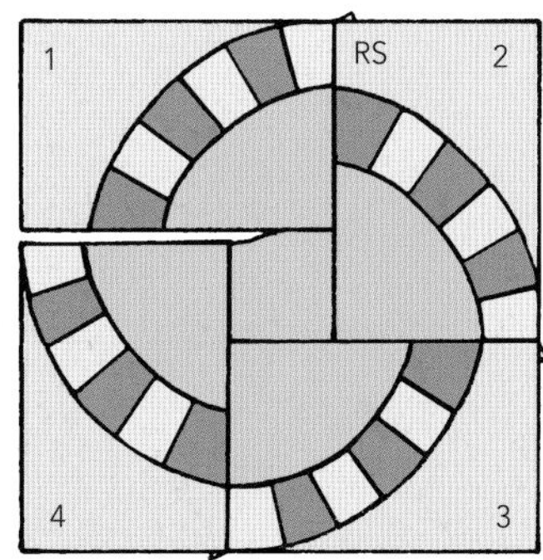

Fig 17

19 *Making the centre circle:* trace the circle in Fig 18 below on to the non-shiny side of freezer paper, or use a pair of compasses to draw a circle with a radius of 1¼in (3.2cm). Cut out the circle exactly on the drawn line.

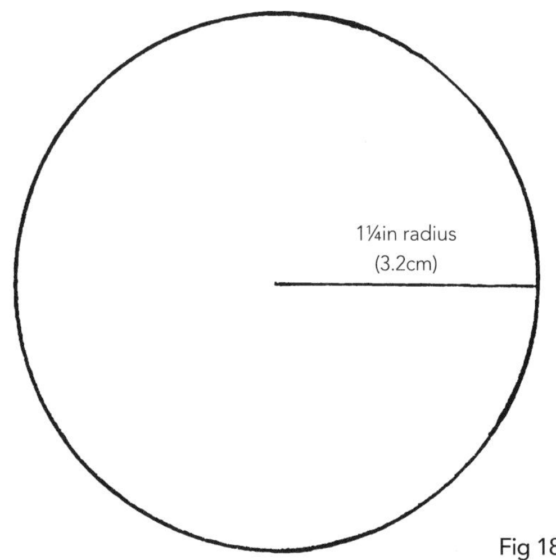

Fig 18

20 Iron the circle shiny side *down* on to the *wrong* side of the fabric chosen for the centre circle in the block. Cut out the circle adding a ¼in (6mm) seam allowance to the fabric (Fig 19).

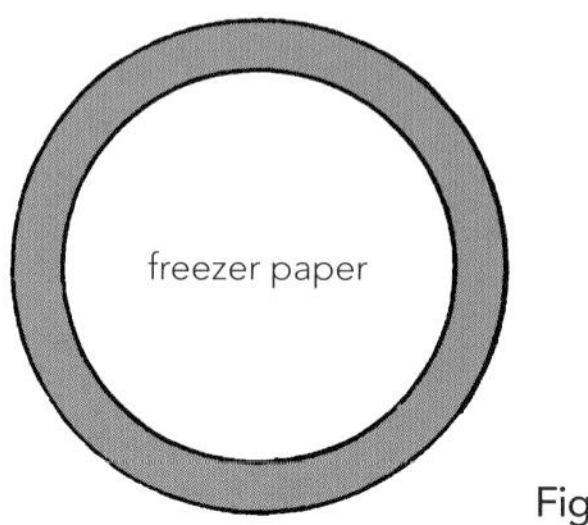

Fig 19

21 Peel the paper circle off the fabric and replace it shiny side *up* on the *wrong* side of the fabric circle in exactly the same position, leaving the ¼in (6mm) seam allowance on all sides. Pin the freezer paper on to the fabric (Fig 20). Using the side of an iron (no steam, wool setting), nudge the seam allowance of fabric over on to the freezer paper, easing in the fullness a little at a time until all the allowance is stuck down on the paper. Keep the curve smooth without any tiny pleats (Fig 21).

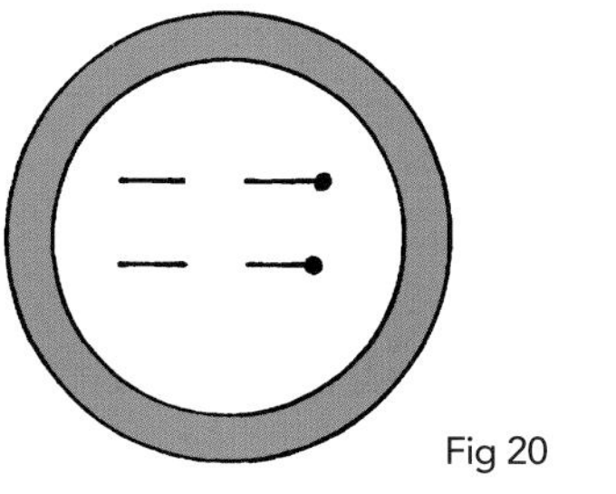

Fig 20

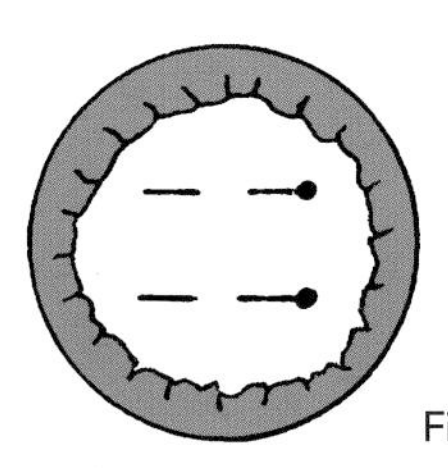

Fig 21

22 Position the fabric circle over the centre square in the block. It can be ironed on but may still need pins to stop it from shifting as you stitch it into place. Match the grain of the circle with the grain of fabric in the rest of the block. Stitch the circle by hand, using small appliqué stitches in a (thread colour to match the circle, not the background.

23 Once stitched, turn the block to the back. Use the stitch lines as a guide to cut away the backing up to ¼in (6mm) from the stitching line of the circle, revealing the freezer paper below. Ease up the fabric from the edge of the paper and pull the paper out. Press the completed block.

24 Add the inner framing strips to bring the block up to exactly 14 x 14in (35.6 x 35.6cm). Finally, add the sashing strips. See page 236 for instructions on framing and sashing.

Fig 3 – Actual size templates

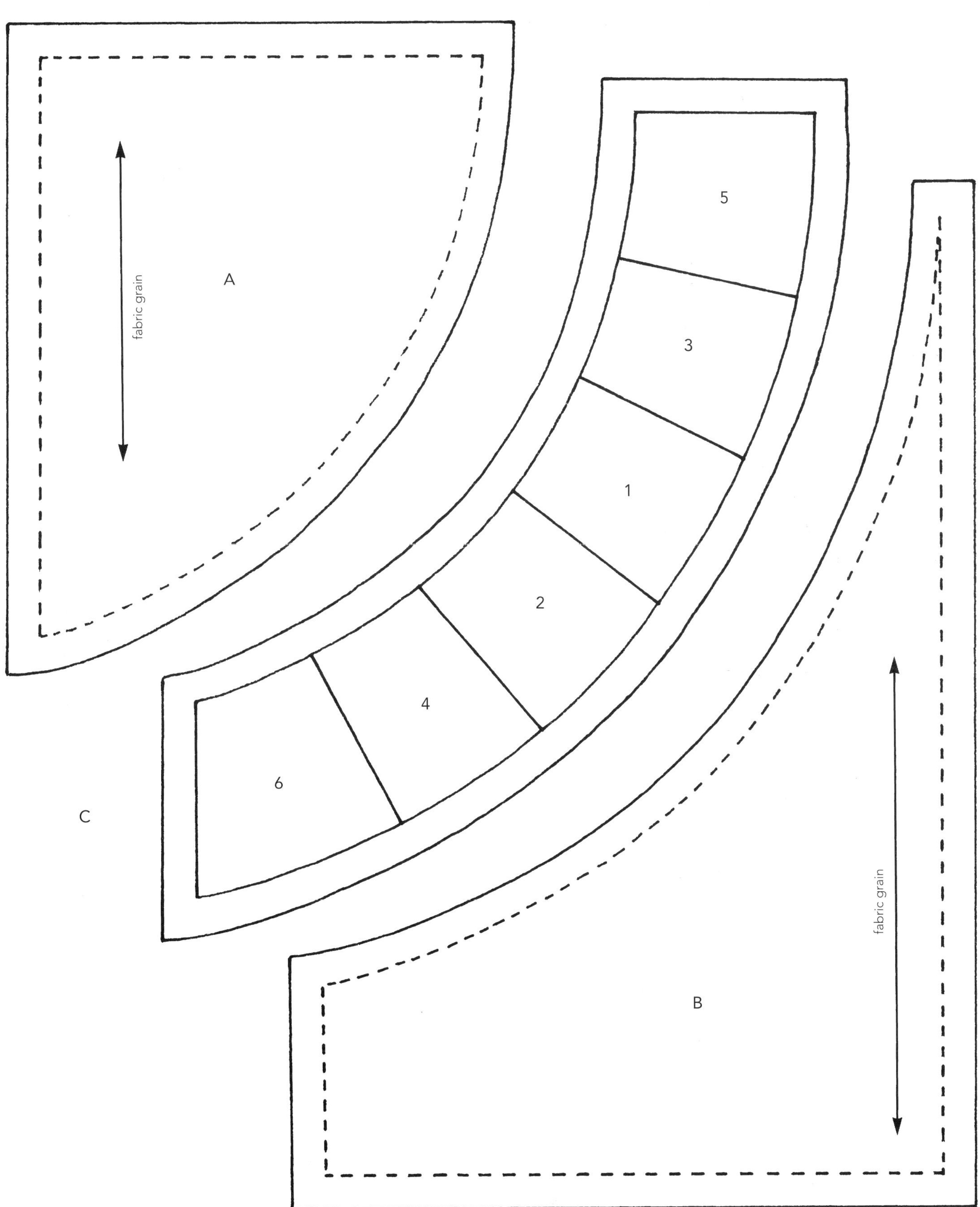

Hand or Machine Appliqué

Alternative Drunkard's Path

This is really a machine technique, using transparent thread as the top thread on the machine and the usual sewing thread in the bobbin. It can be stitched by hand, but if you can master this simple narrow zigzag stitch you will find it really useful for projects where a more durable finish is needed. Exquisite hand appliqué is fine for your heirlooms but is not always suitable for children's quilts or lap quilts that are going to be used and possibly abused.

The Drunkard's Path block (Fig 1) consists of a square with a quarter circle or quadrant set into it. The radius of the quadrant is usually about two-thirds the length of the square (Fig 2). This method cheats in that the units are made four at

a time. A complete circle is appliquéd on to a square and then cut into quarters to give the four Drunkard's Path units (Fig 3). The mathematical amongst you will soon spot that the completed units will not make true quarter circles as they lose a ¼in (6mm) when joined together. The only time this is at all noticeable is when two units are joined to make a semicircle (Fig 4a) or when four units make a complete circle (Fig 4b), as there are slight irregularities in the curve at the seams.

With this technique it is possible to make small Drunkard's Path units, which would not be so easy if the curves were pieced in the traditional way. I have chosen a design of thirty-six units, six in each row. Only twenty-eight are made up of the curved pieces, as eight whole squares are part of the design (Fig 1).

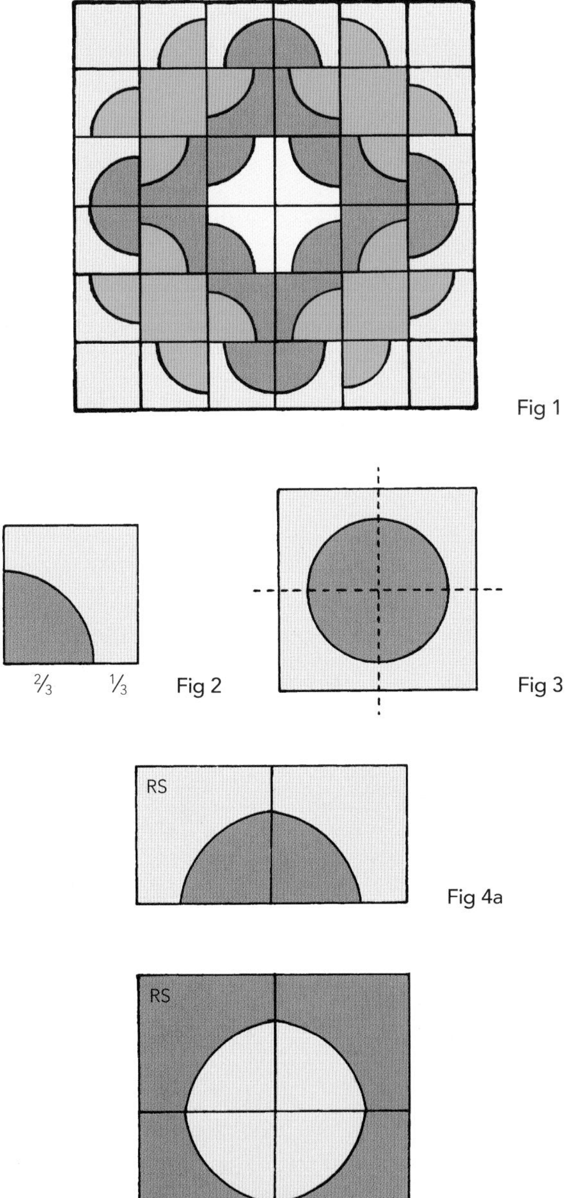

Fig 1

Fig 2

Fig 3

Fig 4a

Fig 4b

Colour Choices

Three fabrics have been used for the design, which is set on a fourth fabric as the background around the outer edge. Choose fabrics where there is enough difference to allow the curved edges of the design to be seen.

Setting up the Machine for Invisible Appliqué

Of course this is not completely invisible, but it is not an obvious edging like satin stitch – the better you get at it, the less it notices. You will need a finer needle when using transparent thread on the machine, a size 70 or 11. The transparent thread has got finer and easier to use in recent years. If the fabric of your circle is very pale, use the clear transparent thread. If using medium or dark fabric, choose smoke-tinted thread. Beware of letting the loose end of thread unravel in your sewing box – it can come off the reel in handfuls if given the slightest opportunity. Stick the end on to the reel when it is not in use with a piece of masking tape. If you are not sure whether a type of nylon thread is suitable, take a thread of it and try to break it with your fingers. If it breaks easily then it will be safe to use and will not damage your fabric. As one American quilter succinctly put it, 'If it snaps, use it; if it doesn't, fish with it...'

Thread the machine with the transparent thread as the top thread. Use a normal thread in the bobbin in a colour that matches your square of fabric. You will need either to tighten the bottom tension or loosen the top tension so that when you stitch, the transparent thread does not pull the bottom thread up to the top surface where it could show on the fabric and spoil the effect. Do a practice piece to test this before starting on the actual block. Like machine piecing, it is a great help if you use an open-fronted foot on your machine so that you can see exactly what is happening ahead of the needle. The zigzag used is so slight a swing that it is possible to use the special ¼in (6mm) patchwork foot that several of the sewing machine companies make without breaking the needle. Set the machine to a short stitch length of about 1½ and a narrow zigzag. I recommend starting with a stitch zigzag width of 1 and edging it down narrower as you get more experienced. Unfortunately many of the all-singing, all-dancing computerized sewing machines jump from stitch width 1 down to 0.5 with no steps in between, so sometimes it is an advantage to have an old steam-driven model! If your machine hates the transparent thread, try using a normal top thread in a colour to match the fabric of the circle as this may well be successful.

Construction

The design for this alternative Drunkard's Path is based on square units that measure 2in (5cm) final size after stitching. To reach this measurement after all the stitching and cutting, the chosen final measurement of the square must be doubled and then 1in (2.5cm) added. Thus for this particular sizing the *starting* squares need to be cut to measure 5 x 5in (12.7 x 12.7cm).

The radius of the quarter-circle used for the design is 1½in (3.8cm) final size, slightly more than two-thirds of the square unit, as I found it looked more effective. The radius of the circle used to make four of these at once needs to be ¼in (6mm) bigger which is 1¾in (4.4cm) (Fig 6).

1 2 3 4

Fig 5

1¾in radius (4.4cm)

Fig 6

1 *Cutting the squares:* Fig 5 shows the design with the fabrics numbered below it. Cut the following squares: From fabric 1, cut one square 5 x 5in (12.7 x 12.7cm). From fabric 2, cut two squares each 5 x 5in (12.7 x 12.7cm). From fabric 3, cut four squares each 2½ x 2½in (6.3 x 6.3cm). From background fabric 4, cut four squares each 5 x 5in (12.7 x 12.7cm) and four squares each 2½ x 2½in (6.3 x 6.3cm).

2 *Cutting the circles:* trace the circle in Fig 6 on to the non-shiny side of freezer paper seven times, or use a pair of compasses to draw seven circles each with a radius of 1¾in (4.4cm) on to the freezer paper. Cut out each circle on the drawn line.

3 Take a piece of fabric 2 (do not use the cut squares for this). Set the iron to a wool setting with no steam and use a firm ironing surface to iron three paper circles shiny side down on to the *wrong* side of this fabric, leaving at least ½in (1.3cm) between each circle to allow for the ¼in (6mm) seam allowances. Cut out each circle, adding a ¼in (6mm) seam allowance as in Fig 7 below.

In the same way, iron the other four paper circles on to the *wrong* side of fabric 3. Cut out each circle, adding ¼in (6mm) seam allowance.

4 Peel one paper circle off the fabric and replace it shiny side *up* on the *wrong* side of the fabric circle in exactly the same position leaving the ¼in (6mm) seam allowance on all sides. Pin the freezer paper on to the fabric. I use two pins to stop the paper moving (Fig 8). Using the side of the iron rather than the point, nudge the seam allowance of fabric over on to the freezer paper, easing in the fullness a little at a time until all the seam allowance is stuck down on the paper. Take care not to press any tiny pleats in the outer edge but keep the curve smooth (Fig 9). Repeat this with the remaining six circles. Remove pins.

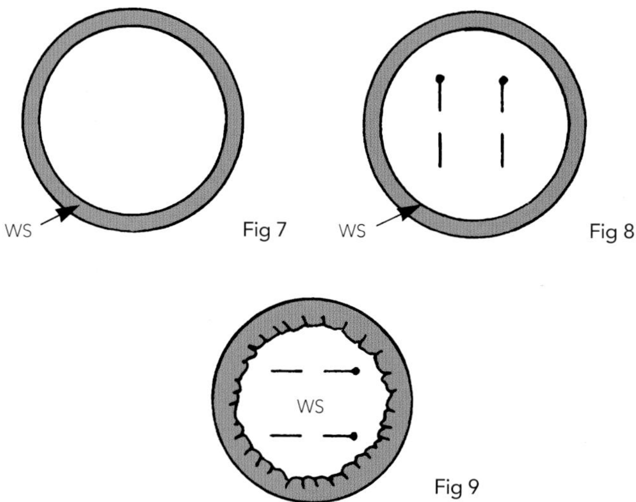

Fig 7

Fig 8

Fig 9

5 Arrange the fabric circles on the cut 5 x 5in (12.7 x 12.7cm) squares as shown in Fig 10 overleaf. To help position the circles accurately, trace the circle and surrounding square from Fig 11 on page 235 on to tracing paper. Cut out the square exactly on the drawn line. Remove the centre circle section by cutting on the drawn line of the circle (Fig 12 overleaf). If you place the tracing paper on a square of fabric, matching the corners and edges carefully, the fabric circle can be positioned in the centre hole. The

"I really enjoyed Lynne's new twist to the traditional patterns. Having decided to stick to my favourite colours, green and fawn, the challenge was to find enough variations of fabric. The quilt was voted People's Favourite at an area quilt exhibition." **Beth Williams**

square of fabric should be lying right side *up* when the circle is placed on it. Turn the circle so that the grain of the fabric matches the grainline marked on the paper square. Press the circle with an iron to fix it on to the fabric square. You could also pin it in place.

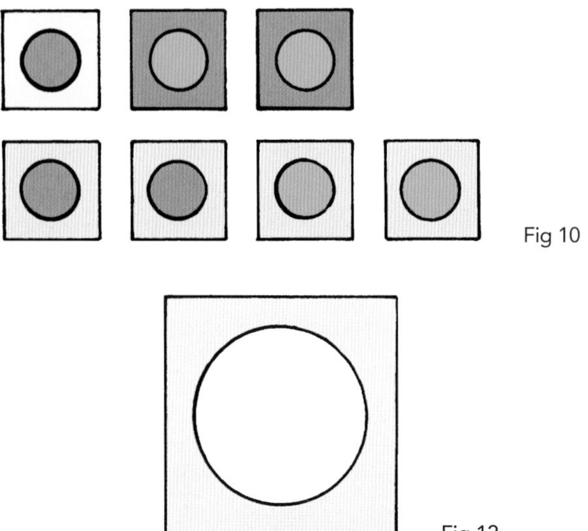

Fig 10

Fig 12

6 *Stitching the circle on the square:* once you have set your machine up for invisible appliqué (see page 231), position the fabric on the machine so that the *left* swing of the needle stitches into the very edge of the appliqué (the circle) (Fig 13a), and the *right* swing or the needle stitches just off the appliqué in the ditch between the appliqué and the background (Fig 13b).

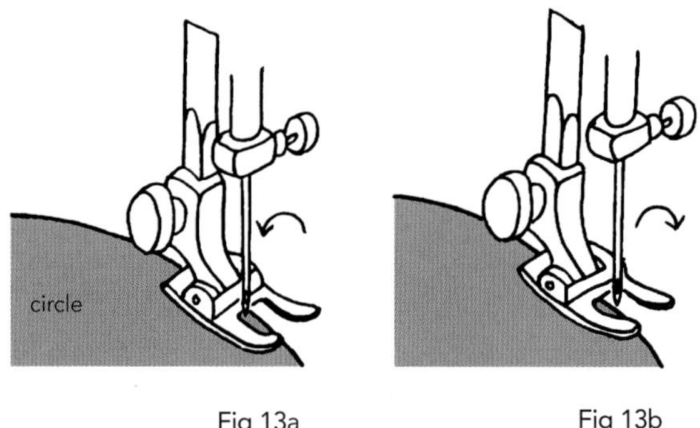

Fig 13a

Fig 13b

7 Start to stitch, taking it very slowly to start with. Do not worry if you miss catching the appliqué occasionally. If a gap is noticeable you can patch it by stitching that section a second time. Try not to stitch both left and right swings of the zigzag up on the appliqué, as this flattens the edge and you lose the soft-edged effect. Transparent thread can easily come undone, so usually the stitches need to be secured at either end of the appliqué by stitching several stitches in reverse. As this design is a continuous curved edge, just begin stitching and when you get round to the starting point again, stitch over the beginning stitches for about ½in (1.3cm) to secure them.

Sewing the Curve by Hand

If for any reason you are not happy with this machine technique, or just because you prefer handwork, the edge of the circle can be appliquéd by hand, like the circles in the Clamshell block on page 166. Because the circle will later be cut into four, it is best not to stitch across these cutting lines. Press and pin the circle on to the fabric square. Place the square on a cutting board and use a rotary ruler to find the halfway point on each side. This is where the block will be cut after stitching. Mark the edges of the circle in these four places (Fig 14). Stitch the circle in place, stitching each quarter circle separately so that when the circle is cut into quarters the stitching will not come undone.

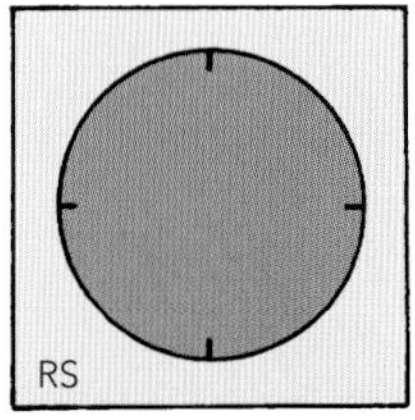

Fig 14

8 Once all seven circles are stitched into position, either by hand or machine, turn each square of fabric to the back and use the stitch lines as a guide to trim away the backing up to ¼in (6mm) from the stitching line of the circle, revealing the freezer paper below. Ease up the fabric from the edge of the paper and pull the paper out.

9 Press each unit from the front and place one on a cutting board. Use the markings on the board and a rotary ruler to find the midline on the square, 2½in (6.3cm) from each edge (Fig 15). Cut the square in half vertically on this line.

10 Take each half square and place it on the cutting board as in Fig 16. Find the midline as shown in Fig 16 and cut each piece along this line to give four quarters (Fig 17). Repeat this process with the other six squares. You should finish up with twenty-eight quarter units, each measuring 2½ x 2½in (6.3 x 6.3cm).

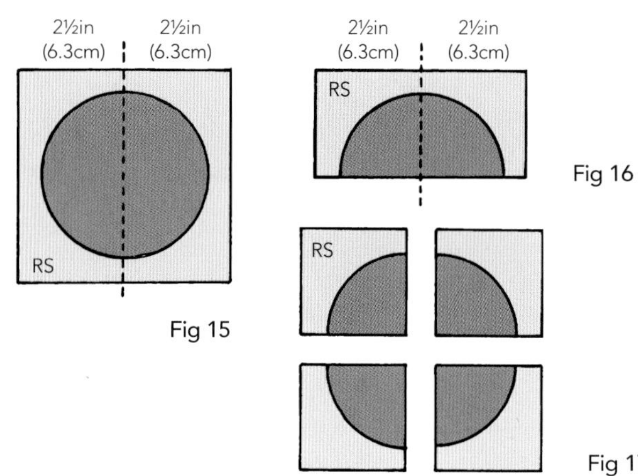

Fig 15

Fig 16

Fig 17

11 Combine these with the eight squares measuring 2½ x 2½in (6.3 x 6.3cm) cut earlier and arrange them to make the design in Fig 5 (page 232). If you prefer an alternative layout, arrange the pieces until you are happy with the design.

12 Stitch the squares of the top row together. Match the two edges of the circle section on squares 3 and 4 very carefully (Fig 18). There are only four places in the design where this match has to be made, so it is worth taking the time to get it right. Press the seams to one side, ironing from the front of the work.

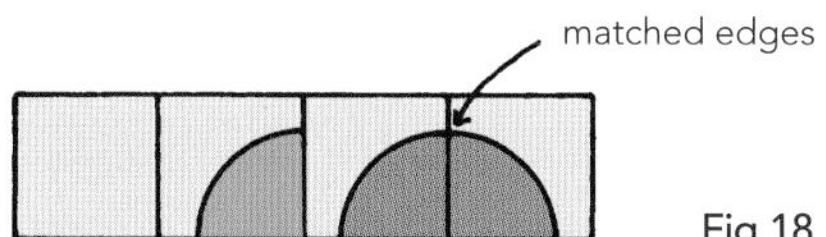

Fig 18

13 Stitch the squares of row two together. Press the seams in the opposite direction to those of row one, ironing from the front. Join rows one and two, matching seams carefully. Stitch the squares of row three together and press the seams in the opposite direction to those of row two. Pin and stitch this row to row two, matching seams carefully.

Continue to stitch together the squares, row by row, and join them to the block until all six rows are joined. Press the completed block from the front of the work.

14 Add the inner framing strips and trim the block to an exact 14in (35.6cm) square. Finally, add the sashing strips. See page 236 for instructions on framing and sashing.

Fig 11 – Actual size template

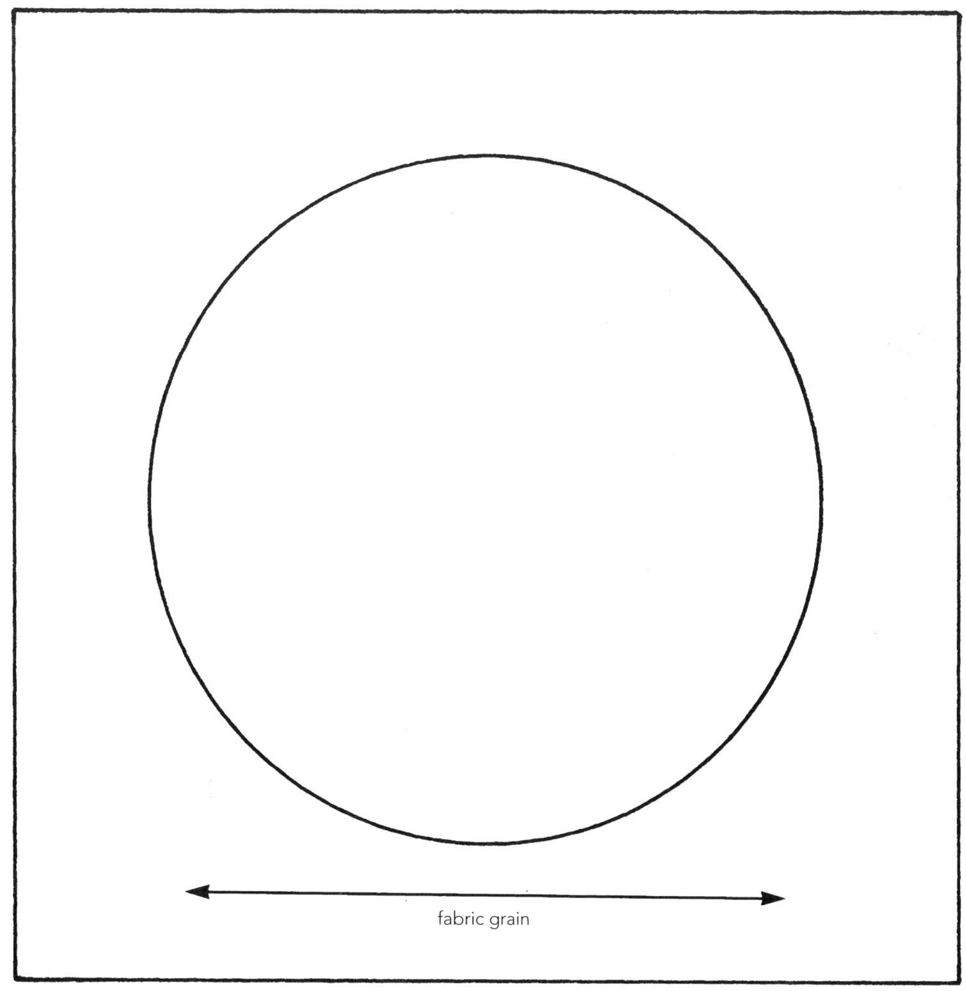

Finishing and Quilting the Blocks

The first twenty blocks in this book and several of the others should all measure 12½in (31.7cm) square at this stage, but the rest of the blocks vary in size, which gives some flexibility to the maker. The original *Sampler Quilt Book* took each block, added an extra narrow border if necessary to bring it up to the required size and then framed it with simple sashing strips. Many of the quilts shown in the first half of the book show this arrangement to great effect. However, if larger designs like Delectable Mountains or Bargello are also used in the quilt, the best way to deal with the different block sizes is by adding an inner framing border that will bring each block up to 14in (35.6cm) square. Then the final sashing strips can be used to join the blocks together. I would really recommend the adding of this extra inner frame to all your blocks, as I think it adds definition to each design and separates it from the surrounding blocks, giving it space within the quilt.

Framing and Sashing

Once each block is completed it is trimmed if necessary and then an inner framing border is added to bring the block up to 14 x 14in (35.5 x 35.5cm) (Fig 1). The block is then sashed with strips and an added feature made with a square of different fabric in each opposite corner (Fig 2). When the blocks are joined, these squares become units of four at each junction, called a Four-Patch (Fig 3).

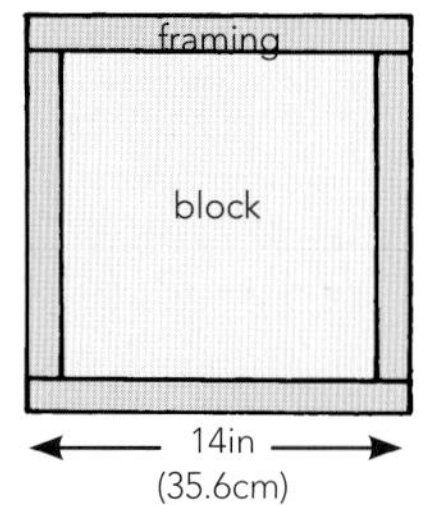

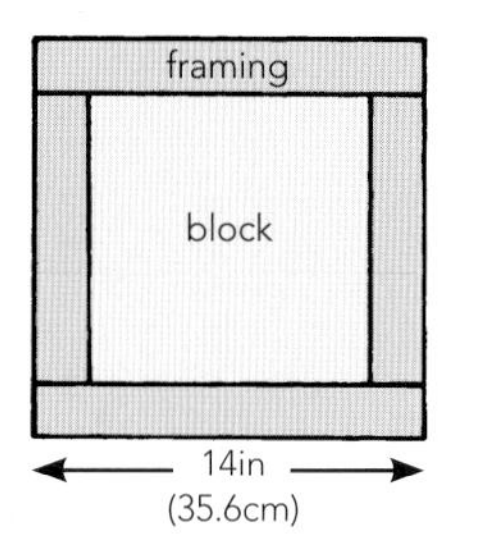

Fig 1

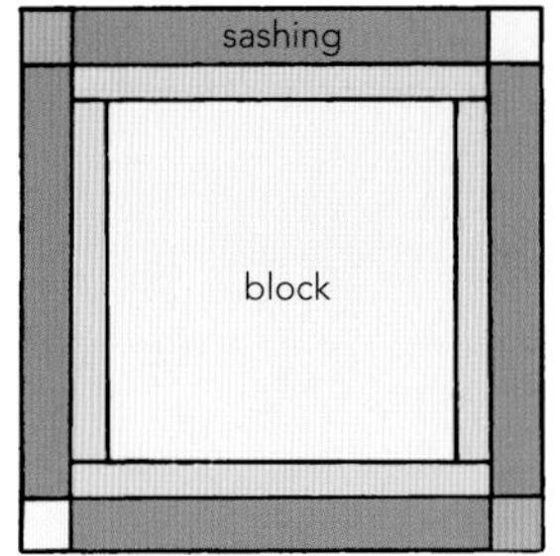

Fig 2

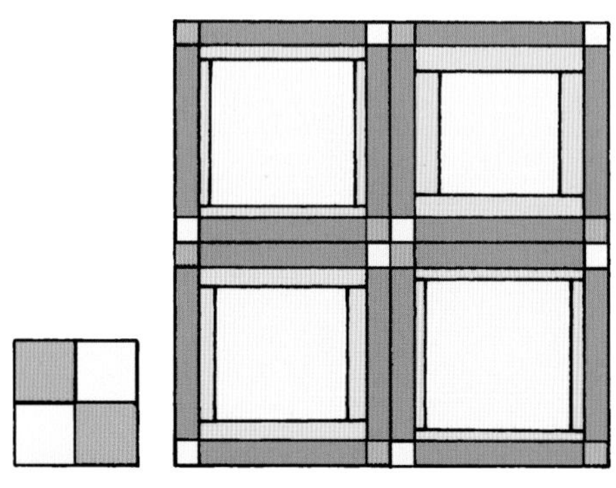

Fig 3

I used a variety of fabrics for my inner frame (see picture, page 2), but many others used the same fabric throughout. About 1¼yd (115cm) in total is needed for the inner frame and about 2yd (182.8cm) for all the sashing strips. If possible, cut all the strips down the length of the fabric parallel with the selvedge edge as it is less stretchy.

Adding the Inner Framing Strips

The block plus inner frame must measure 14 x 14in (35.6 x 35.6cm) *exactly*, including the outer raw edges.

1 Trim the block to a regular square. Do not trim off part of the design and lose corners or points. If necessary use a steam iron to press the block into a regular shape, checking this by placing it on to a cutting board between pressings and using the drawn grid on the board as a guide. The sides need to be vertical and the top and bottom edges horizontal – this seems obvious but it is amazing how many people can ignore this basic requirement.

Blocks that have a central design set in a background need only to be trimmed into a regular square to a size that suits the design before the framing strips are added.

2 The table opposite gives the width of strips needed for an inner frame to bring the block up to exactly 14 x 14in (35.6 x 35.6cm). Do not take a long strip and just stitch it on, trimming the end after stitching. The edges of the block may well stretch as you stitch and will no longer measure a true square when you finish. Cut the framing strips to size and make the block fit them exactly. (If your block does not match exactly the measurements given in the table, see Adding Inner Framing Strips to a Block with an Odd Measurement overleaf.)

3 Pin and stitch the first two strips to the sides of the block (Fig 4). Make the block fit the strips exactly. Press the seams outwards from the block, ironing from the front of the work. The block should now measure 14in (35.6cm) from side to side. If somehow it has turned out wider, trim it down to exactly the right size. If it is smaller, check your seam allowance. I'm afraid your seams probably need to be re-stitched, taking a narrower seam allowance.

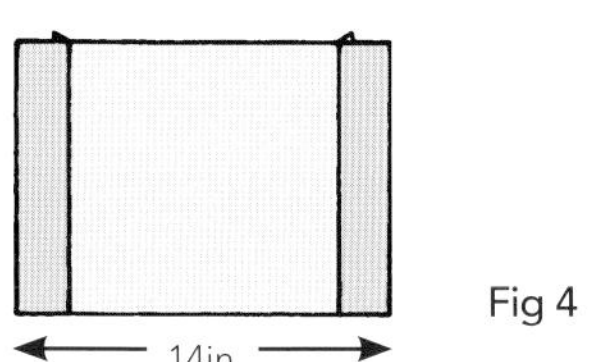

Fig 4

4 Cut two framing strips in the same width as the first pair and 14in (35.6cm) in length. Pin and stitch these to the top and bottom of the block (Fig 5). Press the seams outwards, ironing from the front of the block.

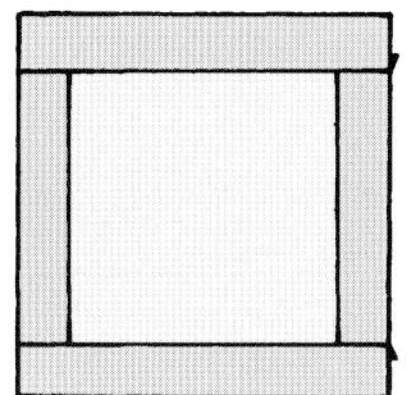

Fig 5

Framing Strips for Blocks

Block Measurement	*Measurement of Framing Strips*
11½ x 11½in (29.2 x 29.2cm) cut size	two strips 11½ x 1¾in (29.2 x 4.4) two strips 14 x 1¾in (35.6 x 4.4cm
11¾ x 11¾in (29.8 x 29.8cm) cut size	two strips 11¾ x 1⅝in (29.8 x 4.1cm) two strips 14 x 1⅝in (35.8 x 4.1cm
12 x 12in (30.5 x 30.5cm) cut size	two strips 12 x 1½in (30.5 x 3.8cm) two strips 14 x 1½in (35.6 x 3.8cm)
12¼ x 12¼in (31.1 x 31.1cm) cut size	two strips 12¼ x 1⅜in (31.1 x 3.5cm) two strips 14 x 1⅜in (35.6 x 3.5cm)
12½ x 12½in (31.7 x 31.7cm) cut size	two strips 12½ x 1¼in (31.7 x 3.2cm) two strips 14 x 1¼in (35.6 x 3.2cm)
12¾ x 12¾in (32.4 x 32.4cm) cut size	two strips 12¾ x 1⅛in (32.4 x 2.8cm) two strips 14 x 1⅛in (35.6 x 2.8cm)
13 x 13in (33 x 33cm) cut size	two strips 13 x 1in (33 x 2.5cm) two strips 14 x 1in (35 x 2.5cm)
13¼ x 13¼in (33.6 x 33.6cm) cut size	two strips 13¼ x ⅞in (33.6 x 2.2cm) two strips 14 x ⅞in (35.6 x 2.2cm)
13½ x 13½in (34.3 x 34.3cm) cut size	two strips 13½ x ¾in (34.3 x 1.9cm) two strips 14 x ¾in (35.6 x 1.9cm)

Adding Inner Framing Strips to a Block with an Odd Measurement

If your trimmed and pressed block doesn't match exactly one of the measurements in the table on the previous page, don't worry. The only thing that matters is that the sides are vertical and the top and bottom edges are horizontal.

1 Place the block on a cutting mat and check that the edges are parallel with the drawn lines on the mat. More trimming or steaming may be needed to get this correct. Measure the block from top to bottom down its centre. Find the block in the table with a measurement nearest to yours but *larger*. Use the width measurement given in the table for your own strips.

2 Cut two strips in this width and in a length to match your own block. Pin and stitch these strips to either side of the block (see Fig 4 on previous page). Press the seams outwards, pressing from the front of the block.

3 Place the block on the cutting board and trim the side strips down equally on both sides so that the block measures exactly 14in (35.6cm) from side to side (see Fig 4 on previous page).

4 Cut two framing strips in the same width as the first pair and 14in (35.6cm) in length. Pin and stitch these to the top and bottom of the block (Fig 5). Press the seams outwards, ironing from the front of the block.

Adding the Sashing Strips

1 For each block cut four strips of the fabric chosen for the sashing, each measuring 14 x 1¾in (35.6 x 4.4cm). Two more fabrics are needed to make the Four-Patch that appears at each junction of blocks. Each of these squares measures 1¾ x 1¾in (4.4 x 4.4cm).

2 Pin and stitch the sashing strips to each side of the block (Fig 6). Press the seams outwards, ironing from the front of the work.

3 To either end of a sashing strip stitch a square of Four-Patch fabric with one fabric used at one end and the other fabric at the other (Fig 7). Press the seams from the front towards the long strip. Repeat this with the remaining sashing strip.

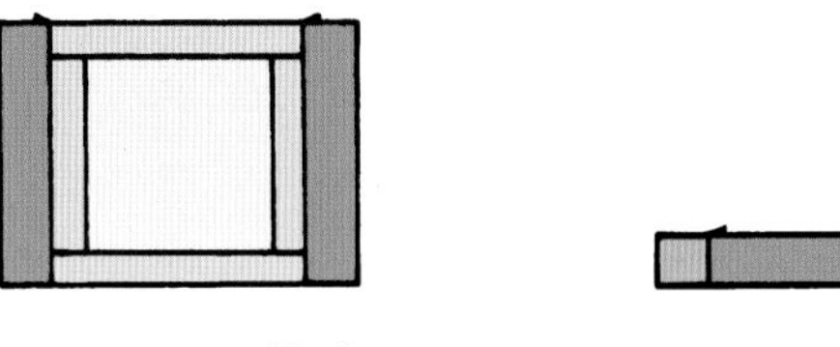

Fig 6 Fig 7

4 Pin and stitch one sashing strip with its end squares (called cornerstones) to the top of the block, matching seams carefully (Fig 8).

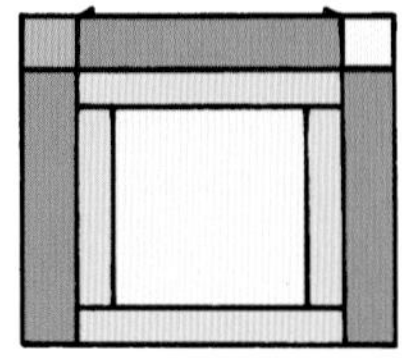

Fig 8

5 Pin and stitch the other sashing strip to the bottom of the block with the two cornerstones in opposite corners to the first pair (Fig 9). Press the seams outwards from the front. Each block should now measure exactly 16½ x 16½in (41.9 x 41.9cm). As you sash each framed block take care that the same cornerstone fabric is always in the top left-hand corner, or your little four-patch design will not work out. Some blocks can be turned through 90° to correct a mistake, but alas, not all of them, so make sure the blocks are the right way up when the cornerstones are added in their correct position.

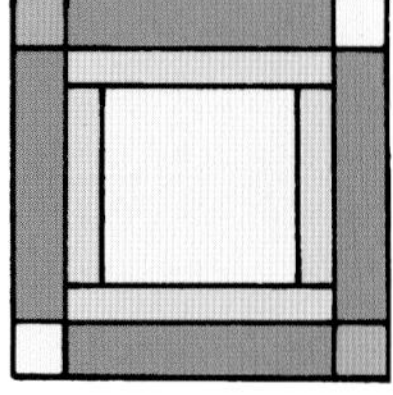

Fig 9

Quilting the Blocks

Once a quilt is pieced together it is backed with another fabric and often an extra layer of padding is sandwiched between front and back. This layer is kept in place with decorative patterns of stitches known as quilting. Hand quilting is a running stitch which makes a broken line of stitches, giving a subtle effect to the quilting design. Machine quilting has a more defined look as the stitches form a continuous line. There is no reason why both hand and machine quilting should not be combined in a quilt. I hand quilted most of my sampler quilt and machine quilted in the seams of the inner frames and sashing around each block.

It is likely that many people tackling this sampler quilt will have had some experience of quilting and already know whether hand or machine work is what they do best and, most important, what gives them pleasure. I like to do hand quilting where it will show on the quilt and enhance the design. Machine quilting I use for stitching in the seamlines (called quilting in the ditch) where it defines the piecing without being noticeable. Hand quilting in seams is quite difficult because of the extra layers and does not show on the quilt, so I avoid it.

Just as the quilt gives an opportunity to try new techniques in the blocks, so it is a good chance to explore and develop quilting skills. Angela Lloyd's quilt, a detail of which is shown on page 242, shows machine quilting in the border and decorative machine stitching along the seamlines. A detail of Jane Brooks' quilt on page 243 shows some wonderful long-arm quilting by Jan Chandler. Hand quilting takes forever to do, but soothes my soul. If you do not enjoy the hand work or you are short of time, work at the machine quilting.

Preparing the Blocks for Quilting

It is very convenient to quilt each block individually as they are easy to take around for hand quilting and a good size to work on at the machine. Some students finished all the blocks, chose the final arrangement and then joined them in rows. Each row was then quilted and the rows joined together afterwards. A few preferred to join all the blocks, add the borders and then quilt the entire piece.

For each block (or larger area if you have chosen to join several blocks before quilting) cut a piece of wadding (batting) and backing fabric each measuring ½in (1.3cm) larger on all sides than the completed block. For a single block this will be 17 x 17in (43.2 x 43.2cm). Layer the backing fabric (right side down) with the wadding and the block placed centrally on it with right side upwards (Fig 1).

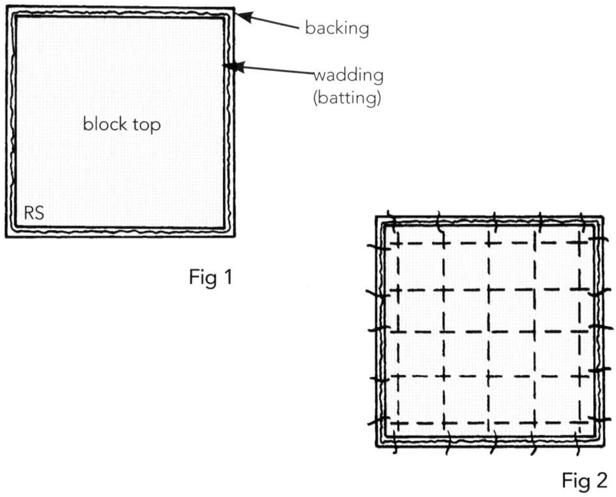

Fig 1

Fig 2

If hand quilting, tack (baste) the layers together with running stitches ¾–1in (1.9–2.5cm) long, using a long, fine needle. Work from the centre of the block outwards in a grid of vertical and horizontal lines about 3–4in (7.6–10cm) apart (Fig 2).

If machine quilting, use 1in (2.5cm) safety pins at a distance of 3–4in (7.6–10cm) over the block. Tacking stitches are not suitable when machine quilting as they catch in the feet while stitching. Keep the pins well clear of the areas to be quilted so that they do not get in the way of the machine foot as it stitches.

Where to Quilt?

Traditionally, hand quilting echoes the lines of the patchwork not in the seam itself but ¼in (6mm) away from it, called outline quilting (Fig 3), while machine quilting is more often in the seam itself. Large areas can be broken up with extra lines or curves which add interest. Do not quilt in the sashing on the block as you will need to fold this part back when joining the blocks together. Study the blocks shown in the quilt photographs throughout the book to get inspiration. Each block should be quilted roughly the same amount, so don't quilt extensively on the first block unless you are prepared to do the same for all twenty blocks.

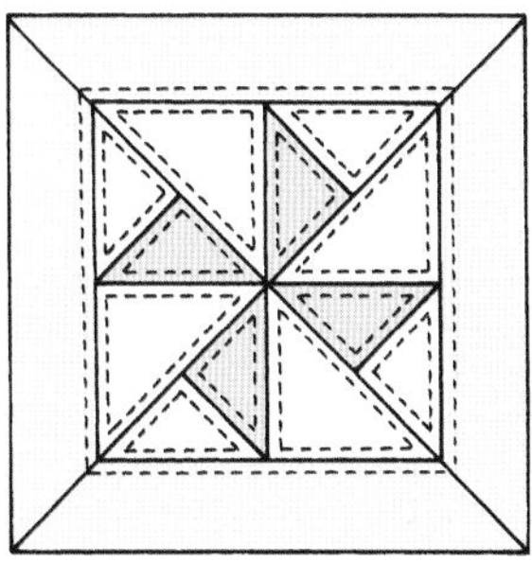

Fig 3

Marking the Design

I try to avoid marking a quilt with pencil lines as much as possible. Outline quilting lines, which are usually ¼in (6mm) away from the seamlines, can be sewn by eye or by using ¼in (6mm) low-tack masking tape. Stick the tape lightly to the surface of the top fabric with one edge against the seamline. Quilt close to the other edge and remove the tape immediately after stitching is completed (Fig 4).

Curved designs can be made by placing glasses, saucers or plates on the fabric and marking around the edge. I marked all the quilting designs on my sampler quilt using a ruler with ¼in (6mm) markings, a set of acrylic circles in various sizes and a marking tool called a hera. This is a gem of a tool that I recommend to all quilters. It has an edge rather like a butter knife that makes a sharp crease in fabric when drawn firmly across its surface. It works well against the edge of a ruler to give straight lines for quilting and even round a curved edge. The line lasts as long as you need it and can be removed just by damping the fabric slightly and letting it dry naturally. If I need to mark with a pencil I use watercolour pencils from an art shop in a colour that tones with the fabric. This wears away in time and washes out.

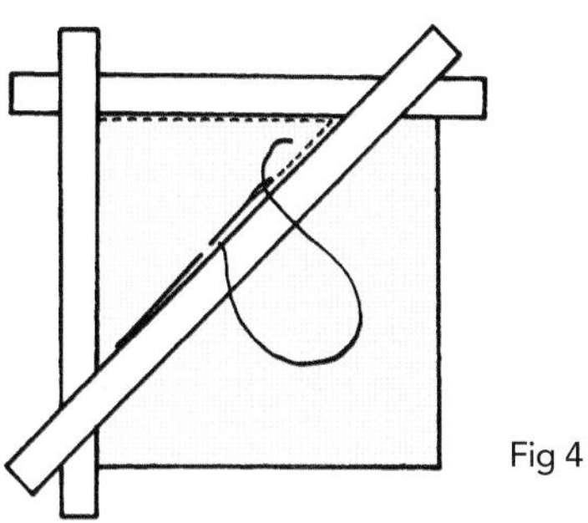

Fig 4

Quilting By Hand

The technique of hand quilting isn't difficult but is easier if the quilt top is prepared well in advance, as follows.

Tacking the Layers

For each block cut a 17in (43.2cm) square of the wadding and backing fabric, so that both are ½in (1.3cm) larger on all sides than the completed block. Place the backing fabric right side down on a flat surface; you may like to anchor it at the corners with masking tape. Lay the wadding on top, patting it into place. Place the block centrally on the wadding (Fig 1). Use a long, fine needle and light-coloured tacking thread and tack, using running stitches ¾–1in (1.9–2.5cm) long, working from the centre of the block outwards across the quilt in a grid of vertical and horizontal lines.

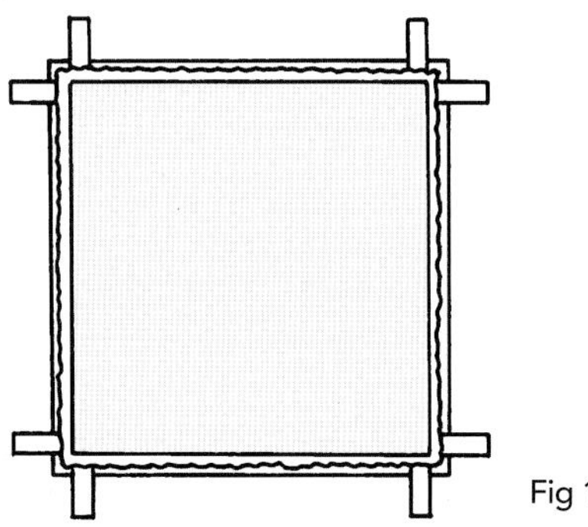

Fig 1

Rather than beginning each tacking line in the centre with a knot, cut enough thread to use right across the block. Begin in the centre, leaving about half the thread as a long end at the start. Tack to the edge, finish with a double stitch and remove the needle (Fig 2a). Re-thread the other end and tack in the opposite direction (Fig 2b). The tacking should be just tight enough to hold the layers together without denting the surface. Continue to tack the horizontal and vertical lines about 3–4in (7.6–10cm) apart to form a grid (Fig 3).

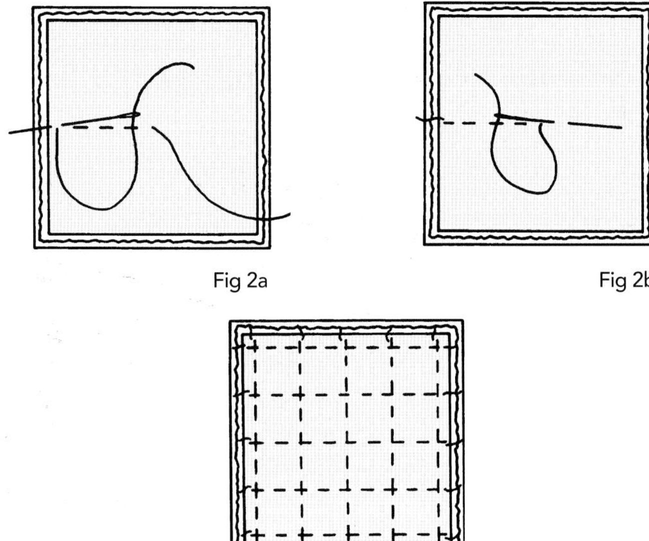

Fig 2a

Fig 2b

Fig 3

Using a Frame

When quilting, I would recommend the use of one of the newer, square plastic frames, as they make a convenient shape to fit around the blocks. A tacked block should never be stretched tightly in the frame – adjust the side clips so the fabric has some 'give', which will make quilting easier. A frame is virtually essential for quilting large pieces.

Starting to Quilt

Begin by cutting a length of quilting thread about 18in (46cm) long. This can be a contrasting colour to your fabric or a shade to blend with the colours of the block. Begin quilting in the centre of the block and work outwards. All starting and finishing is done from the top of the quilt, so make a knot at one end of the thread and push the needle into the top fabric and wadding (not the backing) 1in (2.5cm) away from the starting point, preferably further along the line you are going to quilt. Bring the needle back up to the surface in position to make the first stitch, which I make a backstitch. Pull gently to pop the knot through the top fabric into the wadding (batting).

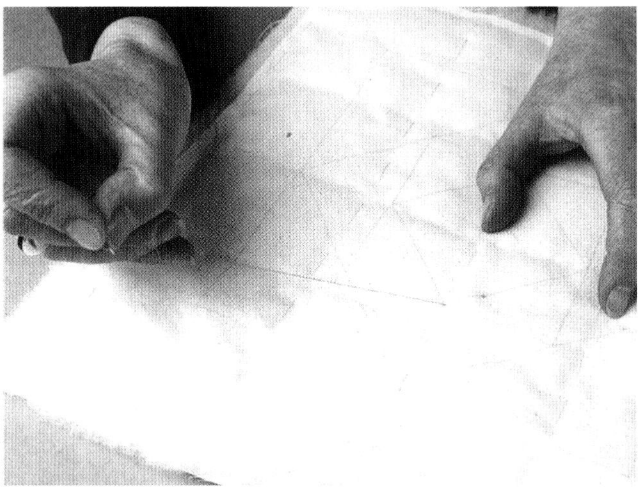

Starting position: the knot is ready to be popped through into the wadding (batting) out of sight.

The Quilting Stitch

Begin quilting each time with a backstitch and a space so that it appears to be a running stitch. When you first quilt it may be easier to make one stitch at a time but with practice you can increase this. It doesn't matter if your stitches are not as small as you would like: what is important is that the stitches are the same size. This becomes easier as you keep stitching and establish a rhythm. Check the back occasionally to ensure that the stitches are being made on that side as well, but don't expect them to be exactly the same size. They are usually smaller, and as long as you are catching in enough of the back fabric to hold it securely in place that will be fine.

Quilting without a frame: it is possible to hold the fabric between the thumb and finger of one hand while quilting with the other, to manoeuvre the layers. To make the running quilting stitch a reasonable size on the back and front, the needle must be pushed into the work as vertically as possible (see picture 1 below) and then swung upwards. This is why it's best to use Betweens needles, as they are short and strong and won't bend too easily. I use the top of a thimble to swing the needle up and down.

Watch the tension of your stitches by pulling the thread to tighten the stitches just enough to draw the top fabric down but not so much that it puckers. When quilting without a frame, always work from the centre outwards. It may be easier to use several threads at the same time while doing this. If you turn and quilt back towards the middle you may finish up with a bulge or a twist in the fabric in the centre.

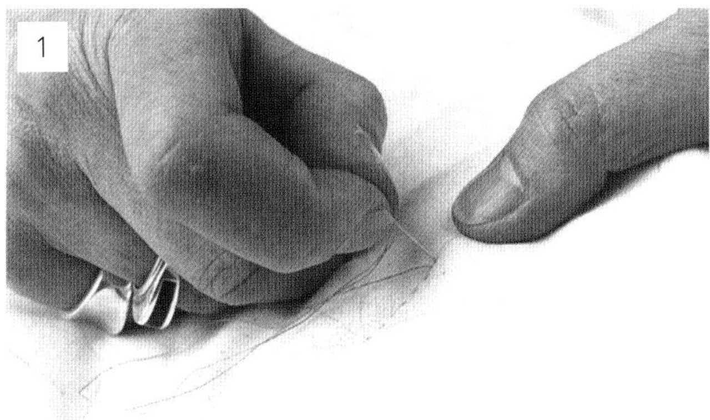

Quilting without a frame: first, push the needle down vertically into the fabric.

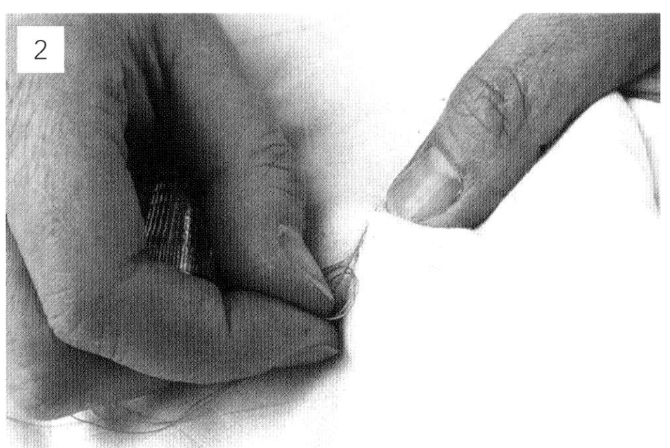

Swing the needle upwards again to make the stitch.

Quilting with a frame: you need a different approach here because the fabric cannot be gathered and held between your thumb and finger while quilting. Place your free hand under the quilt, with the top of your middle finger in the area where the needle should come through the quilt. Rest the top of the needle against the flat end of the thimble and push the needle vertically through the layers until the tip is just (and only just) touching the underneath finger (picture 1 below). Press the layers down ahead of the needle with the thumb of your sewing hand (2). Push the tip of the needle upwards with the underneath finger. At the same time use the thimble to swing the needle head over and forward to help bring the needle tip to the surface (3).

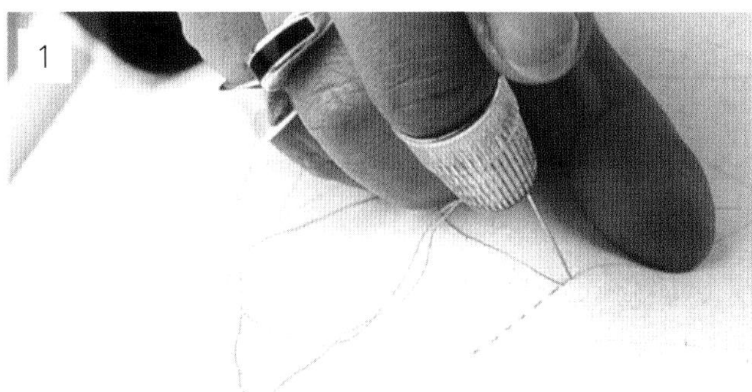

Support the vertical needle with the underneath finger. Press the quilt layers down with the thumb of the top hand.

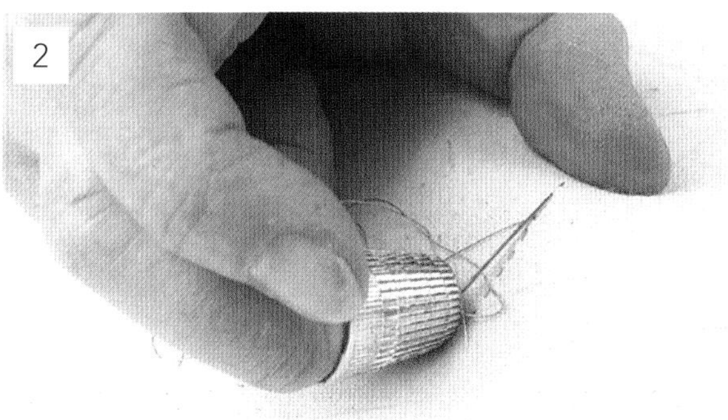

Swing the top of needle down to bring the point of the needle to the surface.

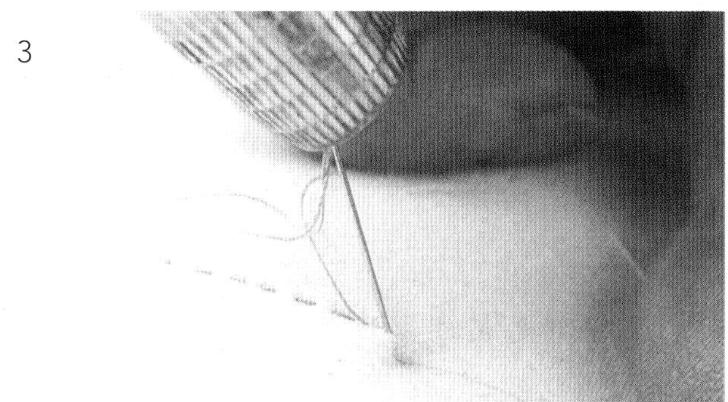

Swing the top of needle upwards to make the next stitch.

Swing the head of the needle upwards to make the next stitch until it is almost vertical, and push down with the thimble until the needle tip touches the underneath finger.

Again, use a combination of the underneath finger and the thumb in from of the needle to help force the needle up to the surface of the work while you swing the needle head down on to the quilt top with the thimble. This rocking action can be repeated to make as many stitches on the needle as are comfortable (4). Pull the needle through the layers, giving a slight tug on the thread to pull the stitches snugly on to the quilt top. Continue in this way until the quilting is complete.

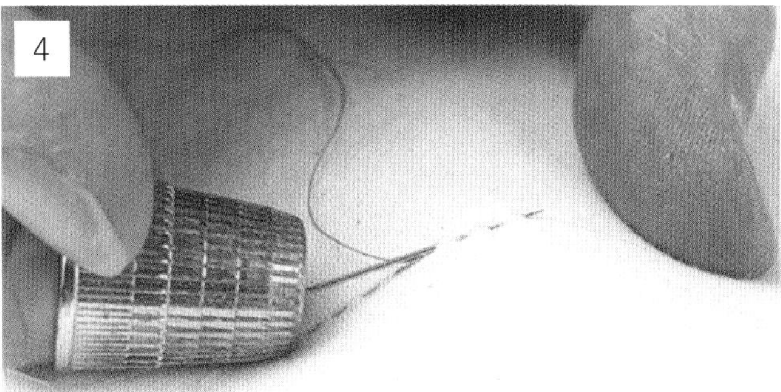

Several stitches can be fed on to the needle before it is pulled through – make as many as you are comfortable with.

To finish off, either make a knot in the thread close to the surface of the fabric or wind the thread twice round the needle and insert the needle into the wadding, running it at least 1in (2.5cm) away from the stitching (5). Pull gently to pop the knot beneath the surface of the top fabric. Cut off the thread level with the quilt top.

I use this same technique to move from one part of the design to emerge at another. Finish with a knot, run the thread through the wadding and emerge at the new stitching line. Remember to always begin with a backstitch before continuing to quilt.

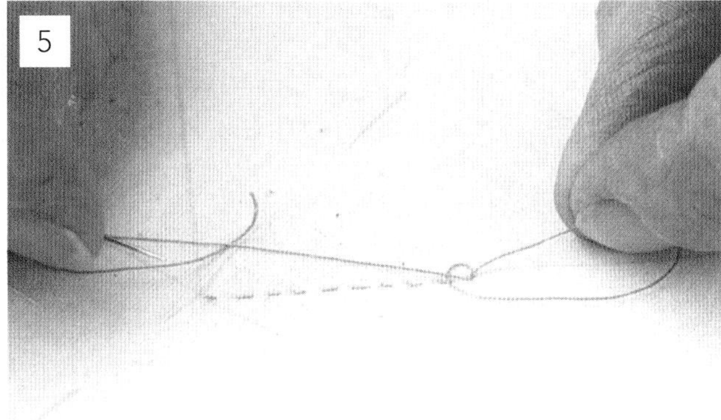

Finish with a knot or by winding the thread twice around the needle and running the needle into the wadding for at least 1in (2.5cm).

Quilting by Machine

One of the most important preliminaries to machine quilting is to get your sewing area comfortable and efficient to work in. I have an office chair that I can adjust to a comfortable height for machine work and sit at a large table with a good light. Beware of working too long at the machine and getting an aching neck or shoulders through tension.

The top thread can be either normal sewing thread to tone with the quilt or the invisible thread described in the Alternative Drunkard's Path block (page 231). Use the normal thread in the bobbin in a colour to match the backing fabric and use a size 9 or 70 needle for invisible thread or a 12 or 80 for normal thread. Try the stitches on a practice piece to check that top and bottom tensions are equally balanced. Use a stitch length that pleases the eye, about the same as for dressmaking or possibly slightly longer.

Angela Lloyd machine quilted the border of her quilt, using a walking foot to stitch the straight lines and with a decorative stitch from her machine along the seamlines.

Quilting in the Ditch

Unless your machine has dual-feed you will need to buy a walking foot for this. These can be expensive but are invaluable for stitching evenly through layers of fabric and wadding. Practise stitching first on a trial sample. Take a piece of plain fabric and stitch several straight pleats in it (Fig 1) using the side of the machine foot as a measurement – you can use the walking foot for this if it is fitted or your usual sewing foot. Turn the fabric over and press the pleats to one side. The seams made can be used for practice in ditch-stitching. Layer a piece of backing fabric, wadding and the prepared seamed fabric and pin together ready for stitching. Aim to stitch as near to the seam as possible, stitching in the single layer of fabric which is lower than the other side. Try not to stitch up on the higher side of the seam, as this is really noticeable.

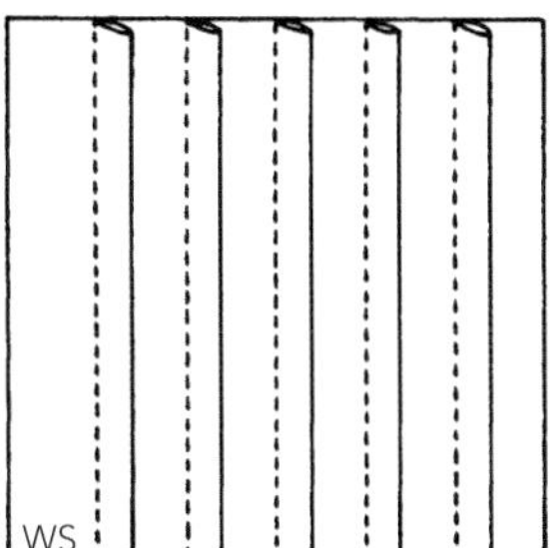

Fig 1

Start and finish your stitches with a series of very short stitches, about six or seven of them. Leave long thread ends, about 4in (10cm), so that the top thread can be pulled through to the back of the work easily. Use a needle with a large eye to pull both threads into the wadding for some distance. Trim off any ends that remain on the surface of the fabric. If you have a 'needle down' option on your machine, use it to keep the needle in position in the fabric when you pause to turn corners or adjust direction round a curve.

Free Machine Quilting

For quilting very curved or complex designs the feed dogs are either dropped or covered so that the fabric is no longer forced along at an even pace. Read your machine instruction manual to see how to adjust your machine for this. Use the darning foot or a special extra-large free-machining foot that can be obtained from quilt shops to fit some machines.

To start, lower the presser foot in the place where you want to begin quilting. Hold on to the end of the top thread and make one stitch. Pull the thread to bring the bottom thread up through the quilt to the top. Hold both threads while you stitch the first few stitches, which should be a series of six or seven very short stitches. Stop and snip the thread ends off close to the stitching.

Place your hands in a C-shape either side of the pressure foot and press down gently to move the layers of the quilt around while keeping the speed of the machine as consistent as you can. Aim to make even stitches of a uniform length. Finish by reducing the length of the last six or seven stitches to the smallest possible size.

To move to a new area, lift the presser foot and position it where you wish to begin stitching. Do not snip the threads, but keep them taut between the two areas. Lower the pressure foot and wind the needle into the quilt by hand. Start to quilt with the usual six to seven tiny stitches, then snip the connecting threads before continuing to stitch. Balancing speed and movement is the real skill and needs plenty of practise. Make up several trial pieces and work through stitching straight lines by eye, curves, writing your name and the overall scribbling effect known as vermicelli quilting. Like hand quilting, machine quilting improves with practise, so put in the time and your confidence and control of the machine will increase. Once you feel ready, start quilting the blocks. Begin with ditch-quilting and any outline quilting using the walking foot, then progress to free-machine quilting in the shapes of the design and finally any quilting to fill in the background areas if desired.

Jane Brooks commissioned Jan Chandler, a very talented long-arm machine quilter, to quilt her sampler quilt in a variety of designs which complemented the blocks and borders beautifully.

Joining the Blocks

Joining the blocks together is not a difficult task but it can be tedious. Still, at least by this stage all the quilting is completed and the quilt starts taking shape like magic as each row is added. The method I use ensures that the joining seams on the back of the quilt reflect those on the front so that the back of the quilt looks as neat and balanced as possible.

1 Arrange the completed blocks in your chosen design. Take your time over this and if possible get a second or third opinion, preferably from a fellow quilter. There may, of course, be a block that just does not fit in and you may have to be brave, discard it and make another. Sometimes, though, the block you have felt uneasy about since it was made fits in the final arrangement perfectly. Only at this stage, when all the blocks are laid out and the overall balance established, can you make these decisions.

2 Take the blocks that will make up the top row of the quilt (Fig 1) and place the first two blocks to be joined right sides down. Pull the backing fabric and wadding back from the vertical sides to be joined on each block front and pin them out of the way (Fig 2).

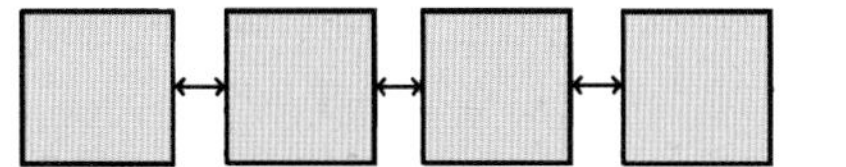

Fig 1

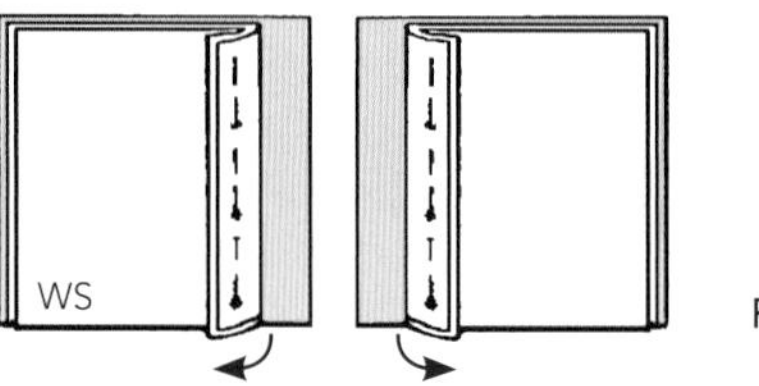

Fig 2

3 With right sides facing, match and pin the two edges of the block fronts together. Machine stitch them together with a ¼in (6mm) seam allowance (Fig 3). Finger press the seam open and press it lightly with the point of an iron from the front of the work. If you try to press it on the back there is a danger of the iron touching the wadding and melting it.

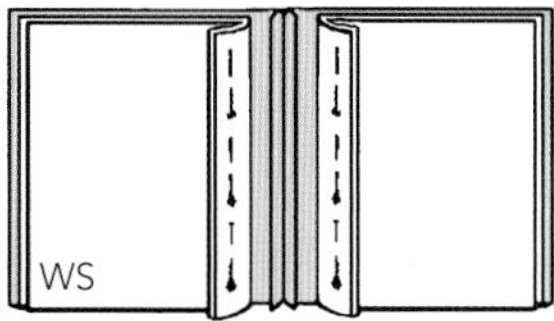

Fig 3

Pauline Bugg used her neutral background fabric for the sashing on each block. Once the blocks were joined, she hand quilted across the joining seams so that they became part of the design.

4 Lay the joined blocks right sides down on a flat surface. Unpin the wadding, but leave the backing fabric pinned back out of the way. Let the two edges of wadding overlap each other and cut through both layers along the centre so that the final cut edges butt together. It does not matter exactly where this cut is made as it will be bidden by the fabric. If you are nervous about accidentally cutting the front of the blocks, slide an ordinary 12in (30.5cm) ruler between the wadding and the block front before you cut so that your scissors cannot come into contact with the block beneath (Fig 4).

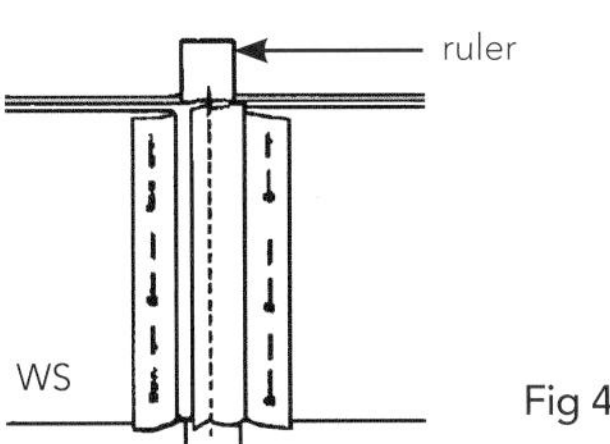

Fig 4

5 Keep the ruler between the layers while you stitch the two butted edges of wadding together. I use a large herringbone stitch as it helps to keep the edges flat (Fig 5).

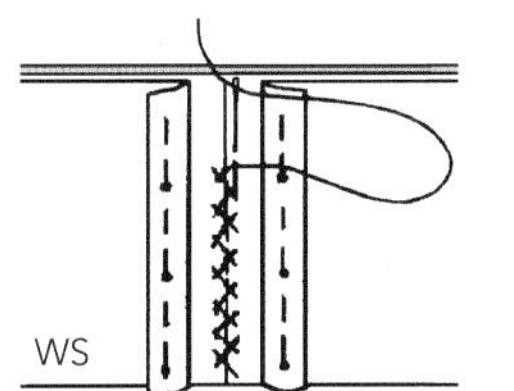

Fig 5

6 Remove the ruler and turn over the joined blocks so that they are now right sides upwards. Push a line of pins through the joining seam and wadding from the front. They should be pushed right through so that their points stand upright when the quilt blocks are turned over (Fig 6a). Avoid using glass-headed pins for this task, as the heads roll sideways and prevent the pins from remaining upright.

7 Turn the blocks over with the backing fabric facing upwards (Fig 6b). Fold each piece of backing fabric so that the folded edge butts up to the line of pins. Finger press the fold and trim any excess fabric to the ¼in (6mm) seam allowance (Fig 6c).

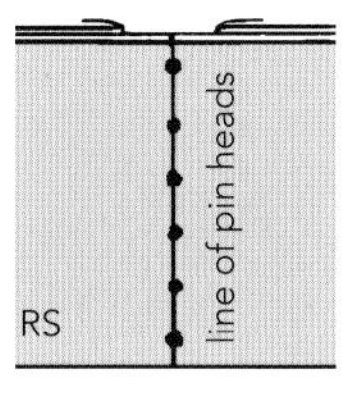

Fig 6a

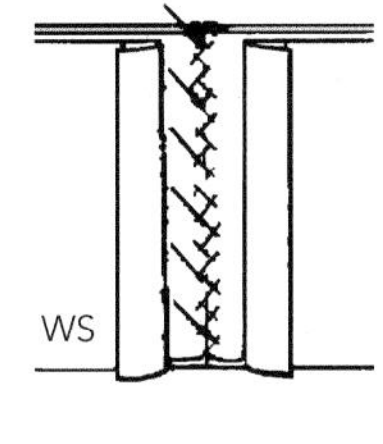

Fig 6b

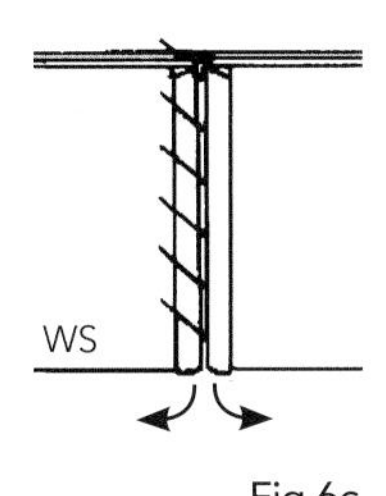

Fig 6c

8 Remove the pins. Unfold the backing fabric of block one and smooth it flat on the batting (Fig 7a). Unfold the backing fabric of block two and re-fold it so that the seam allowance is turned under. Match the fold of block two to the creased line of block one (Fig 7b). Pin together, again putting a ruler under the seam, this time to avoid sewing into the wadding.

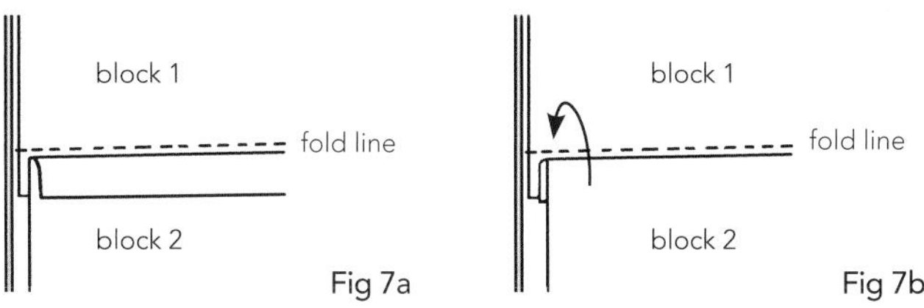

Fig 7a Fig 7b

9 Sew along the overlapping seam with a slip stitch or blind hemming stitch. You can remove the ruler to sew most of this seam, but keep it in place for the first and final 2in (5cm). It does not matter if the stitches penetrate the wadding along this seam in the middle areas, but the end 2in (5cm) have to be kept in separate layers so that they can be joined to the next row of blocks (Fig 8).

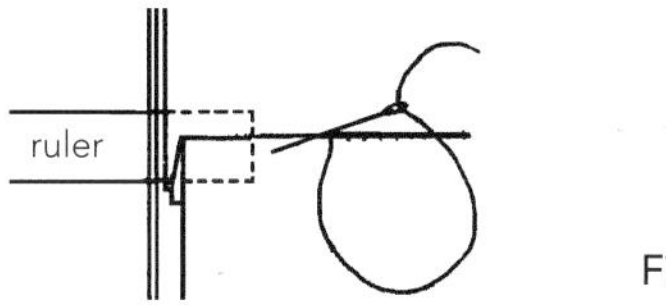

Fig 8

10 Repeat this process to join all the blocks in the top row. Check that the backing fabric is not pulled too tight and that the front sashing strips are well matched and lying flat. Adjust the back seams if they are pulling too tightly.

11 Join the blocks in each horizontal row in the same way (Fig 9). Now join those horizontal rows in exactly the same way, matching seams and borders carefully (Fig 10). The quilt is now ready for its borders and final binding.

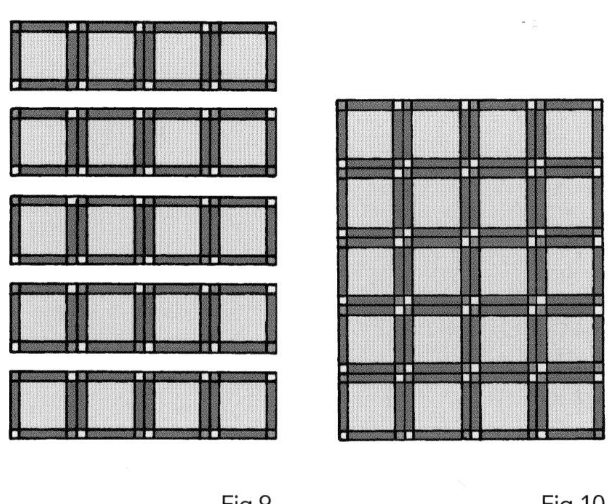
Fig 9 Fig 10

Completing the Quilt

Adding Borders

When the quilt top has been joined together you need to think about the borders. Put the quilt on the bed to see how wide the borders need to be. If the quilt is just going to cover the top of the bed like an eiderdown, it may not need any extra borders.

I began the sampler quilt photographed opposite the title page as the teaching sample for my second sampler course, but as it went on I loved it more and more and determined to use it for the next twenty years or more on our brass bed. I had planned to add two simple framing borders, but found I needed more than this to cover the bed base and look good, so here was a chance to add a border design that I had been admiring for ages. More work, more quilting and a very huge quilt to carry around to classes and exhibitions, but an addition that I am really pleased with.

Study all the photographs in this book – all quilts made by genuine students trying out the sampler quilt course. Some have rich and complex borders, others a simple double border of complementary fabrics which set off the quilt beautifully. As always, the choice of borders is yours and yours alone.

You may be severely restricted in your choice of fabrics by this time. Pieced borders using all the left-over scraps may be the answer, or you could use totally new fabrics. It doesn't matter if a fabric has not been used in the quilt, as long as it looks as though it belongs. The light fabric used around the edge of the pieced border on my quilt is not in the main quilt at all. I had just half a metre of it and was so short of fabric that one of the small squares in the corners is made up from several joined scraps, a real patchwork quilt!

Plain borders cry out to be quilted, although wide patterned borders, if they form the drop down each side of the bed, can look good without quilting. If you have really had enough by this time then add simple borders and keep quilting to a minimum.

At this stage it is easiest to make the borders and join them to the front of the quilt only and not to the wadding (batting) and backing. Ignore the back until all the extra pieces – apart from the final binding – have been added to the quilt top.

Strip Borders

A simple framing border of one or more strips of fabric is very effective (Fig 1). If there is not enough fabric to cut strips for the length of the quilt, you can get away with a few joins, provided they are placed midway in the border or at regular intervals so that they look planned. If you do not have any suitable fabric left for the border you may have to go out and buy something special. It may seem an extravagance at this stage, but any fabric left over will always come in useful for a future project. Another excuse to buy more fabric...

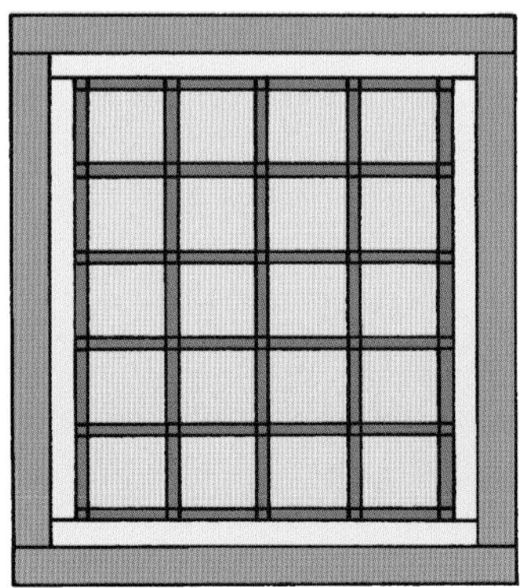
Fig 1

1 Lay the quilt top on a flat surface and measure its length down the centre, not the edge (Fig 2). If you always do this and cut the borders to match the centre measurements there is less danger of the quilt edges spreading to give wavy borders.

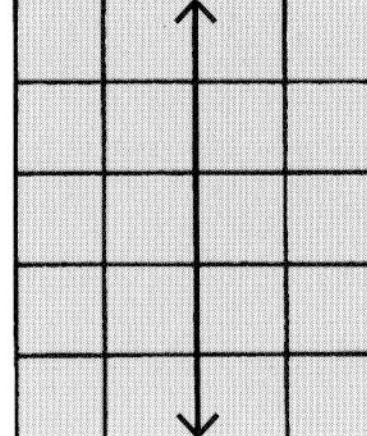
Fig 2

2 Cut two strips of border fabric in the chosen width to match the quilt measurement – these will make the side borders. Pin back the wadding and backing fabric out of the way and pin and stitch each side strip to the quilt top, easing in any fullness in the quilt. Work on a flat surface and match the centres and both ends before pinning the rest. Press the seams outwards, away from the quilt (Fig 3).

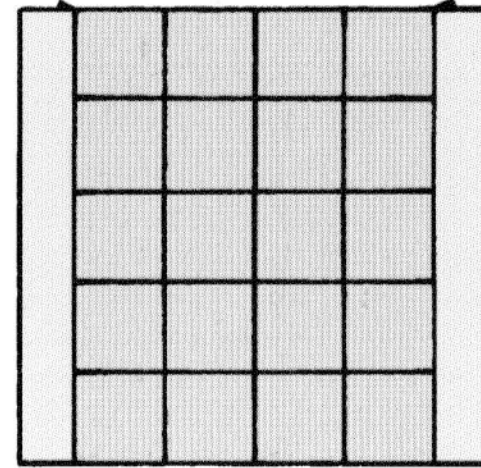
Fig 3

3 Measure the quilt from side to side across the centre (Fig 4). Cut two strips of border fabric in the chosen width to match this measurement. Pin and stitch these to the top and bottom of the quilt, matching centres and both ends and avoiding the wadding and backing fabric as before (Fig 5). Press the seams outwards away from the quilt top.

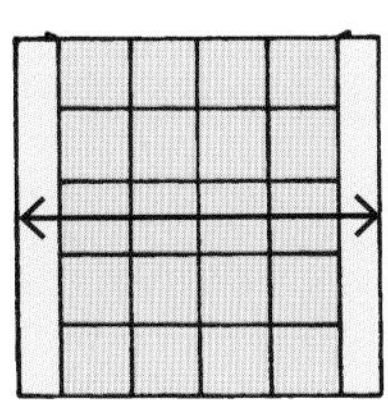

Fig 4

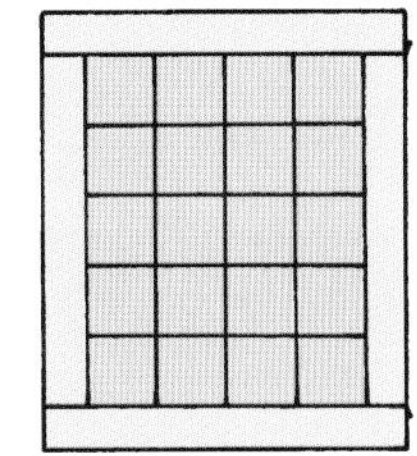

Fig 5

4 If another border is planned, measure the quilt down its centre and repeat the process, sides first and then top and bottom (Fig 1).

5 You may prefer to make your borders with cornerstones, which echo the squares linking the sashing strips. Measure the quilt across its centre in *both* directions and cut strips of the chosen width to match these measurements. Stitch the side strips to the quilt as usual. Press the seams outwards away from the quilt. Cut four squares of fabric for the cornerstones the same size as the cut width of the border strips. Stitch one of these to either end of both top and bottom border strips (Fig 6). Press the seams towards the long strip. Pin and stitch these border strips to the top and bottom of the quilt, matching seams carefully (Fig 7). Press the seams outwards, away from the quilt. If a second border with cornerstones is planned, re-measure the quilt after the first border is added and repeat the process (Fig 8).

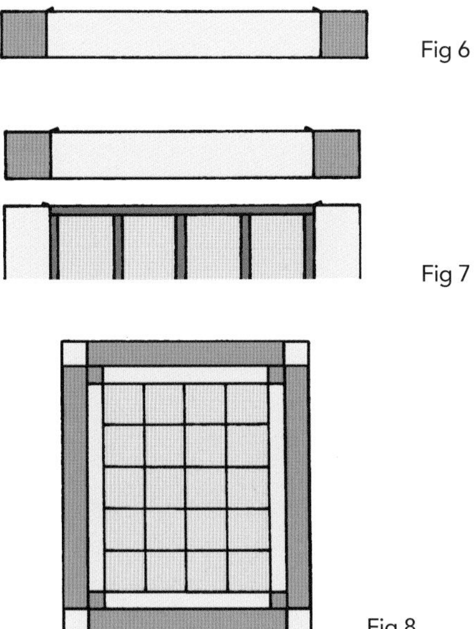

Fig 6

Fig 7

Fig 8

Pieced Borders

Pieced borders made from scraps are an ideal way to use up spare fabric and can greatly enrich your quilt. At this stage the outer edge of the quilt will have only one width of sashing strip around it. With a busy pieced border you may find that a second sashing width needs to be added to the quilt, and possibly even another wider border strip beyond this, before the pieced border is stitched in place. If this is the case, follow the instructions for adding strip borders given opposite.

Both squares and rectangles can be used to make a pieced border. Figs 9 and 10 show suggested designs for using cut squares: 2½in (6.3cm) cut squares are a comfortable size and should fit mathematically around the quilt.

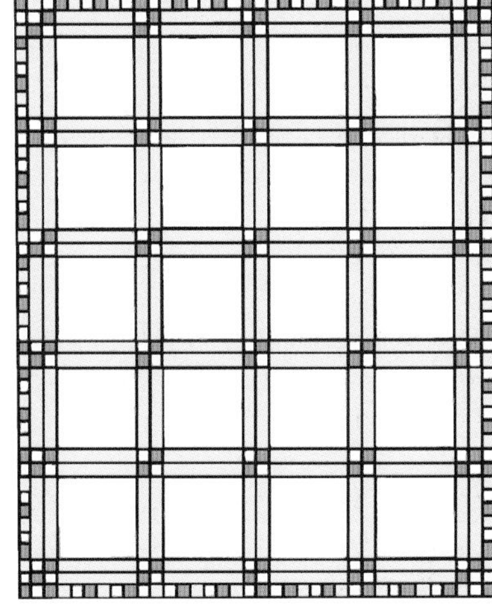

Fig 9

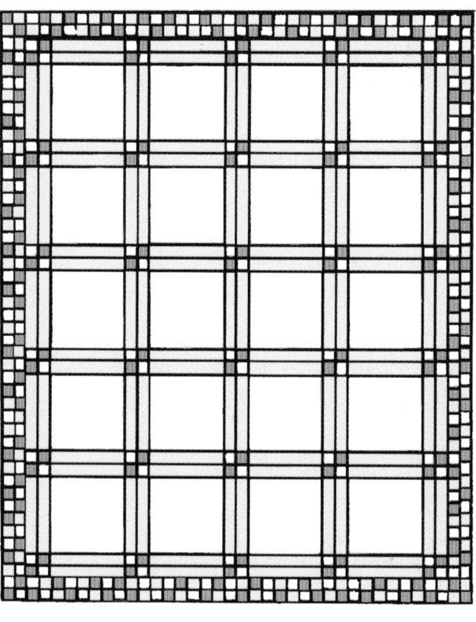

Fig 10

If not, position a seam at the centre of the quilt and trim the two ends to make matching rectangles (Fig 11). Fig 12 shows a design using 2½in (6.3cm) rectangles, cut any length you like, around the quilt.

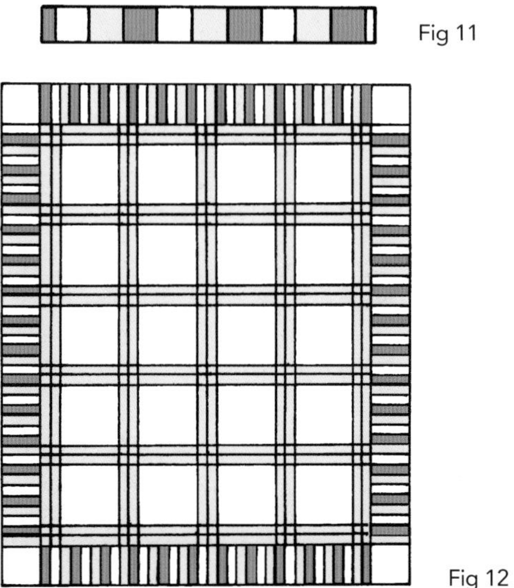

Fig 11

Fig 12

Several students created borders based on larger versions of techniques that feature in the blocks, such as Delectable Mountains or Folded Flying Geese. My own border was based on half-square and quarter-square triangles (Fig 13).

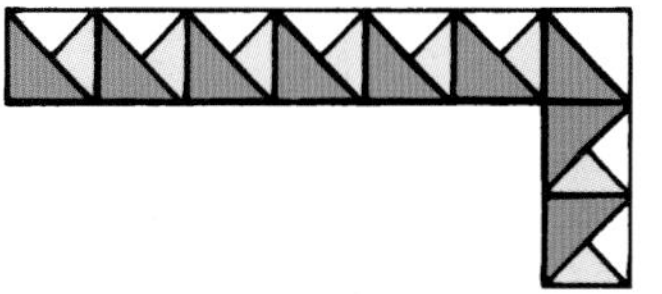

Fig 13

It is not always possible to make repeat designs for border strips in an exact measurement to fit the quilt. My design was based on a 3in (7.6cm) repeat which had to go continuously around the quilt, including turning the corners. One solution is to make the border strips and try them against the quilt as they grow. It may be that by adjusting a few seams or by some creative pressing with a steam iron the border can be made to fit the quilt. I solved the problem with my own quilt by making the borders first and then adding an extra framing strip all around the quilt itself to bring it up to the correct size to fit the borders. Regular repeat designs like Flying Geese can be broken at the corners and midway, where spacing pieces can be inserted to make the sizing correct (Fig 14).

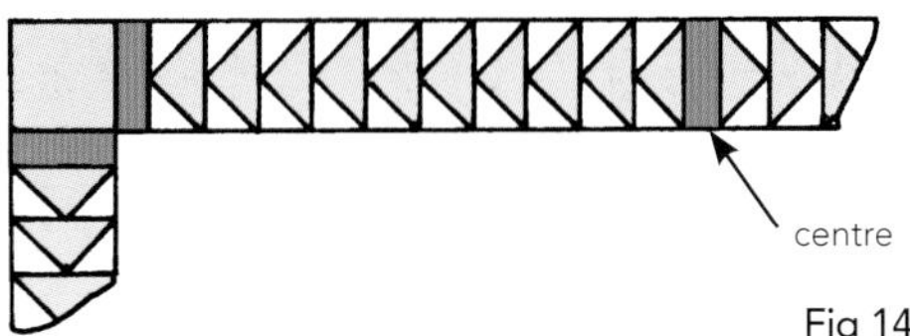

Fig 14

You may want to add another frame beyond the pieced border. Lay the quilt top on a flat surface and measure it again. Work from these measurements when cutting the new strips. If you keep a tight control on the length of each border strip as you add it, you will finish up with a beautifully flat quilt without a hint of a wave or ripple.

Backing the Borders

Once all the borders have been added to the quilt top, extra wadding and backing fabric must be added which extends at least ½in (1.3cm) beyond the quilt on all sides. Join the wadding with herringbone stitch along the butted edges in the same way as when joining the blocks (see step 5 on page 245). Strips of the backing fabric can then be machine stitched to the back of the quilt to make it the same size as the wadding. Join the side pieces first and then the top and bottom strips. Press seams outwards as usual. Any quilting in the border areas should be done at this stage, tacking the layers together thoroughly before quilting. Although the quilt is cumbersome now, at least the extra quilting is all around the edge so should not be too difficult to get at.

Binding the Quilt

I suggest making double-fold binding for the quilt. Strips are cut on the straight grain of the fabric and have two thicknesses on the folded edge, making it more durable. Mitred corners are not necessary as there are no mitres in the blocks or sashing.

1 Before adding the final binding, check that the quilt lies flat and the corners are really square. Tacking with small stitches near to the edge of the quilt will help keep the quilt flat and avoid wavy edges. Trim the wadding and backing fabric down to exactly ¼in (6mm) beyond the quilt top (Fig 1).

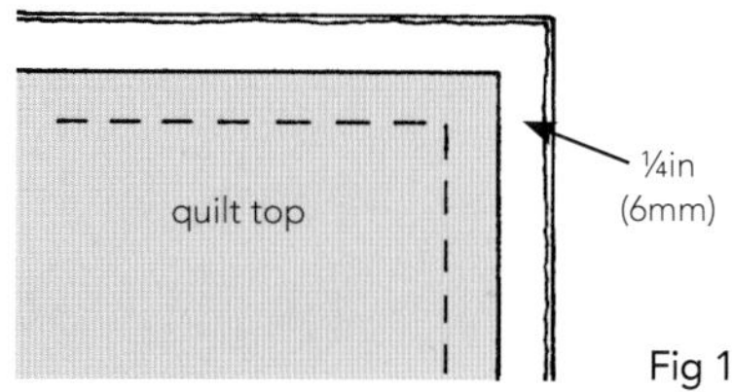

Fig 1

2 Cut four strips of fabric for the binding, each 2½in (6.3cm) wide. The two side strips should measure the length of the quilt from top to bottom. The two strips for the top and bottom edges should measure the width of the quilt from side to side plus 1½in (3.8cm). Shorter lengths can be joined if you do not have enough fabric.

3 Take each side binding strip and fold it in half, right side *outwards*, without pressing. Pin a folded strip to one side of the quilt, matching the edges (see Fig 2). Stitch a seam ¼in (6mm) from the edge of the quilt top through all the layers (Fig 3). Repeat this with the second strip on the other side of the quilt.

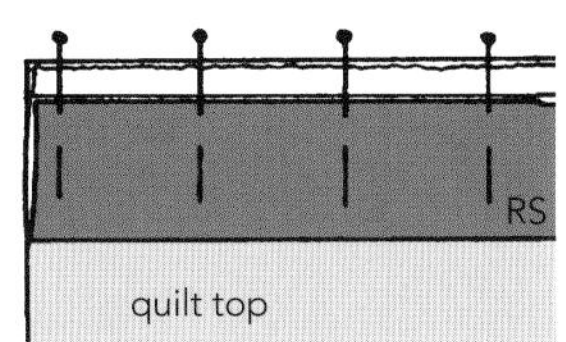

Fig 2

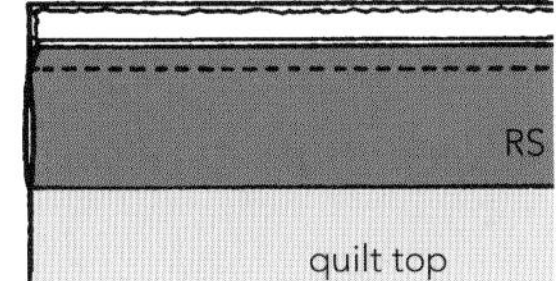

Fig 3

4 Bring the folded edge of the binding over to the back and stitch in place by hand, just covering the line of machine stitches (Fig 4).

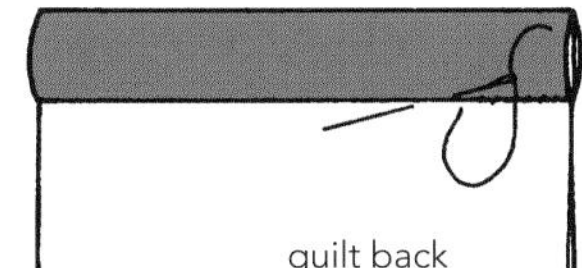

Fig 4

5 Pin and stitch the folded binding to the top and bottom of the quilt in the same way, leaving about ¾in (1.9cm) of binding extending beyond the quilt at each end (Fig 5). Trim this back to about ½in (1.3cm) and fold in over the quilt edge (Fig 6). Now fold the binding over to the back of the quilt and slip stitch it in place (Fig 7). Make sure that the corners are really square before you stitch them.

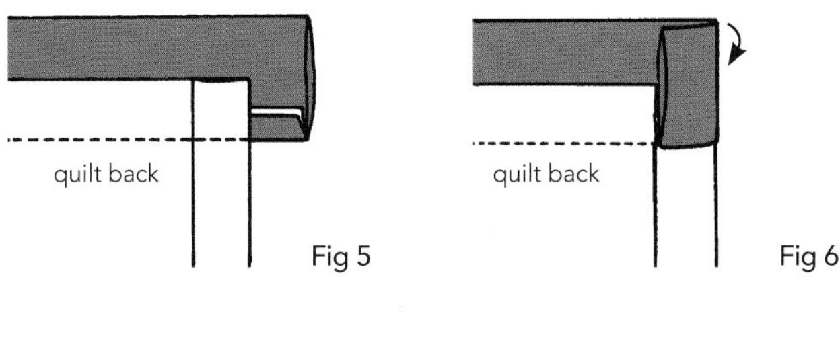

Fig 5 Fig 6

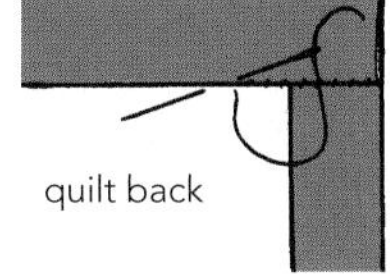

Fig 7

Labelling the Quilt

Quilts should always have the maker's name and date of completion on it – you made it, so make sure future generations know its origins. On the back of the quilt or on a separate piece of fabric write your words either in pencil which can then be covered with stitches or with a Pigma pen, a fine felt pen that will not fade. Owners of hi-tech sewing machines can programme their machine to stitch a label for them while they make a cup of tea.

Quilt Care

The danger with making a rich and precious heirloom quilt is that you are afraid to use it and even more afraid to wash it. Don't worry too much: a well-made quilt will wash and wear wonderfully and if, in time, it shows signs of age that is part of its charm.

If your washing machine is large enough to hold the quilt comfortably, wash it with a low temperature programme and a mild washing agent. A short spin will remove some of the excess water and make the quilt less heavy.

If washing by hand, use the bath and agitate the quilt gently with your hands. Do not let it soak for any length of time. Rinse several times in the bath until the water runs clear. Press out as much water as you can while the quilt is still in the bath. Press towels against the quilt to absorb as much excess water as you can before removing the quilt from the bath.

If possible dry the quilt flat, using a layer of towels or sheets underneath it. Another sheet on top will protect it from birds and other sources of dirt. Keep the quilt out of direct sunlight as this can fade the colours, even in Britain. Once dry, if it needs to be pressed, use a cool iron without steam and just press the unquilted areas where creases may show. A hot iron can cause polyester wadding to bond to the fabric, so use caution and test for the correct heat level for your particular quilt.

When the quilt is in use, beware of sunlight streaming through a bedroom window on to it. Even in temperate climes the sun fades fabric and can spoil a quilt, especially if only a section has been in the sun and it has faded in patches.

A Final Word…

Nobody needs to make a quilt: we do it because we love choosing fabric, handling fabric, arranging fabric and stitching fabric. It is not cheap. It is not quick. Sometimes it is not that well made. Most people cannot understand the pleasure it gives us. Remember, never give a quilt to someone who will not love it in the way you knows it deserves. Keep it yourself until the right owner comes along. That way everyone's happy and you can get busy on the next quilt…

Gallery

Valerie Childs has used a limited palette of colours in her quilt and balanced them beautifully. The addition of so much rich quilting has made her quilt a real heirloom.

"I thoroughly enjoyed making my sampler quilt because I could take some of the blocks to my weekly group. Each block was quilted by hand and the group nicknamed Lynne's book 'the bible'." **Valerie Childs**

An exercise in purely black and white fabrics, Alison Batchelor's graphic quilt makes an elegant and very modern statement. Alison used all the small leftover pieces for a Flying Geese border.

"This quilt was a project with my quilting group, Beacon Quilters of Bodmin, Cornwall. All members completed a quilt using Lynne's books. I added some extra blocks. I chose a black and white theme, mainly because I had a stash of black and white from an unfinished quilt! I was delighted with the finished look of the monochrome tones." **Alison Batchelor**

Elizabeth Tomlinson has taken a group of blocks from the Sampler Quilt and arranged them informally without straight sashings between them, filling the spaces with arrangements of smaller pieced blocks, like half-square triangles and Flying Geese.

"I made all the hand-pieced blocks from Lynne's sampler book through long winter evenings by the fire and then continued with lots of small, hand-pieced filler blocks to complete my own arrangement of machine-joined blocks and finally hand quilted." **Elizabeth Tomlinson**

Daphne Green has reinterpreted some of the Sampler Quilt blocks as an elegant wall hanging. Her use of Celtic motifs in the centre panel is most effective.

"This quilt was a long, drawn-out task, especially deciding on the intermixing of colours and sizes, but I feel that the end result was worth the effort."
Daphne Green

Corinne Bloomfield has used a whole collection of different colours and fabrics in her blocks and combined them skilfully in her version of the Sampler Quilt.

"This was my first patchwork project. I used my favourite colours of blues, purples and a splash of shocking pink. It is the winter quilt on my bed – I am currently working on a summer-coloured sampler quilt."
Corinne Bloomfield

Acknowledgments

My thanks to the following people: to Jane Trollope and Cheryl Brown at David & Charles for making all these books happen, and to Lin Clements, the best editor a girl could wish for.

To all those teachers of patchwork and quilting who have kindly taught beginners using the books in the past and hopefully will continue to do so with this new bumper edition.

To all those quilters who allowed their quilts to be used in this book, and also to the quilters who sent photos but whose quilts were not included, and who at least pretended to be magnanimous and understand that I just could not include all of them, much as I would have liked to.

Contributors

Christine Askew
Barbara Ayre
Judy Baker-Rogers
Alison Batchelor
Corinne Bloomfield
Amanda Boundy
Jane Brooks
Pauline Bugg
Kath Cadman
Annette Chamley
Valerie Childs
Jean Cuthbert
Brenda Day
Lynne Devey
Mary Evans
Jan Evers
Jan Farris
Sue Fitzgerald
Kirsty Gowler
Daphne Green
Pamela Gunn
Jill Harford
Pippa Higgitt
Jeanette Hogarth
Kathie Levine
Angela Lloyd
Alison Maudlin
Karen Moore
Julie Moreland
Jean Parsons
Liz Parsons
Gill Peskett
Linda Riceman
Yvonne Romain
Juliet Simpson
Alison Still
Theresa Stredder
Elizabeth Tomlinson
Bobbie Turley
June Turner
Beth Williams
Jean Williams
Pauline Wilson
Davina Wing
Carol Wood
Honor Woods

About the Author

Lynne Edwards teaches and demonstrates a wide range of patchwork and quilting techniques, both hand and machine. She has written several textbooks that are considered to be definitive works. Her previous books for David & Charles are: *The Sampler Quilt Book* (1996), *The New Sampler Quilt Book* (2000), *Making Scrap Quilts to Use It Up* (2003), *Stash-Buster Quilts* (2006) and *Cathedral Window Quilts* (2008).

In 1992 Lynne was awarded the Jewel Pearce Patterson Scholarship for International Quilt Teachers. This was in recognition of her outstanding qualities as a teacher and included a trip to the Houston Quilt Market and Festival. The award led to invitations to teach as part of the Houston Faculty in 1993 and 1995 and at the Symposium of the Australasian Quilters' Guild in Brisbane in 1993. Since then international teaching trips have included venues in Europe, in Missouri, USA and the National Quilt Show in South Africa. In 2000, teaching commitments included Durban in South Africa and the National Canadian Festival, Canada in 2000. Recent overseas teaching trips include Ireland, France, Spain, New Zealand, Singapore, Dubai, Oman and Kenya.

Lynne's long association with the quilting movement, both locally and nationally, has involved her in the organization of quilt shows – from local village halls to the Quilters' Guild National Exhibitions. She has served on selection committees and is an experienced judge of National Quilt Shows.

She was Senior Judge at the South African Quilt Show in 1998, her first experience of judging overseas. In 2000, Lynne was given honorary lifetime membership of the Quilters' Guild of the British Isles, and in 2002 was awarded the Amy Emms Memorial Trophy for services to quilting. In 2008 Lynne was awarded an MBE for her services to arts and crafts.

Index

Index